PRAISE FOR *HELL'S ANGELS*

"In this epic tale of the World War II aerial campaign over Europe, Marine fighter pilot Jay Stout vividly portrays not only the valiant aircrews, but also the commanders, the maintainers, the clerks, and the magnificent machines themselves. *Hell's Angels* is a gripping and awe-inspiring book." —Nathaniel Fick, author of *One Bullet Away*

"With his superlative 352nd Fighter Group history, *Fighter Group*, Jay Stout raised the bar on WWII unit histories. Now, tackling an 8th Air Force bomb group, he continues cruising in that rarified atmosphere in a detailed, informative, and evocative treatment of the 303rd 'Hell's Angels.' As a former military aviator, Stout knows that the air battle is won on the ground before an engine spools up, and he provides full credit to those who served without pride of Air Medal or hope of DFC. It's all there—the boredom, the devotion, the horror and even the humor in an industrial war fought on a global scale that we'll never see again. Unit histories just do not get any better."
—Barrett Tillman, author of *Whirlwind* and *Forgotten Fifteenth*

"Jay Stout is a triple-threat aviation historian—an experienced combat aviator, a meticulous researcher and a compelling storyteller. His uncanny eye for authentic detail allows *Hell's Angels* to be the incredible story of the 303rd Bomb Group and the bombing campaign that crippled Nazi Germany. Stout makes a hard-ridden topic seem fresh and new again. Highly recommended." —Walter J. Boyne, author/historian

continued . . .

"Jay Stout's reputation as a hard-hitting, authoritative, yet easy-to-read aviation author is upheld with this book. It matches up well with his bestselling *Fighter Group: The 352nd 'Blue Nosed Bastards' in World War II*. The 303rd Bomb Group was one of the top B-17 units in the 8th Air Force, and the basic aspects of its history are well-known, but Stout has used his skills to tell a fresh story. He concentrates on a few men, and tells their stories in depth—some survive, while others, whose luck runs out, do not. This is the way it was. Readers looking for new insights and material will not be disappointed. Highly recommended."
—Donald Caldwell, author of *JG 26: Top Guns of the Luftwaffe*

"A well-researched, beautifully written, and deeply evocative paean to the 303rd Heavy Bombardment Group—and all the young American heavy-bomber crewmen who, from 1942 to 1945, went out, facing a high probability of death or imprisonment, to grind the German industrial base to dust."   —Eric Hammel, author of *The Road to Big Week*

"Jay Stout has done a masterful job. The life and death struggles are told using the mission records, personal writings and experiences of one of the Eighth Air Force's most successful bombardment groups. All who wish a complete understanding of the role played by the Eighth Air Force and the strategic bombing of Germany should read this book."   —Keith Ferris, artist and military aviation historian

HELL'S ANGELS

The True Story of the 303rd
Bomb Group in World War II

JAY A. STOUT

BERKLEY CALIBER, NEW YORK

An imprint of Penguin Random House LLC
375 Hudson Street, New York, New York 10014

ISBN: 978-0-425-27410-1

The Library of Congress has catalogued the Berkley Caliber hardcover edition as follows:

Stout, Jay A., date.
Hell's Angels : the true story of the 303rd Bomb Group in World War II / Jay A. Stout.—First edition.
p.   cm.
ISBN 978-0-425-27409-5
1. United States. Army Air Forces. Bomb Group, 303rd.
2. World War, 1939–1945—Aerial operations, American.
3. World War, 1939–1945—Campaigns—Western Front.
4. World War, 1939–1945—Regimental histories—United States.   I. Title.
D790.253303rd .S76 2015
940.54'4973—dc23
2014029582

PUBLISHING HISTORY
Berkley Caliber hardcover edition / January 2015
Berkley Caliber trade paperback edition / January 2016

PRINTED IN THE UNITED STATES OF AMERICA
6th Printing

Cover design by Diana Kolsky.
Cover photos: Knock-Out Dropper courtesy of USAAF via Steven Mace;
Map and plane courtesy of USAAF.
Book design by Tiffany Estreicher.

Penguin
Random
House

*Harry Gobrecht—writer, historian and combat pilot—
did more than anyone to preserve the legacy of the 303rd.
He also flew thirty-five combat missions with the 303rd as
part of the bloodiest air campaign in history.
This book is dedicated to his memory.*

CONTENTS

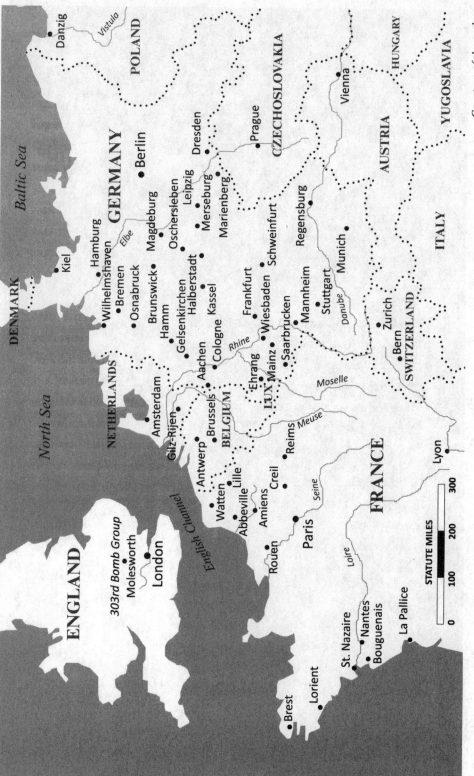

Courtesy of the author

INTRODUCTION

*I surely wish this was all over and we could be
thinking about coming home but there is a long hard
job ahead yet and there will probably be no going home
for many. I just hope that the people back there
realize what everyone is going through for them.*
—**Letter home, John McGarry, February 1944**[1]

ROBERT HALLIGAN STEPPED OUT of the familiar sweat-and-oil-and-cigarette stink of the dispersal tent and into the fresh, gray wet of the English morning. Only a handful of the 303rd's B-17s were visible through the fog. The gray blanket likewise muffled the aircraft-readying noises made by hundreds of maintenance men and their equipment as they prepared more than three dozen bombers for the day's mission.

There had been a mix-up in aircraft assignments, but it was finally settled that the John McGarry crew would fly *Spirit of Flak Wolf* to Marienburg, Germany; Halligan was the crew's navigator. The big ship hulked on its hardstand directly in front of him. Halting rivulets of water traced paths down its sides and gave it a muscular sleekness. Halligan watched the bomber's crew chief walk one of the four propellers through several revolutions to redistribute the oil that had drained into the lower cylinder heads overnight.

Swaddled in layers of flying gear, Halligan clumped to the forward access hatch under the nose of the B-17. He tossed his musette bag through the dark hole, grasped the edge of the opening and swung himself up and into the aircraft. His entry was fluid and easy. Experience had done that. The first time he tried to pull himself through the door—during training back in the States—he flailed and scrabbled and collapsed back to the ground in an embarrassed, out-of-breath heap.

Inside, Halligan collected the bag and ducked onto the narrow catwalk that ran beneath the pilot's compartment. Behind him he heard footfalls and the clanking of metal on metal as the other crewmen readied the equipment at their positions. As big as it was, *Spirit of Flak Wolf* still juddered gently as the men moved about and positioned their gear. Their voices were indistinct mutters that betrayed no emotion despite the fact that the mission was to be the 303rd's longest yet.

It would be Halligan's twenty-fifth mission. Had it been just a few months earlier it would have been his last. But just lately the required mission count had been raised to thirty. Halligan wasn't angry. Rather, he was resigned. In fact, he had been resigned for a long time. But it wasn't a giving-up sort of resignation; rather, it was an acceptance of fate. Whether he died or lived depended not only on his skill and that of his crewmates but also to an enormous degree on considerations over which none of them had control. On luck. Regardless, he was resolved to do his best—he owed it to himself and to his comrades.

Still, the odds seemed to be closing on the McGarry crew. Of the previous twenty-four missions, the men returned to Molesworth with all four engines running on only four. Flak, fighters and mechanical gremlins dogged the crew on virtually every sortie.

Halligan settled himself at the little desk mounted to the left bulkhead of the aircraft's nose. There, he arranged his charts and checked them against the notes he had taken during the early morning briefings. *Spirit of Flak Wolf* was slated to fly near the rear of the formation and consequently, barring a catastrophe, the responsibility for getting to the target would not fall to him. However, it was imperative that he be continuously aware of the aircraft's position. He had to be ready to give McGarry an accurate heading home in the event the ship was separated from the rest of the 303rd.

Kenneth Foe, the bombardier, stepped up from the catwalk and into the nose with Halligan. The two men were joined by the sort of bond created only by shared terror. Together, in the glass-and-aluminum cage that was the nose of the aircraft, they had fought enemy fighters, endured flak and sweated out mechanical failures that could have forced them down over enemy territory, or worse, into the icy North Sea. Too many times they had turned to each other when their very survival was at stake. And although their faces were clamped under oxygen masks and goggles, their eyes had unerringly communicated the fear they both felt.

Halligan and Foe checked the four .50-caliber machine guns for which they were responsible. They heard McGarry and the copilot, Willie Cotham, in the pilot's compartment above and behind them. The flare signaling the time for starting engines was due momentarily. Halligan looked out through the water-spotted glass of the nose and noted that the visibility had not appreciably improved.

There was the flare—a streak of yellow that disappeared immediately into the clouds. McGarry shouted and signaled through the window on the left side of the cockpit, and Halligan saw the crew chief nod and raise a thumb from where he stood outside in the wet. Two other ground crewmen stood ready with fire extinguishers. There was a murmured command in the cockpit, and then the left outboard engine—number one—whined and ticked as it slowly wound the propeller through two or three faltering revolutions. Then, the engine coughed blue smoke, caught and settled into a smooth, syrupy rumble that spun the propeller into a translucent disc. A low, vibrating growl thrummed across the airfield as the rest of the group's B-17s came to life.

The crewmen aboard the bomber were all business as McGarry and Cotham started the right outboard engine—number four. The pilots would taxi the aircraft on only the two outboard engines in order to save precious fuel. The two remaining engines would be started just before takeoff. The interphone crackled as each man double-checked his equipment and reported his status. Halligan, alone in the nose with Foe, felt somehow comforted as *Spirit of Flak Wolf*, with engines running, no longer felt like a cold, inanimate machine. Rather, as did every aircraft, it vibrated with a subtle timbre that was its own—almost as if it were a living thing.

Only a few minutes passed before both the bomber and its men were ready to go. A green flare arced up from the control tower, and the aircraft assigned to the front elements of the 303rd's formation rolled from their hardstands and onto the taxiways that ringed the field. Halligan knew that McGarry was ticking off the different bombers against a list as they taxied. It was imperative that he put *Spirit of Flak Wolf* where it belonged in the long line of big machines.

Finally, McGarry signaled the crew chief and immediately a ground crewman trotted around the left wingtip—clear of the spinning propeller—and pulled the wheel chocks away. There was another exchange of signals, and Halligan felt the aircraft shudder as McGarry advanced the B-17's two outboard engines. He looked left and returned the salute that the crew chief aimed at McGarry. He was never sure if the ground man saw him, but he always returned the salute on principle.

The aircraft ahead of *Spirit of Flak Wolf* blasted up mud and water and small stones. A clump of propeller-blown something made a muddy streak down the left side of the glazed nose. Halligan considered whether or not the climb through the clouds would wash it clean and guessed that it probably would not. Both he and Foe looked up when the aircraft was rocked, as if by a heavy wind. The pilot of another B-17 powered up its engines to pull a wheel clear of the sodden patch where he had let it wander, just off its hardstand. A rock ticked hard against the glass in front of Foe, and he reached up with his forefinger and touched where it hit.

There was another green flare and the mission leader started his takeoff roll. Halligan watched the heavily loaded bomber use most of the runway before pulling itself clear of the ground. A few seconds later it disappeared into the gray murk. The rest of the 303rd's aircraft followed at thirty-second intervals. A short time later McGarry and Cotham started the two inboard engines—number two and number three—finished their takeoff checks, and swung *Spirit of Flak Wolf* onto the runway. They pushed the throttles forward and let the engines settle into a smooth, ready roar before releasing the brakes.

Halligan noted that the aircraft was slow to move; the crew had never flown aboard such a heavily loaded ship. Nevertheless, the bomber did accelerate slowly down the runway. Stuck onto the front end of the aircraft as they were, Halligan and Foe had a view of the takeoff like no one else's. The B-17's initial jouncing damped into a smooth roll as the wings created lift and began to pull the aircraft from the uneven pavement. And then, at a distant point of the runway where none of the crew had ever been, *Spirit of Flak Wolf* was airborne. Halligan watched the ground disappear as the bomber hauled itself into the low-hanging clouds.

There was a sudden, mechanical roar and the aircraft lurched. Halligan felt it yaw even as McGarry and Cotham pushed the engines to full power. An engine had failed. Halligan—even through the din of the hard-pressed motors—heard the two pilots above and behind him strain as they wrestled with the bomber's controls. And then McGarry's voice came over the interphone. He sounded frustrated, but not frightened. He ordered the men to don their parachutes.

Halligan and Foe exchanged their fearful glances one more time. So soon after takeoff there were no oxygen masks to hide their faces. It occurred to Halligan that Foe looked old. And tired. Behind Foe, through the glass nose, Halligan saw the ground again. And trees. The load that *Spirit of Flak Wolf* carried was too heavy for it to climb on only three engines. There was a jolt and the B-17 tipped toward the ground and then bucked nose-high for a long moment before nosing over again. There was another crash, and Halligan blinked reflexively as Foe's body hurtled into his amid a spray of shattered glass and metal.

* * *

DESPITE THE FOG, the thunderclap that *Spirit of Flak Wolf* made when it smashed into the ground near Winwick, on Easter Sunday, April 9, 1944, traveled for miles. The bombs it carried did not explode, but the big ship was ripped into smaller bits that were immolated when the fuel it carried ignited. Halligan, Foe, McGarry and Cotham were all killed, as was the engineer, Henry Grace, and the radio operator, Stephen Stuphar. Miraculously, the four gunners were thrown from the ship and survived, although they were badly burned and injured.

None ever returned to combat operations.

PREFACE

I WAS A FIGHTER PILOT. Like most fighter pilots I was sure that I was the best there ever was. Alone in the aircraft, I controlled my destiny. If I lived or died, there was one person to credit or to blame.

And that is why I am so fascinated by the bomber crews of World War II. Certainly the men who crewed the heavy bombers that were sent against Nazi Germany were flyers, but they enjoyed none of the soaring freedom of flight. Rather, they crawled into primitive, bomb-laden brutes and froze—sometimes to death—miles above the earth in enormous formations while being savaged by antiaircraft guns and fighters. Driven by a visceral loyalty to their comrades and their country, they hunkered down, thrashed through the enemy's defenses, dropped their bombs and fought their way home.

If they weren't shot down.

To some extent their skills and those of their crewmates determined whether they returned home or not. But to a greater degree their survival depended on luck. It was chance that put a bomber in the exact wrong place at the exact wrong time to be caught by a burst of flak.

And providence decided whether or not a mechanical failure forced an aircraft out of formation to be set upon by enemy fighters. And it was fortune that determined if a badly damaged bomber slammed into another. In actual fact, the fates of the bomber men were largely out of their own control.

Indeed, flying heavy bombers against the Germans during World War II was akin to a complex, airborne variation of Russian roulette. And that is why I believe these flyers were the most valiant airmen ever. The decision these men made to climb aboard a bomber, mission after mission, while knowing that a safe return was never certain— regardless of their skill or experience—was a splendidly brave one.

Of more than forty Eighth Air Force bomb groups I chose the 303rd—"Hell's Angels"—for several reasons. Firstly, it was one of the original units to start heavy bombardment operations against Germany. This allowed me to use the unit to provide an overview of the story, from beginning to end, of the Eighth Air Force's strategic bombing effort. Next was the fact that the unit's records are extensive, well orga- nized and readily available. Decades after the war the 303rd formed an association, and many men—Harry Gobrecht chief among them— labored assiduously to preserve the group's legacy. Finally, there was the fact that although the 303rd was a standout unit, its operations were typical of all the Eighth Air Force's heavy bomb groups.

However, that being said, the 303rd's achievements were remark- able. The B-17, *Hell's Angels*, from which the group took its name, was the first Eighth Air Force bomber to fly twenty-five missions. Another of the group's aircraft, *Knockout Dropper*, was the first to surpass both the fifty- and seventy-five-mission marks. The unit was the first in the Eighth Air Force to reach the two- and three-hundred-mission mile- stones. Further, the 303rd flew more missions from England—364— than any other bomb group. And only one other unit dropped more bomb tonnage. Lewis Lyle commanded one of the 303rd's squadrons before becoming the group's deputy commander; he later led his own bomb group. He flew an incredible sixty-nine missions—more than any other

Eighth Air Force bomb group commander. Moreover, the bravery of the 303rd's airmen was never questioned and was personified by Jack Mathis and Forrest Vosler. Both were awarded the Medal of Honor.

Too many histories of the air war over Europe during World War II concentrate only on the terror of air combat. Overdone, this can leave the reader numb, even bored. Consequently, I have worked to describe not only the horrors of the air battles, but also why, how and by whom those battles were fought. I have also gone to some length to describe the roles of the maintenance and support personnel; not a single bomber would have gotten airborne without them. Indeed, for every airman there were approximately ten men who toiled on the ground to support him. Within these pages, for brevity's sake, I have included the various support groups under the 303rd's umbrella. But I believe they merit mention by name at least once. They were the 444th Sub Depot, the 3rd Station Complement Squadron, the 1681st Ordnance Company, the 1199th Military Police Company, the 863rd Chemical Company, the 1114th Quartermaster Company and the 202nd Finance Company.

The 303rd and its support units comprised a bombing organization the size of a large town—approximately four thousand men at any one time. The experiences of those men could fill a hundred or more books. But I could write only one. Although I could not tell the story of every man who served with the group, I am confident that the stories I have aggregated into this book have succeeded in recounting the extraordinary history of the 303rd. Ultimately, my hope is that this work will be regarded as an essential reference for understanding the Eighth Air Force's heavy bombardment operations during the greatest air war that ever was, and that ever can be.

"AND THEN YOU SLEPT IN THE BARN"

"I WAS BORN on the kitchen table of our ninety-acre dairy farm just outside of Smithton, Missouri," said Van White. "It was April 30, 1919, and my birth certificate specified that I was 'Born Alive.' I grew up with an older brother and a younger brother and a sister in that same house with no electricity or running water."[1]

Dairy farming was difficult in good times, but it was almost not worth doing during the Great Depression, when prices plummeted to nearly nothing. "Aside from taking care of the cows and the actual milking, which had to be done twice each day," White said, "the glass bottles had to be meticulously cleaned and sterilized before they were filled and capped. Then we delivered the milk on a small route we had in town—Smithton's population was only about two hundred. We sold the milk for five cents a quart and also sold eggs for six cents a dozen. It was little more than a subsistence living; we were almost destitute, but as kids we didn't realize it because so many of our friends were also very poor.

"Still," White said, "we were envious of our friends who lived in town. They didn't have chores like we did. They didn't have cows to milk and bottles to be sterilized and filled. We did it before school, walked to school and then walked home afterward to do it again. And of course, we had to help with the big vegetable garden we kept. A lot of our meals came from that garden. So, there wasn't much opportunity for us to play sports or participate in other activities."

White's father tried to supplement the family's income as best he could. "At one point my father entered into a contract with a business in Kansas City. They agreed to buy all the rabbits we could raise—rabbit was commonly eaten at the dinner table back then. As it turned out, the company went bankrupt and we were left with two hundred and fifty domestic rabbits. We gave a lot of rabbits away, sold some and ate the rest for a long time after that."

White matriculated through all twelve grades before graduating from Smithton High School in 1937. "I wasn't a particularly good student," he said, "although I did learn to type pretty well, which paid dividends later. I went down to Kansas City to work for Braniff Airways with my older brother. He was making ten dollars a week. I worked as a 'cargo buster.' I handled luggage, gassed and oiled aircraft, and did whatever else I was told. My brother and I shared a room at the airport for free.

"I got it bad for one of the Braniff stewardesses," White said. "Her name was Elisia Romera, and she was from Dallas. She was cute as a speckled puppy under a red wagon, but I didn't get anywhere with her." Still, White did have a brush with greatness. "Jimmy Doolittle was famous as a great air racer during that time. One day he flew a Waco into the airport and taxied off the hard surface onto some wet ground. I helped him park his airplane, and when he climbed out he said, 'Young man, if you wouldn't mind getting a bucket of water and a brush to wipe off the underside of my airplane I'd be most appreciative.' I got the mud cleaned off real nice and he gave me a five-dollar tip! That was close to half a week's pay!"

White joined the Army in 1940. "I was visiting home and was in the barbershop at Smithton when my good friend George Monsees walked in and said that the Army was recruiting for the Air Corps. He wanted us to leave right then to sign up in Kansas City, and I had to convince him to wait until my haircut was finished!" After enlisting that same day, White reported to boot camp at Jefferson Barracks a week later. "It was cold and icy and George got pneumonia and was set back. I finished and was sent to Langley, in Virginia. My Class A uniform was left over from World War I and had been pulled from mothballs. It was the old choker-style jacket and had lace-up puttees to go over my boots. My boots were so old there was mold growing on them. When I got off the train at Langley, a very gruff second lieutenant grabbed me and told me to report to him the next day for a new uniform. It was January 1941."

During the next year, White entertained notions of becoming a flyer, but because he demonstrated a talent for typing he was shunted into clerical work. Specifically, he was made an operations clerk. "So I ended up as a chairborne trooper in the paragraph corps," he said.

"THE ARMY AIR CORPS changed my name for me," said Louis "Mel" Schulstad.[2] It was 1939 and Schulstad had been in the service for only a short time when he stood in line to collect his pay, which, for a private, was $21 per month. According to procedure, when it was his turn, he stepped in front of the lieutenant's desk—which was stacked with cash—and saluted. The attending sergeant told him to sign the payroll. "So, I leaned over and looked and saw that they had spelled my name wrong." Instead of "Lewis," the Army had spelled it "Louis."

Schulstad pointed out the error. "And the sergeant asked, 'Do you want your money or don't you?'" Schulstad declared that he did indeed want his money. "So, the sergeant said, 'Sign it.'" From that point, Schulstad spent the rest of his life with the wrong first name.

He grew up in the small town of Reynolds, North Dakota, and, like many young men of his generation, was inspired by Charles Lindbergh.

"I was bitten by the flying bug," he said. "But it was hard to find the money in 1935 and 1936. I worked as a seventeen-year-old on the farms around my town for a dollar a day. That meant that you were out in the field at six in the morning and you had some lunch and sometimes they brought you dinner—coffee and sandwiches—and then supper at the house at six in the evening. And then you slept in the barn, or if they had extra bedrooms you'd sleep in the house. And you were there for six days a week."

Payday came on Saturday. "Every Saturday night," Schulstad said, "you'd stand there with maybe a couple of other farmhands and the farmer paid you in cash. He'd count out the bills: 'One-two-three-four-five-six.' Six dollars for six days' work." Consequently $6 was a very dear sum to Schulstad.

"I became acquainted with Lester Jolly," said Schulstad. "He had a Piper Cub and gave lessons for eight dollars an hour. I reached an arrangement with him and he agreed to give me lessons—about fifteen or twenty minutes—for two dollars. I'd meet him at the wheat field where he kept his airplane and pay him the two dollars. He'd hand it to his wife, who drove to town, bought five gallons of gas and then poured it into the airplane. And that was our arrangement."

Schulstad's desire for more flying, together with other exigencies, compelled him to enlist in the Army Air Corps. He was determined to become a pilot. Although the odds were greatly stacked against him at the time, there was—assuming he performed well—an official path for him to do so. After completing basic training and other assignments typical for a non-flying enlisted man, he was sent to March Field, in Riverside, California, during 1940. It was there that he saw his first B-17. "Wings you could walk under. And four engines of twelve hundred horsepower each. My God!" Schulstad was excited to learn that, as an armorer, he would fly aboard the massive aircraft.

Schulstad's commanding officer took a liking to him and appreciated the young man's desire to become a pilot. But he knew that

Schulstad would have to pass a rigorous battery of academic tests for which he was not prepared. "I think you've got the potential," he told Schulstad. "I'm going to make you my orderly. That means your job is to come in here at six o'clock each morning and get my office ready for the day. And then, you're going to the junior college in Riverside."

"Well, I didn't have a car," said Schulstad. "But he knew that if I was really serious about passing those tests and becoming a pilot, that I'd find a way to do it. So, I hitchhiked to school every day." In the end, after failing at his first attempt, Schulstad passed the exams.

Schulstad's unit was soon after broken into three parts, which were to form the nuclei for new units. He was sent to Tucson with one of those three parts. The new unit had only a handful of B-17s that it parked at the municipal field. Short on aircraft, it accepted a dozen PT-17 biplane trainers so that its pilots could maintain their currency and earn their monthly flight pay. Schulstad was made a crew chief and subsequently—under the tutelage of an experienced master sergeant—learned a great deal about the little aircraft. "He drank a little bit too much," said Schulstad, "but I admired the old guy."

The "old guy" taught Schulstad quite a bit, including how to adjust the various bracing wires that ran between the wings. "The tension would change a bit depending on the temperature and such, and the old sergeant would get out there with his pliers and hit one of the wires and listen to it as if it were a guitar string or a harp string. And then he'd tell me 'tighten this one,' or 'loosen that one.'"

At the time, the Army Air Corps was expanding rapidly, and Schulstad was promoted from private first class to staff sergeant within just a few months. The extra money was certainly welcome, but Schulstad's job as a crew chief offered other benefits. "I got to know the pilots and they got to know me. They'd take me flying and we flew all over Arizona. We'd do aerobatics or shoot landings. Sometimes if they had a hangover we'd land in a pasture and sleep in the shade under the wing. Often, when they got bored, they'd let me fly. And I learned to do turns and how to land and even do aerobatics. It was a lot of fun." Consequently, when Schulstad was called to pilot training a few months later, he had no problems whatsoever. He was awarded his wings on March 16, 1942, and sent to fly B-17s.

"MY FATHER WAS A BAKER and he delivered pastries in his Willys Whippet to different resorts along the Osage River in Missouri," said John Ford, who spent much of his young life in the west central Missouri town of Warsaw.[3] "But the flour from his bakery got to him. He finally caught pneumonia and went bankrupt at about the same time."

Ford's father recovered and immediately started another career. "He went to barber school," said Ford, "and when he finished he set up a barbershop in Versailles, about thirty miles northeast of Warsaw. I finished growing up there. I was an average student in high school, where I learned to type and also played the saxophone and the clarinet. I played baseball too.

"I joined the CCC when I graduated from high school in 1940," Ford said. The CCC, or Civilian Conservation Corps, was a Depression-era relief program that taught young men discipline and basic skills while maintaining and improving remote public lands. They planted trees, fought fires and constructed outbuildings—among other duties. They were paid $30 each month and were required to send home $25.

"It was essentially a military lifestyle—barracks living and formations and such," said Ford. "We learned quite a bit and it was a good experience. Lots of guys I later served with had spent time in the CCC." Nevertheless, Ford didn't stay in the CCC long before enlisting in the Army. Following basic training at Jefferson Barracks, Missouri, he was sent to Langley Field in Virginia during the spring of 1941. "I wanted to be a pilot in the worst way," he said. "I talked one of the young pilots into taking me flying four or five times in the Waco PT-14. Taking off was no problem at all, but landings gave me problems."

Ford's officers discovered he had typing talent and assigned him to the administrative shop of the 43rd Bombardment Group's 64th Bomb Squadron. The new unit—based in Bangor, Maine—was equipped with B-18s, two-engine bombers that were already obsolete in 1941. Nevertheless, the B-18 was a useful aircraft for antisubmarine patrol work, and following the attack on Pearl Harbor the unit flew missions over the maritime approaches from the North Atlantic.

Bangor was cold and miserable that winter. "Aside from my regular job, I was assigned other duties, just like everyone else. It snowed quite a bit that year, and when I stood guard duty—two hours on and two off—I tramped a trench in the snow about three or four feet deep. During that time I still wanted to fly and applied to do so, but during the interview with my commanding officer he told me that I was too valuable doing what I was doing and he didn't forward my request."

Ford's dilemma was not uncommon—especially among men who could type. Many commanding officers did their best to keep good enlisted personnel in their units. It served them no good purpose to let talented men leave for flight training or for other reasons. Good typists were in especially short supply as the USAAF was in the process of enlarging itself many times over. It was an administratively intensive effort, and administration required good typists.

Ford was stuck.

WHITE, SCHULSTAD AND FORD—and many thousands of young men like them—enlisted in an air force headed by General Henry "Hap" Arnold. They were part of Arnold's plan to grow the service into the largest military air arm in history. It was a plan he had stewarded for several years, and one that had already caused him serious health issues. He was the assistant chief of the Army Air Corps when his boss, Oscar Westover, was killed at the controls of his own aircraft while on a whirlwind circuit to start the buildup that Arnold ultimately completed. Arnold recalled: "Westover worked harder than anybody. Too hard. He flew all over the country, always flying his own plane, landing here and talking to some group or other about airpower while his sergeant got the ship ready for the next hop, then flying on to give another enthusiastic talk to people in another town."

On September 21, 1938, Arnold received a call from the Air Corps representative at Lockheed's factory in Burbank, California. Westover and his sergeant had been killed in a landing crash there. "He said," Arnold recalled, "that as he was talking to me the plane was still burning on the runway. I joined my wife and we went down to wait in the lobby of the Kennedy Warren, hoping to reach Mrs. Westover before she heard about it over the radio."[4] Arnold was made chief of the Air Corps eight days later, on September 29.

At that time the Army Air Corps numbered fewer than twenty-five thousand personnel and twenty-five hundred aircraft.[5] Notwithstanding the fact that the United States was the richest and most industrialized nation on earth, the task before Arnold was gargantuan. Firstly, the government had to make funding available, and Arnold was consequently at loggerheads not only with secretary of the treasury Henry Morgenthau, but also with President Roosevelt himself. The two senior statesmen—unschooled in air warfare—believed that a powerful air force was measured in numbers of aircraft. That notion permeated much of the government, and Arnold tried to educate the President: "The strength of an air force cannot be measured in terms of airplanes only. Other things are essential—productive capacity of airplanes, of pilots, of mechanics, and bases from which to operate. A sound training program is essential to provide replacements."[6]

Arnold didn't argue the point that considerable quantities of aircraft were essential. But he knew that they had to be high-quality machines of the types needed to fight the coming war. Moreover, highly trained men were necessary to crew and maintain them. And those men needed bases from which to operate. Too, specialists such as mechanics, meteorologists, doctors, logisticians, administrators and other uniquely qualified personnel were necessary to support them. Furthermore, an expansive and efficient supply train had to be grown, provisioned and sustained—and it had to reach every man in the giant organization that Arnold and his staff envisioned. Finally, the nation's industries had to be modified and grown to produce everything from electrical harnesses for gun turrets to cathode ray tubes for radar displays. None of this existed in the form and size that was required.

And all of it cost money. Lots of it. Consequently, Arnold's routine included continuous lobbying. His work and the work of his staff and other airpower advocates—together with the exigencies of the coming war—combined to open the coffers not a minute too soon. This was at a time when it took five or more years to design and field a competent aircraft type. And it took approximately a year to train a mechanic or technical specialist, and roughly the same amount of time, or more, to prepare a pilot for combat. Moreover, creating experienced leaders from these cadres of newly trained men took years.

It was demanding work, and it was additionally a politically difficult time for Arnold. He and Morgenthau clashed constantly as Roosevelt had vested the secretary with the power to decide who received what aircraft and equipment. This proved to be nettlesome as various soon-to-be-allies scrambled to purchase whatever American equipment they could while Arnold competed with them for the same equipment to build the Army Air Corps. Arnold's job was made additionally nettlesome by the nation's isolationists who believed that a nation that was equipped for war was more likely to make it.

Arnold and the Army Air Corps, together with industry and the government, worked tirelessly to grow the service to meet the impending global threat. At that point the existing personnel and infrastructure were archaically organized as a defensive arm intended to deter an invasion. It was a preposterous notion for what was essentially little more than a hobbyhorse organization.

Nevertheless, that ill-prepared organization served a purpose. It was the tiny grain of sand about which was created the pearl that eventually grew to be the most massive and modern air arm in history. During 1939, Congress authorized the growth of the Army Air Corps to an unprecedented 24 air groups. Following the start of the war in Europe, the expansion was raised to 41 groups in 1940. The service was charged with training seven thousand pilots *each year*.[7] This was more pilots than had been in the service two years earlier, but it was nothing compared with what was to come. By 1941, authorization had been granted to equip and man 224 air groups.[8] Pilots were needed to fly the aircraft in those groups, and the annual training rate was assessed at *seventy thousand* new pilots per year, together with a commensurate number of other aircrew—navigators, aerial gunners, bombardiers, etc.—not to mention the necessary mechanics, administrators and support specialists.[9]

Such massive growth was mind-boggling even to careerists such as Arnold. In practical terms it meant that virtually everyone assimilated into the growing giant was an amateur. Much learning was done on the job by men who only months earlier had bagged groceries, sold millinery or studied for Boy Scout merit badges. Men who had been in uniform as little as two years were "old hands" who molded newcomers for service even as they learned their own duties.

Arnold's value was unquestioned by the time the Japanese attacked Pearl Harbor on December 7, 1941. Although there were still precious few aircraft available and the training machine was only then getting to speed, there was a guarded optimism that the objectives Arnold and his staff had set could be reached. In fact, even at that point the United States was already producing more aircraft than Germany and Japan combined.

Still, there were setbacks, and painstakingly developed plans were changed and then changed again and again. But Arnold had set the Army Air Corps—newly renamed and reorganized during 1941 as the United States Army Air Forces, or USAAF—on the right path. Ultimately, he oversaw the expansion of the nation's air arm to 2.4 million personnel, and 318 groups. During 1944 alone, the nation's manufacturers produced nearly one hundred thousand aircraft.[10]

But victory was years away when the Arcadia Conference was

convened on December 21, 1941. There, President Roosevelt and Winston Churchill and their staffs met to mature their plan to defeat the Axis powers. A precept of that plan was the concentration of resources and effort against Germany first. To that end Roosevelt and Churchill stressed the importance of heavy bombardment operations against the Third Reich and queried Arnold as to when the United States might join the Royal Air Force—the RAF—in such efforts. "I said," Arnold recalled, "we could not send less than one Group because the Group was our smallest self-sustained unit; that I could probably get the first Group of our bombers over to England by the following March [1942]."[11]

TO PORTRAY THIS MASSIVE GROWTH as anything better than not quite chaotic would be a mischaracterization. For example, William Eisenhart reported for military service to Fort Benjamin Harrison at Indianapolis while wearing a suit and tie. "They took me to a railroad siding on the fort, handed me a shovel and set me to unloading a coal car. In my new suit. It was ruined and I was furious. I still am."[12]

"NO PANTY WAIST UNION HOURS"

THE FORMATION OF THE 303RD Bombardment Group was described by the unit's first official diary entry, dated February 16, 1942, just more than two months after the Japanese sneak attack on Pearl Harbor and America's subsequent entry into the war:

> *In compliance with General Orders No. 5 (confidential), Headquarters Second Air Force, Fort George Wright, Washington, dated February 3, 1942, the 303rd Bombardment Group (H) ["H" for "Heavy"] was activated on February 3, 1942, at Army Air Base, Pendleton Field, Pendleton, Oregon, and was assigned to Air Force Combat Command.*[1]

The 303rd was organized into a headquarters unit, three heavy bombardment flying squadrons and a heavy reconnaissance squadron. The flying units were the 358th, 359th and 360th Bombardment (H) Squadrons, and the 31st Reconnaissance (H) Squadron. On the day of the 303rd's formation the squadrons were little more than placeholders with no personnel, equipment or aircraft. However, men from existing units were assigned to make up a core element, and the 303rd moved its flag to Gowen Field, at Boise, Idaho, on February 13, 1942. The unit received its first aircraft, four B-17Es and three C-39s—two-engine transport aircraft intended for training—on February 16. From that day, personnel and aircraft arrived in increasing numbers as the 303rd started readying for combat. Its parent organization, the Second Air Force, intended it to be ready in time to move overseas and start combat operations beginning in June 1942.

Gowen had been finished for less than a year when the 303rd arrived. Named after an Air Corps pilot from Idaho who had been killed in a flying accident in Panama, it was located just south of Boise. Although it was cold in winter and hot during the summer, flying conditions were generally favorable, and it served as a training base for bomber units throughout the war and beyond.

And the citizens of Boise made the men of those units feel welcome. "I had a good time at Gowen," John Ford said. "We were able to get passes into town and enjoyed ourselves quite a bit. And I had a girl there. There were dances, and places to drink—of course—as well as gambling. It seemed odd to me that the bars and slot machines were always upstairs and never on the ground floor."

At Gowen, the 303rd was—for the most part—formed and trained by amateurs working from Army manuals under the direction of a very few experienced men. This was true of virtually every USAAF unit at that point in the war. Because the service expanded so dramatically and so quickly, there were very few veterans available to season the new units. Indeed, only a sprinkling of men had been in the service longer than a year or two.

John Ford was an example. He had been separated from the 64th Bombardment Group in Bangor, Maine, and sent with several other 64th personnel to help stand up the 303rd. "They assigned me to the 359th Bomb Squadron's personnel shop. By that time I had been in the service for more than a year and was an old veteran compared to most of the guys. Accordingly, I spent much of the time training the administrative personnel from all of the other squadrons as well as the group headquarters. During the time we were at Gowen I was promoted up the ranks from private first class to staff sergeant." Such an advance during peacetime would have taken more than ten years.

Chris Christoff described another example that highlighted the inefficiencies of the USAAF's rapid wartime expansion. Trained as a Teletype maintenance man, he expected to be used as such when he arrived at Gowen. "The Teletype department was operating fairly well without my help. I do nothing for days until someone orders me to report to the motor pool." On arrival, it became apparent to Christoff that the 303rd planned to use him as a truck driver. He wanted no part of it. "I'm thinking if I make a mess or screw up on this driving test they'll not accept me, so I strip the gears a few times while shifting, I hit the curb while turning corners and a couple more minor infractions."[2] He reported back the following day, fully expecting to be sent back to the communications section. Instead, Christoff was issued a motor vehicle operator's permit; he was the newest member of the 303rd's motor pool.

It was inevitable that accidents became commonplace in the rapidly expanding USAAF. In fact, two of every three aircraft lost during the war were destroyed by accidents rather than to enemy action; on average, five aircraft were destroyed each day in the States. The 303rd's first contribution to this statistic occurred on April 3, 1942, when a B-17 crashed near Bridge, Idaho. All eight crewmen were killed.

But accidents weren't confined to flying. Work injuries were common, as were vehicle accidents. The unit diary entry for April 30, 1942, noted a totally pointless mishap that fortunately did not result in death or injury: "During the morning, officers playing with an 'unloaded' gun accidentally shot through a wall and window of the S-2 office."[3]

Accidents notwithstanding, the unit continued to grow as personnel and aircraft converged on Gowen. Whereas the 303rd had only four B-17s when it first arrived in mid-February, it carried eighteen B-17s and two A-20s on its roster by April 6. The A-20s were twin-engine, light attack bombers that the 303rd used primarily as target tugs for gunnery training. They also flew as utility hacks and to maintain pilot currency requirements. Fast and nimble—especially as compared to the B-17—the A-20 was popular with the pilots.

AS THE 303RD continued to form, advance elements of the USAAF began to organize in England. Brigadier General Ira Eaker was put in charge of VIII Bomber Command, the heavy bombardment component of the Eighth Air Force, which was activated at Savannah, Georgia, during January 1942. Eaker, a longtime acolyte of Arnold's, grew up dirt poor in Texas and Oklahoma but excelled as an Army aviator during the 1920s and 1930s. A technician, tactician and logistician, Eaker was also an avid writer and gifted public speaker. Moreover, he was a genuine and charming man who exercised considerable social grace. He worked hard and played hard and—with unstinting aid from the English and his RAF counterparts—was the perfect man to pave the way for America's daytime strategic air war over Europe. He arrived in England with only six men to do just that during February 1942, the same month that the 303rd was activated.

THE 303RD, ITS MEN LEARNING on the job, struggled toward combat readiness as best it could. Shortcomings became evident when the group was inspected by the Second Air Force staff on April 10, 1942. Deficiencies were noted in a number of areas and earlier notions that the group would be ready for combat operations in June began to be questioned.

There was no longer any question when the 303rd underwent a subsequent inspection on April 22. As part of the evaluation the group launched a mock mission that missed its designated target by thousands of feet. An investigation determined that the handpicked crew leading the mission had been wholly unprepared. During earlier train-ing sorties it had achieved satisfactory results by repeatedly bombing the same target using visual cues. However, the target was changed for the evaluation mission, and the crew didn't even use the bomb sight—essentially dropping the bombs on a guess.[4] Consequently, it was deter-mined that the group would not be ready for overseas duty as planned.

Regardless of their performance, there was little for the men of the 303rd to do other than redouble their training efforts. Aircrews con-tinued to fly bombing, gunnery, navigation and formation sorties, while ground crews and support men worked to keep the aircraft flying. All the men attended classes and lectures at the base theater. Subjects ranged from aircraft recognition, to sexual hygiene, to current events. The unit diary entry for May 3, 1942, characterized the tempo during this period: "Sunday—and no slackening in the USA's training program. Seven days a week with no let up, except for physical rest, and with no Panty Waist union hours to hamper the scheduled results desired. 'Keep 'em flying' means just what it says in this man's Army, and no quarter [is] asked or given."[5]

It was during this time that the 427th Bomb Squadron was desig-nated. At its formation the 303rd was composed of the 358th, 359th and 360th Bombardment (H) Squadrons together with the 31st Recon-naissance (H) Squadron and the headquarters element. The 31st was disbanded on March 16 and its personnel, equipment and aircraft were assigned to the 38th Reconnaissance (H) Squadron, which had been attached to the 303rd on March 13. Only a short time later, on May 1, the 38th was redesignated as the 427th Bombardment (H) Squadron. These designations, 358th, 359th, 360th and 427th, were used through the rest of the war. The curious, nonsequential numbering scheme confused friend and foe alike but was not unusual within the USAAF.

The numbering schemes were little more than a distraction to the men as they continued to train. That they needed the training was underscored by a foolish accident that occurred on May 27. While air-borne, a pilot mistakenly activated the bail-out alarm. Although the ship was perfectly airworthy, three of the aircrew jumped from the ship. One of them was killed after landing, when his parachute pulled him over a cliff.

As it was determined that the 303rd would not ship overseas on time, it was imperative that other bomb groups be made ready as soon as possible. To that end, the 303rd was "cherry-picked"—compelled to give up some of its better-trained crews for other duties or to flesh out other units. Indeed, the group was gutted at the end of May by the transfer of seventeen of its aircraft and crews. Many of these were used to reconnoiter weather across the North Atlantic for the 97th Bomb Group's movement to England, while others were assigned to the 306th Bomb Group.

At the same time, most of what was left of the 303rd was moved south to Muroc, California. This movement was connected with Japanese activity in the Pacific. At Muroc, the crews were supposed to receive special training for low-altitude attacks on shipping. As it developed, the great clash at Midway took place during the first week of June, and none of the 303rd's crews or aircraft were sent to the Pacific. Instead, they continued their training with an emphasis on aerial gunnery and bombing. Additionally, the group sent small detachments to conduct antisubmarine patrols from the naval air station at North Island, in San Diego.

This period marked the 303rd's gradual transition from Gowen Field to bases in the Southwest where it conducted more advanced training in preparation for deployment overseas. The first of those bases was Alamogordo Provisional Air Base in southern New Mexico, where the 303rd's first elements arrived on June 17. It was a hot, grimy and primitive post that had been operational for less than a month. It was unpopular with the men, who had grown accustomed to the amenities of Gowen, together with the comparatively temperate spring weather of Idaho.

Moreover, the social scene was markedly different from Boise's. The unit diarist was obviously unimpressed: "The nearest town [Alamogordo] is located ten miles from the post and consists mostly of squat, dusty adobe buildings mostly occupied by U.S. citizens of Mexican decent [*sic*]. Large portions of the town have been declared 'Out of Bounds' for the troops as several knifeings [*sic*] of personnel have taken place in various dark, roudy [*sic*] sections of the city after nightfall."[6] John Ford was likewise disappointed by the place: "It was terrible. And hot. It seemed that there was a sandstorm almost every day."

But aside from occasionally fierce winds that blew sand wherever it wasn't wanted, the flying weather was excellent. Men, equipment and aircraft continued to join the unit, and the number and quality of training flights increased steadily, as did the proficiency of the 303rd's aircrews, ground crews and support personnel. That the group consistently achieved sortie rates in excess of thirty per day reflected well on the maintenance men, especially since there were only ten B-17s on hand.

Still, the place was harsh. The heat was oppressive, and the desert out of which the airfield had been scraped was home to tarantulas, scorpions and snakes. Recon, the 427th Bomb Squadron's fiercely loyal bitch mascot, was bitten by a rattlesnake when she leapt to defend her master, William Nelson. Nelson and his comrades spent several anxious days as the snake's poison worked its worst against their faithful friend. Happily, Recon's resilience won the day as she eventually recovered and was smuggled overseas with the 427th a couple of months later.

More tragic was an incident that occurred on June 27. The 303rd sometimes trucked men to nearby Lake Lucero, where they swam and relaxed. On that day, when it came time to muster for the ride back to the airfield, Clarence Willett, a clerk from the headquarters squadron, was missing. A search was made and his body was found floating in the water. The unit diary noted the loss: "It is believed that he stepped into a deep hole and being a poor swimmer was unable to care for himself. The other men did not miss him until ready to leave the lake."[7]

At least part of the disorder that characterized the 303rd's operations during this early part of its existence was due to the fact that it had four different commanders from the time of its creation at the beginning of February up to mid-July. John Sutherland was the unit's first commander—

essentially, only on paper—during the first couple of weeks. Ford Lauer was the unit's second commander from the middle of February until he was replaced at the end of May by Warren Higgens. Lauer later went on to lead a different bomb group, the 99th, to great success as part of the Fifteenth Air Force in Italy. Higgens led the group for only a week before it was given back to Sutherland, who stayed at its head until July 13 when James Wallace took charge. Wallace was still in command when the group commenced combat operations a few months later.

The 303rd didn't stay long at Alamogordo, and that was fine with its men. At the beginning of August, the unit was ordered to Biggs Field at El Paso, Texas, for the final phase of its training. Biggs, like Alamogordo, had only recently been made operational. It was less than a hundred miles south of Alamogordo and shared the same characteristics as the New Mexico base except that El Paso was a bigger city that offered more diversions.

Nevertheless, the men had little time to enjoy them. After arriving on August 7, the group was put through a hurried set of advanced classes and flights that culminated in a strike against an airfield target complex at San Angelo, Texas, on August 16. Although the event was marked by several failures, orders sending the group overseas were received the following day, and the men enthusiastically readied for the movement. "Packing continued day and night," recorded the unit diary. "Men were becoming tired and grouchy, but, as a whole, they were looking forward to their trip overseas. They went to town, making strange purchases—things to be given to the young ladies upon arrival at the group's final destination."[8]

The unit diary also marked the departure of a particularly disliked individual: "The 427th Bombardment Squadron (H) is gleefully celebrating the transfer to the base of one much hated Master Sergeant Roy Williams."[9] That an official unit diary would carry such a notation is very peculiar and gives a sense of the raw inexperience of the diarists and of the men who led them. Or perhaps, it indicated a singularly magnificent level of loathing for Master Sergeant Williams.

The group was broken into two echelons—ground and air—for the movement to its destination: England.[10] The ground element was scheduled to depart on August 24, while the aircrews, with a small contingent of non-flying personnel, were to proceed by rail to Kellogg Field at Battle Creek, Michigan, to receive new aircraft before crossing the Atlantic. Tragically, just prior to departing El Paso, another aircraft and most of its crew were lost on August 23. The B-17, from the 427th Bomb Squadron, was blasted to bits by lightning while flying near the New Mexico border. Of the nine men aboard, only two survived.

Ehle Reber, a native of Malin, Oregon, was representative of the very finest young men the nation was readying for air combat. The president of his high school's student body, a star football and basketball player, a state champion broad jumper and captain of the University of Oregon's track-and-field team, he was also a pilot with the 427th. His diary entries show him to have been a brash, intelligent and fun-loving young man not yet tempered by the experiences of adulthood. He recalled the accident several days later in his diary entry of August 29, 1942: "Lt. Quentin Hargrove is back from the hospital. Covered with bandages. We call him 'Spook.' Sgt. [Walter] Knox and Lt. [Quentin] Hargove, only survivors, were thrown clear when plane broke in two. Lucky to have silk [parachutes] on. Quite a blow to 427th. Party evening."

In the meantime, the bulk of the squadron's personnel, the ground element, traveled east by rail, having gotten under way during a terrible rainstorm on August 24. The unit diary noted conditions at the train station: "07:00 A.M. The troops are at the train and are awaiting orders to load. It is raining very hard. Water is running down the road, ankle deep."[11]

IRA EAKER HAD BEEN in England for six months by mid-August 1942 as the 303rd readied to leave Biggs. By that time, Carl "Tooey" Spaatz had arrived to take command of the Eighth Air Force while Eaker concentrated on building up the Eighth's heavy bombing component, VIII Bomber Command. The two men, at the head of a fledgling but growing body of men and machines, worked tirelessly to create an air force capable of performing a mission about which nothing existed except theories. They were building the Eighth to conduct precision, daytime, strategic bombing raids deep into the heart of enemy territory.

The notion had more than its fair share of critics. Peter Masefield was the air correspondent to London's *Sunday Times*. Although he was not a military man, he held a pilot's license, had worked as an engineer for Fairey Aviation and, as a journalist, had flown a few operational sorties with the RAF. This gave him the confidence to disparage the two main American bombers, the B-17 and the B-24. He did so with a patronizing smugness that must have infuriated the USAAF's leaders while simultaneously embarrassing top men at the RAF, the USAAF's closest ally.

On August 16, 1942, he wrote: "American heavy bombers—the latest [B-17] Fortresses and [B-24] Liberators—are fine flying machines, but not suited for bombing in Europe. Their bombs and bomb-loads are small, their armor and armament are not up to the standard now found necessary and their speeds are low." Masefield was especially condescending when he wrote, "It would be a tragedy for young American lives to be squandered through assigning either Liberators or Flying Fortresses to raids into the Reich night or day." Ironically, this piece appeared in the *Sunday Times* the morning after the RAF lost five bombers—and many young British lives—on night operations.

In fact, both the B-17 and the B-24 had excellent performance although admittedly they didn't carry payloads as large as some of their big British counterparts. On the other hand, the American aircraft dropped their weapons more accurately. The truth was that no aircraft types at that time were as well suited for a strategic daytime bombing campaign as were the B-17 and the B-24. In terms of technology and ease of production the two aircraft were marvels. None of the belligerents operated anything so capable. In fact, neither the Germans nor the Japanese ever fielded strategic bombers. And the RAF's bombers, although they were excellent aircraft with good performance, were not as rugged as their American counterparts, nor did they have the armament to survive regular daylight operations.

Masefield might be forgiven some of his conceit when it is considered that the B-17 actually had been used earlier in combat over Europe and had suffered badly. RAF's Bomber Command operated twenty B-17Cs from July 8 to September 12, 1941. It was a pitifully small number and the aircraft were dispatched on ridiculously small raids of twos and threes. These—especially the more lightly armed B-17Cs—were relatively easy pickings for German fighters. The RAF lost eight of the original twenty aircraft before ceasing such operations.

The Eighth Air Force—specifically, VIII Bomber Command—flew its first heavy bombardment mission from England on August 17, 1942, the day after Masefield's article was published, and only a week before the first elements of the 303rd left Biggs. It was a small raid of only twelve bombers that hit railroad targets at Rouen, in France. No aircraft were lost and there were no casualties, excepting a bombardier and a navigator on a diversionary sortie who were cut by flying glass when their aircraft struck a pigeon.

The German reaction—flak and fighters—was almost indifferent. That would change dramatically in the coming months. In fact, it wasn't until the Eighth's fourth mission, on August 21, 1942, that the Luftwaffe's fighters engaged the American bombers with any level of vigor. The B-17s were late to rendezvous with their RAF fighter escorts and so were left unprotected as they pressed to their target, the Wilton Shipyard at Rotterdam. After receiving and complying with a recall message, the twelve B-17s were attacked by a mixed force of approximately two dozen Me-109s and FW-190s.

The Germans dogged the retreating bombers for approximately twenty minutes but failed to knock any of them down. The pilot and copilot of one ship were wounded, and the copilot later died, but the formation held its own. This performance certainly must have heartened those who advocated the daytime precision approach to the strategic air campaign. Indeed, it wasn't until the tenth mission, on September 6, 1942, that a USAAF B-17 was lost on combat operations over Europe.

In fact, German fighter pilots were ill-prepared for downing the big American bombers. The USAAF's updated B-17s and B-24s were entirely different from anything they had previously encountered. An element of Jagdgeschwader 26—JG 26—made an attack against a group of B-17s on October 6, 1942, that initially met with little success. The Germans made three attacks, but unused to the massive size of the B-17s they broke away much too early, as described by Otto Stamberger: "We attacked the enemy bombers in pairs, going in with great bravado: closing in fast from behind with throttles wide open, then letting fly. But at first the attacks were all broken off much too early—as those great 'barns' grew larger and larger our people were afraid of colliding with them."[12]

Stamberger finally pressed close enough to do harm on his fourth firing pass. "The next time I went in I thought: get in much closer, keep going, keep going. Then I opened up, starting with his motors on the port wing. By the third such firing run the two port engines were burning well, and I had shot the starboard outer motor to smithereens." Stamberger saw a handful of parachutes blossom from the bomber before it struck the earth near Vendeville, France.

Although the Eighth's first ten or so raids were piddling in size—averaging just more than a dozen bombers each—it was less than two months after the start of operations that, on October 9, 1942, a comparatively massive mixed force of 115 B-17s and B-24s was sortied against steel and locomotive works at Lille, France. However, the abort rate was horrible as thirty-three of the crews failed to drop their bombs. Results against the Lille target were likewise unimpressive as some bombs fell miles from their targets. Indeed, only 9 of 588 bombs hit within fifteen hundred feet of their aim points. There was some damage inflicted on the intended targets, and several other worthwhile targets were unintentionally hit, but up to forty French civilians were killed.[13]

"SHE IS A HELL OF A BIG SHIP"

THE MOVEMENT OF THE 303RD'S ground element was uneventful. Many men were treated to new landscapes and skylines, while others, such as Eugene O'Brien, passed through familiar territory: "We finally came to Chicago and our train stopped to pick up more soldiers. The car I was riding in stopped at 66th Street and Indiana Avenue. I lived at 6936 Indiana, and if it wasn't for the tall trees, I would be able to see my home."[1] By August 27, the train had reached Pittsburgh, Pennsylvania. "05:00 P.M. Are at Pittsburg [sic], Pennsylvania. Stopped to water up the train," recorded the unit diary. "All men are ordered off the train and given exercise. Men enjoyed themselves waving at young ladies."[2] The next day the unit reached Fort Dix, New Jersey, where the men underwent final preparations before embarking for England.

While the ground echelon made its way east, the 303rd's aircrews and a few select ground personnel kept busy. Among other activities the men transferred the group's aircraft to units still in training, typed orders and other administrative directives, packed what they were allowed to take and attended more classes. They also amused themselves as described by

Ehle Reber on September 2: "Ground school in morning. Softball in afternoon with E.M. [enlisted men]—11–0 our favor in 4 innings. Beer Bust afterwards up the canyon. Stock [Donald Stockton] and I killed rattler. I think [Glenn] Hagenbuch is getting married soon. Kidded hell out of him. Hagenbuch, [Lloyd] Cole and [Billy] Southworth become captains tomorrow. Party in order. No flying, no ships."

Reber noted that the expectations of a promotion party were indeed realized the following day after the 427th Bomb Squadron beat the 360th at softball, 6–1. "Captains gave party in evening at Paso Del Norte Spanish Room. Bed late. Bryant and Soha out of this world [drunk]. Some more too. Leave tomorrow. Hagenbuch marriage off. Sad."

The ground element left Fort Dix the next day, September 4, for the port at New York, where the men were loaded aboard a ferry. The unit diary recorded the particulars: "Disembarked from ferry boat onto pier at 08:00 P.M. Boarded the second largest boat in the world— R.M.S. *Queen Mary*. The men were divided into two sections, one section to sleep below deck in cabins and the other section to sleep on deck. Sleeping positions will be alternated every twenty-four hours throughout the trip."

The *Queen Mary* slipped her moorings for the Atlantic crossing the following day and the 303rd's men continued their explorations of her attributes: "Confined investigation of the ship disclosed that she is a hell of a big ship. The halls and passage ways are finished in bird's eye maple. Mahogany, black walnut and crome [sic] plated steel are used throughout the dining hall and stairways. The cabins are beautifully finished and each cabin has a private bathroom with tub."[3]

Despite its fine furnishings, the ship—which normally sailed with a total of three thousand passengers and crew—was overcrowded to an astonishing degree and was much less comfortable than it would have been in regular service. "There are approximately 18,500 people aboard ship. These figures include American troops, R.A.F. troops, nurses and crew." Feeding so many men was an all-day exercise. Men finished one meal only to get in line for the next: "Meals are served twice daily in six settings. Each man wears a button which identifies his setting number."[4]

The voyage was a smooth one for the first few days as described by the unit diary entry for September 7: "Ship still going full speed. Weather holding up fine although it is very windy. Life boat and fire drill[s] were held today. . . . Ship changes course quite frequently. No other ships were sighted during the day. Life belts are required to be worn constantly and quite a number of the men were repremanded [sic] for not complying with the order. Antiaircraft guns were fired today for practice."[5]

But the weather turned poor by September 9. "Sea is getting rough. There was a light rainfall this morning."[6] John Ford, who had been assigned to the captain of the ship as a liaison officer, recalled this point in the journey. "There were two of us and we were berthed on sofas in his cabin. It was a great break as almost all the other men were stacked three-high or more in hammocks on the lower decks. The captain told me to just tell his steward what I wanted to eat and when. I ate my way across the Atlantic on fried egg sandwiches.

"And then we ran into rough seas," Ford said. "And I got seasick. It got so bad that I had to go below decks with everyone else where the motion wasn't so bad. At the same time we were issued 1903 Springfield rifles. They were old World War I weapons covered with Cosmoline—a greasy, waxy, rust preventative—and we had to clean them. I was miserable in my hammock as I scraped and rubbed and polished that rifle."

"Land Ho!" The unit diarist waxed colorful on September 11, 1942. "The men awoke this morning to find several Spitfires and other planes acting as escort. For several hours the ship slowly moved up a channel between green rolling hills and arrived at Glasgow Harbor, Scotland, at about 10:00 A.M."[7] The 303rd's men were ferried from the ship to a wharf at Greenock. John Ford recalled the disembarkation: "When we got to Scotland they made us put on our Class A uniforms. Then they gave us two bandoliers of ammunition for our rifles, formed us up and marched us to the train station. I think they wanted to boost the morale of the locals. At the station, they took away our rifles and ammunition."

From Greenock the men were entrained and sent south. "During the daylight hours," the unit diary recorded, "the men eagerly looked at the countryside. Children lined the tracks every time the train passed a city or town and the boys tossed them candy bars and pennys [sic]. Tinned rations were opened at 2:00 P.M. and again about 9:00 P.M. The men declared them very good."[8] The unit arrived at the small town of Thrapston, in Northamptonshire, early the next morning, September 12. From there, they were taken a short distance by truck to the airfield at Molesworth, officially, Station 107. As ground crews and support personnel, it would be their home for the duration of the war.

The 303rd's men found Molesworth to be a fairly well-prepared base. Built during 1940 and 1941, it was briefly used at different times by the RAF, the RAAF and even a USAAF unit. In fact, the first American raid against occupied Europe—little more than a publicity stunt—was launched from England on July 4, 1942, using borrowed British aircraft. Nevertheless, the base was unoccupied when the 303rd arrived: "The quarters are quite comfortable, far better than any of the men dreamed of getting. There are steel cot beds and mattresses (which are in three sections), stoves and all the other conveniences of home handy. The men are well satisfied."[9]

Regardless of their satisfaction, the men were without most of their gear and equipment. There followed several days during which many of them were at loose ends as they waited for the material they needed to do their jobs. By September 19, they had started to get a toehold: "S-1 is operating, although unfamiliar with base duties; S-2 is operating, although unfamiliar with R.A.F. S-2; S-3 is operating although unfamiliar with R.A.F. S-3; S-4 is operating, although they have nothing to operate with."[10]

Molesworth was a big base, and the men obviously needed to get around to perform their jobs. "We were each given a bicycle when we arrived at Molesworth," said John Ford. "It was part of the Lend-

Lease agreement. But the brakes were set up opposite of how they were arranged in the States. The front brakes were on the wrong side and so there were a lot of wrecks and a lot of guys with scrapes and bruises and stitches during those first few weeks."

PERVERSELY, THE PROGRESS of the 303rd's air element was much slower than that of the ground personnel. The aircrews left Biggs by train on September 4 and arrived at Kellogg Field in Battle Creek, Michigan, on September 7. There, they waited for new aircraft, which trickled in slowly; only three B-17s of an eventual thirty-five were delivered to the 303rd during the first week. The 427th Bomb Squadron received its first, a B-17F, on September 14, and it was assigned to Harry Robey. Ehle Reber mentioned it in his diary on September 16: "Lt. Robey's plane may be rejected as it is incomplete. First plane put out by Douglas."

Because Boeing didn't have the capacity to manufacture the B-17 in the numbers required by the USAAF, both Douglas in Long Beach, California, and Lockheed Vega at Burbank, were contracted to produce the big bomber. The first models produced by those two manufacturers, beginning in 1942, were B-17Fs.

The learning curve for both Douglas and Lockheed Vega was a steep one. Although it didn't take long for both companies to begin producing quality aircraft using Boeing's design, Ehle Reber's diary entries indicate that there were problems early on. On September 17, he wrote: "Lt. Robey's Douglas B-17F was rejected so he received a Boeing this evening." But his entry for September 22 indicated that the unit's rejection of the Douglas-built aircraft was itself rejected by higher headquarters. "Have to keep Douglas B-17F. Hope I don't get it." The feeling seemed to be that a Boeing-built aircraft was the genuine article whereas anything else was an ersatz copy.

But it wasn't long before the quality of the aircraft from all the manufacturers proved to be outstanding. In fact, most crews had no idea which of the three companies produced the individual aircraft they flew on any given mission. Ultimately, of the 12,700 B-17s built, Douglas and Lockheed Vega combined to produce 5,750—just less than half.

The new B-17Fs that were delivered to Reber and the rest of the 303rd's aircrews were the latest iteration of an aircraft that in due course became the icon of the daytime strategic bombing campaign against Germany. Boeing financed, designed and built the B-17 in less than a year in response to a 1934 Army Air Corps tender for a multi-engine bomber capable of reaching targets at what were then considered extraordinarily long ranges. The Army wanted a bomber with a range of two thousand miles and a top speed of 250 miles per hour. Boeing's four-engine entry, the Model 299, flew for the first time on July 28, 1935. The following month the aircraft was flown to Wright Field at Dayton, Ohio, where it dramatically outperformed the two-engine entries offered by Martin and Douglas.

But human error nearly killed the project. On October 30, 1935, shortly after taking off with an Army pilot and a Boeing copilot at the controls, the aircraft crashed. Both pilots were killed and several passengers were badly injured. The gust locks, which kept the flight controls from being battered by wind while the aircraft was parked on the ground, were still engaged. Consequently, the wreck that had been the Boeing entrant obviously couldn't finish the competition and was disqualified. Still, despite the fact that the cost of the big bomber was nearly twice that of the other two entrants, the Army remained very interested in Boeing's design.

Notwithstanding the fact that Douglas was declared the winner of the competition and awarded a contract for 133 B-18s, the Army exercised some legal high jinks and contracted with Boeing for thirteen improved examples of the Model 299, designated YB-17. The program evolved into a regular procurement as Boeing worked with the Army to deliver steadily improved models ranging from the B-17A to the B-17E. The production of these models together totaled fewer than 650 examples, with the B-17C being the first to see combat. The RAF operated twenty B-17Cs with little success during the summer of 1941 before withdrawing them from service.

The B-17F was the first model to see combat in large numbers over Europe. It was also produced in very large numbers, and 3,405 were delivered to the USAAF. With a wingspan of more than 103 feet and a length of nearly 75 feet, it incorporated improvements that made it dramatically more capable than earlier models. It was powered by four Wright Cyclone R-1820 radial engines that gave it a top speed of 325 miles per hour, although such speeds were rarely if ever achieved in combat. It typically cruised at 160 miles per hour and had a theoretical service ceiling of 37,500 feet, a range that ultimately was extended to more than 3,500 miles, and a payload of up to eight thousand pounds. It most commonly carried eleven .50-caliber machine guns: one in each cheek, two in the dorsal turret, one in the radio operator's compartment, two in the ball turret, one at each waist station and two in the tail.

Ehle Reber was assigned a newly arrived B-17F at Battle Creek on September 23. During the next few days he and his crew uncovered a number of discrepancies that required them to fly it to Patterson Field at Dayton, Ohio, on September 27. There were technicians at Patterson qualified to make the needed repairs and modifications.

Reber was the sort of young man who saw opportunities for fun and diversion at every turn. One such opportunity during the flight from Battle Creek to Dayton was the family of Milton Conver, his bombardier: "Finally took off at 17:45 for Dayton and Patterson, via Cincinnati where we buzzed Milt's home. Landed at Dayton. Arranged to have plane fixed. Went with Milt to town where we met his folks at the Biltmore Hotel. Went out to The Farm [Conver's house]. Had a steak dinner and drank Martinis and beer. To bed about 0230."

Reber enjoyed the next night as well. "Went in and checked the airplane until about 1700 then out to The Farm. That nite we went into Cincinnati. . . . Had a wonderful time at the Beverley Hills Country Club over the border in Kentucky. Listened to Guy Lombardo's orchestra.

Home late." And a night or two later: "Stayed at the Netherland's Plaza at Cincinnati last nite. Best in town and really nice. Up at 1130 and then Milt and I met Mr. Conver and went to couple clubs."

Reber and his crew finally returned to Battle Creek on September 30, after having entertained Conver's sister through the previous night. "No sleep. Caught bus at 0500 for Dayton where we met rest of fellas. Took off about 1000. *Jerry Jinx* painted on plane. Landed at about 1130 at Battle Creek. Major Sheridan unhappy." As it developed, Reber's commanders didn't appreciate his extracurricular activities, and he was consequently assigned duty as the 427th's officer of the day for eight days running.

The 303rd's aircrews continued to wait at Battle Creek during the first few days of October while their aircraft were prepared for the trip to England. These were the bombers the men would take into combat, and they began naming and personalizing them right away. Traditionally, the name was the pilot's prerogative, however many of them let their crews decide. Mel Schulstad lined up his crew and asked what ideas they had. "I started with the navigator. He said 'I dunno.' And then I asked the bombardier and he said 'I dunno.' Copilot? 'I dunno.'" The answer was the same as Schulstad queried his engineer, ball turret gunner and waist gunners. Finally, he stood in front of the tail gunner. "He shrugged his shoulders and said 'beats me.' And that became the name of our airplane—*Beats Me!?*"

Finally, on October 4, a total of seven aircraft from the 358th and the 427th flew through foul weather to Bangor, Maine. Bangor was the final stateside staging point for bombers headed across the North Atlantic. The time spent waiting at Battle Creek was excellent practice for what was required of the men at Bangor—more waiting. They dealt with it in their usual way: "Being confined to the post here is rather rugged," recorded Reber. "We get kind of tired in the evening [as] about all there is to do is drink or go to bed. Officers club is pretty nice. Had party in evening."

Reber also noted how the 303rd, composed as it was of four different squadrons, was perpetually in a state of flux as personnel joined and others departed for a variety of reasons—even on the cusp of moving to a combat theater. This also illustrated the point that America's airmen were not always highly motivated or of perfect caliber: "Should get a new assistant radio operator as mine doesn't show much initiative or what it takes. S/Sgt Gray, my radio operator, still in hospital at Kellogg Field with strep infection. May get replacement. Lt. Goodale was transferred out of squadron and Lt. Illgen took his place on Hayes's crew."

It was nineteen days before Reber and his crew escaped Bangor for Gander in Newfoundland. "Gander sure is the last outpost. It is quite desolate here. A few WAACs here, but other than them, women are [at] a premium. Oh! Yes, [movie star] Joan Blondell is here with USO troupe. She stays in our barracks. Shades of civilization. War atmosphere is getting more prevalent the closer we get to England. Not so very cold here yet. The 'Newfies' (Newfoundlanders) all seem to have false teeth. Lack of fresh milk, fruit and vegetables, they say."

Reber was a young man who especially liked the ladies. After nearly a week at Gander—stuck and waiting for weather good enough to cross the Atlantic—he made an observation about the Newfoundland women. His words are insensitive but utterly typical of a self-assured but not yet socially adept or mature young man: "Maybe tomorrow we leave. Women, who were first <u>Haints</u>, are now looking better. Fellas will probably be dating the <u>Newfies</u> soon. A <u>Haint</u>, incidentally, is a girl who could jump over two parked cars and run up a thorn tree and never get a scratch. In other words a <u>bag</u>!"

The 303rd's crews started to leave Newfoundland during late October 1942. A great deal of effort and material had been expended to prepare the route. It featured divert airfields in Greenland and Iceland, and a sophisticated weather forecasting and reconnaissance system. Still, the crossing was treacherous and characterized by unpredictable weather. That weather, especially ice and snow, often clawed aircraft out of the sky and into the icy North Atlantic, where no one could survive. During some of the worst months, losses along this northern route nearly equaled those being sustained in combat. It was a flight that all of the men dreaded.

Mel Schulstad remembered that his crew was especially well prepared before leaving Newfoundland. "They had heard that there was a shortage of booze over there [England] and that getting hold of a good bottle of Scotch or whiskey could be a problem." His crew resolved to do their part to alleviate the island nation's supposed dearth of spirits and bought two cases of various hard liquors. But there was little room for it in the aircraft, which was carrying an extra passenger and other assorted baggage and cargo. "They wrapped the bottles up end-to-end in wool GI blankets," said Schulstad. "And then the flight engineer opened a port on the bottom of the wing. They reached up and fed about ten feet of blanket-wrapped bottles through that port and along the inside of the wing."

Despite the hazards, the 303rd was the first bomb group to make the North Atlantic crossing without incident. But there were close calls. Bill Neff was the 359th's engineering officer and hitched a ride with the Harold Stouse crew. After the takeoff from Gander, Neff grew bored and searched for a place to stretch out and relax. He ducked into the tunnel that ran below the pilot's compartment and into the nose of the aircraft. There he started arranging a canvas engine cover so that he could lie down. In the process he lost his balance.

I reached back to catch it [his balance] and put my hand on the forward access door for stability. The door was not latched and my hand and my ass were, all at once, hanging out in the slipstream, with my neck on one side of the door frame and my legs on the opposite side. I was able to get back inside and tried to close and latch the door by banging it shut in rapid attempts with the aircraft [?] sprung in the flight position. The catch wouldn't catch. The cockpit heard my banging attempts and thought someone was shooting at us in the air. Immediately they took evasive action which startled the whole crew.[11]

Upon crossing the Atlantic, most of the crews landed at Prestwick, Scotland. Van White made the trip with the Carl Morales crew. "We got out of the airplane and it was cold! One of the first things I saw was a little gal at the wheel of an aircraft tug. Her hands were bare and her fingers were purple from the freezing weather. I asked her where in the world her gloves were and she answered in that very heavy brogue, 'I 'aven't got none.'"

"Anyway," White said, "they took us to the RAF mess hall and it reeked of Brussels sprouts and mutton. And that's what I smelled at mealtime for the next several years—Brussels sprouts and mutton." White never got over the stink of what was a ubiquitous meal through the rest of the war.

The group's leadership tried to keep the ground echelon personnel at Molesworth busy with classes and various housekeeping projects, but after nearly six weeks it grew tiresome. Consequently, the arrival of the first aircraft was marked with a certain amount of excitement. "The first section of the Air Echelon, consisting of six B-17F airplanes, arrived over this station at 3:45 P.M. The first plane, Serial No. 41-24608 [named *Yahoodi*], touched wheels at exactly 1551 hours, October 21, 1942. These planes are assigned to the 359th Bombardment Squadron."[12]

Mel Schulstad was part of the 360th Bombardment Squadron and arrived at Molesworth several days later. However, the realities of war hit him before he ever reached the base. Not long after getting airborne out of Prestwick his formation was directed to divert to an RAF bomber base; the weather at Molesworth was too poor to land. The RAF personnel greeted the Americans warmly, fed them and put them up for the night in an old estate house. "A batman led four of us officers upstairs to a room in the corner of the house that had four beds, four tables and four chairs," said Schulstad. "It was obviously occupied by somebody; there were pictures of Mama and the kids, ashes in the ashtrays and the usual sorts of things. And this batman started going around and clearing off all these things and dumping them into sacks that he put out in the hall.

"And I said, wait a minute. You don't have to do that—we're just going to stay overnight. He looked at me and said, 'But they didn't come back last night.'" Schulstad was struck by a sudden realization. "That was the first time it entered my mind that people went out but didn't come back. It was four officers and God knows how many others. That made quite an impression.

"The next morning [October 24, 1942] we had breakfast and went out to the airplane." Schulstad eyeballed some of the RAF's Wellington bombers just returned from the previous night's mission. "They were full of flak holes—shot and torn up." He inspected one particular aircraft carefully. "I looked at the wings and engines and came around to the tail gun position, which was a sort of round, glass cage. And there was a job that hadn't been finished. There were the remains of a human being. They hadn't quite got around to clearing it out yet. And I walked away from there and thought to my country-boy self: My God, people really do get killed, don't they?"

"ONE MUST BE ABLE TO DEPEND UPON HIS CREW"

ALL THROUGH THE FIRST HALF of 1942 the Americans and British toyed with various notions for invading Europe. The Americans were anxious to get forces on the continent as early as that year, but British leaders rightly counseled that such a move was premature as there was no way that they or the Americans would have the necessary material, shipping or trained personnel. And certainly the Luftwaffe could not be neutralized in time for an invasion during 1942.

The focus subsequently shifted to a joint invasion of Northwest Africa by American and British forces. It was intended to achieve several objectives. Most obvious, it would put strong Allied forces to Rommel's rear. Further, it would force the Germans to pour more resources into a secondary theater when they were desperately needed for the fight against the Soviets. Additionally, it would provide an opportunity for the British and Americans to practice and refine joint operations that might be subsequently adopted for the eventual invasion of Europe. Finally, it would be a test; American troops would be blooded for the first time in a major operation against the Germans. There was keen interest at home and abroad in how they would perform.

Of course, the operation—eventually codenamed TORCH—required significant air cover. All eyes turned to the only organization that could provide it: the Eighth Air Force. Consequently, during the late summer and the fall of 1942, just as they were readying to launch their strategic air campaign, Spaatz and Eaker were ordered by Dwight Eisenhower, the commanding general of the European Theater of Operations, to give up many of their combat units as well as the material and manpower necessary to support them. Carefully trained bomber and fighter groups as well as vigilantly husbanded stores were earmarked to support the invasion of Northwest Africa. There was a real fear that the entire Eighth would be dismantled to support the newly burgeoning Twelfth Air Force. That fear was intensified when Eisenhower ordered Spaatz to take charge of the air component of TORCH. Eaker was given command of the Eighth Air Force but was uncertain that there would be anything or anyone left to command.

AS THE 303RD'S AIRCREWS TRICKLED into Molesworth, the greenness of its men sometimes showed itself. Ehle Reber, who didn't arrive until more than a week after Schulstad, recorded the movement of his flight from the RAF field at Sealand to Molesworth on November 2. "Haze again made landing rather difficult, but I was second in. Lt[s]. Stockton, Robey and Broussard fell behind and tagged on to another squadron of B-17Fs, thinking it was us and landed at Grafton Field about 10 miles from here. They should be here tomorrow."

The unit diary entry for October 28 confirmed that the inexperience of the 303rd's aircrews was shared by the support personnel: "The first battle scar was received by one of the planes of the group today. A guard shot a hole through plane 41-24581 accidentally while guarding the ship. Slight damage to the ship."[1]

As green as they were, the 303rd's men readied for combat as

quickly and as best they could. Their training included formation flying, familiarization flights, time in the Link instrument trainer and
classroom instruction. Their counterparts in the Royal Air Force had
already built and handed over Molesworth but were additionally helpful in sharing their expertise during classroom and other training. Ehle
Reber had great respect for his British comrades. "One day a ME109
was seen coming over the field like a bat-out-of-hell several hundred
feet off the ground. About a mile behind were two Spits. They finally
caught the 109 about three miles away from the field and that was the
end of Jerry. The R.A.F. are marvelous fighters after 3 years of experience and hell."

The 303rd's men also learned to adapt to life in wartime England.
Reber went to Kettering with friends on the night of November 10. "The
streets are absolutely void of light except for an occasional flashlite held
by individuals. The lites were very dim and of course my flashlite let out
a beam which was comparable to the beam of an average searchlight on
the east coast of England. Consequently, the first time I flashed it, an
old, bent, cane-aided Englishman gave me hell and so my lite wasn't
much help the rest of the night.

"We went to a dance at the George Hotel Regent Room," continued
Reber. "We were not too much impressed by the English girls so we
spent most of the evening at the pubs. We started drinking raisin wine
and were beginning to feel pretty good until someone found out that
the wine was not intoxicating. We sobered up rather rapidly. We had a
good time."

In fact, because the Eighth Air Force was made up of so many young
men with so much energy and ready cash, heavy drinking while on
pass or furlough grew to be a serious problem, as indicated by a notice
later promulgated by the 303rd's higher command, the 1st Bombardment Division: "A recent survey of the serious crimes committed by
American personnel in this area reveals that over ninety percent (90%)
are committed while under the influence of liquor and that the rate of
cases of drunkenness is increasing. The military police of this area are

instructed to take immediate steps to arrest all American personnel found in a drunken condition. The policy of this Headquarters is to consider drunkenness a courts martial offense."[2] In reality, the policy was unenforceable as the USAAF didn't have enough resources to pursue it.

Still, some men were prosecuted for bad behavior while drunk. For instance, Private First Class Walter Sandage of the 358th Bomb Squadron was charged with striking Private First Class Enrico Caruso of the 1114th Quartermaster Squadron in the head. Sandage pled not guilty but was nevertheless found guilty and subsequently reduced in rank to private, restricted to the base for a month and fined $15.[3]

The USAAF was also especially serious about operational security during this time, and men were forbidden to identify their units to strangers or to say where they were based. And when in town, they returned to Molesworth on a bus or truck with a special name or designator as described in the 303rd's Instruction 80-3, dated October 28, 1942: "An identifying name, such as the name of a state or city, will be given to the truck, and all personnel in it will be ordered to use only that name in attempting to locate or identify it." Indeed, Reber recalled while on a pass that "Our truck was named Arkansas rather than calling out the name of the field for which the truck was heading."

THE 288 DAYS OF TRAINING since the 303rd's formation earlier that year were finally put to the test on November 17. Orders came the previous night ordering the unit to join an attack scheduled against the German submarine base at St. Nazaire. There was a calm earnestness about the men as they performed their particular duties. Everyone pitched in, anxious for the first mission to be a success. Rosters were completed, aircraft were fueled and prepared, and bombs were loaded. The kitchen was made ready to cook the group's first ever pre-mission breakfast.

There is no doubt that men went sleepless that night, but the brief the following morning went well, and the 303rd's commander, Colonel

James Wallace, called out crew names and aircraft assignments. The participating squadrons were to be the 358th, 359th and 360th. The men of the 427th were crestfallen to be left behind as reserve. More details were passed and the targets were reviewed. The primary target was St. Nazaire, while the secondary and tertiary targets were Keroman and Brest. The first of the group's aircraft took off at 0923 and just more than ten minutes later all sixteen aircraft were assembling overhead the field.

While the bulk of the 303rd winged its way east on its first combat mission, the 427th was left behind to fly training operations. Ehle Reber highlighted how the men still made basic mistakes. "I had a good experience when I took off with the pitot tube covers on. As a consequence I had no airspeed indicator." The weather was good, and Reber was able to use engine power settings and visual cues to land, remove the protective covers and take off again. Had the weather been foul, there was a good chance that he might have lost control and crashed. "Of course I gave the engineer hell for he was the one who told me the plane was OK and that the covers were off. One must be able to depend upon his crew for certain duties for there are so many on a Flying Fortress."

While Reber was busy trying to stay alive and his fellow 427th crews were training, the group's other three squadrons joined with forty-seven other heavy bombers that the Eighth was able to get airborne that day. But it was for naught. The target at St. Nazaire was obscured by clouds and the backup targets were left unmolested. The 303rd brought its bombs back to Molesworth. It was a huge disappointment.

Reber's recollection was unkind and he called the raid "a complete flop." He noted problems at the start of the mission that weren't recorded in the official history: "There was a hell of a mix-up on takeoff and in general the show was SNAFU [Situation Normal All 'Fouled' Up]. Stockton and Robey of our outfit went along but turned back when guns failed to operate correctly. On top of that the group failed to find the target. Consequently they landed with all the bombs. Glad the 427th [his squadron] still has a clean slate. I understand we are to lead the raid in the morning on sub pens and docks at La Pallice, France. Here's hoping it turns out better than today's."

EARLIER THAT MONTH, on November 7, Mel Schulstad wrote a letter that made it clear he believed it would be some time before he saw combat. "Right now we are restricted pretty much in camp. General activity is pretty much the same as in the States. Of course, I can't discuss air activity. You know from your papers how successful the Flying Fortress raids have been but I don't suppose I will participate for some time."

In fact he flew his first mission on November 18, the day the 303rd logged its second mission. It was also the first mission for Ehle Reber, the one he had hoped would turn out better than the raid of the previous day. The 303rd—again, led by its commander, James Wallace—latched onto another bomb group and followed it to St. Nazaire, where German fighters were ready and where the flak was heavy although not particularly accurate. There, the 303rd dropped its first bombs in anger. And although good hits were registered by the nineteen aircraft making up the formation, they were registered not only on the wrong target, but on the wrong city entirely.

Instead of St. Nazaire, the group was supposed to have hit La Pallice, a hundred miles to the southeast. It was a grotesquely amateurish mistake. Nevertheless, the group lost no aircraft and a safe return was made to England. Still, whereas the first mission on November 17 had been an anticlimactic letdown, the second on November 18 was simply embarrassing.

Reber made scant mention in his diary of the group's gross navigational error, but rather concentrated on his own sortie. "We were to bomb La Pallice, but ended up by bombing St. Nazaire, yesterday's target. Bombing was quite successful with several good hits noted on photographs. My plane registered several good hits and was thought to have started a fire."

After a mission to Lorient, France, on November 22, the 303rd went back to St. Nazaire—on purpose, this time—on November 23. It was on this mission that the group suffered its first loss when the Arthur Reddig crew, in *Lady Fairweather*, was knocked into the Bay of Biscay by FW-190s. No bodies were ever found although four parachutes were spotted.

Aside from fighters, the enemy antiaircraft gunners also scored hits. And they scored some of them on Reber's aircraft. "While over the target Lt. [Allan] Mitchell and I received quite a scare when a piece of shrapnel came tearing through the cockpit directly beneath our legs and came to rest beneath, one against my oxygen bottle. I picked the piece up and put it in my pocket."

Harold Fulghum, the group's lead navigator, did not return from the mission. "The story has it that the plane in which he was flying [*Holy Mackerel*] was hit by an ack ack shell which burst the hydraulic lines in the cockpit," Reber recorded. "This fluid looks much like blood and it is thought that Harold thought that the pilot and copilot had been killed and before the bombardier could stop him he had jumped. It is thought that he was wounded for the nose of the plane had blood on it and also the door from which he jumped." As it developed, Fulghum was captured and spent the remainder of the war as a POW—the 303rd's first.

WHILE EAKER SPENT much of his energy at the strategic and diplomatic level during late 1942, attention was additionally directed down to the individual combat units of his Eighth Air Force. Eaker couldn't afford for his crews to be anything less than well prepared for combat. They were inspected for the state of their training, their discipline, their material readiness and their morale. The 303rd received a visit on

November 29, 1942, after several days of inactivity due to weather. The inspection failed to impress Ehle Reber:

> *General [Newton] Longfellow and General Cater [Laurence Kuter] paid us a visit yesterday and as a result the post is confined for a week. It seems as though no one saluted him while he was here. Poor boy. I guess they are all childish. It's a wonder he didn't pull out a tire gauge and start checking the air in all the tires on the post. If we go on two or three missions and risk our lives every day and when we come down we don't salute a general as he passes by in his car we get confined. Maybe we should arrange to take him on a couple of them. Maybe he would find out there's a war going on. I'm pished [sic] off.*

On this point, Reber was off the mark. Brigadier General Newton Longfellow did indeed know there was "a war going on." In fact, he had flown a mission nearly three months earlier as an observer aboard Paul Tibbets's aircraft on the 97th Bomb Group's September 7 mission to Rotterdam. The ship, at the head of the formation, was attacked by fighters. A cannon round blasted into the right side of the cockpit, shattered the instrument panel, sprayed Tibbets with shrapnel and tore away the copilot's right hand.

Longfellow came unglued and reached over Tibbets to take control of the aircraft. Tibbets wrestled with Longfellow and somehow kept the aircraft at the head of the formation while also staunching the flow of blood that gushed from his copilot's body. Tibbets finally smashed Longfellow in the head with his elbow and knocked him unconscious. Almost at the same time an enemy round knocked the flight engineer out of the top turret and down atop Longfellow.

Longfellow regained consciousness and collected his wits. Soon after he calmly tended to both the copilot and the flight engineer then climbed into the copilot's seat and helped Tibbets fly the aircraft back to England.[4] Although his performance under fire on his first combat mission was panicked, Longfellow understood the terror of combat at least as well as Reber. And if he wanted to punish the 303rd for a lack of discipline—real or perceived—it was his prerogative to do so.

On the other hand, if Reber believed that Longfellow was not a great leader, he had a point. Longfellow replaced Eaker as head of VIII Bomber Command when Eaker was given command of the Eighth Air Force in December 1942. Longfellow had a tense, dyspeptic demeanor and, as a brigadier general, was known by his staff as "The Shouting Star."[5] Officious and dictatorial, Longfellow was the wrong man for the job. He did not perform to expectations and was later relieved of command.

"I WAS TIRED OF GETTING HIT"

THE 303RD'S MEN went into London on passes of varying durations starting in late 1942. Ehle Reber went on December 2 and checked into the Park Lane Hotel. To that point he had been at Molesworth for one month and flown a grand total of two missions. His recreation in London was typical. Aside from drinking, he and his comrades took in the classic tourist sights: "We saw Big Ben, Westminster Abbey, Buckingham Palace, House of Commons and Lords, St. Paul's Cathedral, Trafalgar Square, Piccadilly Circus; etc."

They were also witnesses to wartime destruction of a sort that had never before been visited on London. "The bombed areas were interesting," said Reber. "Whole blocks were leveled. The ruins were appalling. They [Germans] used the tall church steeples as land marks [*sic*] and the areas around them are scenes of utter desolation. The cabby said that if the R.A.F. had not made their desperate effort, and a successful one, to stop the Jerry raids, England would have folded in about two months. They were on their last legs and no foolin'!"

London's legendary taxi drivers also impressed Reber as "really marvelous. They are mostly driven by old, gray-haired men, and the way they handle the car and the way they get around in traffic is amazing. The cabs are real old and extremely different from anything in the States. They are kept bright and shiny however, and very comfortable. They are also very cheap. Our tour cost us 8 shillings—$1.60."

THE MISSION ON December 6, 1942, was only the 303rd's fifth. That inexperience was apparent immediately after the group got airborne. "A squadron from one of the other fields tacked on our first two squadrons, so Col. Wallace thought he had the group together and really stepped on it," recorded Ehle Reber. "When he saw the other squadron pull out of the formation and he saw us trailing he realized his error and slowed up enabling us to catch him after giving our turbos [engine turbochargers] hell."

Reber described the escort provided by a mix of RAF and USAAF Spitfires. "The Spits were like a bunch of little chicks flitting about the mother hens, the Fortresses. It was indeed a beautiful sight. We were attacked by several FW190's and several ME109's. One FW190 made a suicidal dive through our squadron. It's [sic] guns were blazing, but no hits were made.

"It came very close to my plane. I could almost see the expression on the pilot's face. Lt. [Robert] Swindle gave him several long bursts with the nose guns. One of the planes in our squadron got him as Swindle saw him burst into flames and explode as he struck the earth."

Reber noted—without commentary—that the inexperienced B-17 gunners shot down one of their fighter escorts. "One Spitfire was shot down by gunners on the Fortress who mistook it for a ME109." Sadly, losses to friendly gunfire continued through the war for the same reason—mistaken identity.

THE INVASION OF NORTHWEST AFRICA cost Eaker many of his units, but Mother Nature also upset his plans. The weather over England and

Northern Europe during the fall and winter of 1942 was atrocious; in fact, the Eighth managed to launch only four missions during all of December 1942. It frustrated Eaker, it frustrated Arnold, it frustrated the President, and it frustrated the American public. Most of all, it frustrated the airmen, and Ehle Reber's complaint was typical: "I don't see why in the hell they don't send us to Africa where we would have some flying weather and be able to bomb hell out of the Jerries there."

Evidently, Reber came close to getting his wish. Because of the operational flux in both England and Northwest Africa, the 303rd was alerted to be ready to deploy, as Reber observed in his diary entry for December 8: "Bomb bay [fuel] tanks and baggage racks were taken out to the dispersal area. Maybe we go to Africa pretty soon. An alert was called and then we were released. Everybody is raring to go to the Africa affair. Tanks and racks were not installed, but were to be ready for installation at a moment's notice."

Ultimately, the 303rd did not leave Molesworth. Rather the group stayed put and the men trained as best they could. Reber was in the Link trainer—an instrument flight simulator—constantly. Other men also worked hard to maintain their particular expertise. On December 15 Reber recalled how the top turret gunners practiced their craft while still on the ground: "Upper turret gunners are getting a little practice with the plane on the ground. A couple of cubs [small liaison aircraft] dive down on the planes and the turret gunners track them."

Nevertheless, Reber also noted that the training the men received in another arena—sexual hygiene—did not prove as effective as desired. "Party in the evening. I brought Doris from Cambridge. We had good time. All 48 hour passes have been cancelled as there are quite a few venereal disease cases from the 427th in the hospital."

However, the men were soon allowed to leave the base and Reber was back in London for a forty-eight-hour pass beginning December 29. He and his comrades checked into the Savoy and readied themselves for a good time.

*In the evening we went downstairs to the American Bar and drank
beer and scotch. Had a marvelous time. Met Martha Raye and had a
shot with her. She was going to Africa in the next 32 hours and
apparently headed for a good bender. I proved right later on as we
met her again at the Merry Go Round Club. We were with two
American nurses we had met at the American Bar. Martha was out
of this world [drunk]. She was coaxed (very little) to get up and sing.
She did and it really stunk. She sang "Honeysuckle Rose" and one
other. She really had a whiskey tenor. We tried to get in the Embassy
Club, but without a membership card, it was impossible. The door-
keeper did pour us a spot of tea. Of all things.*

Martha Raye was part of the initial wave of American celebrities
that invaded and continued to overrun England through the war.
Everyone who was anyone in the entertainment world went to
England—usually in the company of the USO but sometimes in uniform. The most famous among them included Bob Hope, James Cag-
ney, Marlene Dietrich, Mickey Rooney, Bing Crosby and Glenn Miller.

Not only did their presence contribute to the morale of their
countrymen—as it was intended to—but for most of the stars it also satisfied a sense of daring and adventure. Crossing the Atlantic, by sea or
air, was still dangerous. And the Germans still made nighttime raids
against London. Too, virtually all of the celebrities felt a very real patriotic obligation to do their part for the war effort as best they could.

A very small number of stars went so far as to serve in combat. Perhaps the most legitimate and well known was Jimmy Stewart. A B-24
pilot, he served as a squadron commander with the 445th and 453rd
Bomb Groups and led both groups multiple times—and to tough targets. He was considered not only an outstanding pilot, but a genuine,
courageous and well-liked leader. He completed twenty officially credited missions with the 445th and 453rd before being transferred to
work as a staff officer at the 20th Combat Bombardment Wing. While

there, he flew several more missions with other bomb groups for which he did not take credit.

Van White enjoyed a bit of celebrity while on pass to London. "I had a little portable RCA radio that ran on dry cell batteries. I carried it on a strap under my raincoat. It measured about three inches by four inches by nine inches and had really nice reception. I had music or news wherever I went. Fred Astaire's sister Adele—the big vaudeville and Broadway star—was quite a popular figure in London during that time and she was just fascinated with that radio. She made me promise to leave it with her when the time came for me to go back to the States. But it wasn't popular when I went into any of the pubs. A license was required to play music in a pub, and the owners always made me turn the radio off as soon as I came through the door. In the end, it was stolen. That was a sad day."

White also remembered a night when a particularly American treat made him popular. "I was sitting in a hotel lobby with a can of Jolly Time popcorn—my mother used to send cans of it to me. While I sat there, two English girls walked up and told me that I was invited to a party that evening. I went out that night to a great house party and I took that popcorn along with me. Later I received a letter from one of the girls thanking me for the wonderful 'pop cakes.'"

Still, White's radio and popcorn didn't always do the trick. "I was spending the evening with a lady friend who shared an apartment with her parents. When the air raid sirens went off, they all left for their assigned bomb shelter under the Mount Royal Hotel. I was left alone in the apartment. I spent the air raid huddled in their bathtub holding an ironing board over the top of my head."

THE 303RD'S FIRST MISSION of 1943 was a disaster, notwithstanding the fact that it included one of the most bizarre incidents to be recorded in combat aviation. January 3 marked the group's ninth mission overall and its fourth to St. Nazaire. During its short combat career to that point, nearly half of its missions had been sent against the enemy submarine base—such was the importance the Allies put on stymieing the German submarine war. That day's specific target was a torpedo storage area, and the group launched seventeen aircraft, three of which aborted.

The weather was cold and clear and offered excellent bombing conditions. Unfortunately, the same superb weather also served the enemy. The fourteen aircraft making up the group's formation encountered intense and accurate flak as well as approximately thirty enemy fighters. *Kali*, captained by William Goetz, simply exploded over the target area. There were no survivors. *Yahoodi*, the first 303rd aircraft to reach Molesworth from the States, was knocked down by St. Nazaire's flak guns. The ship's pilot, Frank Saunders, put it down in the water, where seven of his crew perished. He and two others were rescued and made POWs. *Leapin' Liz* was hit by fighters and likewise went into the water. All the crew was killed.

Alan Magee was the ball turret gunner aboard Arthur Adams's *Snap, Crackle, Pop!* It was his third trip to St. Nazaire. "Near the target and on the bomb run, there was so much flak and the B-17F seemed to be going so slow that I felt like getting out of the plane and running ahead, telling it to catch up to me. It seemed like we were standing still."[1]

Magee's apprehension was justified. "All of a sudden I was hit in the face, and the turret sight was knocked out. With the front glass broken out it was impossible to stay in the turret to operate it." Magee's eyes were peppered with slivers of glass and he had difficulty seeing. He advised Adams of his situation and was told to climb out of his position. "When I was out of the turret and went for my chest pack [parachute]," Magee said, "I saw it had a large hole in the middle of it and one end seemed to have been damaged. I didn't bother putting it on."

He moved forward past the open bomb bay and saw the radio operator readying to jump from the aircraft. "The B-17F was now on fire and in bad shape. We seemed to be getting hit at will. We never got the alarm to bail out."

There was a clattering racket and Magee felt shrapnel punch into his body. Almost immediately afterward the aircraft fell off to the right and went into a spin. Magee was pinned against the roof of the radio compartment near the top hatch.

"The next thing I remember," he said "was trying to reach the open hatch. I don't know why I wanted out without a chute on but the plane was on fire and going down. I blacked out at this point, not having an oxygen mask on since leaving the turret." Something hit Magee again and he briefly regained consciousness. He did not know what hit him, but he grew weary of the repeated blows: "I was tired of getting hit."

Magee passed out once more as his body accelerated in its fall toward St. Nazaire. From twenty thousand feet gravity pulled him earthward. He fell past *Snap, Crackle, Pop!*, which drifted away in a spin toward the coast.

The glass and bracings that made up the roof of St. Nazaire's train station gave way to Magee's body. Physics demanded it. But physics also somehow played a role in an incomprehensibility. When workers climbed up into the roof's support structure to pull free what they were sure was a corpse, they were stupefied to discover Magee still alive. Although he wore a parachute harness, there was no parachute to be found.

The workers brought him to the ground, but it wasn't until midnight that he reached a hospital. His body bore twenty-eight puncture wounds, his left arm was nearly torn away, he had a broken leg, a smashed ankle and a shattered knee. His face was smashed, and his teeth rattled loose—barely in their sockets.

A German physician attended him. "The doctor who did the operation on my face, nose, arm and back couldn't speak English," Magee said. "He told the nurse who did speak English he would try to save my arm, and if he couldn't, it wasn't because I was an enemy." The operations went well. "I was in the hospital a month and a half," said Magee. "The German doctor did a great job on my face, putting my arm back in good shape and leg, knee and ankle." Magee additionally marveled that the doctor even saved his teeth. "I was treated well by the Germans in the hospital," he declared.

Magee made an excellent recovery. In fact, he was not repatriated back to the United States through the Red Cross as badly injured POWs often were. Rather, he was put into a POW camp where he remained until the war ended.

"A CHARMED LIFE, MAYBE"

EHLE REBER, ALTHOUGH SCHEDULED to fly on the January 3 mission to St. Nazaire, never got airborne. "As I sat there waiting to join in taxiing for takeoff, I suddenly heard a loud explosion." Stunned, Reber checked his engine instruments and rubbernecked over the rest of the aircraft as best he could from the cockpit. The engines seemed to be operating normally, and from where he sat there was no indication of what was wrong. "I looked at the tires and they were OK and then the smoke came filtering up front. It was gun smoke."

Reber went to the back of the ship, where he found two of his gunners bleeding as they exited the aircraft. One of the waist gunners, Victor Hand, had inadvertently fired five .50-caliber rounds into the bomber. "He did not have it pointed out of the window at the time. It was in its carrying rack so that when it went off it tore several large holes in the rear door, went through some armor plating, through the horizontal stabilizer and elevator. It caused more damage than any raid I've been on.

"I was supposed to have flown Lt. [Frank] Saunders' position. He took my place when I failed to get off. That's the second time the plane that took my place on a raid has been shot down. A charmed life, maybe—huh. In the evening we had a party at the Club. Everyone was out of this world and forgot their sorrows."

Reber's recollections also confirm that the group's crews were well aware of the beating they were taking. "The 303rd has now lost 25% [emphasis in original] of its air echelon in two months of operational flying. Nine crews and 11 airplanes, including Hayes [who was temporarily interned after mistakenly landing in the Irish Free State]. However, he should be back one of these days. Rapid turnover."

The group's experience to that point indicated the need for a modification to the B-17's defensive armament: "It is apparent that the B-17 is in dire need of a nose gun or turret of some kind," wrote Reber. "The enemy planes can come in from level at about 10:30 to 1300 [from head-on and slightly to either side] and can pound the fortresses unmerciful[ly] without accurate fire being placed upon them."

The top turret, although it could be aimed directly ahead, could not depress its guns enough to bring them to bear against these sorts of attacks. The ball turret likewise was limited, as described by Reber: "Lower turret gun cuts out here when bomb bay doors are open and also for the props so it has only a small area it can come directly to the front, but only to the side and forward about 45°." Various ad hoc nose gun arrangements were tried at the time but were not especially effective. Something more and better was needed.

AS THE EIGHTH'S raids grew in size, one of the problems the pilots encountered that hadn't been carefully considered previously was that of prop wash. This was the wake, or disturbed air, an aircraft created as it motored through the sky. The bigger the aircraft, the greater the prop wash. It could cause trailing ships to be rocked, or tipped, or otherwise thrown off course. Staying in tight formation while dealing with prop wash was not only difficult, it was dangerous.

This danger was underscored during the mission to Lille on January 13, 1943. "The mission was extra tough," recorded Ehle Reber, "because of the continual prop wash of the group [306th] ahead of us. In fact it was so bad that two 17s collided in mid-air just ahead of me and the one plane broke in two and they both went down. It was really a horrible sight to see. Some parachutes were seen to come from the plane."

The effects of prop wash—which descended below the elevation of the aircraft that created it—could be mitigated by increasing the lateral or vertical separation between aircraft and groups of aircraft. This was effective, but it dissipated the defensive firepower against enemy fighter attacks. Too, such offset formations were more difficult to maneuver and they also made it difficult to achieve tight bomb hit patterns. Ultimately, a blend of formation arrangements and spacing helped reduce the problem, but it was never completely eliminated and it vexed aircrews until the end of the war.

The 303rd's only casualty on the raid to Lille was not due to enemy action. "Stock's [Donald Stockton] tail gunner [Paul Ferguson] died from lack of oxygen on the trip," recorded Reber. "He pulled out of formation over the Channel and hurried to the field in an effort to save him but the lack of oxygen and the extreme cold temperature was too much and he died."

VIRTUALLY NONE OF THE 303RD'S men knew or cared, but at the time the unit first started flying missions, the strategy behind those missions was being questioned at the highest levels of Allied leadership. As early as America's entry into the war, Great Britain's political and military leaders expressed doubts that the United States could successfully prosecute a daylight precision bombing campaign against Germany. The RAF had already tried—and failed miserably—to bomb Germany by day. Although the intensity of their insistence varied, many of Great Britain's leaders were very keen to have the USAAF join the RAF in its night bombing operations.

Indeed, during mid-September 1942—a month after the Eighth's inaugural raid and the same month that the 303rd arrived in England—Churchill wrote, "It is a great pity that General Arnold does not try first to send us two or three hundred of his big American bombers to expand our Bomber Command, after they have been adapted to night fighting. Failing this, he should send us as many American squadrons as he can to operate from this country, and teach them to fly by night. So far, his day bombing operations have been on a very petty scale."[1]

Certainly Churchill was correct when he observed that the size of the American raids was trifling; creating an organization as large and powerful as the Eighth Air Force would eventually become could not happen overnight. Indeed, when the 303rd started operations during November 1942, it was one of only four USAAF heavy bombardment groups available to Eaker. Other groups already part of, or slated for, the Eighth were being sent or diverted to North Africa to support TORCH, an operation that Churchill heartily supported.

At the time, the Eighth had been flying operations for only a few months. Although the missions were small and failed to inflict crippling damage or even to touch Germany, they did give an indication of the potential of daylight precision bombing. From them could be extrapolated what might be possible once the planned force was in place and missions of hundreds, or even a thousand or more, bombers were launched.

Some among the British, to include Chief of the Air Staff Charles Portal and Assistant Chief of the Air Staff John Slessor, did indeed come to recognize the potential of daylight precision bombing. Or at the very least, they believed that the Americans ought to be given a chance to try it. In fact, during mid-December 1942, Slessor wrote a draft intended for Churchill: "No one can say for certain until it has been tried—and tried repeatedly." He also offered: "And they will only learn from their own experience. In spite of some admitted defects—including lack of experience—their leadership is of a high order, and the quality of their aircrew personnel is magnificent."[2]

But still, Churchill outranked everyone else in Great Britain, and Arnold and Eaker worried that he might convince Roosevelt to order the USAAF to transition to night operations. In fact, alarm bells went off when Eaker received a message on January 13 ordering him to travel from England to Morocco and report to the Casablanca Conference. It read, in part: "Conference involves method of air operations from United Kingdom."[3]

Arnold traveled to Casablanca from the States and was there when Eaker arrived on January 15. The two men, among other ranking American staffers, confirmed that Churchill did indeed plan to pressure Roosevelt on the daylight bombing issue. It was decided that the best defense was a good offense, and Eaker prepared a one-page statement for the prime minister together with a larger, more detailed report. Eaker's paper minced no words and listed a number of reasons why the USAAF should conduct operations during the daytime. The finishing argument opened with the following sentences: "Day bombing is the bold, the aggressive, the offensive thing to do. It is the method and the practice which will put the greatest pressure on Germany, work the greatest havoc to his wartime industry and the greatest reduction to his air force."[4]

Eaker had an audience with Churchill on January 20 during which the prime minister read his paper. One of its points was that—with the RAF flying missions at night and the USAAF conducting operations during the day—Germany would be, at least notionally, under continuous attack. This idea of "around-the-clock" bombing resonated with Churchill. He said to Eaker, "Young man, you have not convinced me you are right, but you have persuaded me that you should have further opportunity to prove your contention." The Prime Minister declared that he would "withdraw my suggestion that U.S. bombers join the RAF in night bombing."[5] The notion was never seriously raised again.

So at Casablanca it was made substantially clear that the Americans were to be left unmolested—at least by their allies—to execute a strategic daylight bombing campaign against Germany. But in addition, the

British and Americans agreed in principle to better coordinate their efforts. Tacit accords were reached to form what became known as the Combined Bomber Offensive. Shortly after, the British articulated the goals of the Combined Bomber Offensive in what became known as the Casablanca Directive:

> *The progressive destruction and dislocation of the German military, industrial and economic systems and the undermining of the morale of the German people to a point where their capacity for armed resistance is fatally weakened. Every opportunity to be taken to attack Germany by day to destroy objectives that are unsuitable for night attack, to sustain continuous pressure on German morale, to impose heavy losses on German day fighter force and to conserve German fighter force away from the Russian and Mediterranean theatres of war.*

Officially, it was the basis for the subsequent combined Anglo-American air offensive against Germany. In reality, it was a mutual permission slip for the two nations to prosecute the air war however they wanted. It would be several more months until they directed their combined efforts on a more focused objective.

THE ME-109 AND FW-190 were the primary fighters the Luftwaffe used against the Eighth Air Force through the entire war. The Me-109 was the most produced fighter in history, with nearly thirty-four thousand examples built from 1935 to 1945. Introduced to combat for the first time during the Spanish Civil War, it was fast, nimble and relatively easy to fly, although its narrow-tracked landing gear caused considerable losses during takeoff and landing. A small aircraft with a very cramped cockpit, it was continuously modified and improved.

Risking pilots and wasting resources to engage the big American bombers with inadequate firepower was foolish. Consequently, many of the improvements were to the Me-109's armament that, in various versions, ranged up to 30-millimeter cannons, although 20-millimeter cannons were more commonly used. Rockets were also tried, although they were heavy and limited the aircraft's maneuverability when compared to American fighter escorts. Fitting the Me-109 with big enough weapons to deal with the bombers while preserving enough performance to defend itself against the American fighters was a challenge for which the Germans never developed a good solution.

Although the design was showing its age during the latter stages of the conflict, the Me-109 was still capable of meeting the best American fighters on near-equal terms when flown by a competent pilot. And it continued to kill bomber crews to the end of the war.

The FW-190 was a newer design than the Me-109 and was in many ways superior. It was easier to fly, offered the pilot better visibility, was more maneuverable and generally carried more armament. In fact, Adolf Galland, the commander of the Luftwaffe's fighter arm and an Me-109 pilot for much of his career, proposed to end all Me-109 production in favor of the FW-190. His pitch was not accepted.

The FW-190's chief shortcoming was that its performance dropped off at the high altitudes where the USAAF's heavy bombers typically flew. This was not a critical fault so long as its pilots had the time and freedom to climb into an advantageous position from which to attack. However, they were at a disadvantage if bounced by American fighters.

Like the Me-109, the FW-190 was greatly modified throughout the war. One particular variant, the *Sturmböcke*, was especially armed and armored as a heavy bomber destroyer. The most dramatic change to the FW-190 was the replacement of the BMW 801 radial engine with a more powerful inline Junkers Jumo 213 engine that gave the FW-190D a "long nosed" look. Again, similar to the Me-109, the FW-190 was capable against the best American fighters when flown by a good pilot.

The Luftwaffe also used multiple types of twin-engine aircraft against the USAAF's heavy bombers, to include the Me-110, the Me-210, the Me-410 and the Ju-88. Although typically slower than the Me-109 and the FW-190, they generally carried bigger, harder-hitting weapons such as rockets. On the other hand, they were bigger targets and were more manpower-intensive as they were typically crewed by two or more men. Additionally, their larger size and multiple engines made them more expensive. Their use against the USAAF's heavy bombers was significantly curtailed as the American fighter escorts—to which they were easy prey—grew more prevalent and capable later in the war.

Although the character of air combat aboard the bombers could be appallingly gruesome, the nature of the fighting between the combatants was most often starkly impersonal. Men were generally killed from long range rather than at close quarters. An American bomber crew might straggle out of formation and perish in a burning aircraft miles from where a German fighter attacked it. And flak gunners firing through overcast skies might never know they had scored. Likewise, German pilots were sometimes killed as they streaked through the bomber formations, yet the gunners had little or no indication of their success. And of course, the bomber crews—unless they were shot down—never saw the effects of their missions up close.

But occasionally the fighting offered more human and personal perspectives. George Ashworth, a radio operator with the 427th Bomb Squadron, recalled an aerial clash during which he was reminded that he and the men he was fighting shared human characteristics. "A Ju-88 was going down so close that I could see the rear gunner's face. He looked as scared as I was."[6]

And Russell Ney recalled an escorting fighter pilot joining the formation during a bomb run. Fighter pilots—enemy and friendly—normally distanced themselves from the bombers as they approached the target, because the flak was so intense. "He slowed to our airspeed, rolled his canopy back and waved to us."[7]

"THE KRAUT FIRED A BURST INTO THE SKIPPER'S CHUTE"

THE 303RD'S MISSION scheduled for January 22 was canceled due to foul weather. Ehle Reber recalled: "This morning we were to be the first American attack on Germany. We were to bomb some sub[marine] pens and workshops northwest of Bremen 7 miles. The area is very highly defended with heavy flak and JU88's and ME110's as well as FW190's."

It was anticipated to be a fiercely defended target. "I think we have the same target for in the morning," Reber wrote. He was wrong. Rather than Bremen, the mission of January 23, 1943, was scheduled against Lorient in northwest France. Lorient was a major submarine base and critical to Germany's war in the Atlantic. Germany's U-boat fleet—much of it serviced at Lorient—had a stranglehold on England during the early years of the war and Churchill was keen to neutralize it. Indeed, if the Allies were to defeat the Nazis, they had to mitigate the U-boat threat. The day's mission to Lorient was part of that mitigation.

The 303rd got airborne with twenty-one ships, one of which turned back early due to mechanical issues. They were part of a larger formation of seventy-three B-17s led by the 305th Bomb Group. After crossing over Land's End, the train of bombers headed to sea. The water was shrouded by a bright white undercast that grew patchier as the formation approached the enemy-held coastline.

Antiaircraft fire peppered the sky as the American bombers neared the target. It was described as intense and accurate, and one group reported that several of the flak bursts were pink.[1] Regardless of color, it was deadly, and the aircraft of the 303rd started taking hits almost immediately. *Green Hornet*, piloted by Ellis Sanderson, fell away from the formation with three engines knocked out.

At the same time the 305th's lead bombardier had equipment issues and was unable to get his bombs onto the primary target at Lorient. Consequently the 305th turned for the secondary target at Brest, sixty-five miles to the northwest. The 303rd continued to the target at Lorient, but the situation deteriorated badly. Another bomb group—out of position and above the 303rd—dropped its bombs through the formation.

Mel Schulstad was back in Molesworth that day, grounded by the flu. But his aircraft, *Beats Me!?*, piloted by Joe Haas, was on the mission with most of Schulstad's crew. A bomb smashed *Beats Me!?* in the tail and knocked it upside down. The rest of the 303rd scattered. Charles Roth, the crew's radio operator, nearly fell from the upside-down aircraft, through the hatch at the top of his compartment. Haas managed to wrestle the badly mangled aircraft upright, but it was barely controllable and fell from the protection of the formation.

"After Lt. Haas righted the plane," said Roth, "I got up from the floor and assisted the ball turret gunner, Sgt. P. [Peter] Soria, out of the turret and put his chute on him. He headed for the rear escape door. I then noticed that the right waist gunner, Sgt. J. [John] Sherman, was hanging outside the plane, I went to help him, but, as I reached for his leg, his body fell away from the plane. Surely, he was unconscious or dead."[2]

Roth looked toward the tail and saw that the shoulder of Wayne Stevens, the tail gunner, was shot away; he was obviously dead. Roth donned an oxygen mask and manned Sherman's waist gun against a pair of FW-190s that made repeated passes against the staggering bomber. The running battle lasted more than five minutes before *Beats Me!?* nosed over, out of control. Haas and his copilot, Roy Christianson, were probably shot dead by the attacking fighters.

Roth left his waist gun and headed for the escape hatch on the right side of the rear fuselage. Along the way he noted that Peter Soria, the ball turret gunner, had not bailed out but was either unconscious or dead. Roth struggled with the handle on the hatch before he was able to get it open. Still, he fought to get clear of the falling bomber. "It seemed impossible. I was half in and half out when something came off the wing, probably part of the deicer boot, and hit me in the head, knocking and jerking me out.

"I thought surely I must be close to the ground. I was spinning around very fast and pulled the rip cord, opening the chute too soon. The tremendous jerk broke a leg strap, and whipped off a boot and a shoe. Worst of all, a long tear appeared in the top of my chute. It was difficult to control. A German fighter pilot circled me, and was close enough that I could see his face. As he circled the second time, I saluted him. He saluted back and flew off." After being recovered by French farmers, Roth was picked up by German soldiers that same night and spent the rest of the war as a POW.

A French farmer, Maurice Deimat, recalled watching *Beats Me!?* fall to earth:

I realized that the plane was about to crash, although the B-17 went on flying straight ahead. She actually lost speed until she reared backwards and turned on her left wing, then finally dived toward the ground. Her engines made a terrible noise. For a few minutes, as I saw her getting bigger and bigger, I thought she was going to fall on my head! Eventually she crashed at 500m from where I was—in a terrific explosion. A huge black cloud rose high in the sky, whereas

the earth was shaking under my feet. I was astounded and scared;
nevertheless, I decided to run toward the spot. People came from all
around.[3]

In the meantime, Ellis Sanderson's *Green Hornet*—flying on only
one engine—fought against gravity. Worse, FW-190s made head-on
attacks and raked it with machine gun and cannon fire. Sanderson
ordered everyone to bail out. However, for whatever reason, there was
only one parachute between him and his copilot, Howard Bowman.
They stayed with the aircraft and crashed it at Kergolay, where both
were injured; Sanderson lost several fingers. Both were captured.

Hell Cat, captained by Oran O'Connor, was also knocked down by
enemy fighters. Of the crew, two evaded capture and returned to
England less than two months later. The rest became POWs.

Most of the guns on *Werewolf*, piloted by George Oxrider, froze or
were otherwise inoperative. Moreover, the left outboard engine was
damaged by flak and lost manifold pressure. *Werewolf* couldn't keep
up with the rest of the formation. "I cut the corner," Oxrider said,
"planning to rejoin them on the flight back, and ran into a mess of
FW-190s. They got the #4 motor and then the #3 motor, setting them
both afire [engines were numbered thusly: #1 was the left outboard, #2
was the left inboard, #3 was the right inboard and #4 was the right
outboard]. The FW's stayed with us until we reached the Channel, and
then they had to turn back because they were out of ammunition."[4]

Sebastian Vogel, the radio operator aboard *Susfu*, manned the
.50-caliber machine gun that protruded through the open hatch at the
top of his radio compartment. A bitterly cold slipstream buffeted him
as he watched for enemy fighters. "As we neared the target the flak was
getting thicker; in fact, as I looked out to the rear through the top
hatch it looked like you could walk on it. At that time I saw one of our
B-17s go down. I still remember the sick feeling as I watched her go
down because I did not see any of the crew bail out. Then I saw a

Focke Wulf [190] blow up and saw the pilot bail out and disappear below. Every gun on the ship was firing at fighters; they were all over us like flies.[5]

"A fighter came in at one o'clock level and hit and demolished our top turret," said Vogel. "He killed our bombardier [Roy Moser] and also took the nose glass out." Vogel and the left waist gunner, Val Hannon, watched their rounds tear pieces from another FW-190 diving down from *Susfu*'s left side. "Shortly after that encounter I heard a loud thump on the side of our ship then I heard the pilot feather the prop on one of the engines. As I looked out to the rear of the ship through the top hatch, I could see that the vertical stabilizer was gone. Then the ship started to climb, it kept on climbing, the engines roared as it climbed then it stalled out and went into a dive. I started for the bomb bay where I was to bail out."

Val Hannon fell on top of Vogel when he opened the door at the rear of his radio compartment. "I tried to get him out [of the aircraft] by yelling at him and pounding on him but it did no good. We went into several spins and I was thrown around the plane, hitting my head several times. I was very dazed. I did not know if he [Hannon] had been shot. I was so concerned with getting out myself I did not try to be the hero and see if I could get him out or at least see if he had been wounded.

"When I went to the bomb bay," Vogel said, "I should have taken the emergency oxygen bottle, which was strapped on my leg, and opened it and put the tube in my mouth, but I forgot. When I got into the bomb bay I was having difficulty moving because of lack of oxygen. When I finally got on the bomb bay catwalk the crew chief [Francis Sulkofski] had just come down out of the upper turret and was pulling the release on the bomb bay doors. The doors opened up when he pulled the release, but blew back shut."

Vogel struggled with the doors. Toward the front of the aircraft he saw the copilot, Mark McDermott, bail out through the forward crew hatch. The pilot, Harry Robey, followed a few seconds later. Vogel grew increasingly hypoxic. "I thought I was going to go down with the ship. I thought that I had had it. A strange feeling of peace came over me and the thought that it was not going to be so bad after all. I figured I wouldn't feel anything when we hit the ground. My thoughts wandered to back home. It bothered me that Kathie [his wife] would probably feel bad and Mother and Dad and the rest would hear that I didn't make it and it would be like a funeral around home."

It was at that point that Sulkofski coaxed the bomb bay doors open again. "As soon as the doors dropped open he went out," said Vogel. "All I can remember about getting out was the wind hitting me in the face and I could see that I was hanging out of the ship and my foot was caught in the door. The next thing I recall is that I was hanging in midair; the ship was making a hell of a noise and heading for the ground. I knew that I had to pull the ripcord to get the chute open but I couldn't get my hand on the ring."

Vogel wore a seat parachute. He twisted about until he spotted a white handkerchief his wife had given him when he was still in the States. It was tied to the ring at the end of the parachute's ripcord. He grabbed it and pulled. "I pulled it so hard that I ripped it clear out and I could see it flying off in the distance with the ring. My chute opened with a big bang like popping a paper bag full of wind. At first I was swinging back and forth making a big arc. As I was swinging I could see our ship heading for the ground and it looked like it was about to hit. I didn't see it hit the ground because I looked the other way. I knew some of the crew were still in it.

"Just as the ship crashed into the ground a Kraut fighter came so close to me I could smell the exhaust from the engine. He didn't bother me but he came in on the skipper [Reber's friend, Harry Robey] whom I could make out quite a ways below me. The Kraut fired a burst into the Skipper's chute then disappeared."

Vogel, like virtually all of the 303rd's men, had never before made a parachute jump. "It was fascinating even though I was very scared and worried about the fighter. By this time I was down where it was much warmer and everything was quiet except for the wind whistling through the chute shroud lines. When I got down to a few hundred feet from the ground it seemed to be coming up to me at a pretty fast rate. When I got to treetop height the earth seemed to come up and hit me."

JERRY JINX, PILOTED by Ehle Reber, was mortally hit. German fighters continued their attacks on the aircraft until it was well out over the Bay of Biscay, where nine parachutes were spotted as they blossomed from the descending aircraft. A short time later one more airman, presumably Reber, was seen to parachute from *Jerry Jinx*. None of the crewmen were recovered and it is believed their bodies sank into the sea.

The ragged remains of the 303rd's formation straggled back to England. John Castle made a wheels-up landing with *Thumper* at Lulsgate Bottom after ordering the crew to bail out. Billie Stander, the crew's right waist gunner, was killed when his parachute failed to open. The legs of Emilio Yannie, the radio operator, were crushed so badly upon landing that he was hospitalized, returned to the States and discharged.

George Oxrider and his copilot, Don Hurlburt, wrestled *Werewolf* across the English Channel back to England. Both engines on the right wing were dead, as was the left outboard engine. There was no stopping the B-17's descent. Oxrider ordered his crew to bail out of the shot-up ship and headed for a hole in the clouds below.

When they were all gone, I shut off the alarm bell—it made a hell of a racket—and slipped the plane through the hole in the overcast. My one engine [left inboard, #2] was purring beautifully—it never did get hot. After two or three circles, I leveled off to land on a rugby field, coming in pretty fast. And then out of nowhere, a bunch of kids appeared in the middle of the field. Down at one end, there was a wooden flagpole, a hedge, and beyond that, another field with several roller coaster bumps in it, and a tree-lined wall at its end. I gunned the motor for what little it would take, cracked off the end of the flagpole, skipped the hedge, and set the plane down fast. It was an alfalfa field. I landed on one rise, went up and down to the next, up and over that one, and then I shoved the stick forward, so that the wheels would plow into the ground.

Werewolf came to a stop just in front of a stone wall, with its nose between two trees. Almost immediately it was swarmed by a terrifically curious crowd. Oxrider was no doubt stunned when—upon his climbing down—they straightaway bombarded him with questions and exclamations as they touched and felt and crowded around his ship.

George Oxrider had put *Werewolf* down on the grounds of one of England's largest mental hospitals—Langdon, at Dawlish.

The mission, the 303rd's eleventh, was a disaster and marked the group's blackest day to that point. Curiously, it was the only group that lost aircraft on the mission. This was due in some indeterminate degree to simple bad luck, but it can also be attributed in part to the fact that the group's formation—understandably—came apart when it was bombed by another group and *Beats Me!?* was hit. Consequently, much scattered, the 303rd's B-17s were more vulnerable to enemy fighter attacks. Aside from the five aircraft that were lost, four other badly damaged aircraft recovered at locations other than Molesworth. Only eleven of the twenty aircraft that crossed the Channel to Europe returned home. Almost all of them were damaged.

Ehle Reber had been one of the 427th Bomb Squadron's original ten pilots. His diary captured much of the color and character of the men who made up the organization that was the early 303rd Bomb Group. He and Harry Robey were the second and third of those ten original pilots Killed in Action, or KIA. By the first part of October 1943, six of the ten were dead. As much as Eaker or Arnold or anyone else might have wished otherwise, the strategic air war over Europe was—and would continue to be—a horrific destroyer of American lives.

In fact, it wasn't until the very beginning of 1943 that direction, or even careful consideration, was given to what number of bombing missions would constitute a complete combat tour. Ira Eaker recognized that flying his crews until they were shot down or physically or mentally exhausted would cripple morale. He addressed the subject on January 3 in a letter to George Stratemeyer, Arnold's staff chief.

Within the next sixty days we shall face a very critical period. We will arrive at the time when many of our combat crews will have to be relieved by reason of having completed their operational tours. They will be tired, war weary and punch drunk and they will have to be relieved whether there are replacements or not. As Tooey [Spaatz] cabled you, he, [James] Doolittle and I went over the situation very carefully and decided that the operational yardstick should be 30 missions and 200 hours maximum, with 25 missions and 150 hours minimum, giving the tactical commanders leeway within these limits.[6]

"I LIKE TO THINK SHE WAS PRETTY"

SEBASTIAN VOGEL, THE RADIO OPERATOR aboard the wreck that had been *Susfu* on January 23, hit the ground long before Reber's crew was shot down or any of the remaining 303rd aircraft reached the English Channel. "When I hit, I flexed my knees to reduce the impact as much as possible," he said. It wasn't enough, and he broke his left ankle when he struck the ground. "I landed in a small plowed field with a thick hedge around it on all sides. No one was near me in this field but I could see a crowd heading for the field across the hedge."

He also spotted another parachute being collapsed and gathered. It belonged to Francis Sulkofski, *Susfu*'s engineer—or, crew chief—and top turret gunner. "He landed just a few minutes before me," Vogel said. "The ladies were all taking turns hugging and kissing him as he was pulling in his chute. He was pale as a ghost and airsick; the swinging in the chute when it popped open after he pulled the ripcord got to him. He looked at me and asked, 'Where are we? In Ireland?' I have no idea why he thought we were in Ireland."

Immediately three Frenchmen helped Vogel out of his flying gear and dressed him in civilian clothing. "This was done to make it easier for them to help hide me if the Krauts happened to show up on the scene," he said. His rescuers didn't match his preconceived notions of how the French people should have looked: "Many of the young ladies were blonde and I thought pretty. They all wore wooden shoes.

"After leaving the area where we came down we walked about a half mile then stopped at a place along the road. It was a house and barn building which was owned by an elderly couple. The old woman was a very pleasant person. She had tears in her eyes as she hugged me and seemed to be happy for me making it to the ground in one piece. Apparently she had seen the action up in the sky and saw us get hit. Now I just began to realize that I was on the ground and still alive. It seemed like a moment of great joy that I had made it this far. I guess I even wept a little inside."

Vogel and Sulkofski were unsure of their location. "We didn't know what part of the country we were in; we were pretty busy in the ship after leaving the target plus getting out of the ship after it was hit. I opened up my escape kit which all airmen carried on raids and took out the cloth map of France. I laid it on the ground and tried to get one of the French guys to indicate on the map where we were." The men were in a sparsely populated part of the countryside approximately twenty miles east of Brest.

Worried that the near-festive atmosphere might attract the Germans, one of the Frenchmen shooed off the others and escorted Vogel and Sulkofski to another farmstead about a mile away; Vogel was not able to go any farther on his broken ankle. Injured, tired and still somewhat in shock, the two Americans bedded down in a pile of straw. Vogel awoke that night to find that the French had brought in Mark McDermott, his copilot. "His leg was in bad shape and he could not walk," Vogel said. A short time later the crew's ball turret gunner, Wilbur Hummel, arrived on horseback.

"A little later a Frenchman came back to the barn," said Vogel, "and indicated to us that they had found one of our fellows and that they had laid him out on a slab in the small funeral parlor near the local church. He conveyed the idea that he wanted one of us to come over there and see him and identify him." Sulkofski and Hummel trailed the Frenchman to the town of Pleyben and discovered that the dead man was their pilot, Harry Robey. A bullet had entered his temple and exited his neck. Vogel recollected how Robey was killed: "When I was coming down in my parachute the skipper [Robey] was not very far away from me when the Kraut fighter came by me, then fired a few rounds at the skipper." The French people gave Robey a funeral mass the following day and buried him near the church. That both Sulkofski and Hummel attended the funeral is an indicator that the Germans were not omnipresent in the area.

The four men stayed put for a couple more days after Robey's body was interred. The French tended their injuries, hid them and fed them. Vogel was especially impressed by the local bread. "Real homemade wheat bread. They didn't slice it, they just broke off chunks and put some butter on it and dipped it into the coffee."

Despite the kindness of their helpers, it became apparent that the men couldn't stay long. "On the third day a man came and told us that two strangers were seen in the little village asking the youngsters if they had seen any American soldiers around there. This fellow could manage some English and sort of conveyed the idea that it might not be too safe to hang around there too long."

The French agreed to try to get McDermott more care for his leg while Vogel, Hummel and Sulkofski prepared to leave. The three of them settled on a plan to walk ten or so miles west to Châteaulin and from there get a boat, follow the Aulne River to the sea and sail for England. However, Vogel's ankle became too painful almost immediately after they started. "The guys tried to help me walk and insisted that I go along with them," he said. "But I decided it was no use. My leg couldn't take it even with their help." It was only after much back-and-forth arguing that Hummel and Sulkofski agreed to continue without Vogel.

"Now I was alone and began to feel it," Vogel said. "It was very cold and getting dark, but I managed to head back to the barn on my own, taking it very slow." As he approached the barn where he had spent the previous few days, Vogel spotted flashlights and lanterns. "I thought they might be Krauts so I headed for the hedgerow. The hedges seemed to be hundreds of years old and spread out quite wide. I had not gone too far until my leg gave out so I crawled under the hedge hoping that if the Krauts were looking for me they might not find me because I was pretty well covered up. My heart was pounding so hard I figured that if they were Krauts and anywhere near they could hear it."

Vogel shivered in the dark and cold. "Then I heard a noise which seemed to be someone crawling along the hedgerow behind me. It was getting close and I was sure it must be a Kraut." Vogel heard a voice call out "*Mon chéri*," and then a young woman squirmed through the hedge to him with a container of heated wine. "She gave me a couple of cups of it which I drank. This hot wine took the shivers away; boy how I needed that!" The girl kissed him on both cheeks before she left. "It was so dark I really never saw her face very clearly," Vogel said. "I know she was quite young and I like to think she was pretty."

Vogel was reunited with McDermott at the same barn on the following day. There they remained another night. At daylight, a Frenchman stopped at the barn and put the two Americans on a pair of horses and led them away. "We came to the town of Pleyben, in Finistère," Vogel said. "I have no idea how far we rode those horses, but we were on them for more than an hour. We stopped at a small house with a slate roof owned by Madame and Monsieur Bernard Gilberte. They were an elderly couple. The man was slim with a moustache and his wife was very pleasant looking and rather heavy. She spoke some English words along with her French. It was almost dark again when we sat by their fireplace and talked. The lady tried to tell me about when she was a young girl during World War I when she met an American officer. I don't really know what she was telling me, but Bernard was shooting some pretty heavy glances at her while she was telling me about it."

Vogel and McDermott stayed in the Gilbertes' attic. "There were no windows up there, but there was a piece of glass laid in with the slate shingles so light came in and we could see down on the street. They had stored some potatoes up there and quite a lot of hedge clippings which they used for fire wood in the fireplace." Had the two men been caught by the Germans, it is likely that the elderly couple would have been executed. Nevertheless, the Gilbertes not only sheltered them at great risk to themselves, but also shared their food. "They had a fairly large chicken tied up by one foot in their entrance shed," said Vogel. "Whenever the chicken laid an egg they cooked it and brought it up to us."

Still, the men grew bored quickly. "During the day," said Vogel, "I spent a lot of time looking out through the glass onto the street below. Once in a while I would see the Krauts moving troops and equipment along the road." Restless as the men were, they welcomed any diversion, so long as it wasn't German soldiers. "A young lady from the town came up to see us on the third day. She was a nice looking blonde lady who lived in Pleyben. Her husband had been taken by the Krauts and put in a labor camp. Marie came to visit us several times. She had an English-to-French dictionary, which we communicated with. We spent an hour or so talking in this manner with her when she came to visit us. It was always good to see her as she helped pass the time."

After several days it became known about town that the Gilbertes were keeping Vogel and McDermott. Staying was too dangerous for everyone and a plan was made to move them. "This was a sad time," said Vogel. "I had grown to like Bernard and his wife and really appreciated what a chance they took looking after us. They were such nice people."

Marie and a handful of other townspeople came to help the two Americans move on. After dodging German trucks loaded with men and equipment, the small party headed for the edge of town. "A little farther down the road," said Vogel, "we met a small truck that looked very much like a Model A Ford. It was pulling a small trailer-type charcoal generator. The charcoal gas that the trailer unit produced was used to run the truck engine. We got in the truck after the usual good-bye routine with both the men and the women and left Pleyben."

The driver took the men to the town of Le Cloître. They were moved into a three-story apartment building, the basement of which housed a bakery. "The baker was working with several ovens; he had a long pole with a large flat end which he used to reach way back into these large ovens and bring the loaves out. The place brought back memories of home when we came into the house on a cold winter's day after we had been in the woods most of the day—cutting logs or some other cold job—and smelled the fresh bread my Mother baked."

The building was large, with many tenants, and Vogel and McDermott had to guard against being discovered. "We had to move very quietly through the narrow halls especially when we passed the room where one elderly woman was sleeping," said Vogel. "She was a Kraut who had been married to a Frenchman. The room they took me and Mac to had a large double bed with a very large feather pillow laying on it. The linens smelled fresh like they had been washed in some kind of cologne water."

As before, the two Americans were restricted in their movements, and Vogel had little to do other than observe the daily rhythms of the town's life; they still continued despite the war. "The next morning I was awakened by what sounded like ten head of cattle running down the street. The noise was made by fifteen or twenty kids heading for school. The people in this part of France wore wooden shoes. That same day, in the afternoon, the kids returned home and they sang some French song that was slightly familiar."

It was just a few days later that Vogel and McDermott were moved again. "The old lady who was supposed to be an ex-Kraut was already getting suspicious," said Vogel. "About ten o'clock one night the people came into the room and told us we were going to have to get out of this town because two strangers were asking the kids if they had seen any Americans. Before we left they took us into a room where there was a bedridden elderly woman who was probably the grandmother of many of the women that were in the house. She spoke very good English and had a rosary in her hand—she said she was praying for our safe journey. She had tears in her eyes when she said goodbye to me which moved me a lot."

The two Americans were hidden under straw in a horse-drawn cart and taken out of town, where they met a truck loaded with oyster baskets. "They had these baskets stacked across the rear of the truck bed so that they completely filled the back," Vogel said. "From the rear it looked like the truck was completely loaded with the baskets." Vogel and McDermott were hidden under stacks of the baskets, and the truck rattled north toward the coastal port of Carantec.

It went only a short distance before it was stopped at a German checkpoint. "My heart was hammering so loud I'm surprised the Kraut didn't hear it," Vogel said. "Apparently the driver knew what to tell the Kraut because we took off after a few minutes. Every few miles after that we were stopped and had to go through the same routine. Each time I thought that we'd had it. One time the Kraut walked around the truck and lifted up the canvas and shined his light but all he saw was oyster baskets.

"We finally arrived at Carantec very cold and very scared," Vogel said. He and McDermott were ushered into a house close to the water. Soon they were joined by a Frenchman, George Coste, who welcomed them with a meal of fresh shrimp. "Mac and I started to eat the shrimp but I had a tough time getting them down. Mac did alright with them.

"After George gave us the shrimp he left the house by the back door," remembered Vogel. "There was a bed on the second floor so Mac and I finished the shrimp and went up there and were about to hit the sack when George came back with two bottles of champagne. He talked with us a little, then left. We opened the champagne, it was really good stuff. No off flavors, just plain good and smooth. We ended up drinking the two quarts before we hit the sack. I slept very good that night but the next morning I got up and wanted very much a drink of water. Boy, I was thirsty and the French did not drink very much water; in fact I don't think I ever saw anyone over there take a drink of water."

George Coste returned the following morning with his girlfriend— a striking blonde woman in her mid-thirties. "She could speak English very well," said Vogel. "She made a comment when she came into the room about me being just a boy. After some conversation we all went down to the kitchen and made some coffee and had some of their terrific bread which she had brought.

"We saw a great deal of George and his girlfriend while we were there," Vogel recalled. "We talked of many things—about how the Krauts had taken most of the food, about how they used up much of their cattle, and about how hard it was to find such things as cigarettes and tobacco. She told how they saved their cigarette butts and took them to a tobacconist to have them rerolled into cigarettes and repackaged. She gave me one of these cigarettes, I lighted it and one drag on it just about put me under."

Vogel and McDermott were with Coste only a few days when they were told to get ready to sail for England. "The girl asked if she might get something for us to take back as a souvenir," said Vogel. "I gave her all of the French money that was left in my escape kit—I have no idea how much it was. She left and when she came back she had purchased a ceramic doll. I accepted the gift even though a ceramic doll was about the last thing I needed at that time."

Vogel and McDermott were moved to a building next to the docks. "There was a lot of seagoing gear and oyster baskets and other equipment in the back yard," said Vogel. "Inside the house several men sat around a table drinking wine. A lady came in from the kitchen with a big platter loaded with oysters in the shell from which some seaweed was still hanging. I was very hungry, so when we were invited to sit down with them I thought I would try to eat some of the raw oysters. But I could not get these to go down, so I took a big gulp of wine and got rid of one of them."

The tide rose enough to float their escape craft at dusk, and Vogel and McDermott were taken to a dock. The vessel was a fishing boat just more than twenty feet in length, with a mainsail and a jib. "There was a small four-cylinder gasoline engine hooked to a car transmission which was connected to the propeller," said Vogel.

Vogel's bad ankle still bothered him and he had trouble getting into the boat. "Then a big six-foot-three-inch French guy with a crew cut picked me up and sat me down in the boat with Mac." Vogel and McDermott were not the only evaders the French were sending to England. There was an RAF radio operator—Jerry Smith—as well as two French soldiers and a French officer. "They had served on the Maginot Line," said Vogel, "but managed to escape when the Krauts took over. I have no idea why they were trying to get to England." The rest of the passengers included two wealthy Frenchmen, a French submarine sailor and someone named "Rodger."

The boat was loaded with loaves of bread and bottles of wine and cognac. Finally an elderly fisherman climbed aboard. "The ex-soldiers spoke fairly good English so they were able to explain that the old fisherman was going to sail us out of the harbor," said Vogel. "Then he would return by the small rowboat that he had tied behind the sailboat.

"After a lot of goodbyes we took off with the jib and the main sail [sic] for power," Vogel said. "There were many huge rocks sticking out of the water in the harbor so the old fisherman had to pick our way through them. This is why we left just a little before dark. The wind was beginning to pick up and the surf was rolling in. When we got past the rocks after about an hour of sailing the old fisherman got in the small boat and headed back through the rocks."

George Coste took over as captain and had Vogel start the boat's engine. The wind picked up, and the tiny boat was tossed by increasingly rough waves. "The Krauts must have found out that we were out there because they started to shoot up star shells that lit up the sky," recalled Vogel. "It had started to rain fairly heavily so I expect this offered some help to hide us from the shore. We pulled the jib down right after the first shell burst; this was done to give us a lower profile on the water. After the second burst we shut down the engine on account of the noise which George thought they might pick up on the shore. It was raining a lot and the wind was blowing pretty hard, which is probably why the Krauts did not send a patrol boat out to find us."

The weather grew worse. "The waves hit the bow of the boat so hard that I thought it was going to be split in half," remembered Vogel. The water also doused the engine at frequent intervals, and Vogel took responsibility for restarting it until he could no more. "Another big wave hit the bow sending a large amount of water back over the engine which shut her down again. I took the distributor off and started to wipe it dry but the center contact point in the distributor cap jumped out and fell into the engine cooling pit. The contact point was a small round piece of carbon about a half-inch long mounted so that it was spring loaded. I spent a long time feeling around the water in the cooling pit but I could not find the thing and I knew the engine would not run without it."

The men huddled against the wind and rain and sailed the tiny boat as nearly north as possible. "It was a long night," Vogel recalled, "but daylight finally came and we had a look at the sea we were riding on. I couldn't believe what I saw. The waves were so high and the troughs were so deep it was unreal. We kept busy bailing water out of the boat and watching for anything that might be out there on this big sea aside from us."

Vogel, who had survived attacks by enemy fighters as well as a desperate parachute jump—not to mention time spent hiding from German troops and spies—feared his end might come in the icy waters between France and England. "The day was very cloudy and cold and often raining. Time seemed to stand still. It seemed like we had been on the boat forever. George was hanging on to the tiller; it seemed to be most difficult to keep the bow into the waves and keep the compass on due north. The sea water was creating a large black ulcer on his hand." Vogel checked his own hands and noted they were no better.

"The second night was just as long as the first," remembered Vogel, "with the endless sea banging away at the bow of the sailboat. None of us felt like eating anything and it was good we didn't because the bread was soaked up with sea water. The salt pork looked alright but no one ate any of it. During the night George and one of the ex-soldiers were talking. First one would say a few words which I did not understand then the other would utter a verse or two then repeat the cycle over again. I was sure something had gone wrong until I figured out they were saying the rosary in French. Then I really got worried. I was frightened enough so I joined in."

The third day dawned calmer and clearer, but the men aboard the small boat worried about their whereabouts. Powered only by sail and with nothing more than a compass for navigation, they might easily have been blown well off course. Too, despite the breaking weather, the cold and wet and physical punishment of the waves took a toll. "I think the worst thing about being cold and wet was that there was no place to go to get warm and no prospect of ever reaching a warm place again," said Vogel. "I got terrible chills that I couldn't shake. I shivered a lot then seemed to have needles going through my mouth."

On the fourth day, February 8, 1943, Coste skippered the little boat to the mouth of an estuary. The men still had no sure idea where they were. They watched a patrol boat nose through the waves at them. "When the launch approached our boat," Vogel recalled, "there were three sailors aboard and one of them had a Lewis gun [machine gun] pointed at us. The other two had rifles. We identified ourselves, hoping they were Englishmen and not Krauts. As the boat pulled up alongside, their stern swung around so that I could see the British flag. As soon as their bow was next to our boat I jumped, bum leg and all, into their boat. As I hit the deck one of the British sailors said, 'You can't get on here.' I was already on so I asked, has one of you guys got a cigarette?"

Vogel and McDermott and the other men were safe. They were taken to a naval station at Salcombe on the Kingsbridge Estuary in southwest England. Coste's navigation had been good as Salcombe was just more than a hundred miles due north of Carantec. The men were initially kept under guard as a precaution against them being spies, but were given a chance to get warm and clean. "The Commander told us that he would have someone bring us some dry clothes as soon as possible," said Vogel. "We were standing by the fireplace in the raw feeling much relieved from the itching, when the door opened and in walked a Wren [a member of the Women's Royal Naval Service—WRNS]. She was carrying a tray with a teapot and some chocolate bars on it. The four of us were standing next to the gas fireplace trying very hard to be less exposed. She never batted an eye, just came and said, 'I have some tea and chocolate for you; this will warm you up.' She turned around and left the room as nonchalantly as she came in."

Although it had seemed to him like ages since he had been shot down on January 23, Sebastian Vogel was back in England just more than two weeks later. He was the first USAAF enlisted airman to evade back to England after being shot down. As such he was somewhat of a curiosity, and he found himself dressed in a borrowed Class A uniform at Eaker's headquarters a couple of days after returning.

Vogel was to be decorated with the Air Medal and the Purple Heart. Before the small ceremony he was invited to visit with Eaker. "General Eaker was a very personable guy—not at all like I expected a general to be. He shook hands after returning my salute and told me to make myself at ease and asked me if there was anything he could get me. I said, No sir nothing, I am just fine." Eaker encouraged the young airman to relax, and Vogel reconsidered. "Well, it has been a long time since I had a good scotch and soda." Eaker sent his aide after a bottle of Scotch, and the three men enjoyed a drink together.

Following the short awards ceremony Vogel spent a few supervised days in London before being returned to the 303rd. "The General and his staff made it clear that they wanted me to go back to the squadron as soon as possible," said Vogel. "It seems that of all the guys that went down over occupied territory, I was the first non-commissioned officer to get back." Eaker and his staff believed that it would be good for morale if Vogel was seen safe, and relatively sound. Vogel, in person, validated the notion that it was possible to be shot down and still return to England.

His comrades at the 427th Bomb Squadron were happy—and almost unbelieving—to see him. "The guys back at the combat barracks were all very helpful getting my bunk and clothes back. The second morning that I was back they called a raid so I got up and went to the briefing with the crews and went out to the ships with them and watched them take off. I was glad that I didn't have to go with them. I stayed at the squadron for about a week then I got orders to go to the States."

Sebastian Vogel returned to the United States in March 1943. At that point, most of the airmen who eventually served with the 303rd hadn't even finished their training. Vogel was a pioneer of sorts as he was among the first of seventy-three men from the 303rd who evaded capture and returned to Allied hands.

ONE OF THE HOLLYWOOD luminaries who spent time with the 303rd was Clark Gable. He was assigned to the 351st Bomb Group, but because that unit hadn't yet started operations he flew his very first mission with the 303rd, aboard *The 8-Ball Mk II* on the mission to Antwerp on May 4, 1943.[1] "He was a gunnery officer and spent quite a bit of time with us," said John Ford. "At the officer's club one evening he was teased quite a bit and fed a bunch of Irish whiskey."

Gable stumbled out of the club and into the dark sometime later that evening. "I was walking along the road," said Ford, "when I heard some moaning and then a small voice said, 'Won't someone help me back to my quarters, please?' I checked the ditch and there was someone all in a heap. I helped him out and was surprised to see it was Clark Gable." Ford escorted the movie star back to his hut and made certain he came to no harm.

"The next day," Ford said, "I took a shortcut to the mess hall and stumbled right into the set where Gable was filming the movie *Combat America*. The colonel in charge really chewed me out—I had ruined whatever scene they were shooting. It was then that Gable walked up. I snapped to attention and gave him a smart salute. He recognized me right away and returned my salute with a big wink."

"HOW ABOUT *HELL'S ANGELS*?"

JACK MATHIS APPROACHED ROBERT YONKMAN on March 17, 1943. Both men were bombardiers with the 303rd's 359th Bomb Squadron. "Jack's brother Mark, who was a B-26 bombardier [and a veteran of combat in North Africa], came to the base to visit Jack," said Yonkman.[1] "They would have a couple of days to visit together. Jack came to me bearing a bottle of rum and asked me if I would take his mission for him so he could be with Mark." Yonkman agreed and went to bed. A short time later Mathis woke him up with news that the squadron commander promised him a few more days with his brother, so long as he went as the lead bombardier on the next day's mission. Mathis thanked Yonkman and retrieved his bottle of rum.

The next day's mission was to the submarine construction yard at Vegesack, near Bremen. Heavy flak burst among the B-17s of the 303rd's formation as they neared the target. Jack Mathis was bent over *The Duchess*'s bombsight when an enemy round shattered the nose, blew him away from his position and ripped his body with great, mortal wounds. Seconds later Mathis got to his hands and knees and—in the bitter cold cyclone of glass and debris—single-mindedly crawled back to his undamaged bombsight. Once there, with one good arm, he fine-tuned *The Duchess*'s course and at the correct instant released the big ship's bombs. Rather than "Bombs away," the crew heard Mathis utter, "Bombs . . . ," over the interphone. And then nothing else.

Eldon Audiss was the crew's engineer. Following a fighter attack, Harold Stouse, *The Duchess*'s pilot, sent Audiss to check on Jack Mathis. Audiss found Jesse Elliot, the navigator, wounded and white with shock, but alive. "I rushed to Jack," Audiss said, "rolling and lifting and with my knife, cut as necessary his parachute harness that had pulled into the bombsight mechanism. I checked for [a] pulse. There was none. I opened his jacket and found the wound on his side, four to five inches across that was full of clotted blood."[2]

The target was smashed. Mathis—seconds from death—had performed his duties to a degree that was nearly beyond credible. And *The Duchess* survived the mission. "When we returned to Molesworth," Audiss said, "we shot a red flare over the field and landed. We were greeted by Jack's brother Rube [Rhude Mark Mathis] who was waiting anxiously to greet him. It was a bitter welcome."

For his heroism, Mathis was posthumously awarded the Medal of Honor. His brother, Rhude Mark Mathis, asked for and received a transfer to his dead brother's squadron. Tragically, he was also lost after flying only five missions, when *FDR's Potato Peeler Kids* was shot down on May 14, 1943.

THE *MEMPHIS BELLE* and the Robert Morgan crew of the 91st Bomb Group are popularly commemorated as the first bomber and crew of the Eighth Air Force to achieve the seemingly unachievable goal of twenty-five missions. Morgan reached the mark on May 17, 1943, and the *Memphis Belle* did so two days later on May 19. The milestone was celebrated with great fanfare and a certain amount of relief by Eighth Air Force headquarters. It was a boost to morale as the casualty rate during that period was such that many men believed the goal was impossible.

The Eighth, which was desperate for positive news, sent the men and their aircraft home on a public relations swing that canvassed the United States. The results were spectacular; war bonds were sold in unprecedented numbers, and the boon to the USAAF's recruiting effort was palpable. It was a public relations home run.

But, as is so often the case with promotional extravaganzas, everything was not as it seemed. In fact, the *Memphis Belle* was not the first Eighth Air Force bomber to complete twenty-five missions. Neither was Morgan or his crew the first to reach that goal. The truth was that the 303rd's *Hell's Angels* reached the mark on May 13, six days before the *Memphis Belle*.[3] Indeed, by the time the *Memphis Belle* completed twenty-five missions, *Hell's Angels* had notched twenty-eight. And the 303rd's Irl Baldwin reached the magic number on May 14, three days before Morgan.

So why did the *Memphis Belle* get all the publicity? It's difficult to say with certainty. It seems hardly likely that Eaker's staff did not know of the *Hell's Angels* and its record. In fact, the 303rd aircraft's mission count never trailed the *Memphis Belle*'s after February 26. Likewise, Baldwin's number of combat sorties surpassed Morgan's beginning on March 8. So, the Eighth's public relations machine had plenty of time to prepare for the crowning of the eventual "winner."

The true reason was probably the fact that the *Memphis Belle* and the admittedly quite capable Morgan had been the subject of a documentary film by William Wyler since February. Wyler—serving as a major with the First Motion Picture Unit—was a veteran Hollywood producer and director whose works to that point included *Wuthering Heights*, *Mrs. Miniver*, *Dodsworth* and *The Little Foxes*. Wyler's film crews actually flew at least six missions with the 91st, several of them aboard the *Memphis Belle*.

The documentary, eventually named *The Memphis Belle: A Story of a Flying Fortress*, had been ordered by Arnold and was intended to convey to the public the bravery of the USAAF's airmen in the savage skies over Europe. The fact that Wyler, who had actually visited the 303rd, chose the 91st and the *Memphis Belle*, might have been influenced by the fact that the 91st's base, Bassingbourn, was built before the war. Accordingly, it was not built in a hurry and featured permanent brick structures, groomed grounds and other amenities. It was much more comfortable than Molesworth, which was widely derided as "Mudsworth."

So then, although no one denied that the 303rd's *Hell's Angels* and the Irl Baldwin crew were the first to fly twenty-five missions, neither was the fact widely trumpeted. Instead, it actually made sense from a publicity perspective to send the *Memphis Belle*, Morgan and his crew back to the States. There they could tour as the stars of an upcoming motion picture that would show the American public just what their sons and brothers and husbands were enduring over Europe. And if people believed that they were the first to reach the twenty-five-mission mark, well, what harm did it do?

Essentially, the accomplishments of the 303rd's *Hell's Angels* and her air and ground crews were strangled at the altar of public relations expediency.

The ship actually began its combat career without a moniker. It wasn't until its fourth or fifth mission that the crew agreed upon a name when, during a slow period, Baldwin asked, "How about *Hell's Angels*, after the movie?"[4] He referred to the Howard Hughes World War I epic of the same name, which was released in 1930. Eventually, after flying forty-eight missions, the aircraft and its ground crew were in fact sent back to the States to fly a bond-selling tour similar to what the *Memphis Belle* had done earlier. The results were also similar.

It is worth noting that the nature of the bombing missions throughout the war was such that no one crew flew the same bomber on every mission. Aircraft often needed extensive maintenance and so were not continuously available. Likewise, every crewman was not available for every mission, and so the compositions of the crews—and the numbers of missions flown by various individuals—varied. Accordingly, neither Baldwin nor Morgan was the pilot on every one of the missions flown by "their" aircraft, although Baldwin flew all but one mission at the controls of *Hell's Angels*. This was, in itself, a remarkable achievement and one that likely was never equaled.

THAT THE EARLY FIGHT was a meat grinder was borne out by the 303rd's losses. Of the original forty pilots, fully 45 percent, or eighteen, were killed. And an additional seven, or 17.5 percent, were shot down and made POWs. Of those original pilots, fewer than four of ten men completed their twenty-five-mission tours.[5]

Indeed, the losses during that first year were terrible for all the crewmen, original or not. The casualty statistics can be spun, ciphered, diddled, qualified and asterisked, but the awful truth was that a bomber crewman in the Eighth Air Force stood about a 50 percent chance of being shot down during the period from the beginning of operations in 1942 to at least the early part of 1944.

THE EIGHTH AIR FORCE and RAF's Bomber Command essentially pursued their own goals in their own ways during the several months following the Casablanca Conference. Nevertheless, Allied leaders recognized that more dogmatic and focused air operations were essential to winning the war. And that the war could not be won until Europe was invaded. And that Europe could not be invaded until the Luftwaffe was destroyed, or at least neutralized. Accordingly, after a great deal of collaboration and coordination—much of it led by Eaker—the POINTBLANK directive was issued on June 10, 1943.

POINTBLANK mandated attacks against seventy-six different targets making up six different systems or sets. Submarine targets were still part of the mix, but there was more emphasis on other target types, to include the aircraft industry, oil production, and ball-bearing plants. The target selection was biased not only toward those that were related to the aircraft industry, but also toward those that the Luftwaffe was expected to defend with vigor. After all, if Germany's airmen rose to fight, they could be killed. And if enough of them were killed, the Luftwaffe would crumble.[6]

The Eighth Air Force started to hit its stride during the summer of 1943 as POINTBLANK was planned and executed. Enough crews and aircraft were in place to launch more than three hundred bombers—B-17s and B-24s—on thirteen different missions beginning in June and continuing into mid-August. These were in addition to many smaller raids.

But as much as the Eighth was growing, it was doing so behind schedule and not nearly fast enough for Arnold back in Washington, or for Roosevelt and the American public. Arnold constantly badgered Eaker to put more bombers into the air, and to do it more often. Arnold's zeal and dedication came at the price of great impatience—especially with Eaker, who was running the biggest show in the USAAF. And although direct attacks by the press were rare, there were great expectations for the men and equipment the nation was sending to England.

Eaker, for his part, was doing the best he could with the resources he had. Although more men and aircraft were pouring into England, the skilled technicians, the parts and the material to maintain them in operational status—especially heavily damaged aircraft—lagged. Eaker's staff found that only one of every 2.6 bombers was ready for a mission at any given time.[7] Accordingly, although the Eighth had approximately eight hundred heavy bombers on hand, it struggled to sortie more than three hundred on a raid. And following those raids it took time to reconstitute the resources necessary to mount subsequent missions. Moreover, maintenance and material and manning issues aside, the weather continued to be a factor in the Eighth's operations, although it was less perverse than it had been during the previous winter.

"WE CHECKED OUR PARACHUTES"

EDDIE DEERFIELD WAS BORN in Omaha, Nebraska, on August 24, 1923. "My father emigrated from the Ukraine to the States and was naturalized in 1920. My mother was from Poland, and they were married in 1921."[1] His name was Eddie rather than Edward or Edgar or Edmund. "Eddie Cantor was a popular singer, dancer and comedian of the time and was a favorite of my parents. He had big brown eyes, as I apparently had when I was born. My folks made the connection and I was named Eddie. But even though my birth certificate clearly showed my name as Eddie, it was commonly assumed to be a nickname." Indeed he was often misidentified as Edward Deerfield on various lists and rosters. "This continued all through my military service and beyond."

Deerfield's father moved the family from Omaha to Chicago in 1927. There he worked at the grain mill in the Union Stock Yards. "My parents moved to Chicago from Omaha in hopes of making a better life, but I don't remember that anything really changed. We were poor and lived in an apartment in northwest Chicago," Deerfield said. "But everyone around us was poor as well. Most of my friends were first-generation Americans whose parents came from all over Europe; there were Irish, Germans, Russians, Poles and many others."

Then, as poor as they were, things got worse. "My father lost his job at the grain mill during the Depression," Deerfield said. "So, to make a living he rented a horse and wagon from which he sold fruit and vegetables—summer and winter—on the streets of Chicago. I helped him on many weekends while I was a teenager. I weighed and bagged the produce while he collected money for the purchases. I enjoyed the times we stopped and shared a lunch together; that was special to me.

"My mother and father kept things going, although I must admit that poverty was always an embarrassment for me when growing up. Still, my brother and sister and I were loved and I know things could have been a lot worse.

"I was a very good student in grammar school," Deerfield said. "I wrote poems and was invited to recite them at school assemblies and also appeared in school plays. When I was twelve I wrote and published a four-page neighborhood newspaper that I sold for two cents a copy.

"The problems started when I was a senior at Tuley High School on Chicago's northwest side. I was invited to join a local theater group that presented one-act plays to raise funds for various charities. I never knew very far in advance when they would call me to perform, so I had to cut a lot of classes. I enjoyed acting and felt good about what we were doing."

Deerfield loved reading, writing and acting but was not only bookish. "I liked to box. I represented the Deborah Boy's Club on the northwest side and fought for the welterweight championship against the boy from the American Boys Club on the west side. I had a great left jab and he wasn't able to handle it. I hit him so much that he reeled around the ring and the referee shouted to stop the fight early: 'Ring the bell! Ring the bell!'

"Ultimately," Deerfield said, "I earned just enough high school cred-its to graduate. Still, the five hundred students in my class elected me as one of the two orators to speak at graduation. It was an unexpected honor. Following high school—during the summer of 1941—I worked as a copy boy at the *Chicago Daily Times*. I had always looked forward to a career as a journalist, and this was a great beginning. But, by the end of the year," he recalled, "there was the Japanese attack on Pearl Harbor and I was anxious to enlist."

Eddie Deerfield went into the USAAF during the summer of 1942 at the same time that the 303rd was struggling to get ready for combat. "I rode a Greyhound bus from Chicago to Jefferson Barracks near St. Louis, Missouri, for basic training. From there, in the fall, I was sent to Las Vegas, Nevada, to train as an aerial gunner. At that time, it was just a small desert town—the bright lights and gambling casinos came much later. But, the gunnery training was excellent. We started with BB guns and advanced to firing shotguns from the bed of a moving pickup truck at clay pigeons hurled into the air along the route."

While he was at gunnery school Deerfield and his classmates endured one of the brutish fools that seemed to be a feature in every military organization. "We all arrived as buck privates. They put a little corporal in charge of our class and he lived in the same barracks. He wasn't a gunner or a flyer; he was just an administrative type. The guy was a tyrant and really enjoyed giving us a hard time. He drilled us and called formations and made us do stupid little tasks in the barracks. He was a little Napoleon."

Nevertheless, Deerfield and his comrades quickly progressed through the training. "During the final period of our instruction," Deerfield said, "we shot a .30-caliber machine gun from the back of an AT-6 advanced trainer at a target sleeve towed by another AT-6." This was a doubly exciting event for Deerfield. "Not only was I shooting for score, but it was the first time I had ever been in an airplane or wore a parachute. It was that way for a lot of guys.

"We fired bullets that had been freshly painted. One guy's bullets were one color while another guy's bullets were a different color and so on. When the bullet hit the target sleeve it left some paint behind so that when the sleeve was brought back the umpires could tally our hits." Deerfield performed well: "I scored eighteen hits the first day and twenty-three the second.

"Immediately after we finished our training," Deerfield said, "we were promoted from private to buck sergeant. So we finally outranked our tyrant. But it didn't matter a bit to this guy—he just continued to order us around. Finally, the guys put me up to go to the captain. I went in and gave him a really snappy salute and explained that we really thought that the corporal ought to respect our rank. And actually, things changed quite a bit after that during the short time we had left at Las Vegas."

Following aerial gunnery training, Deerfield was sent to Salt Lake City for schooling as a radio operator. "The instruction at Salt Lake City was also very good," he recalled. "I had no problem there at all. In fact, the biggest eye-opener for me was the fact that they billeted us in the horse paddocks at the state fairgrounds. Believe it or not, it was the first time I had ever used an outdoor privy. This was during January and February of 1943—and it was cold!"

Deerfield subsequently received orders to Blythe Army Air Base in California, where he joined a new B-17 crew. Because the crew already had a radio operator, he was assigned as the ball turret gunner. "I was a little disappointed because I had been trained as a radio operator and knew I could handle the responsibilities of the position. Aside from that, I was a little too big for the ball turret—it just wasn't a good fit in terms of my training, my desires and my size." Nevertheless, following additional training at Blythe, and Pyote, Texas, Deerfield and the rest of the crew took a new B-17 across the Atlantic during May 1943.

It was unusual when a crew remained intact through an entire combat tour. The composition of most crews changed due to injuries, sickness, reassignments and requests for removal from combat status—among other reasons. Eddie Deerfield transferred to another crew almost immediately upon arriving at Molesworth. "I learned that another new crew needed a radio operator. I volunteered for that position and no one objected—there were no hard feelings. The crew I joined was just fantastic, and they were led by a pilot that I believe was among the best there ever was, Robert Cogswell." The admiration between Deerfield and Cogswell was mutual. Cogswell wrote home: "I have a new radio operator from Chicago. He is, at present, as good a man as I have on my crew. He has a good head on his shoulders, and knows how to use it, plus plenty of initiative."[2]

First missions were especially anxious events, to which the men reacted in various ways. Eddie Deerfield recalled his feelings: "I had been training for more than a year. I had been through basic training, gunnery school, radio operator training and phase training on the B-17. All of this training was undertaken to prepare me for combat. As the time for my first mission approached, I looked forward to it not with fear but with a sort of curiosity. What was it all about? What was I getting into?" He learned soon enough.

As the radio operator on Robert Cogswell's crew, Deerfield flew his first combat mission on July 10, 1943. Following that first mission the Cogswell crew flew on four of the 303rd's next six missions and was airborne again on July 30. The target was the Fieseler Aircraft Works at Kassel, Germany. Fieseler produced not only its own design—the Fi 156 utility and observation aircraft—but more importantly, it manufactured Me-109s and FW-190s under license. As the Allies were anxious to not only destroy the Luftwaffe's fighters, but also neutralize Germany's capacity for aircraft production, the Fieseler complex was a prime target.

The 303rd's takeoff, rendezvous and flight across the North Sea was fairly unremarkable, although four of the group's aircraft aborted for mechanical reasons. Deerfield remembered that Cogswell's crew, flying aboard *Upstairs Maid*, very nearly aborted as well. "At the Belgian coast the outboard engine on the right wing, number four, developed a malfunction and began consuming gas at an alarming rate. We heard the copilot, Paul Tippet, question Cogswell about whether or not we should continue as there was a real danger that we wouldn't have enough fuel to complete the mission." Every man on the crew strained to hear Cogswell's response. "Cogswell's answer was unequivocal," Deerfield recalled. "He said that the target was too important to miss and that we'd have to take our chances. None of us said a thing. I remember shrugging my shoulders and uttering a ridiculously long sigh of resignation. We checked our parachutes and settled in for a rough go."

The opposition got stiff as the bombers penetrated into Germany; they were without fighter escort. The crews counted more than a hundred single-engine fighters making seventeen different attacks against the 303rd. *Upstairs Maid* was the object of several firing passes. "We were hit by FW-190s and Me-109s over the target and on the way out," Deerfield said. In fact, the fighters attacked from every direction and holed the bomber badly. Shrapnel from heavy antiaircraft fire added to the maelstrom. It was a near-miracle that no one aboard the staggering aircraft was hit.

"The attacks forced Cogswell and Tippet to use violent evasive action, which caused the engines to use even more fuel than they normally would have," Deerfield said. "Cogswell asked the flight engineer, Gilbert Bengston, to transfer gas from the number four engine to the others—he planned to shut down the number four engine and return on the remaining three. Bengston told him there wasn't enough gas left on the entire aircraft to transfer anywhere.

"We finally fell out of the formation as we neared the Dutch coast with only two engines running," said Deerfield. "We were in such bad shape that the German fighters left us alone—it was obvious to them that we weren't going to make it." Nevertheless, Cogswell's crew didn't give up. "By that time we were over the North Sea, and we dumped anything that wasn't attached to the aircraft—to include guns and ammunition." Despite their efforts, it soon became apparent that *Upstairs Maid* was not going to make it back to England. It had lost too much fuel, and the remaining two engines, operating at high power, were consuming what little remained at a rapacious rate. Cogswell ordered the crew to prepare for a water landing. "I set my transmitter to the emergency frequency, and began tapping out the letters 'S-O-S' on my Morse code hand key while the rest of the crew got ready for ditching," Deerfield said.

DITCHING A LARGE AIRCRAFT like the B-17 was no easy task. In the water, most aircraft were little more than leaky, winged, metal tubes encumbered by heavy and useless equipment. Indeed, aircraft in the water tended to obey the laws of physics and sink quickly. Because the USAAF knew that ten ill-prepared men rattling around inside a ditched bomber stood little chance of surviving, it gave its crews training to maximize their chances against a water landing.

Each crewman had specific duties during a ditching that were unique to his position. Among the pilot's duties, aside from actually flying the aircraft and landing it on the water, was to sound the signal bell—six short rings—and ensure via the interphone that the crew was prepared. Just prior to touching down he was to order the crew to "brace for ditching" and give one long ring on the signal bell. Once the aircraft stopped moving, he was supposed to exit through his side window, proceed to the inflatable dinghy on the left side of the aircraft and take command. The copilot was tasked with assisting the pilot. Upon landing he was to take charge of the raft on the right-hand side of the aircraft.

The flight engineer was responsible for assisting the rest of the crew as they jettisoned guns, ammunition and loose equipment well prior to touching down on the water. He was also tasked with pulling down the escape hatch cover at the top of the radio compartment and putting it in the rear of the aircraft, where it was out of the way. Except for the pilot and copilot, the entire crew was supposed to gather in the radio compartment during the ditching; the hatch was the main escape point. If the cover was left in place, there was a good chance that it would jam and become immovable as the aircraft bent and twisted on impact with the water. Following the ditching, as the last one out, it was the flight engineer's duty to help boost everyone through the radio compartment hatch.

The bombardier was tasked with jettisoning the bombs if they hadn't already been dropped, and with making certain the bomb bay doors were closed. He was additionally responsible for destroying the bombsight and taking the first aid kits into the radio compartment. Once the ditching was complete, he was to climb out the top hatch, receive equipment and rations and assist the other crewmembers as they exited.

The navigator was charged with calculating an accurate position prior to the ditching and passing it to the radio operator for transmission to Air/Sea Rescue. He was also to destroy any secret papers, gather up his maps and celestial equipment and give the wind speed and direction to the pilot. Following the ditching he was responsible for passing rations, survival radios and other gear out of the radio compartment to the bombardier.

The radio operator was the crew's connection to the pilot and copilot, as well as to the organizations whose job it was to rescue them. He stayed on interphone with the pilots before they put the aircraft into the water and relayed their orders to the rest of the crew while also transmitting SOS messages via Morse code. On the pilot's orders, just before the ditching, he clamped the transmitter key down, which ensured that a constant tone was broadcast until either the radio was disabled or the aircraft sank. Shore-based radio direction finders used the tone to get a final fix on the aircraft. Aside from these radio operator duties, Deerfield was also the crew's medic.

The two waist gunners, the ball turret gunner and the tail gunner were largely responsible for securing their positions so that nothing loose could hurt anyone during the ditching. Well prior to the water landing, the waist gunners jettisoned their guns and ammunition and, in later model aircraft, closed their windows to help reduce the volume of water entering the aircraft once it was ditched. The tail gunner manually cranked the tail wheel down while the ball turret gunner turned his guns rearward and sealed off the turret.

By the time the men gathered in the radio compartment they were to have shed their oxygen masks and ties—if they were wearing them—so that they didn't get caught on anything. Likewise, they were supposed to loosen their collars so that they had greater freedom of movement. Too, winter flying boots were to be removed so that they didn't become waterlogged and drag their wearers down.

The radio compartment was not a large space. Everyone except the pilot and copilot, and the radioman—who remained strapped to his seat—sat on the radio room floor. A few of the men braced their backs against the forward bulkhead and clutched other crewmates who sat between their legs, facing away. To lessen the chance of injury they were instructed to tuck parachute pads and other soft articles around themselves.

"WE WERE AT about three thousand feet when the engines quit," recalled Deerfield. "The B-17 was a noisy aircraft, but when those engines stopped the silence was eerie." With its engines dead, *Upstairs Maid* was little more than a spectacularly shot-up, four-engine glider. The sound of nothing but the slipstream was strange to the men—it was something they had never experienced. Regardless, Cogswell and Tippet wrestled with the powerless ship as it descended toward the water.

The navigator, Edward Cobb, and the bombardier, John Kennedy, came back from the front of the aircraft and entered Deerfield's radio compartment along with the flight engineer, Gilbert Bengston. The ball turret gunner, Paul Davis, the two waist gunners, Alvin Etheredge and Elmer Peterson, and the tail gunner, Harold Timm, entered through the rear door. They quickly reviewed their assignments and took positions on the floor. "On Cogswell's signal," Deerfield said, "I locked the transmitter key so that a continuous signal would mark our position. At the same time I strapped myself into my radio operator's chair and made a mental note of the location of the ration kits, a battery-operated Gibson transmitter and a first aid box—we would take them with us after we ditched.

"At that point there was nothing more that any of us in the radio room could do," said Deerfield. "It was up to Cogswell and Tippet. Shortly thereafter Cogswell called me on the interphone—I was the only one still in contact with him. He told me to relay our altitude to the rest of the crew as he called it out in hundred-foot increments. And then, just before touching down on the water, he'd signal us with the bell."

Deerfield called out as they descended through a thousand feet. "I remember that P. J. Davis, our ball turret gunner, raised himself up as if he was going to brace himself better. Then he changed his mind and settled back. I continued the countdown, and a few seconds after we passed through a hundred feet the warning bell sounded." Procedures directed the pilots to land parallel to the waves rather than run the risk of smashing directly into the face or reverse side of a crest. The pilots were also instructed to ditch while still powered by the engines.

That option wasn't available to Cogswell and Tippet. Nevertheless, they put the aircraft down perfectly. The aircraft shuddered as the tail section hit the waves. At the same time a tearing shriek ripped through the *Upstairs Maid* as its wings and fuselage struck the water. The sudden deceleration slammed the men forward as the aircraft went from flying speed to a full stop almost immediately.

Water rushed down into the radio compartment through the top hatch. "Instinctively," Deerfield remembered, "I unsnapped my safety belt and tried to stand, but the water rushing through the open hatch pushed me back down. I struggled against it and then fell back exhausted. I thought that the aircraft was already sinking and that it was a hell of a way to die."

The rush of water stopped almost as suddenly as it began. The men in the radio compartment leapt up and sloshed around in water up to their knees. "The plane was motionless," Deerfield said, "and we realized that the water that came through the hatch was part of a huge wave formed by the wings as they churned their way over the surface of the sea." Although it was filling with water, the big bomber was still afloat.

The men moved quickly to get out of the aircraft. There were two life rafts aboard the bomber, located in compartments above the wings. When Paul Davis pulled the release handles, they sprang out and away, and inflated automatically. The men helped one another out of the radio compartment through the top hatch and were met by Cogswell and Tippet. Of the ten men, Edward Cobb, the navigator, was the only one hurt; he had a broken leg, a smashed nose, a cracked tooth and various contusions. "He was only semiconscious, and blood ran from a gash on his forehead and down his face," Deerfield said. "I helped lift him up through the hatch, and they carried him to the raft that was floating just off the left wing. After he was clear, the rest of us grabbed the first aid kit and the emergency transmitter and hauled ourselves out."

Some of the men clambered into the rafts while Deerfield and others jumped into the water and pulled the rafts away from the bomber. "Cogswell shouted out, 'There she goes,'" said Deerfield. "I got turned around in time to see the vertical stabilizer rise up high in the air as the aircraft went down nose first. And then it slid beneath the water almost without making a ripple."

It was high summer, and the water, while not warm, was not as brutally cold as it was during the spring and winter months. Deerfield's crewmates pulled him aboard the raft in which Cobb was settled. "As the crew's medic," he said, "I gave Cobb a shot of morphine to help get him comfortable and then pinned the syringe to his shirt. It wasn't long after that when Paul Davis sprang up, almost upsetting the raft, and pointed toward the horizon. There was a tiny black speck barely recognizable as an airplane." The men held their breath and hoped that the approaching aircraft wasn't German.

The speck grew larger and proved to be an American P-47 that was soon joined by a wingman. "One of them climbed," said Deerfield, "while the other circled us in our rafts and waved encouragement." That encouragement was well founded. Less than an hour after Cogswell and Tippet put *Upstairs Maid* into the water, an RAF High Speed Launch—specifically, HSL 2562, commanded by John Shanahan—motored into view. The craft was an Air/Sea Rescue vessel based out of Felixstowe in Suffolk, England.

"They were very professional," remembered Deerfield, "and helped us get Cobb aboard first. They recognized right away from the empty syringe on his shirt that he'd already been administered one dose of morphine, and made sure that he was made secure and comfortable." The RAF crew gave warm blankets and glasses of brandy to the rest of the wet Americans. Both warmed their bodies and spirits considerably.

Although *Upstairs Maid* was irretrievably gone, the big bomber had stayed airborne long enough to get Cogswell's crew to a point twenty-two miles from the English coast, well more than half the distance from Nazi-occupied Belgium. That every one of his men survived was due in large part to Cogswell's skillful piloting and the leadership he had imparted to the crew, along with, perhaps, a small dose of good luck. Cogswell wrote home about the mission: "I guess it won't be violating military censorship to let you know that I went down in the drink last week. Yes, the water was fine; practically tepid. I brought my entire crew out of it, though, so everything is fine and dandy. It was a real adventure—hell while I was going through it, but quite interesting in a way.

"For some strange reason," Cogswell continued, "I had faith that everything would turn out all right. It is this faith for which I am thankful. . . . Supplementing this faith is the realization that I am fighting for the right side, the right things, the right ideals, and as long as I retain this [realization], there will never be fear."[3]

Surviving a ditching and the subsequent time adrift on the water was not a foregone conclusion. Through the course of the war, twenty-four B-17s from the 303rd went into the water. The casualty rate was more than 50 percent: 138 men were killed or drowned or died of exposure, whereas only 99 men were rescued by Allied or German forces.[4] Crews shot down over Germany had better survival rates.

Cogswell's crew owed its rescue almost entirely to the British. The Air/Sea Rescue organization and equipment were products of the British experience during the early part of the war. Although the RAF and the Royal Navy had dedicated organizations, aircraft and boats in place at the opening of hostilities, they proved to be wholly inadequate for the scale of the fighting. In fact, the RAF's losses over the water during 1941 averaged two hundred men each month.[5]

Such a waste was a moral and practical tragedy to which the British responded with purpose. Many more aircraft and boats were procured and delivered to a revamped and enlarged Air/Sea Rescue organization. New equipment was developed, including improved rubber dinghies, dye markers, portable radios, air droppable survival kits, moored rescue pods and signaling equipment. Homing pigeons were tried aboard some aircraft.[6] Aircrew training was likewise dramatically improved.

Key to rescuing downed airmen was accurately determining their locations. The British created a system of "fixing" stations that received radio signals from crews in distress. Control stations collected and triangulated those signals, plotted positions and forwarded the information to control staffs that coordinated the launching of aircraft and rescue boats. It was a system that was operational and proven by the time the USAAF began operations during the second half of 1942.

Air/Sea Rescue was initially not high on the USAAF's list of priorities; the service's focus was on destroying targets. However, it didn't take long for the American leadership to realize that it was an enormous waste to abandon men to the sea—or if they were lucky, to the Germans—who might reasonably be rescued. Consequently, within a few months the Americans were keen partners with their British allies in Air/Sea Rescue and contributed greatly in terms of men and equipment, ultimately setting up their own separate service.

The results were tremendously encouraging. Whereas only about 6 percent of USAAF flyers who went into the water were rescued during the first half of 1943, 40 percent were pulled out of the water during the latter half of the same year.[7] During the summer of 1944, when the water was warmer and the various organizations were more mature, rescue rates exceeded 50 percent. Aside from the value gained by returning highly trained personnel to service, morale was also improved by the knowledge that rescue from a water landing was not only possible but realistic.

"COULD WE KEEP IT UP?"

AS THE EIGHTH AIR FORCE expanded through the summer of 1943, its planners explored various ideas for how to use it; it was critical to extract as much effectiveness as possible from the burgeoning force. Henry Arnold, President Roosevelt and the American people demanded it. At the same time, it was essential to prosecute the objectives of the Combined Bomber Offensive and POINTBLANK.

Thus was born the notion of a simultaneous strike to Regensburg and Schweinfurt. Regensburg was a primary manufacturing center for the Me-109, and Schweinfurt produced most of Germany's ball bearings. Aside from the obvious disadvantage to the Luftwaffe if Regensburg's Me-109 plants were smashed, USAAF planners also theorized that Germany's war industries would be brought to their knees if Schweinfurt's ball-bearing facilities were destroyed.

The scheme for the mission was relatively complex and had the look and feel of a "trick play." Eaker was not an advocate of the idea but was pressured—presumably by Arnold—to carry it out. "We were pushed into this before we were ready," he later said, "and I protested bitterly."[1]

Eaker's chief worry was that the participating forces would not be large enough to penetrate so deeply into Germany without suffering outsized losses.

The plan was for one group of 146 B-17s, led by Curtis LeMay, the commander of the 4th Bombardment Wing, to attack Regensburg. Then, rather than turning back for England, the formation was to continue south and cross the Mediterranean to USAAF bases in Algeria. A second formation composed of 230 Schweinfurt-bound B-17s was to follow closely behind along much the same route. The hope was that they would be unmolested during that brief period when—having spent their fuel and ammunition during attacks on LeMay's force—the defending German fighters would be regrouping on the ground. Too, it was hoped that LeMay's unexpected track to the south, concurrent with the second group's approach from the north, would confuse the German defenders. After being canceled on August 7, the mission was scheduled for August 17, 1943; it was the one-year anniversary of the first mission to Rouen.

As it often did, weather upended the Eighth's plans. Fog and low clouds mantled most of England, and LeMay's takeoff was delayed more than an hour. However, the Schweinfurt force, instead of taking off soon after LeMay, did not get airborne until more than three hours later. That interval was more than sufficient for the Luftwaffe to savage LeMay's formation and subsequently land, refuel, rearm, attend to biological imperatives and prepare for the Schweinfurt bombers.

The result was predictable and horrific. Fighter escorts took LeMay's bombers as far as the German border, but from that point the B-17s were left to the Luftwaffe. During a ferocious running battle that lasted ninety minutes, approximately fifteen bombers from the Regensburg force were knocked down by fighters prior to reaching the target. Another nine B-17s—already damaged for the most part—crashed after hitting the target.

It was long after LeMay's formation dropped its bombs on Regensburg when Robert Williams, the commander of the 1st Bombardment

Wing, led the Schweinfurt-bound force over the continent. As with the Regensburg force, Luftwaffe fighters were waiting for the B-17s when the escorting P-47s, low on fuel, turned for home. Not only were the German units that had attacked LeMay's formation refueled, rearmed and ready, but so were additional units that were raised in anticipation of hitting the same bombers as they returned to England. However, LeMay's force hadn't turned back, but instead was on its way across the Mediterranean. Consequently, the Schweinfurt-bound B-17s became the sole focus of the German fighter pilots.

The 303rd was part of that effort. Eddie Deerfield, aboard the *Iza Vailable* with the rest of the Robert Cogswell crew, remembered when the P-47s wagged their wings in salute before leaving the bombers. "There were deadly Me-109s and FW-190s joined by the relatively cumbersome Me-110s and Ju-88s. The Germans were throwing everything they had at us." Only moments later a cannon round holed *Iza Vailable*'s right wing, barely missing the fuel tanks. Another smashed into the number two engine.

The fighting continued all the way to the target and its savagery was confirmed by Deerfield:

> The box formations out on the far left and far right seemed to be getting most of the attention, and Fortresses were falling everywhere. As they dropped out of the protection of the formation, the enemy fighters roared in for the kill. Parachutes started peppering the sky as American airmen jumped from their burning B-17s; what sickened me to the point of tears was the Fortresses that exploded in mid-air, giving the crews no chance of escape.[2]

The 303rd, in two separate formations, was toward the rear of the attacking force. The route was marked by the white blossoms of parachutes and by the orange-and-black pyres of burning aircraft. In fact, twenty-nine aircraft from the 1st Bombardment Wing were knocked down on the way to the target. As the formation approached Schweinfurt, it was apparent that the raid had degenerated into chaos. The bombs from earlier groups were scattered across a broad area, and clouds of dust and smoke obscured the three separate ball-bearing plants. German smoke generators further degraded the visibility. Still, Kirk Mitchell, the pilot of the 303rd's lead aircraft, declared that he saw the target at a distance of twenty miles and that the group's bombing accuracy was outstanding. "I'm not making any excuses for that one," he said. "We really knocked holy hell out of the place."[3] That the group achieved such results is all the more remarkable because Mitchell's bombardier was hit by flak. Only the navigator's quick reflexes and good sense got the bombs away before it was too late.

German fighter crews, as described by Deerfield, renewed their attacks as the bombers turned for England: "Then the Me-109s and FW-190s swooped in again. Our aircraft suffered no hits on the return journey, but B-17s in other formations were being pounded unmercifully. It was a bloody reenactment of the inbound flight as American parachutes filled the air and more B-17s plunged to earth or became fireballs." The Germans knocked down nine more bombers during the retreat. The carnage only ceased when P-47s met the bombers over Belgium.

The final reckoning revealed a debacle unlike anything the Eighth had ever experienced. In fact it was the greatest beating that any American raid had ever sustained. The mission cost the Eighth 60 aircraft— 24 from the Regensburg force, and 36 from the formation sent to Schweinfurt. It was a 19 percent loss rate. Crew losses were tallied at 552 men killed or captured. Salt in the wound was the fact that the battle was so lopsided. Although the bomber crews put in claims for 288 enemy aircraft shot down, actual German fighter losses—at 27— were less than a tenth of that. And only 16 enemy pilots were killed. The Luftwaffe had had a very good day.

The bombing results were mixed. The Messerschmitt plant at Regensburg was well and truly plastered. However the capacity was quickly reconstituted both on-site and at dispersed locations. This notion of relocating manufacturing capability to smaller, not easily bombed shops—rather than massive factories—was one that the Germans began to practice with vigor in the coming months. In reality, the Regensburg raid did not have much of a practical impact; the Luftwaffe was not forced to curtail operations because it lacked aircraft.

Definitively determining the impact of the Schweinfurt raid was more difficult. Although many of the groups dropped their bombs far from their targets, the different plants did sustain some damage. Estimates ran to as much as 34 percent of capacity. However, the Germans dipped into existing stocks while they rebuilt their factories. Ball-bearing supplies from Sweden also mitigated the effects of the strike. Ultimately, the raid did not achieve the effects that the USAAF's planners had hoped for.

There was no sugarcoating such middling results against the gruesome outlay in men and machines. Nevertheless, the 303rd played little part in paying the butcher's bill. The group lost no aircraft. Jack Timken, the pilot of the 358th Bomb Squadron's *Sky Wolf* said, "There was a big air battle going on. I saw my first enemy plane go down and there were plenty of them going down. It wasn't any rougher than the Ruhr for me, thank God."[4]

Why the 303rd was spared when so many other groups were brutalized is open to speculation. It might have been that its position toward the rear and the center of the formation made it less vulnerable compared to other groups that were more exposed. Or perhaps its pilots flew tighter formations; aircraft grouped closer together put up more concentrated defensive gunfire and were consequently less liable to be attacked. Or it could be that the 303rd was simply lucky on that particular day.

That Arnold—the USAAF's chief—was flummoxed by what his forces in Europe could or could not do is evidenced by what he recorded in his memoirs soon after the war: "Could we keep it up? . . . To this day, I don't know for certain if we could have. No one does."[5]

Yet, despite the slaughter the Eighth endured that day, it was apparent that the USAAF's leadership believed that its bomber crews could defend themselves against concentrated enemy fighter attacks. An example was the mission to Stuttgart three weeks later on September 6, 1943. During that raid 45 of 338 bombers—again, unescorted—were chopped out of the sky. Worse was to come.

ROBERT COONEY WAS A TAIL gunner and part of the 303rd's original cadre. Consequently, he flew many of the group's most dangerous missions, to include the first raid to Schweinfurt on August 17, 1943. He was young, and one particular recollection put his age—and that of his peers—in context. He was awarded the Distinguished Flying Cross by Brigadier General Robert Travis, the commander of the 303rd's parent command, the 41st Combat Bombardment Wing. "The general had been a friend of my father for many years and when he was presenting it to me, he said, 'Bob, I should be giving you your high school diploma; you are the youngest man that I have ever awarded the Cross to.' I was 19 at the time."[6]

The 303rd's target on August 19, two days after the raid to Schweinfurt, was Gilze-Rijen, in the Netherlands. Although the group didn't lose a single aircraft during the splendidly tragic raid to Schweinfurt, the men were nevertheless somewhat rattled and more than ready for a milk run. Gilze-Rijen looked as if it would fit the bill as the route was relatively short and did not penetrate Germany. Certainly the men did not believe that the ferocity of the defenses at Gilze-Rijen would equal what they had endured on their way to Schweinfurt and back.

The raid was to be Louis Moffatt's first. In fact, he wasn't a trained crewman, but rather was the 359th's assistant engineering, or maintenance, officer. He had asked permission on August 10 to go on a raid as an observer. In his request, he outlined why he believed it was important for him to go on a combat mission: "As [the] Assistant Engineering Officer, I should like to observe airplane and engine performance on extended high altitude formation flights and to observe what troubles are encountered with oxygen systems and electrically heated clothing." In order to dispel the notion that Moffatt's request was a gutsy lark, his command endorsed his request with the following statement: "The interest of the Government is the dominant and controlling factor in this request."[7]

In truth, Moffatt probably could have gotten all the information he needed simply by debriefing with the crews. But he was like many of the support men; through choice or chance they were not selected to fly in combat. Nevertheless, either to satisfy a sense of adventure, or mindful of how they might reply after the war when asked about their experiences, many of them made requests similar to Moffatt's.

Indeed, there are stories of men—cooks, clerks, mechanics, etc.—who went on missions as stowaways, or who were allowed onboard, outside of official channels, by crews who were sympathetic to their cravings "for some action." These accounts are probably apocryphal. First, it is very unlikely that a pilot would risk disciplinary action, and his career, by allowing an untrained man aboard his ship for a combat flight. Additionally, an extra body would have simply been in the way. During combat, there was no advantage in having someone aboard the ship that was not only in the way, but who also required special care and attention. Finally, if an aircraft was shot down with a stowaway aboard, it is likely that the man would have been listed as a deserter; there would be no way to know that he had been airborne on a mission.

The takeoff and assembly went well, and none of the 303rd's twenty aircraft aborted en route to the target, which was a German airdrome and its storehouses. However, sun glare and haze conspired to stymie the crews sent against it that day. The lead group failed to find the target and did not drop its bombs. When the rest of the wing gave up on the mission, the 303rd turned back for another try. It likewise was unsuccessful, although half the crews released their bombs, likely in frustration.

Alone after their desperate try, the 303rd's crews finally headed home. It wasn't long before the group was attacked by a formation of approximately thirty German fighters. After-action reports remarked on the aggressiveness of the enemy pilots, noting that the crews had never seen enemy fighters come so close during their firing runs; this, two days after the Schweinfurt raid. The B-17 piloted by James Nix was hit in the wing and caught fire. Likewise, the nose of the ship was hit and the bombardier was trapped by an oxygen fire. The ship exploded and killed four of the crew, including Nix, but not before seven of the men, including Moffatt—who had gone on the mission "to observe what troubles are encountered with oxygen systems and electrically heated clothing"—bailed out. These men were made POWs.

Aside from Nix's ship, eleven aircraft were hit by light but accurate flak near Antwerp. One of them, *Stric Nine*, of the 427th Bomb Squadron, was knocked down. Only four of the ten-man crew survived to become POWs. Of the dead, four bodies later washed ashore and were buried in Dutch cemeteries.

The result of the day's mission was that the 303rd lost two of twenty aircraft on a short mission to a wholly unremarkable target. It was a bitter irony when compared to the group's experience during the horrifying mission to Schweinfurt two days earlier. The caprice of providence in the skies over Europe was mystifying.

RECON, THE 427TH'S MASCOT, had been smuggled to England by William Nelson in his "A" bag when the group made the move aboard the *Queen Mary* the previous year. The effects of the rattlesnake bite she had sustained while protecting Nelson at Alamogordo were long gone, and she had little trouble making canine friends in her new home. She whelped a litter of pups during the spring of 1943.[8]

"GOD WILL FIND OUT"

MANY CREWS GREW a special affinity for a particular aircraft. Somehow, a bomber could just "seem right." It might be a nuanced feel at the controls, a certain treble in the interphone system, the contoured familiarity of a seat or even a unique smell. In some instances the attraction was almost immediate, but in others the aircraft earned its way into the hearts of the crew only after bringing it through multiple missions—some of them harrowing. The Robert Cogswell crew was especially attached to *Iza Vailable*. A reclining, bare-breasted beauty dressed its nose. "It became part of our family. We respected it just as we would a father, a mother, a sister or a brother," said Eddie Deerfield, the crew's radio operator.

But just as harm could befall a family member, the same could happen to an airplane. The attack against the German V-1 infrastructure at Watten, France, on August 27, 1943, was the first of the Eighth's missions specifically directed against these types of targets. It was a short run across the English Channel—only eighteen miles inland from Calais on the French coast. Nevertheless, it was not the milk run that some of the crews thought it might be. Heavy antiaircraft fire and fighters hit the 303rd hard.

The Cogswell crew was part of the formation. The men had flown four combat missions since being knocked into the North Sea by fighters the previous month. The German defenders around Watten threatened to do them similar hurt. "We were in our favorite bomber, *Iza Vailable*," said Deerfield. "The flak was thick and deadly accurate." Enemy fighters also swept the formation, although escorting Spitfires provided some protection.

"*Shangri-La Lil* was flying nearby and was hit by flak," Deerfield said. "The plane simply exploded in midair. But we counted four parachutes." The men aboard *Iza Vailable* didn't have time to dwell on the downed bomber. "We were also getting hit by flak bursts." The rattle and ring and ping of shrapnel hitting and sometimes piercing *Iza Vailable* put the crew on edge.

Cogswell and his copilot, Hershel DeWall, were busy in the cockpit. Although they weren't long over the target, *Iza Vailable* was badly hit. The controls to the left outboard engine were knocked out, the left inboard engine was set afire, and the oil lines on the right inboard engine were severed. "We all thought back to the previous month when we had to ditch in the North Sea," said Deerfield. "It wasn't something we wanted to go through again."

As soon as he thought it safe to do so, Cogswell dropped the struggling aircraft out of formation. "Our pilot did a fantastic job maneuvering that shot-up B-17," Deerfield said. "Bob made an emergency landing at the Royal Air Force base at Manston. When we got out and walked around the plane, we counted more than two hundred holes from flak and German fighter fire. Yet none of us suffered so much as a scratch."

"That night," Deerfield said, "the RAF noncommissioned officers on the base hosted us at their club. They treated us like absolute royalty and had a splendid little string quartet that entertained us through the evening."

Although it had safely brought its crew back to England, *Iza Vailable* was decidedly not. "They eventually got her patched up and back to Molesworth," said Deerfield. The ship underwent repairs for more than a month and wasn't returned to service until after more bad things had happened to the Cogswell crew. "We sure were sorry to lose her," Deerfield said.

The maintenance men also developed kinships with particular machines. They came to know every inch of their aircraft; they understood its quirks and its history. They knew what it needed and what it didn't, and they grew protective of it against crews that might treat it roughly. Essentially, their lives in the 303rd revolved about their assigned bomber. It represented their contribution to the war.

In fact, especially during the 303rd's early combat career, when spare parts were scarce, crew chiefs were reluctant to allow their ships to be taken to the main hangar for repairs. There the aircraft might be—with or without official sanction—stripped of parts in order to keep other bombers airworthy. In the event that there was no choice but to move an aircraft under cover, crew chiefs often posted men to guard the ship against unauthorized cannibalization by other maintenance men.

Fabian Folmer, the crew chief of the famed B-17, *Hell's Angels*, described how the aircraft—after they were repaired and serviced—were prepared for the following day's mission:

The engineering officer checks each crew chief—"Is your ship okay?" And then we give it a last minute check. Oxygen. Get ready for the armament man to put the bombs in. We wait until all the civilian workers finish their day and leave the field. Security. And then the bombs are loaded on. We don't have anything to do with the loading. Sgt. Tooey is our armament man. Each ship has two of them usually. . . . They have a tough job, especially in the winter. There is a specialist for the gun turrets. Another for oxygen equipment. We check the troubles, report, then see that the specialists do the work on our ship. And then, bed. Up about three to four hours before takeoff. Ready the ship. Crew chief preflights the engines, warms

GOD WILL FIND OUT" 125

*them up after the ground crew "pulls the props through." The crew
chief walks his bomber out of the hardstand, waves so long. Then the
real work starts—the sweat of waiting for their ship to come home.*[1]

Eddie Deerfield's recollections underscored this attachment of the
ground crews to their aircraft: "We got to know them pretty well. To
an extent, our lives depended on the work they put into the airplanes.
As we came in to land after each mission, and as we taxied back, I
looked out through my window in the radio compartment and saw
their white, upturned faces as they scrutinized each bomber, looking
for their own. When we returned, they were always quite happy to see
us—they treated us like long lost brothers."

But just as some crews seemed jinxed or cursed with bad luck, so
did some aircraft—no matter how much time or energy the men spent
to make them right. Jim O'Leary of the 427th Bomb Squadron remembered one such aircraft:

*As I recall there was a donkey painted red with both heels in the air
on the nose of the aircraft and the tail of the fuselage was painted
red also. The* Red Ass's *ground crew hated that airplane with an
unswerving passion . . . they hated to see her come home. Those
poor guys were always working on that flying machine. You'd see the
lights on full blaze near their hardstand every night . . . they were the
most embittered ground crew that I ever remembered having anything to do with. We were leery about flying her even to slow-time an
engine (which was frequent) because we feared that the mechanics
were tempted to sabotage it.*[2]

Ultimately, *Red Ass* was shot down by flak during the raid to Bremen on November 29, 1943; five of its crewmen were killed. It was the
ship's thirty-sixth mission.

At the other end of the spectrum was a recollection by Willis Meyer,
the crew chief of the 360th's *Quinine—Bitter Dose*. "I was lying on

my bunk thinking about my brother Bill who I heard had been shot down on a mission. I was wondering if he was dead or a prisoner of war, when the door opened and an officer came in. My first thought was that he had come to tell me Bill had been Killed in Action."

The officer was a pilot, George Stallings. "He told me that he had gone to see Major Walter Shayler, the squadron CO, to tell him how pleased he had been with the mechanical condition of *Quinine—Bitter Dose*, the B-17 he had been flying. Shayler said 'Tell it to the crew chief.'

"Stallings hugged me," said Meyer, "and gave me a kiss on the cheek. He was emotional. I was real proud. When he finished his combat tour, he gave a party for all the men in the ground crews of the B-17s he had flown on missions. One swell guy!"[3]

It is understandable that it is the men and aircraft that interest most students of the air war over Europe; there is a visceral connection to the visual and human aspects of the great air battles. But the men could operate those machines only if they were supported by a very robust and complex logistics organization. The 303rd's B-17s, for all their magnificence, might be grounded—rendered impotent—for lack of any number of obscure components, some no larger than a coin. Supplying the maintenance men with the thousands of different parts necessary to keep the aircraft operating was a largely thankless job performed by thousands of men organized in largely forgotten units. Nevertheless, without them the war would not have been won.

And then there were the men who made contributions that were difficult to characterize or describe, but which were exceedingly important. Indeed, behind the achievements of many great organizations there are often unheralded individuals without whom the organization's successes might not have been so pronounced. The 303rd's Russell Seaton was one of these men. "The 303rd was always noted for having really high morale," said John Ford. "And one of the reasons for this was the behind-the-scenes work that Russell Seaton did. He was a master sergeant before the war, but was so good at getting things done that he was made an officer so that he'd have more clout and could get more and better things done. He climbed through the ranks to become a major very quickly.

"He took the time to do things for the men that commanders didn't think to do, or didn't have time to do," Ford said. "For instance, early on we had to carry our own individual mess kits to the mess hall. After we ate, we scraped out the scraps into trash bins then dipped them in a series of barrels with hot water and soap to clean them up and rinse them. It wasn't very convenient, nor was it particularly sanitary. Russell Seaton fixed this. He went inside and outside of channels to get dishes and trays and commercial dishwashing equipment so that mealtime became much less of a hassle and, at the same time, more enjoyable." Ford didn't note it, but Seaton's work likewise kept more men healthy.

"He also revamped the different duties. No one was eager to do KP—or especially latrine duty—for obvious reasons. But he arranged for volunteers to be promoted to corporal and fixed their schedules so that they were on duty for a period of days and off duty for a period of days. It was a pretty good deal. And because the payroll always came with a certain amount of change, he also took that change and split it among the volunteers. Consequently, the people he had on duty were motivated to do it, and they also got really good at it because it was their full-time job.

"He did a similar thing for the men who stood charge of quarters, or CQ," said Ford. "These were the men who, among other things, were in charge of waking the crews for missions. Traditionally, they were temporarily pulled from their regular jobs—as mechanics, for example—and assigned to CQ for a short period. It was disruptive, and every time someone new was assigned they had to learn the job from scratch. Seaton got volunteers by promoting them to sergeant and keeping them on CQ full-time. He also had special little cottages built for them, which was an additional incentive.

"He found good people and kept them working for him," said Ford. "There was a mechanic who had been a master carpenter as a civilian. Seaton had him promoted and kept him busy building things all over the base. This was the guy who built the bar in the enlisted men's club from the crates in which the GB-1s [guided bombs] were shipped. Ray Dusman was a supply sergeant and was one of Seaton's best men—he could get hold of things that others never could. Seaton often got his crew together and sent them out into the surrounding countryside to trade cans of gasoline for eggs and whatever else could be used in the mess kitchen; the farmers were happy for the gasoline, which was strictly rationed.

"Seaton was actually assigned to the 359th Bomb Squadron," said Ford. "But a lot of the things he did benefitted the entire group and were copied by the rest of the squadrons. He got the PX—the post exchange—built and was instrumental in getting the two base theaters into place. His work was so important to the command that he was made the squadron's executive officer. This was done despite the fact that the official table of organization had no billet for an executive officer."

Seaton was with the 303rd from its beginning in the States and through the group's entire tenure at Molesworth. Many of the aircrews—the pointy end of the spear—arrived and were gone in six months or even less. Most of them never knew Seaton or understood enough of what he did to appreciate it. But that wasn't the case with Seaton's fellow support personnel. "I'll never forget what he did," said Ford. "His efforts played a tremendous role in the welfare of our lives and to some degree in what the men flying the bombers were able to accomplish."

JUST AS THE 303RD'S CREWS sometimes recovered to RAF bases when in extremis, RAF bombers likewise occasionally landed at Molesworth. Curtis Olsen recalled one such occurrence that took place during the summer of 1943. On that evening the group's officers hosted a party to which every available female in the region was invited. "As always," Olsen said, "the officers outnumbered the invited girls and I was in the forefront of those trying to claim the sole attentions of any one of the guests."[4] In the meantime an RAF Short Stirling heavy bomber—with one engine out—made its way through the dark toward Molesworth.

Olsen didn't know and didn't care. He was elated when a young Irish nurse agreed to return to his Nissen hut with him.

Through the most urgent, passionate and imaginative pleading/ cajoling/coaxing—ad nauseum, I'm sure—I managed to get the partially undressed nurse into my bunk and was attempting to get better acquainted. She was adamant that she had gone as far as she was about to venture, repeating, "God will find out." I was understanding of her concern, but desperately trying to find a way around it. No matter what I said, the answer was, "God will know." Finally I resorted to that old argument, "It is all part of His scheme of affairs for men and women."

The Almighty was apparently unimpressed by Olsen's case. The massive British bomber continued its approach to Molesworth. At that moment Lawrence Whippo and Kenneth Kallstrom were biking back to their quarters after working late into the evening on a set of balky bomb racks. They heard the Stirling before they saw it and pulled off the perimeter track to watch it land. A few seconds later it became apparent that the British bomber was off course and that they were in danger of being flattened. The two men abandoned their bicycles and sprinted for the protection of a nearby mess hall. "We hadn't got too far before we heard the brakes start screeching, then just a rumbling sound, then all hell broke loose."[5]

Meanwhile, the spirited and sexually charged debate in Olsen's hut was interrupted by a massive, scraping bang on the roof. The young nurse pulled away from him and shouted, "I told you he'd know!"

"At her words," Olsen said, "a hunk of plasterboard fell from the ceiling atop the bed. We both leapt to the floor, me groping for a flashlight, she groping for her uniform." The Stirling rumbled to a halt atop a pile of broken concrete adjacent to where the 427th Bomb Squadron's officers—including Olsen—were billeted. One of the aircraft's wing-tips had smashed into Olsen's hut. His hopes for a sex romp were ruined. "The worst part of the episode was that I had to load the young lady on my bike and pedal her back to the officer's club where the party was still in full swing, but sans liquor."

The Stirling's crew escaped the accident unhurt. And after being dragged from its awkward perch, the British bomber was patched up and sent on its way only a couple of days later.

THE 303RD WAS SENT to the port area of Nantes, France, on the afternoon of September 26, 1943. The mission got off on time but was recalled after nearly two hours because of cloud cover over the target. Robert Cogswell's crew was flying aboard *Lady Luck*. It occurred to the crew that the ship was not particularly lucky at all when the propeller of the right outboard engine ran away. Efforts to feather it failed and the engine caught fire. "The aircraft was vibrating so badly that rivets were popping out," said Eddie Deerfield. "It looked like the right wing was cracked and about to break off. As we crossed back over the English coast near Southampton, Bob Cogswell ordered us to bail out."

The two waist gunners, the tail gunner, the ball turret gunner and Deerfield, the radio operator, readied their parachutes and clustered around the waist door on the right rear side of the fuselage. "No one wanted to jump," Deerfield said. "We all wanted to take our chances with Bob Cogswell and trusted him to make a safe landing." That trust was especially notable considering the fact that the aircraft was still loaded with bombs.

Deerfield was the only one in the rear of the aircraft still in contact with the pilot by interphone. "I called Bob Cogswell and told him we knew he could get us back to base, and asked if we could stay onboard. He said that we might want to reconsider as he planned to bail out. I turned to the four men around me and gave them a thumbs-down sign."

Deerfield checked his parachute. "The two waist gunners and tail gunner jumped," he said, "and we saw their parachutes open. P. J. Davis, the ball turret gunner, was next to bail out. When his parachute opened, it looked to me like his head was ripped off." Stunned, Deerfield followed Davis out the door and pulled the ripcord of his own parachute.

The burning aircraft, still carrying a load of ten five-hundred-pound bombs, fell toward the town of Alresford in the south of England. Cogswell, now the only one aboard the ill-fated bomber, wrestled it onto a different course and stayed with the plane until he was certain the town was safe. Finally, with the ground only a few thousand feet below, he bailed out of *Lady Luck*. The big ship crashed clear of the town, just east of Old Alresford Pond, where it struck and killed several cows.

The crew landed in the area around Winchester, south of Alresford. "We came down into trees, on rooftops and into open fields," said Deerfield. "I came down backward and was stunned when I slammed into the ground. When my head cleared, there was a farmer standing over me with a pitchfork pressed against my chest. He had seen all the parachutes in the air and thought we were German paratroopers invading England."

When the crew had been collected and brought back together, Deerfield was relieved to learn that the ball turret gunner's head had, in fact, not come off when his parachute opened. "What I thought was P. J.'s head was actually his helmet! The worst thing about the bailout was that pilot Cogswell was badly hurt. When he jumped, the aircraft was in a dive near the ground. The shock of his parachute opening and the hard landing injured his back. He was hospitalized and it wasn't certain when he might be released."

Cogswell's description of the ill-fated flight in a letter home was magnificent in its simplicity: "I'm afraid that we've had another shaky deal. Once again I was able to save everyone on my crew, but the *Lady Luck* will be hauled away in a bushel basket." He also asked a rhetorical question that was entirely reasonable. "Well, now I've ditched, crash-landed and parachuted. What more is there to do?"[6] The obvious answer, unarticulated, was to be shot down and killed.

As it developed, Cogswell was released for flight duty less than two weeks later, in time for the October 4 mission to Frankfurt. His crew rejoined him, but fuel problems forced an abort. Notwithstanding the fuel problems, it was apparent that Cogswell was not fit for duty as his back had not fully healed. He was pulled from flight status for an indeterminate period.

It was at that point that the close-knit crew began to unravel. "We were hit so badly during our early missions," Deerfield said, "that our crew simply started to fall apart. We had ditched in the North Sea, crash-landed at a Royal Air Force base, bailed out from a burning aircraft and suffered flak and fighter damage on almost every mission.

"After the aborted mission to Nantes on September 26, which would have been our fourteenth as a crew," said Deerfield, "and after the aborted mission to Frankfurt a few days later, some of the guys on the crew asked to be removed from flight status permanently. I guess they had talked to the flight surgeon. P. J. Davis, our ball turret gunner, asked for temporary release from flight status until Bob Cogswell's return to duty as a pilot. I did the same. We wanted to be with Cogswell—the only pilot we had flown with in combat—when he left the hospital and formed a new crew. Our requests were granted. Our navigator, Edward Cobb, flew as a replacement with another crew and was shot down and made a POW."

Cogswell's reflections in a letter home provide insight into the mind of a young man whose job was among the most terrifying in the world. "When I come to the moment when I must balance the ledger, I will look back on the career of R. W. Cogswell very much alone. I, alone, can judge whether the good deeds outweigh the bad, whether I have made the most of the life that God bestowed upon me. It is sometimes simple to fool others, but to fool oneself is sheer folly."[7]

"YOU COULD HAVE HEARD A PIN DROP"

THE EIGHTH'S FIRST ATTACK against Schweinfurt's ball-bearing plants on August 17, 1943, had been only marginally effective. Production climbed toward normal levels during the following weeks as the factories and machinery were speedily repaired. So then, Germany's ball-bearing production capacity still needed killing. The industry remained critical, and both sides knew that if it were ruined, Germany's ability to manufacture the machinery required to make war—to include aircraft, tanks and submarines—would be crippled. Consequently, the Americans prepared to hit Schweinfurt again while the Germans stood ready to defend it.

The mission was scheduled for October 14, 1943. It was to be Bill Eisenhart's seventh. The copilot from the 359th Bomb Squadron recalled the briefing: "When they pulled the curtain back so that we could see the target, there was some murmuring, and then it got kind of quiet."[1] Pilot Bill Heller of the 360th Bomb Squadron had a similar recollection: "You could have heard a pin drop."[2] Major General Frederick Anderson, the commander of VIII Bomber Command, ordered a message read at all briefings that morning: "This air operation today is the most important air operation yet conducted in this war. The target must be destroyed. It is of vital importance to the enemy. Your friends and comrades, that have been lost and that will be lost today, are depending on you."[3]

The weather matched the mood. It was gray and misty, with low-hanging clouds. "We thought the mission would be scrubbed," recalled Eisenhart. "And some guys were hoping that it would be." It wasn't, and after a delay of more than an hour the group taxied in heavy rain and visibility so poor that the crews couldn't see the end of the runway. Nevertheless, the 303rd got airborne without incident and broke out above the clouds at approximately seven thousand feet.

The 303rd—as part of the 1st Bomb Division—took its position toward the rear of the lead column of B-17s. The 1st Bomb Division and the trailing 3rd Bomb Division—a total of 291 B-17s—winged their way from England toward Germany. An additional sixty B-24s from the 2nd Bomb Division were unable to form in the poor weather; the twenty-nine aircraft that did manage to join together flew a diversionary mission north toward Emden rather than proceeding to Schweinfurt.

RAF Spitfires escorted the bombers across the North Sea and VIII Fighter Command P-47s picked them up as they crossed the coast into Europe. Various fighter elements of the Luftwaffe were already airborne, and rather than waiting to attack the bombers until the escorting P-47s reached the limits of their fuel, several units hit both the bombers and their escorts. The American fighters claimed thirteen German fighters, while losing one of their own.

Nevertheless, the P-47s didn't carry enough fuel to escort the bombers all the way to Schweinfurt. Upon reaching Aachen, on the German border with Belgium and the Netherlands, they turned back for their bases in England. It was then that the German fighters hit the bombers in earnest. Near the front of the column, ahead of the 303rd, the sixteen aircraft of the 305th Bomb Group were savaged by frontal attacks. It was pure carnage; thirteen of the 305th's B-17s were knocked down.

The ferocity of the attacks was described by Eaker in a cable to Henry Arnold, the head of the USAAF.

Yesterday he [the enemy] ran off the full scale dress rehearsal perfectly timed and executed as follows: a screen of single-engine fighters flew in from the front very close firing normal 20mm cannon and machine guns. These closely followed by large formations twin-engine fighters in waves, each firing large numbers of rockets suspended under wings. Firing began at long range and twin-engine planes broke away further back than single engine planes. Rockets were lobbed in barrage quantities into formation. . . . Single-engine fighters than [sic] refueled and attacked from all directions to engage our gunners. These followed closely by reformed formations of twin-engine rocket carriers attacking principally from the front and rear.[4]

Mathias Kremer of the 303rd's 358th Bomb Squadron was the ball turret gunner aboard *Joan of Arc*. Kremer recalled what happened when the escort fighters turned for home. "They [German fighters] lined up out of reach of our guns. Then, ten or fifteen at a time, they would come in to attack us. I was in the ball turret. My intercom was shot out in about the second attack, so I was on my own down there." In the thick of the battle, inside the little motorized steel-and-aluminum-and-glass bowl that was his ball turret, Kremer was isolated from the rest of the crew. "It was really lonesome without the chatter from the rest of the crew."

Bill Eisenhart was Thomas Quinn's copilot aboard *Wallaroo*. "There were Me-109s, FW-190s, Me-110s and Ju-88s and they kept after us the entire time," he said. In fact, the Luftwaffe launched 547 sorties over a period of nearly three-and-a-half hours. Many of the German pilots exhausted their ammunition and fuel, landed, refueled and rearmed, and then took off again. *Wallaroo*—like all the bombers—shuddered repeatedly as her gunners fired on the attacking fighters. "There were aircraft, both ours and theirs, falling out of the sky almost continuously," remembered Eisenhart. "And it was noisy as hell."

William Heller, the pilot of *Thumper Again*, recalled the chaos: "It was amazing to me that aircraft weren't running into each other. The Germans flew through our formation very close to us and to each other. And they seemed to fishtail as they came through. It looked as if they were kicking their rudders so that they could see behind them as they dived. Likewise, we all maneuvered whenever we came under attack." Indeed, notwithstanding the danger of midair collisions, the sections of the bomber column that came under fighter attack appeared to shiver and tremble as individual aircraft maneuvered—as much as their pilots dared—to evade the enemy fire. Adding to the terrifying panoply were short streaks of white and gray that hung motionless in the air. They were smoke trails that marked the points where German fighters had fired their guns and rockets.

Heller recalled, "I saw a Fort up ahead start to smoke—the next instant a sheet of flame, then nothing! I saw a Fortress fly upside down in a very slow roll then dive to earth." He counted ten parachutes—the entire crew—blossoming from the doomed aircraft. The crews of the 3rd Bomb Division, in trail of the 1st, noted that they needn't have brought their navigators. The route to Schweinfurt was marked by the smoking wrecks of the 1st Bomb Division's B-17s.

Heller and his copilot worked hard to keep their ship from becoming one of those wrecks. Two of their bomber's engines started to lose power, which forced Heller to demand more from the other two engines. Those engines—forced to carry an extra load—were consequently in greater danger of failing. Worse, *Thumper Again* was still under attack. "Jack Coppom was my copilot and he or my other crewmen called for me to maneuver one direction or another as the fighters made their passes. It's how we stayed alive."

But they couldn't stay alive if they didn't stay with the rest of the formation. Even with the two good engines pulling hard, Heller's aircraft lagged. "As much as we wanted to hit the target, we were going to get shot down if we fell back from the protection of the formation. So, we jettisoned our bombs." Free of its load, *Thumper Again* regained its position. The only good Heller's crew could do at that point was add its defensive fire to that of the other bombers.

Still, the formation's .50-caliber machine guns were useless against the antiaircraft fire that dogged the American bombers along much of their route. It intensified around the target and continued to harry the formation as the aircraft released their bombs and turned toward England. Aboard *Wallaroo*, Bill Eisenhart recalled: "Our number three engine was hit and caught fire internally. We couldn't control it and we couldn't feather the propeller—we were sure the engine was going to throw the propeller right into fuselage."

The fighter attacks continued. "A shell came up through the flight deck and shot out the radio as well as part of the oxygen system," Eisenhart said. "The pilot, the navigator, the engineer in the top turret, the right waist gunner and the tail gunner were all without oxygen. My pilot, Tom Quinn, passed out. During this time the cord on my earphones came loose and I couldn't figure out what was going on. I was shouting over the interphone and the crew was responding, but I couldn't hear them. I just thought that they weren't answering me—it was very confusing.

"Joe Vieira, the radio man, and Oscar Howlett, the navigator, were heroes," Eisenhart said. "They grabbed oxygen walk-around bottles, left their positions and got them to the crewmen who were without. In the meantime, Jim Reynolds, the left waist gunner, and Joe Vieira were wounded.

"The number three engine slowed us down. That propeller still wouldn't feather and hadn't torn loose and was creating a great deal of drag. We weren't able to stay with the group and fell back and tucked into the group behind us until they also pulled away." *Wallaroo* slipped back through the column of bombers from group to group and miraculously remained unmolested as it slid through the gaps alone.

The crew of *Joan of Arc* wasn't so fortunate. Mathias Kremer, the ball turret gunner, saw a twin-engine fighter attack the B-17 and knock out its rudder and elevator. "Now the pilot couldn't keep up with the formation and we fell behind."[5] *Joan of Arc* was set upon from all quarters. "I was firing at a plane coming in at me," remembered Kremer, "and it started to go down in smoke. I followed it with my turret to make sure I had gotten it. That is when a twenty-millimeter shell came in behind me and went through my elbow and into my leg. Everything in the turret was bloody!"

Kremer rotated his turret down, opened the door and crawled up into the fuselage. "As soon as I got my eyes level with the floor of the plane I realized that everyone was parachuting out." Kremer had disconnected his oxygen when he cleared the turret and had to hurry before he blacked out. "I had to put on my parachute with just one hand; since my left hand was useless. I almost had it on when I was hit in the back with shrapnel from a shell. It knocked me down and I had to start over with getting the chute on my back. By now, all four engines were on fire and I knew they could blow up anytime. I finally got my chute on and headed for the door."

Kremer jumped clear of *Joan of Arc* just as the big bomber nosed over into a dive. As he plummeted through the thin, icy air, he noted a German fighter circling him. "When I opened my parachute, he saluted and left."

Heller and his crew, aboard *Thumper Again*, made it across the coast and over the North Sea. The weather was foul, and Heller's windscreen and instrument panel were shot out. Moreover, the left horizontal stabilizer was badly shot up and the fabric covering the top portion of the vertical stabilizer was torn away. Nevertheless, with his bomber's fuel nearly exhausted, Heller pushed it down through a hole in the clouds. "We found a small RAF field [Kenley] just outside of London. The RAF immediately gave us a clear runway. A doctor and a chaplain met us at the flight line. We needed neither, thank God, but these actions boosted our admiration of the RAF."

Aboard *Wallaroo*, Eisenhart and his pilot, Tom Quinn, nursed their bomber to the North Sea still under the protection of the last group of bombers. "We made it back to Molesworth," remembered Eisenhart.

"And that damned propeller stayed attached to the number three engine through the entire mission. When we finally got the engines shut down, that propeller hung loose just like a big, limp . . . noodle."

The 303rd survived one of the most spectacular air combats in history—and as in the earlier mission to Schweinfurt it returned home relatively unscathed. Despite the fact that it was part of the heavily engaged 1st Bomb Division, the group's only loss over the continent was *Joan of Arc*, although the crew of *Cat-O-Nine Tails* bailed out near the base at Molesworth when its pilots couldn't bring the battered bomber down through the weather to land. A third bomber was so badly damaged it was written off upon landing. These losses were considerably less than the 40 percent loss rate of the 1st Bomb Division as a whole.

Notwithstanding the group's relatively low loss rate, the surviving crews were glad to see the end of the mission. "We all quickly decided that we didn't want to do that one again," said Bill Eisenhart. James Teno, a ball turret gunner with the 427th Bomb Squadron, was injured by 20-millimeter cannon fire. It was his second mission. He commented, tongue-in-cheek, "Oh well, the first twenty-five missions are always the hardest."[6]

AFTER PARACHUTING FROM *Joan of Arc*, badly wounded Mathias Kremer crawled to a nearby road. There, a farmer with an ox-drawn wagon picked him up and headed toward the nearby town of Sindringen. Kremer was shortly joined by a pair of German soldiers. "They took me from the wagon and helped me to the aid station. Nearby, were about twenty German civilians in the street with guns and pitchforks." Kremer, who grew up in a German-speaking household, listened closely to what they said. "I heard one of them say in German, 'We should shoot the S. O. B. in the back.' The two German soldiers turned around, pulled their side arms, and cleared the street."

Kremer was briefly reunited with his pilot before being taken to a hospital. He was put in casts but otherwise left untended for a week before being moved—this time by a horse-drawn cart—to a hospital in Ludwigsburg, north of Stuttgart. There he was put under the care of a Polish doctor named Zenowksi, who was also a prisoner. Zenowski held out little hope for Kremer and had an orderly put him out of the way for the night.

The next morning, when Zenowski found Kremer still alive, he removed his casts, cleaned his wounds, extracted some shrapnel, broke and reset his arm, put him in new casts and hoped for the best. But there were complications. "About two weeks after I got to the hospital, my leg started to hurt real bad. Doctor Zenowski announced that he had to take off my leg because it was gangrenous. He promptly took me to surgery at 0800 and at 0814 I woke up in my bed. The doctor explained that he had to work real fast because he couldn't give me much ether, since he was afraid the ether would kill me."

After he was healthy enough Kremer was moved to a POW camp. During the summer of 1944 he was taken to Sweden as part of an exchange of badly wounded prisoners. He arrived in New York that fall, about a year after he had been shot down, and was discharged from the USAAF in February 1945.

THE SECOND ATTACK on the Schweinfurt ball-bearing plants was effective; the bombers hit the target with remarkable precision. Germany's minister of armaments, Albert Speer, estimated that 67 percent of the complex's production capacity was ruined. He was fearful of what follow-on raids would do to the Reich's ball-bearing manufacturing capacity even as work got under way to repair the damage and disperse the production nodes. One or two more raids might totally destroy the Schweinfurt plants.

He needn't have been so anxious. The Eighth Air Force was so badly mauled that it didn't return to Schweinfurt until the following February. Of the attacking force of 291 B-17s, sixty were shot down. An additional seven were so badly damaged that they were scrapped after recovering to England. Of the remaining bombers, more than half were damaged and needed repair. In contrast, the Luftwaffe lost approximately forty fighters.

The truth was that the Eighth did not have the capacity to mount a sizeable raid until nearly a week after Schweinfurt when 282 bombers were sent to Düren on October 20. In practical terms, the one-in-five loss rate at Schweinfurt was terrifying not just to the crews, but also to the USAAF's leadership. The mission finally and irrevocably drove home the fact that the heavy bombers could not defend themselves against the Luftwaffe. Even the most ardent bomber advocates gave up the notion of the self-defending bomber.

Eaker cabled Arnold the following day: "This does not represent disaster; it does indicate that the air battle has reached its climax." He then outlined a list of what he needed to successfully prosecute the air campaign against Germany. Aside from replacement aircraft and crews he wrote: "Send every possible fighter here as soon as possible. Especially emphasize earliest arrival of additional P-38s and Mustangs."[7] Both types had better range than the P-47s the Eighth was then operating.

Indeed, following the second attack on Schweinfurt, except for a few unique exceptions, the Eighth never again sent the bombers without fighter escorts. Therein was the rub. At that point in the war the most important targets were beyond the ranges of the fighter aircraft that were available. Essentially, for the next few months, the Eighth Air Force was a strategic air force that was incapable—without sustaining prohibitive losses—of hitting strategic targets. In short, it could not do what it was intended to do.

It was a problem that the USAAF's leadership had seen coming for some time. In fact, on June 22, 1943, Henry Arnold had told his deputy, Barney Giles, "You have got to get a fighter to protect our bombers. Whether you use an existing type or have to start from scratch is your problem."[8] Accordingly, a number of options were reviewed to extend the ranges of the service's three leading fighters, the Republic

P-47 Thunderbolt, the Lockheed P-38 Lightning and the North American P-51 Mustang.

The P-47 was the Eighth's primary fighter during 1943 and well into 1944. The largest single-engine fighter fielded by any combatant during the war, it was built like a cinder block—big, strong and ugly. Notwithstanding its size and appearance, the P-47 was an excellent performer. No other fighter was as maneuverable at the high altitudes where it escorted the Eighth's bombers. It was also fast, and nothing could escape it in a dive. At lower altitudes it was marginally outperformed in some respects by the Luftwaffe's Me-109 and FW-190, but not so much that it was not competitive. Moreover, its eight .50-caliber machine guns packed a terrific punch and it could absorb seemingly impossible levels of damage. But it suffered from short legs. When P-47 groups began operations during the spring of 1943, they were able to escort the bombers only a short distance over the continent.

The twin-engine P-38 had already proven effective in the Pacific, North Africa and the Mediterranean. It had good range, heavy armament and was fast. Although early models suffered from compressibility in high-speed dives, when flown well it could hold its own against its German counterparts. On the other hand, for a variety of reasons, it proved to be mechanically unreliable when operated in the cold and wet conditions typical of Northern Europe. Too, it wasn't nearly as numerous as the P-47 and didn't become operational with the Eighth until the day following the second mission to Schweinfurt.

The P-51 started life as a bastard child of a foreign parent. When the British were shopping for someone to license-produce P-40s for them during 1940, North American offered the P-51 design instead. Designed and built in record time, it was first fielded by the RAF in 1942 and, after some reluctance, by the USAAF a short time later. It proved itself as a superb low-level fighter with exceptional range, but its performance dropped off at high altitude. This problem was solved when its Allison engine was replaced with the excellent Rolls-Royce Merlin. It subsequently began long-range bomber escort missions in

December 1943 and eventually became the dominant fighter in the European Theater of Operations.

Giles and his staff responded to Arnold's orders with remarkable energy and speed. Close cooperation with the different aircraft manufacturers compelled them to increase the internal fuel capacities of all three fighters. Likewise, work at home—and collaboration with the British in England—yielded externally carried, droppable fuel tanks in a variety of sizes that further increased the ranges of the fighters. Finally, tactics and procedures were developed and refined that likewise gave the fighters longer legs. Chief among these was the relay system. This concept allowed relays of fighter groups to fly profiles that conserved fuel while penetrating deeper into Germany than ever before. Additionally, separate, detached fighter sweeps not in direct support of any particular bomb group allowed the fighters to reach even farther.

The eventual result of all these efforts was a fighter escort force capable of taking the bombers anywhere they needed to go. Certainly there were lapses in protection for any number of reasons. But those failures were never again because the fighters were incapable of going where the bombers went.

The improvements became apparent to the 303rd's men beginning at the start of 1944 as the Eighth started to fly into Germany again. Indeed, the mission to Kiel on January 5 offered a fine example as noted by Edward Carter, the engineer aboard the 359th's *Baltimore Bounce*: "Two JU-88s dove down on us and then two P-51s dove on them. In a few seconds, all that was left in the air were the two P-51s and just scattered bits of the two JU-88s."[9] John Manning, the pilot of the group's lead ship, observed that enemy fighters were not a factor: "We hit flak all over the area, but fortunately didn't see many fighters. I really expected to see a lot of them because it was a beautiful, clear day and we were the last ones over the target. However, I only saw about a dozen and they didn't bother us much."[10]

On another mission Mel Schulstad was gratified to see the 303rd provide some protection to one of its fighter friends. "I got a kick out of a

P-38 [pilot] who had an engine knocked out at the target. He immediately flew up under a cluster of Forts and stayed there all the way back. Those boys have been giving us good protection. I felt pretty good about being able to reciprocate the favor."[11]

Later, during early 1944, the Eighth's fighter pilots were allowed to range farther away from the bombers and—as they returned to England—to pursue the Luftwaffe wherever they found it. This included great aerial chases as well as impromptu attacks on German airfields. Indeed, the fighter pilots were encouraged to shoot up whatever military targets they found, or anything that might be useful to Germany's war effort. Accordingly, locomotives became a favorite target. It all added up.

THE B-17, WITH its four engines, its defensive armament, its highly trained crew and the maintenance and logistics train that supported it, was still nothing more than a bomb delivery machine. It existed for no other reason other than to put bombs on the enemy and the things with which he made war. But without an accurate means of putting the bombs where they needed to be, the big ships were still incapable of executing the USAAF's vision of precision daytime bombing.

The Norden bombsight was that means. It was the product of an evolutionary development, largely driven by the Navy, which traced its roots back to at least the 1920s. Not just a simple sighting device, it was a fifty-pound analog computer made up of more than two thousand components, including gears, motors, gyroscopes, levers and optics; it was among the most complex and sophisticated machines of the day. The Norden compensated for a number of variables, all of which could cause bombs to drop significantly far from the target. These variables included the aircraft's altitude, airspeed and aberrant motion, as well as the type of bomb being dropped and wind speed and direction. In testing, the Norden demonstrated the ability to put half of its bombs—from relatively high altitude—into a circle with a diameter of one hundred feet.

And beginning in March 1943 the Norden was demonstrating excellent results in combat when it was connected with the aircraft's flight controls through the AFCE, or automatic flight control equipment. This coupling allowed the bombardier to "fly" the aircraft from his position in the nose. Once coupled, and upon reaching an exactly determined point, the system dropped the bombs automatically.

Nevertheless, it was a complex system that demanded not only precise care and maintenance, but a bombardier who had the intelligence and training to operate it effectively. Bombardiers were carefully screened, and their training ran up to four months. The B-17 pilot training manual made the bombardier's importance very clear to the pilot:

Accurate and effective bombing is the ultimate purpose of your entire airplane and crew. Every other function is preparatory to hitting and destroying the target. That's your bombardier's job. The success or failure of the mission depends upon what he accomplishes in that short interval of the bombing run. When the bombardier takes over the airplane for the run on the target, he is in absolute command. He will tell you what he wants done, and until he tells you "Bombs away," his word is law. A great deal, therefore, depends on the understanding between bombardier and pilot.

Aside from successfully operating the Norden, the bombardier was required to fuse and arm the bombs, set the bomb release intervals and make certain that the bomb bay and the bomb racks were ready for operations. Additionally, he was responsible for readying the cameras that many ships carried to assess damage to the target. Before a mission, he typically received a special bombardier briefing that followed the standard briefing, and then requisitioned a Norden from the unit's "vault." At the aircraft, he installed the device and prepared it for the mission. Once airborne he worked with the pilot to ensure that the bombsight was "leveled" and that it was synchronized with the aircraft and the autopilot.

Achieving good results against the target demanded that the aircraft remain as steady and stable as possible during the bomb run. If it did not, the Norden could not generate a good solution and the bombs would miss the mark. This was emphasized by the pilot training manual: "Wavering and indecision at this moment are disastrous to the success of any mission, and during the crucial portion of the run, flak and fighter opposition must be ignored if bombs are to hit the target."

Just prior to starting the bomb run, the bombardier made final inputs to the Norden, and then, during the run itself, he made heading corrections via the autopilot to "kill the drift" caused by winds at altitude. Finally, he identified the specific target. Even though he would have studied target photographs beforehand, finding the target was often not an easy task, even when the weather was clear. And it was very difficult when the target was partially obscured by clouds, haze, smoke screens or by dust and smoke from the bombs of preceding formations.

Such was the case during the mission to Düren on October 20, 1943, less than a week after the Black Thursday mission to Schweinfurt. The 303rd was attacked by Me-109s and lost two aircraft en route to the target. As described by the group leader, Walter Shayler, they failed to avenge their loss as they closed on alternate targets in the Netherlands.

Without warning, the [Combat Wing] lead ship fired a red flare and announced over VHF, "Turning on IP." I took interval and instructed my bombardier to look for the target. We could not determine whether the target was going to be Weensdrecht or Gilze-Rijen. My bombardier picked up the airdrome at Gilze-Rijen and we started to make a bomb run on it. The lead Group fired a red flare and dropped a phosphorus bomb before the bomb release line, but I was unable to see any other bombs drop from the lead Group. My bombardier asked if he should drop his bombs and I instructed him not to, unless he was sure it was the target. We did not drop our bombs.[12]

The men carped about the failure during the debriefing. "Several crews complained about the lack of Combat Wing leadership and wanted to know why the bombs weren't dropped."[13] Aside from this very legitimate objection, they also griped about the "no good" orange chocolate bars they received as onboard rations and the "greasy" French toast and bacon they were served at breakfast.

Petty protests about food aside, the failure to drop bombs over the target was demoralizing—the 303rd existed for no reason other than to bomb the enemy. It was the motivation behind the turn of every wrench, the clack of every typewriter key and the expenditure of every drop of fuel and each round of ammunition. Men endured fighter attacks and antiaircraft fire, sometimes giving their limbs and their lives so that the bombardier could work his trade. He shouldered a mighty burden.

In actual combat, the accuracies achieved with the Norden bombsight were not remotely close to the results obtained during stateside testing under controlled conditions. Rather than a circular error probable, or CEP, of one hundred feet, typical results were closer to one thousand feet or more. This was attributable to a number of factors, including human error, poorly calibrated equipment, problems with identifying the proper target and maneuvering during the bomb run. Too, bombing altitudes during combat were typically greater than those flown during testing, and errors were consequently magnified.

Days when targets could be visually hit with the Norden were made rare by the regularly dismal weather over Northern Europe. Further, the Germans, not content to rely on the vagaries of the weather, added to the bomb aiming problem with man-made smoke. Indeed, they manufactured specialized smoke generators made up of two containers, one of which contained a mixture of chlorosulfonic acid and sulfur trioxide. The other held pressurized air. These were typically arranged at intervals of about seventy-five yards around the most valuable targets. Upon receiving notice of an inbound air raid, the Germans opened the container valves and the compressed air quickly transformed the chemical mixture into a dense, non-caustic smoke that, under no-wind conditions, remained suspended for up to four hours.[14]

The 303rd's men made frequent references to the smoke screens and to their effectiveness. James McCormick was the bombardier aboard the lead ship during the mission to Emden on December 11, 1943. "We got a good break on weather and were able to make a nice bomb run. I followed my bombs down and they went right into the dock area. There was a good smoke screen over the target, but it didn't bother us."[15] In fact, something bothered someone, because the 303rd's bombs landed in open fields. Whether or not this was due to the smoke screen can't be known, but it is certain that the smoke screens were effective on many occasions.

As the pace of operations gained momentum, it became apparent that there was no need for every aircraft to carry a Norden bombsight. The groups released their bombs while flying tight formations, and it was not only unnecessary, but also dangerous, for each aircraft's bombardier to execute his own bomb run; theoretically, they would all arrive at the exact same point in the sky when it came time to release their bombs. In practice, the bombardier in the lead aircraft of each squadron controlled the bomb run, and the rest of the bombardiers in the formation released their bombs when they saw his fall away.

It did not take long to recognize that the dearly bought skills of the bombardiers—who were officers—were not being used to their fullest. Consequently, a gradual transition was started during the spring of 1944 that ensured, at a minimum, that the lead and deputy lead aircraft of every squadron was manned with a trained bombardier equipped with a Norden bombsight. However, it became more and more common to crew aircraft farther back in the formation with "toggliers," rather than bombardiers. Toggliers were enlisted crewmen, usually gunners, who were taught to perform the same duties as the bombardiers, with the exception of bomb aiming. These men checked and armed the bombs and otherwise prepared them for release. Then, over the target, they "toggled" the bomb release switch as soon as they saw the lead aircraft's bombs fall away. Ultimately, it was an arrangement that worked fairly well and reduced the requirement to train bombardiers.

THE STATESIDE TRAINING of all the 303rd's crewmen was dangerous, exhausting and—at times—emotionally numbing. Bombardier Philip Peed recalled that a fellow student was killed one night in miserable weather when his pilot crashed into a hill in desolate West Texas:

> *The pilot's brother found the wreckage the next morning. They were twins and it was a real rough time for everyone. Our flight C.O. [commanding officer] asked if I would go to the mortuary and identify the bodies. I did and it wasn't a very good place to go for me. I accompanied the body [of his friend] back to his home and I had to go back in the baggage car . . . every stop of the train to West Warwick, Rhode Island. It was a closed casket funeral and I really had a time with "Joe's" mother to keep her from opening the casket.*

Peed recalled that after the rigor of the trip and the emotional delivery of his comrade's body, he was, "whipped out and down."[16]

"I VOWED THAT I WOULD NEVER TURN BACK"

MISSION ABORTS, OR "ABORTIONS," occurred on virtually every 303rd mission. And of course, the group was not unique in that regard. Aside from weather that occasionally forced the entire group to return to base, most aborts were motivated by mechanical issues. The B-17 was a big and complex machine made up of many components that had to work properly together. It was rare when an aircraft didn't have at least a few minor "gripes" or issues. These usually weren't of great importance and didn't keep the aircraft from flying. But if there were significant problems, the aircraft stayed on the ground until it was repaired.

More problematic were malfunctions that manifested themselves once an aircraft was airborne. The pilot was responsible for making the decision as to whether or not to continue the mission. That judgment could be easy and obvious or it might be very complex and nuanced. For example, the decision to abort after an engine fire was an easy one that typically raised no questions.

But other situations weren't so black-and-white. For instance, an engine with oil pressure that was just below limits but running fine would cause some angst. There was a good chance that the aircraft would complete the mission without incident. There was also a chance that the engine would fail. And if it failed, it was quite possible that one or more of the other engines—operating under increased strain to make up for the lost engine—might also fail. Added anxiety came with the fact that the pilot was responsible for not only his own well-being, but also that of his crew.

No doubt, the phase of the war also influenced the decision making. A failure of the top gun turret during early 1943 when German fighters were so prevalent would probably have compelled a pilot to turn around prior to crossing over enemy territory. However, that same failure during the latter part of the war when enemy fighters were less frequently encountered would not have been so compelling. Another consideration later in the war was that large areas of Europe were under Allied control and a pilot might be motivated to take greater risks, especially when he could land at a base in France or Belgium or in Soviet-controlled territory, rather than crossing the treacherous North Sea back to England with an ailing ship.

The point at which a malfunction was noted also influenced a pilot's decision to abort. It was much safer to turn back to base when a problem became apparent before crossing over hostile territory. Indeed, this was when most aborts occurred. However, once the enemy's defenses were breached, it was generally safer for a pilot to trust to fate and the protection of the formation. If it was impossible to stay with the rest of the group, the best option was generally to head for England within the protection of a cloud deck. David Michael noted that his pilot made an extremely risky decision during the mission to Augsburg on March 16, 1944: "We aborted 125 miles into France and returned by ourselves. Escorted by 4 P-47s. LUCKY!!" Michael also made an additional annotation lower on the page: "P-47s are the most beautiful thing in the world!"[1]

The particular target also played into the equation. It is certain that a small number of pilots discovered reasons to abort when the group was headed to a target with a particularly tough reputation. On the other hand it is quite likely that pilots pressed on to those same fear-some targets when they should have aborted, simply because they didn't want to be derided by their peers as shirkers or cowards.

However, the reputation of a target didn't always hold true. There were times when missions to the "big name" targets were cakewalks, and there were also instances when the most innocuous objectives were vicious. "Early on, we used to worry about what the target would be—we'd really sweat out the pre-mission briefings," recalled Eddie Deer-field. "But, after a while I took a more detached view. It didn't matter where the target was because there was nothing we could do about it; we had to go. And, it often didn't turn out as anticipated anyway. For instance, on my first mission to Berlin, our B-17 suffered very little damage. On the other hand, we were almost shot down on what should have been a 'milk run,' a short trip across the English Channel to attack German V-1 bomb sites at Watten, France."

There were other factors too. *Sack Time* went an incredible 110 missions without an abort before it was finally shot down. As that mission count reached very high numbers, it is quite likely that there were occasions when the pilot should have aborted but didn't; no one wanted to be known as "the guy who broke *Sack Time*'s streak." Too, pride and reputation played a role. There is no doubt that pilots who had experienced several legitimate mechanical aborts subsequently stuck with missions in bad aircraft because they didn't want to be characterized as weak or gutless. John St. Julian, a pilot with the 360th, described his experience:

We aborted on a raid to Mersburg because of a runaway propeller. Upon landing with our bomb load, the squadron brass were waiting for me. They took the plane up for a test flight as I returned to the barracks, fell into my bunk and went to sleep. That afternoon I was awakened by one of our officers who informed me that I should have reported to Group Headquarters on landing. He told me to blame the squadron for not having me read the SOP [Standard Operating Procedures]. I did that, and the C.O. [commanding officer] nearly

had a heart attack. I was grounded and instructed to read the Stan-
dard Operating Procedure to get my crew back. I vowed that I would
never turn back from a mission again unless an engine fell off.[2]

One pilot who did not have to weigh a sackful of borderline considerations was George Oxrider of the 358th Bomb Squadron. As the
303rd crossed over the English Channel on the mission to Wilhelmshaven on January 27, 1943—the first mission to Germany by the Eighth
Air Force—the gunners tested their weapons. The top turret guns
aboard Oxrider's ship, *Spook*, vibrated the life raft loose on the aircraft's left side. The raft crashed into the waist gunner, Wilmer Raesley,
and knocked his gun out of his hands. The gun subsequently fired a
number of rounds into the side and rear of the ship. Two of them holed
the right buttock of the tail gunner, James Sadler. Oxrider's decision to
abort the mission and return to Molesworth was an easy one.[3]

The 303rd's abort rate on the July 17, 1943, mission to Hanover bordered on absurd. Before takeoff, one aircraft's engines would not start.
Another aborted immediately after getting airborne, when an engine
ran out of control. Soon after, a ship turned back due to a broken oil
line. The next aircraft to turn back did so when the tail gunner showed
signs of anoxia. Nearly across the North Sea, another pilot left the formation when a gunner's heated suit failed. It wasn't long before a runaway engine forced another ship back. An additional five bombers
returned to base when they failed to find the main formation. Gunners
suffering from the aftereffects of vaccinations caused two more aircraft
to turn around, and another runaway engine forced a final ship back.
Ultimately, poor weather caused the entire mission to be recalled even
though it had already penetrated well into enemy-controlled territory.[4]

The issue of aborted missions was one that the commanders had to
handle carefully. Aborts reflected badly on them. Their leadership, in
part, was measured by tons of bombs dropped and other inflexible
metrics. Certainly, weak-spirited pilots had to be made right or sent
away, but caution also had to be exercised so that conscientious pilots

with bad luck weren't maligned. Most commanders reviewed the circumstances associated with each abort quite carefully. Indeed, aborting pilots were required to make formal statements and to complete official forms that reviewed the conditions that had caused the abort.

The issue also affected the ground crews. Aborts for imagined or pretended faults caused the maintenance men to work needless and frustrating hours. It was costly in terms of effort expended as well as aircraft parts and material—not to mention trust and respect. But in most cases the ground crews were genuinely concerned, and sometimes embarrassed, by real mechanical breakdowns. This was especially true when a fault could be traced to their work rather than to material failure.

Bert Hallum, a pilot with the 360th, described one of the rare episodes when a ground crew failed to do right: "We were taking off in breaking daylight, and I had just got airborne when one of my crewmen called, 'Lt. Hallum, we're leaking gas pretty bad from the left wing!' Fire was coming from the exhaust of the engines. I looked out and saw fuel all over the place. I cut the throttles and settled back to the runway. We went over to the end of the overrun. It didn't hurt the airplane, but we were in the boondocks. What had happened when they gassed that airplane was that they had not put the cap back on the tank."[5]

In truth, virtually no pilot wanted to abort a mission. Motivated by personal integrity, duty and comradeship, most were ready and willing to fly; it was why they were in the 303rd. And all that aside, logic told them that there was no way to finish their tours if they didn't fly their missions. Aborting was a double-edged sword that got them no closer to that goal.

The 303rd's mission reports note that aircraft sometimes aborted when heated flying suits malfunctioned. Indeed, frostbite was deadly and caused casualties that were only exceeded in number by those caused by flak and fighters. Crewmen whose heated suits malfunctioned were hard-pressed to keep their fingers and toes, much less perform their duties. The B-17 was unpressurized and, for the most part, unheated. As Mel Schulstad noted, "If it was thirty-five degrees below zero outside the airplane, it was thirty-five degrees below zero inside the airplane." Indeed, temperatures of sixty degrees below zero were encountered on some raids.

The men's bodies, exposed to super-cooled air, reacted by restricting blood flow to the extremities in order to preserve their core temperatures. Robbed of warm blood, tissue in the fingers and toes, face, and even the hands and feet, froze. Recovery was a long and painful process, and the damage to nerves was often permanent. If the freezing went too deep, the flesh was destroyed, gangrene set in and amputation was often the only option.

The special clothing the men were issued was intended to guard against frostbite and to keep them warm and comfortable to the maximum extent possible. Firstly, they had woolen long underwear that they wore next to their bodies. Over this they layered electrically heated jackets and trousers. Over the electrically heated garments they wore standard trousers and jackets or one-piece flying suits. Parachute harnesses and life preservers went over it all. On their feet they wore heavy flying boots over heated felt boots that were laced over one or more pairs of socks. Their hands were protected by silk or rayon gloves, and heavier, electrically heated gloves, and mittens. For added warmth, each aircraft carried several hand muffs. Soft, fur-lined flying helmets helped to keep their heads warm.

The various electrical garments were connected together, and a master cord was plugged into a receptacle at the crewman's position aboard the aircraft. A rheostat at the position was rotated to control the temperature. The electrical clothing was generally satisfactory but was far from perfect. It did warm the men, often to the point that they were soaked with sweat. But when the electrical current to the suits was interrupted, as it sometimes was either through failure or battle damage, the sweat froze and made the men miserably cold and especially vulnerable to frostbite. Too, the suits often heated unevenly and hot spots were created, especially when men sat down and the heating elements pressed against their bodies. And sometimes the suits simply caught fire.

Although there were standard configurations of cold weather clothing, updated articles were continually introduced, and the men often held on to older pieces. Further, the men frequently wore personal articles, and scarves and hoods were issued upon request. Because the boots were designed for warmth rather than walking, many men carried their regular shoes or boots with them in the event they were shot down. Additionally, they often wore less or more clothing than prescribed, depending on their individual preferences. The result—as often evidenced in photographs— was that virtually no two men dressed identically for combat.

Sadly, there were occasions when the suits were of little value against the brutal cold. One such instance took place during the mission to Bremen on November 26, 1943. German fighters blasted the nose out of the 358th's *Stardust*, killing the navigator. The bombardier, Charles Spencer, was also hit, and his oxygen mask and helmet were torn away. Unconscious, he sprawled faceup fully exposed to the icy blast that shrieked through the shattered nose.

The engineer, Grover Mullins, found Spencer a short time later, but the cold had already worked its damage. "His face was so swollen I could hardly see his nose," said Mullins.[6] Mullins dragged Spencer underneath the pilot's compartment and tried to administer oxygen to him, but Spencer's face was so misshapen that it was difficult. He left Spencer and climbed up to the pilot's compartment to attend the copilot, who was also unconscious. When Mullins returned to check on Spencer, he found that the bombardier had crawled back into the nose, released the ship's bombs and collapsed at his guns. It was a staggering feat of will and endurance.

Upon the *Stardust*'s return to England, the doctors found Spencer's face and hands destroyed by frostbite. "My facial features, nose and ears—new ones were made—were frozen," he later recalled.[7] "My hands were so frozen that the fingers had to be amputated. The tips of my toes were frozen. One eye had to be enucleated, the other was impaired." Spencer was sent home to his new wife and a hellish string of surgeries that numbered in the dozens. Later his palms were sliced in half so that he could use them as pincers.

"HE WAS LYING ON HIS BACK HOLDING HIS GUN"

CHANCE, FATE, DESTINY AND PROVIDENCE. It went by those names and others, but however it was characterized, it played an enormous role in what happened to the men. It was there when a flak burst missed one bomber but blew another into flaming pieces of bodies and wreckage. It was there when a cannon round struck an aircraft but failed to explode. It decided when—and where—a critical engine or aircraft component failed. It decided what motivated the leader of an enemy fighter unit to direct an attack against one formation of straggling bombers rather than another. It drove the physics—down to the sixth decimal point or beyond—that determined how an enemy fighter's machine gun round missed a crewman's head by less than an inch. Or didn't.

James Geiger, a pilot with the 360th Bomb Squadron, remembered an instance when a cannon round smashed into *Sack Time*'s windscreen immediately in front of his copilot's face. "I had just told my copilot to get my parachute and the only thing that saved him was that he was ducked down to get it, otherwise he would have been hit right in the face. . . . There must have been two bushels of glass fragments in our laps."[1]

Indeed, fate came into play in many situations and ways. Eddie Deerfield remembered one: "I was sitting in my Nissen hut when an orderly came in looking for me. There was a new crew going on a familiarization flight and they needed a radio operator. I held off on volunteering. Our crew might be called for a combat mission in the morning, and I felt enough was enough.

"There was another fellow in the hut who was a radio technician. We called him 'Tex.' He wasn't on a crew, but he was happy to go flying and volunteered to go in my place. The plane clipped a set of power lines, caught fire and crashed. Everyone was killed."

Sometimes, but not always, the crews overcame the cruelty of chance with teamwork, skill and the sort of comradely love for one another understood only by those who have served together in combat. One such instance occurred during the mission to Bremen on December 20, 1943. Bremen, on Germany's northern coast, was the site of a number of important targets, including a port, shipbuilding works, submarine pens, steel mills and aircraft factories. The city was heavily defended, but in seven previous missions the 303rd had lost only three aircraft.

The group's assembly and route across the North Sea were unremarkable, although two aircraft aborted early during the mission. A layer of clouds blanketed the sea during the first part of the mission, but it dissipated as the bombers neared Germany. However, dense and persistent contrails clouded visibility and the pilots worked hard to maintain position.

Real trouble found the 303rd as it approached the target at twenty-six thousand feet. Intense and accurate antiaircraft fire rocked the formation, and more than a hundred enemy fighters attacked from all directions. Donald Gamble was in the lead aircraft, *Sky Wolf*: "We were doing fine until we started the bomb run. The formation was perfect. As soon as we got over the target, they smashed hell out of us. That flak was pretty accurate and there was lots of it. Our escort tried to keep the fighters out, but they sneaked through the contrails where we couldn't see them."[2]

The 303rd's mission summary report noted that Ju-88s and Me-210s fired rockets from approximately a thousand feet astern. Additionally, other Me-210s dropped small, dynamite stick–sized bombs from approximately five hundred feet above the formation. These miniature "bombs" were observed to "explode at once." Although it was unnerving, no damage was reported from the air-to-air bombing. Rather the 303rd was savaged by more conventional fighter attacks with guns and rockets, and by antiaircraft fire.

The 427th Bomb Squadron was hit especially hard. The B-17 captained by Franklin Leve, perhaps damaged by flak or suffering from mechanical failure, struggled to hold its position on the right side of the formation. Ahead and to the left of Leve's bomber was John Barker's *Flying Bitch*. An Me-110 attacked it and then made a hard, right-hand turn and hit Leve's ship in the rear fuselage with two rockets. Leve's ball turret gunner, Edward Drees, shot off the Me-110's left wing and it spun earthward, out of control.

Leve's ship was subsequently attacked by another enemy fighter. Mortally damaged—with its two inboard engines afire—it went into a near vertical dive before leveling off and then gently descending into a cloud deck. No parachutes were observed. The aircraft crashed a few minutes later. All but two of its crew perished.

Alexander Alex's crew aboard *Santa Ana* was on its first mission. Positioned at the right front of the 427th's formation, *Santa Ana*, like Leve's B-17, was brought down by a combination of antiaircraft fire and fighter attacks. At the head of the 427th's formation was Edward Woddrop's *Spirit of Wanette*. A wingtip was blown off the ship, an engine was destroyed, and the chin and ball turrets were rendered inoperable. The tail gunner and waist gunners lost consciousness due to lack of oxygen. Moreover, the electric flying suit of the copilot, Grover Henderson, went up in flames and had to be doused with a fire extinguisher. Twice. Nevertheless, Woddrop—a former flying sergeant with the Royal Canadian Air Force—brought the ship safely back to Molesworth.

Jersey Bounce Jr. was part of the 358th Bomb Squadron, which was at the head of the 303rd's formation. It was piloted by John Henderson and Merle Hungerford. Henderson was relatively new to operations, having flown only four missions previously. Hungerford was an instructor pilot flying in the copilot position. Just prior to their reaching the target, an antiaircraft burst knocked out the left outboard engine and set it afire. The right outboard engine was likewise destroyed soon after the 303rd dropped its bombs.

The ship could not stay in formation with only two engines and was left behind. Henderson and Hungerford rolled the aircraft into a dive to the left, hoping to escape the attention of enemy fighter pilots. As much as Henderson and Hungerford hoped that diving away would save the ship, it did not. Isolated and with no friendly fighter escorts, *Jersey Bounce Jr.* was set upon by a mixed group of Me-109s and FW-190s. Cannon and machine gun fire ripped the flagging bomber, and George Buske, the tail gunner, called over the interphone that he was hit.

Forrest Vosler, the crew's radio operator, was also wounded.[3] Chunks of jagged metal penetrated through his several layers of clothing and punched into his chest, legs and feet. Blood ran down his legs and into his boots. Although badly wounded, Vosler stood up, charged his gun and fired it at the waves of enemy fighters that dived on *Jersey Bounce Jr.* Farther forward, in the upper turret, was the flight engineer, Bill Simpkins. Simpkins fired his guns in quick staccato bursts as he worked to fend off the dogged enemy pilots. A short time later Simpkins was called back to check on George Buske in the tail turret. The left waist gunner, Stanley Moody, climbed into the unmanned turret, shot up an Me-110 and then literally blasted an Me-109 pilot out of his aircraft. Moody, from Lewiston, Maine, hadn't even told his mother he was flying in combat.[4]

In the meantime, Simpkins found that the tail gunner's position was essentially destroyed. Buske was flayed open, bloody and near death. Great wounds exposed the inside of his chest while his intestines pressed through another equally gruesome gash in his abdomen. Simpkins dragged Buske out of the tail turret and to the waist gun positions, where there was more room to tend him. He put compress bandages over the gaping holes in Buske's body, defrosted a pair of morphine syrettes in his mouth, then stabbed them into his wounded comrade's body.

Henderson and Hungerford wracked the shot-up bomber through near-continuous evasive maneuvers. Vosler, from the radio compartment, fired his gun at the attacking fighters but was hit in the chest, face and eyes. Although he didn't know it, the inside of his right eye was dribbling down his face.

"As soon as I could I came down from the turret and looked back through the ship at Vosler," said Stanley Moody.[5] "He was lying on his back, holding his gun. In a few minutes I managed to get back for another look, and although he had been hit again, he had somehow pulled himself up on his table and was manning his gun to protect our defenseless tail."

Moody recalled that the fighter attacks lasted more than an hour. "By the time they had finished, part of the control cables had been shot away, the ship was flying at a very bad angle, there were very few instruments left intact and four of us had been hit. The pilot told us to move everything moveable up to the front of the ship to try to level it out." It wasn't long however until the pilots realized that *Jersey Bounce Jr.* had to be lightened if it was to stand any chance of getting back to England. "So everything that could be lifted was thrown out," said Moody.

Vosler turned to his damaged radio equipment and worked by feel to repair it. If *Jersey Bounce Jr.* made it past the enemy-held coastline, the crew stood a chance of rescue. Their odds would be better if Vosler could send SOS messages. In the meantime the German fighters inexplicably left the crippled bomber to its own fate. It is likely the enemy pilots believed it was incapable of returning to England. Or perhaps they were out of ammunition.

Stanley Moody entered the radio compartment to assist Vosler. "Every time Vosler wanted to turn himself around to change a tuning unit," said Moody, "I had to move his leg for him. I must have done it about fifty times. When he tried to turn by himself, the leg just stayed where it was. I waved my hand in front of his face but he didn't flinch, so I knew that he was blind."

By that point *Jersey Bounce Jr.* was so low that it drew small arms fire as well as attention from larger antiaircraft guns. Finally, badly holed and struggling, it reached the North Sea. It was then that a lone Me-109 made a single, ineffectual, nose-on firing pass and disappeared. The crewmen aboard the bomber who could still move continued to toss every nonessential item overboard.

"I called the pilot and told him that we were ready for ditching," said Moody. "Vosler, who had overheard part of the conversation, asked me if I had thrown everything out. I told him yes, all except the pilot and copilot." Vosler asked Moody if he remembered the conversation they had shared during which Vosler declared he wanted to be pushed out of the aircraft—with a parachute—if ever he was badly wounded. "Now he told me to do it," Moody said.

"I told him that we were over the North Sea and that there wasn't a hope of his being picked up in that condition. He said that he didn't care, but to throw him out with or without a chute. He said it would lighten the ship and make the gasoline last longer. He wasn't morose about it. He'd been thinking and he said he was blind, his leg was no good and he'd probably be dead by the time we got back to base anyway. We argued a long while but I wouldn't do it."

Vosler's radio set still did not operate properly. Moody helped him locate the correct frequency module, and Vosler put it in place. When the equipment still failed to work, he located and fixed a loose fitting by touch alone and then transmitted the SOS signal.

Air/Sea Rescue aircraft rendezvoused with *Jersey Bounce Jr.* as the bomber drew closer to England. There were two Spitfire Mk IXs, an Avro Anson and a Walrus. Henderson and Hungerford fired a red flare to declare their intentions to the pilots of the other aircraft and then put the B-17 into the water near a Norwegian coaster. The aircraft sliced into the cold water and almost immediately shuddered to a halt in a cascade of white-green spray.

Then, it started to sink. Bill Simpkins, with aid from the others, lifted the grievously wounded Buske out through the radio compartment hatch and settled him onto the right wing. Simpkins then turned his attention to the life rafts. Vosler moved to the hatch in the roof of his radio compartment and crawled out on his own. Once atop the fuselage he looked to the right where the sea was about to float Buske off the wing. He shouted a warning, but the rest of the crew was distracted with readying the bomber's two life rafts.

Unattended and incapacitated, Buske was in danger of being swept away and drowned. Vosler, badly wounded himself and mostly blind, scrambled to rescue his comrade. He grabbed the wire antenna that ran from the top of the vertical stabilizer to the fuselage near the radio compartment. At the same time, he jumped from the top of the fuselage and grabbed Buske just as the waves lifted him into the water. Shortly after, *Jersey Bounce Jr.* lifted its tail and slipped nose first under the water.

Vosler and Buske were pulled into one of the aircraft's two life rafts. The crew of the Norwegian boat subsequently brought the men aboard and shortly thereafter transferred them to a British patrol boat. The misery of the mission was extended when one of the boat's engines caught fire and the transit to Great Yarmouth was delayed. Vosler and Buske suffered in silence. It was nearly dark when the boat was finally berthed.

THE HORRIFIC SORTIE WAS OVER, but the ugliness of it was far from finished. George Buske, the injured tail gunner, was more dead than alive. No one who saw him held out any realistic hope that he could survive. His right lung and diaphragm were visible through an enormous sucking chest wound. Moreover, his liver was torn and bleeding. His intestines protruded through another wound in his lower abdomen. A third, massive gash on his left side exposed his ribs.[6]

He was nevertheless moved the short distance to Great Yarmouth Hospital, where—suffering from blood loss, exposure and shock—he received multiple transfusions and was rushed into surgery. A hurried examination showed that bullet fragments were lodged near his heart and that one of the machine gun rounds that had torn open his chest was embedded in his back. The British surgeons controlled the bleeding from his liver, reattached his diaphragm and closed the massive wound on his right side. The other two wounds were treated with sulfanilamide, packed with gauze and left open. Near death, Buske was evacuated to the U.S. Army's hospital at Botesdale.

The rest of the crew was kept overnight. All but Vosler were released the following day. Vosler was moved to a hospital at Northhampton before being sent to the States, where his injured eye was removed during a long hospitalization.

ALTHOUGH OPERATIONS AT THE END of 1943 continued to take a toll on the 303rd, the size of its operations—coincident with the growth of the Eighth Air Force—continued to increase. Presumably, so did the effects against the Germans. Aside from the size of operations, other changes were made during this period.

Perhaps foremost was the creation of a new counterpart to the Eighth Air Force on November 1, 1943. The Fifteenth Air Force, headquartered at newly seized Bari, near the heel of the Italian boot, was intended to augment the Eighth's operations against Germany. From bases in Italy—which enjoyed better weather than England—it was assumed the Fifteenth would be able to fly when the Eighth could not. Too, the Luftwaffe would be forced to disperse its forces in order to defend against USAAF attacks from two different directions. Moreover, the Fifteenth would be able to hit targets in the south and east of Europe that were beyond the reach of the England-based bombers.

Another big change made during early 1944 was the creation of a new command, the United States Strategic Air Forces, or USSTAF.

Headed by Carl Spaatz, who returned to England to command it, the USSTAF coordinated and commanded both the Eighth Air Force and the Fifteenth.

Possibly the most emotionally charged change was Arnold's removal of Ira Eaker from command of the Eighth Air Force. Done in part on Spaatz's recommendation—perhaps under pressure from Eisenhower—the decision was controversial. Eaker, who got along famously with his British counterparts, had led the formation of the Eighth from essentially nothing at the outset of 1942. Finally, as 1943 transitioned to 1944, it began to meet expectations. Aside from increased numbers of bombers, long-range fighter escorts were finally being introduced. These were the final ingredient needed for the Eighth to succeed over Germany.

So, just as the Eighth was poised to achieve greatness, Eaker was removed from its head.

He felt betrayed, especially as Arnold had earlier told him that he would be the first to hear—and directly from Arnold—"if there was anything detrimental to be said" about his performance.[7] Eaker straightaway cabled Arnold: "Believe war interest best served by my retention command Eighth Air Force: Otherwise experience this theater for nearly two years wasted. If I am to be allowed my personal preference having started with the Eighth and seen it organized for major task in this theater, it would be heart-breaking to leave just before climax."

Others—both British and American—championed Eaker's cause, but Arnold's decision stood. Instead, Eaker was given command of the Mediterranean Allied Air Forces, or MAAF. Technically, it was a promotion; the MAAF was actually the largest air command in the world in numbers of aircraft and personnel, but no one pretended that the Eighth and its bombing organization was not the big show. Even Churchill appreciated Eaker's frustration. "I can understand your disappointment, young man [Eaker was 48!], at having to leave the Eighth Air Force just when it's achieving its maximum effect on the war effort." Churchill also validated the arguments Eaker had made in favor of precision daylight bombing at Casablanca earlier in the year: "I no longer have any doubt that they will prove completely valid."[8]

Haywood Hansell played key roles in developing the USAAF's strategy against Germany. And he had served under Eaker as both a staff member and a combatant commander. Moreover, he had worked on Arnold's staff. There were few if any people more qualified to comment on Arnold's handling of Eaker. "Arnold was terribly impatient. He just did not understand air combat. His crews, led by Ira [Eaker], were doing a simply astonishing job. I marveled at their willingness to keep on fighting." Hansell offered that "Arnold just never understood what Eaker was up against," and that "I think that Arnold treated Ira very badly."[9]

Eaker's replacement was Major General James "Jimmy" Doolittle— the same celebrity whose aircraft Van White had wiped clean of mud before the war. He had led the daring raid against Tokyo on April 18, 1942, at the head of a flight of sixteen USAAF B-25 medium bombers. Since then he had commanded the Twelfth and Fifteenth Air Forces in North Africa, the Mediterranean and Italy. During that time he had worked closely with Eisenhower, who was impressed by his dynamism and abilities, and who wanted to continue the working relationship as the time for the invasion of Europe approached.

Eaker and Doolittle were friends. Of the change, Doolittle wrote, "I was pleased that I had finally sold myself to Ike [Eisenhower], but was sensitive about Ira's feelings. He had done a magnificent job of getting the 8th started, and I didn't want anyone to forget that. I hoped I could do as well."[10]

These organizational changes meant little to the 303rd's men. To their minds the missions would be no less dangerous simply because there was a new air force being formed in Italy, or because the commander of the Eighth had changed. Accordingly, they carried on as they always had.

"THIS IS THE TIME WHEN I GET SCARED"

THE 303RD HELL'S ANGELS are sometimes mistakenly associated with the motorcycle gang of the same name. There is no connection. The 303rd antedated the gang by a number of years, and there is no record of former 303rd servicemen being members. Moreover, the Howard Hughes film of the same name reached theaters in 1930 and is what really brought the name into public awareness. Too, the 303rd was hardly the first military unit to use the moniker. Indeed, one of the squadrons making up the famous Flying Tigers was named Hell's Angels during 1941.

The actual numeric designations of USAAF units in England were classified. For that reason—and for purposes of morale and informal recognition—many units adopted nicknames. The 303rd considered the matter seriously beginning in late 1943 and settled the matter on January 7, 1944, with a vote by the squadron commanding officers and select group staff. The name they chose was Hell's Angels. Aside from its dramatic and warlike connotations, the moniker also honored the group's B-17F of the same name that had been the first Eighth Air Force bomber to complete twenty-five missions. Its reputation as a steady and stalwart performer was one the 303rd's men sought to emulate.

Regardless of what was or was not emulated, the newly renamed Hell's Angels of the 303rd continued to bend their necks to the harness that was the air war. Killing, or at least neutralizing, the Luftwaffe was a prerequisite for the invasion of Europe. Doing so required the Eighth to hit all manner of targets, not least of which were Germany's aircraft production plants. Accordingly, plans were drawn up to hit manufacturing facilities at Oschersleben, Halberstadt and Brunswick on the morning of January 11, 1944. It was to be a deep penetration; Oschersleben, the farthest of the three targets, was only a hundred miles southwest of Berlin. That fact notwithstanding, the bombers were scheduled to have fighter escorts, to include the new P-51 Mustang, along the entire route.

Brigadier General Robert Travis, the commander of the 41st Combat Bombardment Wing, was at Molesworth the night before the mission. Along with many of the men he watched a movie and recalled the cold and the stink of the place: "The theater consisted of a Nissen hut with a concrete floor, and was unheated and poorly ventilated; the only heat coming from the bodies of the military personnel present, which also exuded a distinct masculine odor."[1] The night's showing was interrupted many times by shouted announcements for the men of various units to report to their posts. It was obvious that there was a mission scheduled for the following day. Travis didn't wait for the movie to end but instead gathered his staff and returned with dimmed headlights on blacked out roads to Brampton Grange, where the 41st was located. Aside from the 303rd, the other bomb groups making up the 41st included the 379th and the 384th.

The initial battle orders made it clear that the mission was a deep penetration. Travis suspected that it might be Berlin and called the 1st Bomb Division, his higher headquarters, to politick. He wanted to fly the lead aircraft at the head of the division for what promised to be a historic mission. He was given reassurances but no promises; he had to wait until the detailed field orders were transmitted. Travis hung up the phone, stepped outside and looked at the cold but clearing sky. "Far off to the east could be seen occasional flashes, where the British were practicing night bombing or a Jerry was putting on a nuisance raid. Search lights came on for short periods, fingered the sky, and disappeared into oblivion."

The field orders came chattering across the Teletype a short time later. Travis hurried inside and reviewed them: "It was to be the Fock-Wulfe [sic] plant at Oschersleben, just south of Berlin, which so far had been untouched by our bombers. To reach this objective meant breaking through the concentric rings of fighter interceptors which the Hun had placed about Berlin and her important industries." Oschersleben wasn't Berlin, but Travis knew it would be a rough mission nonetheless. And he was assigned to lead it. He left his staff to finish their work and walked to his quarters filled with a mixed sense of anxiety and excitement.

At Molesworth, men scrambled to get the machine that was their bomb group ready for the coming mission. Van White, the operations clerk with the 358th Bomb Squadron, recalled his duties: "We matched crews to aircraft and assigned substitutes as required. We called the bomb loaders to let them know how many bombs of which type were required, and we also let the mess hall know what time breakfast had to be ready." Required fuel loads were also passed. Veteran crews knew how long—and dangerous—the next day's mission might be by how long the fuel trucks took to service each aircraft.

"We also assigned men to wake-up duty and we put together the flimsies for the crews," said White. These "flimsies" took their name from the thin, onionskin paper on which they were printed. On them were printed the mission particulars such as aircraft assignments, engine start, taxi and takeoff times, formation positions and radio particulars. Additional details included the assigned routes and altitudes, the group's position within the overall formation, various rendezvous points and basic target information. A flimsy was essentially a mission briefing on a slip of paper.

While support personnel hurried through the cold and dark at Eighth Air Force bases across southeastern England, Travis laid out his flying gear; he wanted to ready himself quickly when his wake-up call came. On his table were an escape kit, cigarettes, identification tags, a silk scarf, emergency rations and other sundry items. On the floor he put his heavy flying clothes, to include a flak helmet, a protective vest and a heated flying suit, among other articles. "Alongside of this flying equipment was a special target folder in which my Intelligence Officer had placed a route to and from the target with check points and fighter rendezvous points marked thereon. Also was included aerial maps of the area and large scale identification photographs of the actual target."

Finally, Travis reminded his aide to wake him at 0330 and put himself to bed.

This is the time when I get scared, not on the mission. Lying there in my bed and attempting to relax, my imagination runs wild. Being aware of the opposition and the problems of such a mission, I start thinking of all the things which can go wrong. I remembered that I volunteered for the damn mission and that it was not necessary for me to go at all as I had already done more than my share. I remembered my duty to my wife and children and how little money they will get in case I am killed. I wonder whether my sense of duty has caused me to go, and not just the desire for excitement and adventure. The net result is that I never sleep soundly but toss from one side to another in the bed until I hear the approaching feet of the Charge of Quarters to tell me it is time to arise.

After too little sleep, Travis climbed out of his bed. At the same time, a short distance away at Molesworth, Van White and his comrades made their rounds. They went into clammy, dark Nissen huts and shoddy barracks where the men made murmuring sleeping noises, or rocked the early morning with great, rumbling snores. The air stank of flatulence and sweat, and of bed linens and clothing long overdue for laundering. The waker-uppers swept their flashlights across foot-lockers and compared the names against those on their rosters. Then, with gentle hands, they woke the crews. Some rose with a start; others required more persistent attention. Few were cheerful.

More than four hundred crewmen were roused. It was common for the clerks to feel a sense of fretfulness about the duty. "There was a chance that the men I touched in the morning were going to be dead by the end of the day," said White. "They might never come back to that bed again."

On the day of the Oschersleben mission White experienced an "it's a small world" episode of the sort that happens only once or twice in a lifetime. "I woke an officer for the mission. His name was J. B. Lewis Halliburton and he was a navigator for Aubrey Emerson's *Sky Wolf.* As he got up, I noticed a portrait of a woman on his locker; it was Mary Catherine O'Rourke. I knew her when we were based at Gowen Field in Boise. She was very much interested in Adagio dancing, and we had exchanged a few letters since that time.

"I told Halliburton that I thought I knew that girl. He said, 'Oh no, you wouldn't know her. She's from Boise.' I told him that yes, of course she was from Boise, and that her address was 1107 Pueblo Street. He looked at me kind of confused and I showed him the photo of her I had in my wallet. It was a smaller version of the same portrait he had on his locker. He said, 'Well, that's my wife!'"

White and Halliburton exchanged notes before White departed to finish the rest of his wake-up roster. "Halliburton was shot down that same day," White said, "and he was made a POW. After the war it all worked out for Mary Catherine and him."

Travis saw to his morning ablutions. Freshly scrubbed, his spirits lifted and his excitement grew during the short drive to Molesworth. At thirty-nine, Travis was ancient compared to many of the young men who were also readying for the mission. A West Point graduate, he had been commissioned into the infantry in 1928 but went almost immediately to flight school. His prewar service included more than a dozen different assignments of increasing responsibility. He had arrived in England the previous August to take command of the 41st Combat Bombardment Wing.

The son of an Army general, Travis was a tough, competitive man. Although he could relax in social settings, he demanded strict military professionalism on the job. One account noted how he crept about the flight line with a measuring tape to discipline anyone who broke regulations by smoking within fifty feet of an aircraft. He was a perfectionist with a strong personality that affected people differently; he was variously loved, loathed, respected and feared.

Travis ate in the 303rd's mess hall, where real eggs were served; it was traditional to do so on the day of a mission. He normally ate carefully as he believed he tended toward obesity, but on this morning he ate with gusto. In the event he was shot down and survived, it might be his last good meal for a while. Some of the men shared his attitude, while others—anxious and fearful—had no appetite and barely looked at their meals.

From the mess hall the men made their way to the 303rd's briefing building. It was still dark but the Eighth's meteorologists predicted clear skies over Germany—perfect for the precise visual bombing required for the day's effort. Inside the briefing hall, behind the speaking platform at the front of the room, a map was covered by a curtain. Clots of men were scattered around the big room. They talked nervously. Many of them smoked. "One young pilot saw me enter the room," Travis wrote, "and realizing that I only went on visual missions of great importance that involved deep penetration said, 'We have had it. The Old Man is going.' Everyone took their seats with a sense of expectancy. The room was bitterly cold and damp. In the far corner one Sibly stove struggled valiantly against the winter climate of England. Many of the crews were suffering from colds as was apparent from their almost constant coughing."

The briefing started. It was a scene that was being repeated at virtually all of the Eighth's heavy bomber bases. Thousands of anxious, cold and sleepy men watched as maps were uncovered and targets were revealed.

Of the three targets—Oschersleben, Brunswick and Halberstadt—the 303rd was being sent against Oschersleben. Specifically, the 303rd and the rest of the 1st Bomb Division was assigned to attack the AGO Flugzeug-werke at Oschersleben. The factory had been producing aircraft since before World War I and by early 1944 manufactured a significant number of the Luftwaffe's FW-190 fighters. The 303rd's crews would be facing those same fighters later that day.

Following the main briefing, most of the men were released while the various squadron leaders and other key personnel received ad-ditional instructions. From that point, the crews had about an hour to take care of last-minute personal preparations, catch a ride to their assigned aircraft, organize the equipment at their positions and be ready when the signal to start engines was given. Travis rode in his staff car to where his assigned aircraft, *The 8-Ball Mk II*, was waiting. He sat in the warmth of the idling vehicle as the ship's crew readied it for the mission.

Darrell Gust was *The 8-Ball Mk II*'s navigator that morning; he hadn't flown in combat since the October 8, 1943, mission to Bremen, when he had completed his requisite twenty-five missions. As the group navigator—responsible for planning missions rather than flying them—he had been asked to fly the Oschersleben mission because of its impor-tance. "Station time was 07:00 and as I arrived at the aircraft, my nervous stomach started doing flip-flops because of the importance of the mission and the fact that it had been months since my last combat mission. I went behind *The Eight Ball* [*sic*] and tossed my cookies."[2]

Then, it was time. Travis stepped out of his car and introduced him-self to the rest of the crew. Although he was leading the entire 1st Bomb Division, he would be riding in the copilot position with William "Cal" Calhoun, the commanding officer of the 303rd's 359th Bomb Squadron. High-ranking leaders such as Travis left the nuts-and-bolts flying of the aircraft to more current and experienced unit pilots, while they were charged with the overall execution of the mission.

Travis climbed aboard the bomber. "As usual I found considerable difficulty in working my large body with all of its winter flying equipment and paraphernalia up through the emergency exit and into the copilot's seat. Calhoun, who is to be my pilot, followed me and seated himself on the left. We both spent several minutes arranging such things as binoculars, maps, parachutes, and so forth, at conveniently located spots about us in the cockpit. On my left front a white rocket shoots skyward and bursts in a shower of small stars, which is the signal to start engines. Immediately the entire airdrome throbs to life with the powerful deep-throated roar of 160 engines. Normal checks are made, wheel blocks removed, and the [ground] crews stand back in readiness for us to taxi."

The ground crews peered through the dark and gave their aircraft a final, cursory inspection. The pilots aboard each B-17 watched the movement of other aircraft against the briefed taxi plan then throttled up their own engines when it came time to join the line of slow-moving ships. The first two aircraft took their places next to each other—one on each side of the runway—and waited for the signal to take off. "At the green flare," Travis wrote, "Cal fed full power to our B-17 and we slowly gained momentum as we rushed into the dark. It always seems as though these ships will never leave the ground and the last few moments are anxious ones as we approach the end of the runway and see ahead of us a line of trees, which we never clear by more than a few feet. Slowly we climb in circles while each succeeding airplane cut short their turns and fill into proper positions until we have a group of eighteen ships flying a normal combat formation several thousand feet in the air." Below and behind the 303rd's first group of bombers, a second group of eighteen 303rd B-17s—plus spares—formed.

Jack Fawcett, *The 8-Ball Mk II*'s bombardier, sat at his station in the nose of the aircraft, in front of, and below, Travis and Calhoun. His recollection underscored the notion that the skies over southeast England came alive when the Eighth mounted a mission: "As we assembled over the field I wanted to steal a few winks, but in the dawn's grey brown I had to keep alert for wandering aircraft from other squadrons and other neighboring airfields. I could see the winking Aldis lamps and the pyrotechnic flares, their colors denoting the different groups. It was an early, busy sky."[3]

It took hours for the aircraft making up the mission to take off and assemble prior to pushing east across the North Sea and over Europe. Individual aircraft took off from their airfields and joined in squadron formations that came together in bomb group formations. Bomb groups assembled into combat wings and combat wings merged into bomb divisions. The time was 1001 when Travis led the 1st Bomb Division—with the 303rd at its head—across the English coast north of Felixstowe on course for a landfall over the Netherlands. Along the way, four of the 303rd's aircraft aborted for various reasons; their places were taken by spare bombers.

"Well out over the North Sea," Travis recalled, "I give the order to check our guns. Even though I expected the firing, I always jump when the twin 50-caliber machine guns of the top turret fire just above my head. The whole cockpit vibrates violently while they discharge. Dust floats down through the rays of the sun and the shadow of the twin barrels swings across the nose of the aircraft as the gunner tries out his turret."

German intelligence was likely aware of the raid as soon as most of the American crews. Radar and radio listening stations monitored the progress of the massive formation as it formed and flew toward Germany: "Beginning at 0828, German radio reconnaissance detected the assembling of a force of approximately 500 American bombers in the area south of Ipswich. The first bombers, accompanied by a large fighter escort, were reported at 1010: their position was given as 150 kilometers west of the Dutch coast, with course towards the east."[4]

Fighter and flak units were alerted. On that day, three German fighter divisions had a total of 239 fighters available to oppose the Americans. They were ideally situated at Deelen in Holland, Stade on the Elbe, and Döberitz just west of Berlin. Thusly located, they could keep up a steady stream of attacks on the bombers as they motored to and from their targets.

And they did. Jack Fawcett described the initial action: "We were hardly across the Zuider Zee, when I looked up to discover what seemed like hundreds of planes milling around. Friendly or enemy? A formation of enemy fighters pulled up at nine o'clock level, ten o'clock; then at eleven o'clock they peeled off and came at us in threes and fours—in rapid succession. This wave barely engulfed us before another was positioning itself for attack. Some squadrons had twelve planes, others had thirty."

Travis, at the very front of the formation, felt especially vulnerable as the German fighters made their attacks. "From this time on action became so violent and combat so exciting that it is difficult to tell a cohesive story. The enemy aircraft continued to climb and pull ahead of us until there were two columns of pursuit ships of approximately twenty-five each, strung out just outside of machine gun range. Drawing ahead of us four or five miles the ends of the columns turned in 90 degrees across our course, peeled off in elements of five, which flew in abreast wing tip to wing tip head on to our formation; successive waves of fighters being so close that when our gunners fired at the first wave, the next two waves would get through unmolested. Every gun in the formation was firing continuously."

Jack Fawcett emphasized the ferocity of the fighting: "I don't know how long these attacks continued. The General [Travis] was calling them fast and furious until one gunner, not knowing who was calling fighters, said in exasperation, 'Yes, yes, but don't call them so fast; I can't shoot at 'em all anyway.'"

Bad Check was a 303rd B-17 that had been financed by San Quentin Prison inmates through war bond purchases. It was so named because a check written against insufficient funds—a bad check—"always comes back." John Kaliher was the ship's navigator. His official statements provide a spare but gruesome picture of what happened aboard the ship which was flying at the rear of the low group's formation. "Our plane was attack[ed] first by 3 waves of 4 single-engine German fighter planes. This first attack put out both our top and ball turrets; started a fire in #1 engine and dumped much of our ammunition out of holder[s] due to violent evasive action. We lost about 1,500 feet altitude and were immediately attack[ed] again both from the front and rear. A large shell or rocket from one of these rear attacks destroyed most of our oxygen containers; tore open the right side of the plane from the bomb bays to the nose escape hatch; also tore away most of the right wing root and part of #3 engine so that the propeller windmilled. We ended up flying in a banked circle with no flying speed and constantly losing altitude."[5]

George Callihan, *Bad Check*'s radio operator, was killed by the first wave of German fighters. Barnell Heaton, the left waist gunner, recounted in his official statement: "I personally saw Callihan hit by 20mm burst[s] in [the] shoulder, mid-section and legs. There were three or more of these bursts."[6]

The flight engineer, David Tempesta, manned the top turret and was injured during the initial attacks by shrapnel that knocked him down. Despite his wounds he climbed back into the turret and resumed firing at the enemy fighters. Kaliher reported, "A 20mm shell burst inside Tempesta's chest." He was killed instantly.

Bad Check was mortally hit, and Kaliher climbed back from his position in the nose of the aircraft, up onto the flight deck. George McClellan, the pilot, stood behind his seat and asked Kaliher to find his parachute. Kaliher quickly located it and helped him put it on. The crew's copilot, William Fisher, was on his first combat mission. He was still in his seat, and Kaliher retrieved his parachute and put it in his lap. At that point McClellan ordered Kaliher to bail out, which he did with Merlin Cornish, the bombardier. Ultimately, McClellan and Fisher, for reasons unknown, failed to jump from *Bad Check*. The Germans found their bodies—with Callihan's and Tempesta's—in the ship's wreckage later that morning.

Other 303rd crews suffered similar fates. Vern Moncur was the pilot of the *Wallaroo*. He recounted the savagery of the fight as Travis led the bombers to the target: "The first pass made at our group included thirty to thirty-five ME-109s and FW-190s. The low group, to our left, had three Forts go down from this first pass. We also saw three German fighters shot down by this group during this time. The No. 4 ship, lead ship of our element and on whose wing we were flying formation, had its No. 1 engine hit. It immediately burst into flames and dropped out of formation. A few minutes later, this plane exploded. Soon afterward, the No. 3 ship ahead of us also caught on fire in the No. 1 engine and peeled out of formation. This ship exploded, also."[7]

Fred Reichel was a radio operator with the 303rd when it was initially formed. He was detached from the unit during April 1942 for pilot training and by a quirk of fate was reassigned to the 303rd during November 1943. On January 11, 1944, he was the copilot aboard *S-for-Sugar*, which was hit hard by the attacking FW-190s. He bailed out with the rest of the crew and came down in a snow-covered clearing. Shortly thereafter he was captured by a German ski patrol made up of young boys and old men. The youngsters were equipped with machine guns, while the old men carried heavy sticks.

"The old men wanted to beat me," he said, "but the kids pushed them away. I was taken to a farmhouse where there were a grandmother, mother and three girls. One, about eight years old, asked me in perfect English, if I'd like some coffee. We had been briefed that Hitler had told the German people that U.S. airmen were gangsters recruited from American cities to bomb innocent women and children."[8]

Reichel was wary of being poisoned. "I asked her to drink first. She jabbered in German to her mother then she drank, telling me it was alright. So I thanked her and drank it. I then reached in my flight jacket and offered her some gum. Without batting an eye, she said, 'you chew first.' I took out a piece, it was Beechnut, and chewed it and then handed her the pack. She again conversed with her mother; handed it back saying, 'No thank you. Have you got any Wrigley's?' . . . Deep in the heart of Germany and she knew Wrigley's."

As aircraft were shot out of the sky, the 303rd's formation shrank and the remaining ships closed in tighter on Calhoun and Travis in *The*

8-Ball Mk II. Moncur moved up in *Wallaroo* until he was flying on the lead ship's left wing. The low group was so badly shot up and had so few aircraft remaining that it climbed and joined the high group.

While the Eighth's three bomb divisions pressed toward their targets, the weather over England deteriorated. This presented James Doolittle, the Eighth's new commander, with a nightmare dilemma: There was the very real possibility that a large mission such as the one airborne that day might hit its targets, return to its bases and be unable to land through heavy clouds, fog and rain or snow. Low on fuel, the crews would be faced with either bailing out or making desperate, last-ditch attempts to land. England and the surrounding seas would be littered with wrecked aircraft. Losses in such a scenario might exceed 50 percent; recovering from that sort of disaster could take months.

Wracked by indecision, and having been at his post for less than two weeks, Doolittle finally recalled the mission. Parts of the 2nd Bomb Division, and all of the 3rd, reversed course and motored back to England. The 1st Division, with the 303rd at its head, continued toward Oschersleben. Travis was within ten minutes of the initial point—the final turn toward the target—when his radio operator, Kenneth Fitzsimmons, informed him of the recall. It was unclear at the time whether or not the 1st Bomb Division had been specifically directed to abort the mission. Travis recalled his decision: "Though we had received no instructions, I was left with the decision as to whether to proceed on to the target or return to our bases with the main force. I fully realized that should I proceed I would become the sole target of all that remained of the Luftwaffe and their undivided attention would almost certainly wipe out what was left of my force. Visibility was excellent and it appeared that the target would be visual. I felt that our losses had been so great that success of the main mission must be accomplished. I informed the Combat Wing and my crew that we would continue and attack as briefed."

The crew aboard *The 8-Ball Mk II* missed the initial point to the south but corrected back on course. The pilots of the remaining aircraft moved closer together; a tighter formation would ensure a more focused and effective bomb pattern on the target. The Germans continued to press their attacks as Calhoun passed control of the aircraft to the bombardier, Jack Fawcett. The entire weight of the mission was now on Fawcett. Whether or not he appreciated the import of it just then cannot be known. But the reason that men were dying that very moment—the reason behind all the dead sons of so many mothers— was because the Eighth's leadership wanted bombs put into the AGO factory works. Were it not destroyed, everything would have been for naught. Fawcett remembered:

> Then we were off to the target. Surprising view . . . thirty miles away was the forest near which my factory target was located. The woods showed up clearly, but the little town was lost in a grey haze. So I put the sight on it and just waited. In fact I had time to set up my camera so I could possibly get some target pictures. As we approached, I had time to check my pre-set drift, etc. It was all good. Soon, I could discern the runway, the town, and then the target. I had plenty of time and good visibility, so my synchronization was good. Because of the time we had, everything was quite deliberate; I would have no excuse for missing. I had one eye on the indices, and one on the bomb rack indicator. The indices met; the lights disappeared. No, two lights remained, so I jumped my salvo lever to make sure all the bombs dropped. With the plane again in Cal's [Calhoun's] hands, I grabbed my camera and crawled under the bombsight, camera poised for my bomb-fall. Oh, boy, there they were, right in the middle of the assembly hangar I had aimed for. The nose glass was smeared. . . . But I watched the bomb pattern blossom, covering the target completely. . . . That FW [Focke-Wulf] shop would be closed—for a long time.

The 303rd and the rest of the 1st Bomb Division turned for England. Travis was excited about the results of the bombing: "I sent a WT [wireless transmission] Message to the Division reporting the target bombed visually with excellent results. A quick survey was made to determine the number of aircraft still with me, their condition, and the ability of the stragglers to keep up. Four ships could be seen with feathered props. Many were having difficulties in conserving what gasoline was left to get home. Despite my reluctance to remain over Germany any longer than necessary, I reduced power, slowed down the formation to keep it compact."

One of the reasons that friendly fighter cover was so thin during the retrograde was that several of the P-47 fighter groups had turned for home when the recall was sounded. It was likely that the pilots were not aware that the bombers needed help. A P-38 group simply never climbed out of the clouds, and its pilots also returned to base. The one fighter group that had the range to cover the bombers over the target was the P-51-equipped 354th—a Ninth Air Force unit on loan to the Eighth. It did not obey the recall, but its forty-nine aircraft were hardly enough for the job at hand. Nevertheless, Major James Howard, separated from the rest of the 354th, single-handedly provided protection to the 401st Bomb Group, and was credited with four aerial victories. After the mission he declared: "I seen my duty and I done it."[9]

Virtually all the bomb groups airborne over Europe during the return were under attack of some sort, either by German fighters or antiaircraft fire. Gerd Wiegand was flying an FW-190 with JG 26 as the bombers retrograded. "West of Nordhorn, nineteen B-17s sighted without escort!"[10] Contrails marked the path of the heavy aircraft.

The German fighter pilots took their time and maneuvered to set up simultaneous flanking attacks on the American bombers. Finally set, Wiegand and the other Luftwaffe pilots arced toward the B-17s. Wiegand held his fire until his target grew large in his gun sight, while the gunners aboard the bombers ripped the sky around him with thousands of rounds of .50-caliber machine gun fire. Still, he concentrated on his target: "Fire at 20 degrees deflection, 10 degrees elevation,

1½ sight radii—the B-17's left wing falls off and strikes the next B-17—I split S—Attack another B-17 from the rear—Shoot off the third B-17's elevator, am almost struck by it."

Although Wiegand missed being hit by the piece of the disintegrating bomber, his aircraft was nevertheless struck in the oil cooler by something—probably gunfire. He dived for the underlying clouds to assess his situation. Continuing down, he made out familiar landmarks through the murk; he opened his canopy and readied to bail out if necessary.

Finally, at less than a thousand feet, Wiegand's engine stopped. With the runway at Deelen in sight, he elected to stay with the powerless aircraft, dumped the landing gear and expertly hauled it through a low-altitude turn and set it down. When the aircraft finally coasted to a stop, he heard a beautifully melancholic tune playing over the airfield's loudspeaker system. It was, "Sing, Nightingale, Sing."

German fighters continued to harry the bombers all the way to the North Sea, where they were met by flights of P-47s that had not complied with the recall or were unaware of it. Vern Moncur recorded the action: "As we approached the German border, two more Forts in our group were lost—only two or three men got out of each ship. I also saw another Fort (ahead and to our left) do a very steep wingover, nearly going over on its back, and then go down in flames. About this time I saw a German fighter get hit by a flak burst and explode. This made us all chuckle! High above and ahead of us, a P-47 hit a German fighter, and the Jerry's plane exploded. And to our left, a P-47 knocked down a JU-88 at about the same time."

The leader of Germany's fighter forces, Adolf Galland, recounted the successes of his units: "In the sectors of Rheine-Osnabruck, Hildesheim and over the target areas there were heavy dogfights, in which we were very successful. On their way back the bombers were again attacked by our fighters on their second sortie. They attacked from south of Bremen up to the Dutch border, where the bombers met their fighter escort."[11]

Finally, with the appearance of the American escort fighters, the Germans left the bombers to face a new enemy. As Doolittle feared, the weather had worsened over England. Crews that had literally fought for their lives during the previous several hours had no choice but to grope their way down through thousands of feet of clouds and fog to find a place to land. And they had to do it before they ran out of fuel. And without colliding with one another or the ground.

Jack Fawcett, aboard *The 8-Ball Mk II*, described the scene at Molesworth: "Cal was flying at close to stall speed and only 300' off the ground. He spotted a runway, flew up one side, and turned sharply around for position to land. As we came in, we found a ship just ahead, and planes were appearing from every which way. But we settled on the runway behind three other ships. Good piloting and safe at last! As we rolled down the runway, we could see that landed ships were sitting everywhere on the field. Some wheel-deep in mud."

It had been the 303rd's grimmest mission to date. The group lost eleven of the forty bombers that crossed into Europe. It was a 27 percent loss rate. Moreover, there were many wounded and two dead on the ships that managed to get back to England. The 359th Bomb Squadron's commander, William Calhoun, pilot of *The 8-Ball Mk II*, said that although the mission had been the roughest he had ever experienced, the bombing results made the sacrifice worthwhile. Not all of his men agreed.

For a number of reasons the Eighth's headquarters was slow to release the details of the raid. Consequently, with no official statements on which to base their work, American news writers repeated German propaganda claims that declared that 123 Eighth Air Force bombers had been knocked down. The Eighth remained silent on the following day, January 12. Conversely, the Nazis shrilly recounted their successes and upped their claims to 135 American bombers shot down.

Speculation ran rampant and rumors flew that the Eighth's leadership was trying to cover up an unprecedented air disaster.[12] It wasn't until January 13 that details were released about the losses sustained on January 11: Of the 663 bombers that got airborne, 238 pressed into Germany to release their bombs despite the weather recall. Of those 238, 60 were shot down. Of the nearly 500 fighter escorts that took off in support of the mission, 5 failed to return. It was the most vicious beating the Americans had sustained since the second mission to Schweinfurt on October 14, 1943.

German aircraft losses were far smaller. The Distinguished Unit Citation awarded to the 1st Bomb Division credited it with 210 German aircraft destroyed that day. This number was grossly overblown, as German sources indicated that only 207 aircraft actually made contact with the Americans. Of that number only 39 were shot down.[13]

The calculus of determining whether the mission was worth the cost was complex. There was no question that the Focke-Wulf plant at Oschersleben was smashed; Jack Fawcett, the 303rd bombardier aboard *The 8-Ball Mk II*, had done good work. The 1st Bomb Division—with the 303rd in the lead—put 51 percent of their bombs within one thousand feet of the prescribed aim point.[14] Although it is impossible to determine the mission's exact impact on German fighter production, it certainly was significant.

Moreover, the elements of the 2nd Bomb Division that continued to their targets at Brunswick that day were equally successful. However, making the case that it was worth sixty bombers and their crews was a hard sell; it was essentially equivalent to sixty American hometowns losing their high school baseball teams. And likewise, each bomber cost as much as a small town. It was a loss rate that simply could not be sustained.

Ruby Side Thompson was a fifty-nine-year-old Englishwoman who lived in London during the war. An intelligent and thoughtful woman, she had kept a diary for decades. On January 14, 1944, she made an entry that referenced the Eighth's January 11 attack on Oschersleben:

This infernal war goes on and on. On Tuesday we were told that the American's [sic] had made a big daylight raid over Germany, but no facts were given, which was ominous, and portended a failure of

*some sort. This morning "corrected" figures were given out. We lost
sixty bombers out of a company of 700 sent out, and five fighters. . . .
General Arnold, Chief of the U.S.A.A.F. has stated that the huge air
battle over Germany inflicted one of the hardest blows yet struck
against the German Air Force, at a cost of approximately five percent
of the American aircraft making the attack. I can't see how sixty out
of seven-hundred is only five percent, but there you are, reporting.
Probably all the escorting fighters are counted in, and we are not told
how many of these were sent out. War, damnable war. It is intolera-
ble, and yet the fool world of men goes on with it.*[15]

Likewise, the attack received significant coverage in the States. The
Associated Press filed a story carried by newspapers on January 14—
the same day as Thompson's diary entry. The article in the *Joplin
Globe* was headed with the declaration: 3 ENEMY AIRCRAFT CENTERS
WRECKED. The piece definitely did not underplay the action: "American airmen shot down at least 152 German fighters at a record cost of
60 bombers and five fighters in history's greatest sky battle Tuesday,
and blasted two other targets besides shattering the three aircraft centers southeast [southwest] of Berlin, it was disclosed officially tonight."

It is interesting that, only three months since the October 14, 1943,
raid on Schweinfurt, the Associated Press declared the January 11
action to be "history's greatest sky battle." The AP's reporters in London were seasoned and understood the air war as well as most, but
Schweinfurt emerged as the more memorable mission.

The article also described the damage caused by the raid: "The
Flugzeugwerke AMG plant at Oschersleben, 90 miles southwest of
Berlin, believed to be the most important producer of Focke Wulf
190s, was well covered by a heavy concentration of high explosives
and incendiaries loosed by the Americans who tore through swarms of
rocket-firing German fighters."

Ultimately, however, it wasn't enough. The Eighth's bombers would
attack Oschersleben seven more times.

* * *

ROBERT LIVINGSTON WAS a waist gunner aboard *S-for-Sugar* on the mission to Oschersleben. He was made a POW after the ship was downed, but caught pneumonia and died two months later. His family had served in every conflict since the American Revolution; he was the first who did not return home. He—or rather, his family—was awarded the Citation of Honor, as were all USAAF men who died in the line of duty. The citations carried the same message, which read in part: "He lived to bear his country's arms. He died to save its honor. He was a soldier . . . and he knew a soldier's duty."

His parents would have rather had their son.

EVERY FLYER IN THE 303RD was a volunteer. In fact, every flyer in every branch of every American armed service was a volunteer. None of them had to go into combat. Nevertheless, virtually all of the men fulfilled their obligations. This was particularly remarkable during the early part of the bombing campaign against Germany, when the odds against completing twenty-five missions were so poor. Indeed, it is arguable that the greatest acts of bravery were performed by the flyers not while they were fighting miles-high battles against the Germans. That sort of bravery was almost instinctual—it was about self-preservation. But it took tremendous courage to consciously put oneself in such a situation to begin with. In effect, simply climbing aboard a bomber before a mission—knowing the grim odds against survival—was where the real bravery was exercised.

This was especially so because the men sometimes saw firsthand the horrible aftermath of air combat. Clifford Fontaine, a waist gunner with the 427th, described such an instance: "358th ship lost a tail gunner by a direct hit from flak. It blew the whole tail gunner's position right off the ship. After we landed the ship was in the hangar and you could see the T.G.'s [tail gunner James O. Williams] meat and blood and bone bits stuck to the sides of the Fort."[16] Indeed, the violence of the explosion blew one of the gunner's kneecaps forward into the radio compartment.

Hal Gunn, copilot to Ray Jess of the 358th, recalled a particularly gruesome incident from only his third mission. The crew's bombardier, Charles Box, was hit by fire from enemy fighters.

He was lying in a pool of blood. He was in a bad way. He had been hit in the left ear and it had exited out his right cheek. The wound on his cheek ballooned out and sprayed blood when he coughed. He was choking on his own blood. He was thrashing around, which made it impossible to apply any pressure to the wound. We had to quiet him down so that we could attend to him. I had heard that morphine was not good for head wounds, so I gave him a partial shot of morphine from the first-aid kit in the nose of the plane, just enough to quiet him down. It quieted him down, but he was still choking. We decided to get him up and hold him in a sitting position, leaning forward, on the navigator's table.[17]

Miraculously, Box lived. But there can be little doubt that Gunn recollected the bloody terror on every subsequent mission he flew until his ship was shot down the following month.

Van White's observations while serving as an operations clerk underscored the terrible anxiety that some of the men felt: "Before missions there were always a few guys who went behind their aircraft and upchucked; it didn't matter if they were officers or enlisted men. Or whether or not they were veterans. The risks of being killed on every mission were so terrible that throwing up was a natural reaction."

George Morrison, a tail gunner with the William DaShiell crew, told his story in a letter to the mother of a lost comrade. The crew flew their first combat sortie on Thanksgiving Day, 1943. They were shot up on that mission and on several subsequent missions. Morrison, who had been sick with an unspecified illness that caused him to miss several raids, wrote that he was knocked out of his position, but not badly injured, during the mission to Ludwigshafen on January 7, 1944.

However, he was still not medically cleared to fly on January 11, as his crewmates readied to fly the mission to Oschersleben. "It was a chilly, foggy morning, the ground covered with frost," he wrote. "I arose with the rest of the boys, had breakfast with them, went to the briefing, and before the takeoff I helped them dress. They were all lighthearted and in a good mood, doing the usual kidding and fooling around. I walked out to the ship with them, saw them go aboard and wished them Godspeed and a safe return.[18]

"After they left, then began my worst part of the trip, sweating out their return. I went back to the barracks, made up the beds, hung up their clothes, and tried to stay busy so that the time would pass more quickly. Came the time of the afternoon when they should return, so I hurried down to the end of the field so that I could spot them the instant they hove into view.

"Finally, I spotted one from my squadron [358th] and as soon as it had rolled to a stop I ran over to see what had happened. I asked the pilot of this ship where my ship was and he pointed in the direction from whence he came and said, 'Out there. They got every plane in our squadron but ours.'"

Morrison's guts wrenched. "That was the end of my world," he wrote. "The war to me was over. From then on I lost interest in planes and bombing. Our barracks housed twelve men, the noncommissioned members of two crews. Neither of those crews returned that day and I alone was left in the barracks that night—a night that was the longest and the loneliest of any I hope I ever must have. The next day I packed their belongings and saw to it that they were properly taken care of. Later that day I was moved to the hospital."

Morrison was evacuated to the States three months later. There, he spent time recovering in various hospitals and rest homes before returning to duty as an instructor at a gunnery school. As it developed, no one from the DaShiell crew was made a POW; they were all killed on the raid to Oschersleben.

SUPPORT PERSONNEL OBVIOUSLY did not face the same risks as the bomber crews. Consequently, many of them felt a certain amount of anxiety, if not guilt. Logically, they knew the jobs they were doing were crucial to the war effort even if they did not involve direct combat with the enemy. Still, many had an irrational sense that they were not contributing as much as they should. Conflicting with that sensibility was another. It was relief at not risking their lives mission after mission. Nearly all of them had friends among the combat crews who never returned. All of this created a certain self-conscious unease.

There were times when the fretfulness came to the surface. Van White remembered the Oschersleben mission: "One in four of the men who left that morning didn't come back, and I knew a lot of them. It was heartbreaking. I was upset and angry and sad and felt like I had to do something. I told my officer in charge, Glenn Shumake, that I was going to volunteer for flight duty. He was a pilot and we had worked together in operations since Gowen Field in 1942. He knew me pretty well and understood what I was feeling, but he also knew what it took to run a bomb squadron. He told me, 'You stay here, Rip [White's nickname]. We need you here and you're more valuable doing what you're doing than you would be as a gunner or something else.' I understood what he meant, and although part of me felt like I should have been flying missions anyway, I continued to work in operations."

White's reactions weren't unique. Other men on the base who did not go into combat felt the loss of their comrades very keenly. Lucius Arnold worked at the post exchange, or PX: "I was transferred to the 427th Squadron for [living] quarters. Four of us were put in one end of a combat barracks. We were told to stay away from the combat personnel because they and the ground personnel did not mix. That was false and we did become friendly. I was happy to do small favors for them in my work at the PX. I came back to the barracks one night from my job to find the entire combat personnel had gone down. It was a devastating experience and I did not get over it for some time."[19]

WEATHER SUCH AS THE 303RD encountered on its return from Oschersleben was a regular feature of the European air war. But aside from clouds and fog and rain—and sometimes sleet and snow—wind was also troublesome. Most dangerous were unexpectedly high winds against which the bombers flogged after hitting the target. Many fuel-starved aircraft of all types fell into the sea short of England.

The wind could be vexatious in other ways. During late January 1944 the Ken Edwards crew was newly assigned to the 303rd and sent for an area familiarization flight. Accompanying the new crew were Tommy Quinn and Joe Vieira. Quinn was an experienced pilot, while Vieira was one of the group's veteran radio operators. Coleman Sanders was the new crew's navigator. "We flew around the area so that they could show us the prominent landmarks," Sanders recorded.[20] "When it was time to return to base the group was returning from a mission and flying control needed us out of the way while the planes landed. We flew around, climbing through the overcast to about 5,000 feet."

With the aircraft in close proximity to Molesworth, Sanders relaxed. He assumed that his duties as navigator were complete and didn't know that a very strong wind was blowing from the northwest. "When it was time for us to let down through the clouds, Quinn asked me for a heading back to Molesworth, I looked down as soon as we broke out and saw London below. Joe Vieira, our radio operator, heard my report to the pilot and came on the intercom with, 'London doesn't have an Eiffel Tower!'

"At first I thought he was joking, but sure enough it was Paris, not London," Sanders said. The unarmed bomber attracted a pair of German fighters that raked it with machine gun fire before Quinn climbed the ship back into a cloud layer and escaped. The shaken crew returned to Molesworth without sustaining further damage but ultimately had to admit their folly; there was no good way to explain away the bullet holes in the aircraft.

"HE WAS MAD AS FIRE"

THE MAGIC MISSION count for heavy bomber crews in the Eighth Air Force until early 1944 was twenty-five. When a crew completed twenty-five missions, they were eligible—and usually allowed—to stop flying combat. However, Arnold was concerned that the combatant forces would be shedding experienced combat crews too early. He directed his numbered air force commanders to change their policies, and this was an order that Doolittle obeyed. He promulgated a policy that made the heavy bomber crews "eligible for relief from further combat duty" following the completion of thirty missions. This meant that they might be kept on duty to complete more than thirty missions. That number was raised to thirty-five missions in July 1944 and stayed at that point until the end of the war. The men were assured that they would not be compelled to involuntarily fly more than thirty-five missions without being individually evaluated as to their capacity to do so.[1] As it developed, no heavy bomber crews in the Eighth Air Force were required to fly more than thirty-five missions.

Don Stoulil, like many men who were assigned to the Eighth during the same time frame, was caught up in a cruel chase to complete the required number of missions. "When I got to the 303rd in November 1943 a combat tour was twenty-five missions—and a lot of guys weren't making it. And then as I got close to twenty-five the number was changed to thirty. And then a short time later it was raised again to thirty-five. I wondered if I'd ever get out of there. It sure felt like the odds were against me."[2]

It seems that there was confusion during the spring of 1944 as to what the required mission count actually was. This is indicated by the diary entry of Clifford Fontaine. On June 7, 1944, the day after D-Day, he wrote: "Today was number 30 for me but because of the invasion, I must keep on flying. SOME SHIT!"[3] If Fontaine was surprised by the requirement to continue flying, it was indeed "some shit"; in his line of work it took only an instant to be killed.

Officialdom recognized the value of the rotation policy. After extensive combat operations many men really did reach the ends of their tethers. "At Redistribution Stations routine examination of returnees sent back on rotation policy after completion of prescribed tours of operational missions indicates that such a policy is absolutely essential for maintenance of flying personnel in the theaters. This examination shows that sometimes as high as 30 per cent of returnees are suffering from operational fatigue, moderate or severe. The remaining 70 per cent are usually badly played out even if they are not demonstrating actual symptoms."[4]

MEN SOMETIMES FAILED to take care of themselves hygienically. It wasn't just that the showers were sometimes cold, or that the men were too exhausted to clean themselves. The fact was that, in some instances, they simply didn't care. "There was one guy in our hut who just would not take a shower," said John Ford. "He smelled like high heaven and his long handles [long underwear] were just black with filth. The stink of him just became absolutely unbearable.

"There were a bunch of us who came back to the hut one night after having had a few drinks. We decided right then and there that we'd clean him up. So, four of us dragged him to the shower and held him down while a couple of guys scrubbed him down. He was mad as fire and fought us the whole time. We got him cleaned up, but the next day he complained and was transferred out of our hut. Of course we were happy about that."

That happiness was short-lived. "We caught crabs from that guy when we showered him up," Ford said. "We were just covered. We tried to pick them off and get rid of them—we'd throw them on the stove and they'd pop like a firecracker. But it didn't work because there was just too many of them.

"Normally," remembered Ford, "the medical folks prescribed a blue ointment that was rubbed all over the body for several days. We didn't want to go through that. There was a guy who had been in the Army for about ten years, and he said that they used to get rid of crabs in the old days by rubbing themselves with gasoline."

Ford and his friend opted for the gasoline cure. "We went over to where the *Knockout Dropper* was parked nearby. There was a can with gasoline that the ground crew used to clean parts and tools and their hands and such. We rubbed ourselves down with gasoline from that can and it worked great. It sure killed the crabs."

But it didn't occur to Ford and his friend that the gasoline in the can was 100-octane aviation gasoline rather than standard motor gas of the type used by automobiles. "It burned our skin red and it felt like we were on fire. It was almost worse than the crabs. It hurt so bad that it was dreadfully painful just to have clothes on." Ford and his companion eventually recovered.

PROTECTING AIRCREWS WITH BODY ARMOR became an imperative even before the Eighth Air Force and the 303rd began combat operations in earnest. Aside from protecting the men for their own sakes—a goodly and Godly endeavor by any measure—such equipment offered tangible advantages to the men who planned for and managed the resources necessary to wage the war. For instance, men hospitalized or killed were obviously not available to fly missions. And where it was possible to cannibalize useful parts from aircraft too damaged to ever fly again, such actions were obviously not an option with trained crewmen. Consequently, anything that kept men in combat also eased recruiting and training stresses. This was especially critical as the USAAF struggled to meet its demand for replacement aircrews through much of the war.

It was recognized that many of the sorts of projectiles that injured the men—shell shrapnel and pieces of aircraft blown loose by fighter and antiaircraft fire—could be stopped by protective equipment that was reasonably wearable in the line of duty. Moreover, nearly 80 percent of all injuries were caused by these sorts of missiles. Although traditional steel helmets modified with earphone holes and metal earflaps were available early on, more specialized head protection and other equipment started to reach units at the end of 1942. Within a year the gear was readily available.

Flak suits were the primary protective article. These were essentially plates of overlapping manganese steel sewn into padded vest (M-1) and apron (M-3) combinations that were worn as a top layer. At nearly twenty-six pounds in total, they were heavy and consequently were not personal issue equipment, but remained with the aircraft at the individual crew stations. They were rigged so that, in extremis, the wearer had only to pull a single red strap for both pieces to separate and fall away.

Flak suits aside, aircraft were also fitted with special screens and pads that were effective in blocking or absorbing the same sorts of projectiles. Seats were also armored and were resistant to rifle-caliber machine gun rounds and similarly sized shell fragments, but were of little use against cannon fire.

The suits were bulky and heavy, and although the 303rd's airmen intellectually understood the imperative of wearing them, the discomfort of doing so often overrode the logic. So did the sense of invulnerability and the notion that "it'll happen to someone else" that was common among some of the men. Indeed, it took a particular incident to motivate Dick Johnson, a pilot with the 427th Bomb Squadron, to wear his: "Part of our protective gear was a skull cap of flak resistant plates that we wore under our fifty mission caps. It was a heavy and uncomfortable thing, and since I had never seen a hole in the top of a B-17 there were times that I would take it off and place it under the pilot's seat with my parachute."[5]

During one particular mission, the antiaircraft fire was heavy, but Johnson did not feel the need to wear the armored skullcap. And then a burst of flak punched a hole down into the left inboard engine, causing a drop in manifold pressure. Johnson scrabbled around under his seat, extracted his "flak beanie" and slapped it onto his head. "I wore the beanie on all my remaining missions."

William Malone, a navigator with the 427th Bomb Squadron, recalled when another crew also felt the imperative to don protection during the heat of battle rather than beforehand: "On [the] bomb run, some fool almost collided with us. Both the pilot and copilot were putting on their flak suits and missed us by only an inch or so."[6] Vern Moncur observed: "Those flak suits are a healthy thing to be wearing when the Jerries put up a barrage. They are heavy as heck, but they feel like feathers when the flak starts bursting around you."[7]

The protective gear saved many men from injury or death. But sometimes the protection was only just barely enough, as described by Edgar Miller, a pilot with the 360th Bomb Squadron during a mission to Leipzig. Miller wrestled mightily to bring his badly damaged ship, *Flak Hack*, home from Germany. "When we arrived back at Molesworth, I was shocked to find that my flying suit was bloody when I got out of the aircraft.[8] I had evidently been hit with a piece of oxygen bottle when it exploded, as it went through the bottom of my flak suit and hit me in my scrotum.

"When I got to the hospital," Miller recorded, "it was determined that I had just a superficial wound—just enough to make it bleed but hardly disabling. They wanted me to report the wound so that I could get the Purple Heart Medal but no way was I going to do so. What if someone asked me where I was wounded during the war?"

Aside from the obvious physical protection provided by the gear, a postwar study noted that it contributed significantly to morale: "The protection that newly-developed body armor, for example, gave to bomber crews of the Eighth Air Force in December 1942 yielded benefits that were mental as well as material and led to wholesale adoption of the new life-saving equipment. There was no hiding place in a B-17 and any gadget or garb that lessened a crewman's feeling of naked vulnerability to all missiles was bound to have a comforting effect."[9]

After enemy action and frostbite, lack of oxygen—or anoxia—caused the most casualties. At the rarefied altitudes the 303rd flew, an extra supply of oxygen was required to stay alive: "Anoxia overtakes one without warning," declared the group's Standard Operating Procedures, "and will result in anything from slight inefficiency to death. It is nearly always caused by carelessness on the part of the individual concerned. Remember, that an individual at 30,000 feet has useful consciousness for approximately 48 seconds if additional oxygen is not supplied." Confusion and stupefaction were common symptoms prior to losing consciousness. If an unconscious crewman did not get oxygen soon enough, the result could be permanent brain damage or death. Consequently, crew checks over the interphone were made every five minutes to ensure everyone was conscious and coherent.

A confused, stupefied or unconscious crewman was obviously of no use in air combat. Clifford Fontaine recorded his experience when he had trouble with his oxygen system: "We had a lot of trouble, the other waist gunner had an attack of appendicitis and my mask froze up and I passed out. The ball turret man came up and passed out. I passed out 8 times in the waist and once in the radio room. . . . Passed out so much that I didn't know where we were till we were on our way back. From just before the target til after we left it us three were passing out!!!"[10]

Operations at such high altitude were new, and equipment was still not fully developed and reliable. The A-8B oxygen mask with which the 303rd's airmen started operations forced oxygen into the crewman's face and was prone to ice blockages when the water vapor in the user's breath froze. It was replaced beginning in late 1943 by the improved and less balky A-14, which supplied oxygen only as the crewman breathed. With weep holes, the A-14 was less prone to ice blockages. The men could attach their masks to walk-around bottles in the event that the main oxygen system failed or if they needed to leave their positions. To the USAAF's credit, new equipment and better training reduced the cases of anoxia significantly during the last year of the war.

Aside from their physical well-being, the Eighth Air Force was also interested in the morale and spirit of its men. USO shows, furloughs, gyms, decent food, recreational facilities, rest homes and more were all part of the effort to keep them pleasantly distracted, rested and fit. However, there was little that was more important than mail from home: A postwar report on morale in the Army Air Forces noted the effects of letters from home on airmen, maintainers and administrative personnel alike:

> During leisure hours, when there was time to take off the blinders of routine and look away from a world circumscribed by pistons, flak, and third carbons [typewriter copies], the thoughts of thousands of airmen turned first and foremost toward home. Therein lay the importance of mail to morale. Letters (with the usual snapshots enclosed), personal parcels, and periodicals not only linked men overseas with the people and places they had left behind, but served also as tangible symbols of that idealized promised land of America for which airmen longed with an aching desire that at times bordered on the obsessive. Mail from home was not, however, an unmixed blessing. Letters bearing news of feminine faithlessness and other calamities like family illness and death hit the men who received them hard.[11]

Along with his flying duties, Dick Johnson was periodically assigned to censor mail. "The letters had to be written on one side of the paper so that offensive or obscene words or confidential matters discussed in the letter might be cut out with a razor blade. There were a few high spots in the duty, as some of the letters were very entertaining." One young enlisted man loved the ladies—apparently all of them. "The best was from a Lothario who wrote a very passionate love letter to a girl in the States," Johnson said. "I had nothing to censor, so I picked up his next letter which was almost identical to the first but addressed to another girl. And then a third which was identical to the other two but addressed to a third girl." Johnson briefly considered swapping the letters into different envelopes.

He also remembered another letter in which a disenchanted enlisted man complained about virtually everything. "In one letter the writer was complaining about everything that he could think of, including all the saluting that was required. He said, 'This place is just a bunch of bull shit.'" As required, Johnson dutifully wielded his razor and excised the world "shit."[12]

Some of the men felt compelled to make more of their service and duties than was actually the case. "Another enlisted man wrote that he was in a foreign combat area that was Top Secret and he couldn't reveal his location. I knew that this wasn't the case, so I took my censor's pencil and wrote the word, 'England' across the top of the first page."

The smallest details from home were dear to the men. James Geiger recalled being confused by one note: "Got a letter from Bill Crumpacker about Doc Powell quitting drinking. I had no idea what he was talking about until I got a copy of the *Valerian* [Valier, Montana] that said Doc Powell had died."[13]

"OUR FORCES ARE FIGHTING A HOPELESS BATTLE"

BY FEBRUARY OF 1944, Spaatz and Doolittle had more and better bombers available than ever before. Too, the USAAF's fighter escorts were more numerous, more effective and more aggressive. Still, although more and larger missions were being flown deeper into Germany, the overarching objective of POINTBLANK—the destruction of the Luftwaffe—had not been achieved.

The notion of a great surge to achieve that goal—a concentrated all-out effort—had existed in various forms since November 1943. It envisioned a maximum effort including coordinated strikes between not only the Eighth and Fifteenth Air Forces, but also RAF's Bomber Command. By design, the raids, codenamed ARGUMENT, were intended to cause massive damage to various German manufacturing centers.

But perhaps as important, or even more important, was the supposition that the Luftwaffe would be compelled to defend against the raids. Allied intelligence indicated that the German daytime fighter forces were increasingly stressed. Indeed, administrative and support flights were curtailed in favor of fighter operations. At the same time, seasoned veterans were ordered to stay on operations for longer durations. For instance experienced pilots, who normally would have been sent to training units to get a break from the stresses of combat as they passed their expertise to neophytes, were kept on combat duty. And many of them were killed. Consequently, the quality of the Luftwaffe's new pilots suffered while the ranks of their skilled men were inexorably thinned. Allied planners hoped that the German fighter arm, already under tremendous pressure, might be broken by ARGUMENT.

Accordingly, when it appeared that the weather would allow several consecutive days of operations, Spaatz ordered the effort to begin. The first missions in support of ARGUMENT were launched on February 20, 1944. The 303rd was in the thick of it and flew missions to Leipzig and Diepholz on February 20 and 21.

On February 22, the group put thirty-six bombers airborne early as part of the attack against the Junkers complex at Aschersleben. "This was the third mission in three days," recalled Vern Moncur, the pilot of the 359th's *Thunderbird*. "And we were plenty tired before we even started out." Tragedy struck early as the group assembled after take-off. *Hell's Angels II*, piloted by John Stuermer, collided with a B-17 from the 384th Bomb Group, which was based out of Grafton-Underwood, only ten miles west of Molesworth. *Hell's Angels II* was cut in half, and only the right waist gunner, David Miller, bailed out. Two crewmen from the 384th ship survived.

This accidental yet terrifying coming together of different bomb groups had a nickname. The crews called it "shuffling the deck." Despite prescriptive procedures intended to prevent them, these tragedies continued throughout the war. They were inevitable when so many bomb groups were based so closely together. In fact, the bomber bases at Glatton, Kimbolton, Polebrook, Grafton-Underwood and Chelveston were all located within a dozen miles of Molesworth. That there weren't more midair collisions between the groups is remarkable.

Aside from the loss of *Hell's Angels II*, mechanical issues forced three aircraft to abort. The rest of the group was engaged by German fighters beginning over the eastern Netherlands at Nijmegen. Accurate flak harried the formation as it crossed the Ruhr and continued to the target.

German fighters exploited gaps in the fighter escort coverage: "Since weather conditions were favorable and high-altitude visibility good, our [German] assembly maneuvers were carried out smoothly and without interference from the enemy. Although, on the whole, the American fighter escort was a strong one, during the time from 1350 until 1415 the bomber formations were flying without escort. Thus our fighter aircraft, approaching from the north, were able to make repeated attacks on the bombers and succeed in bringing down a goodly number, while keeping their own losses to a reasonable minimum."[1]

The 303rd bore a share of those "repeated attacks." William Werner was the tail gunner aboard the 427th's *Luscious Lady*. The aircraft was under constant fighter attack for much of the run to the target. For his performance that day he was awarded the Distinguished Service Cross, one of only four awarded to men from the 303rd. His citation read, in part:

Before reaching the target Sgt. Werner was seriously wounded by a 20mm. shell. He realized that with most attacks being made from the tail the ship would be doomed unless a steady stream of fire was maintained from the tail gun[s]. In spite of his painful wounds he stayed at his post and destroyed at least one enemy fighter. Although wounded again by anti-aircraft fire and becoming weaker from loss of blood, he heroically stayed at his guns until all fighter attacks ceased before letting crew mates give him first aid.

Orvis Silrum was the right waist gunner aboard the *Luscious Lady*. "He [Werner] was able to crawl back to my position. I noticed he was not wearing his oxygen mask. I assisted him with my own mask and relocated him forward into the radio compartment where T/Sgt. Wayne Magner gave him first aid. I remained at both waist positions while the other waist gunner, S/Sgt. Sam Ross took over the tail gunner position."[2]

As it developed, *Luscious Lady* made it back to Molesworth and Werner recovered. His recovery was due in some measure to the fact that his wounds froze and stopped him from bleeding to death.

The ship captained by Charles Crook was also hit hard. Much of the aircraft's fuel escaped through a hole in one of the wings. As Crook considered his options, it became apparent that the aircraft wouldn't make it back to England, or even to Sweden. Nevertheless, with no other good choices he turned west and descended. He did his best to keep the B-17 hidden in a deck of clouds, but the cover finally dissipated and he had no choice but to continue in clear skies. It wasn't long before the crippled bomber was spotted by an FW-190 pilot.

"He came from below and at the rear," recalled the engineer, Louis Breitenbach.[3] "The rear guns were out and he was too low for the other gunners to shoot at. He gave us a burst of machine gun fire and the shells ripped through the ship. Our pilot [Crook] was doing some beautiful flying, but we were defenseless and the German came in from the left and to the rear again."

Crook's B-17 was doomed, and two of the crewmen bailed out. He ordered the rest of the men to stop firing and ready themselves for a crash landing. "We were all crouched down and waiting for the first bounce," said Breitenbach. "It came and plenty hard. We bounced up into the air, came down again with a loud crash, and were sliding along the ground, taking fences and everything along with us. Things were flying all around inside the ship: ammunition, radio sets, flares, and boxes of all kinds."

Broken, twisted and holed, the aircraft finally stopped. "The front of the plane was in the water of a pond and the tail was bent and pointing into the air," Breitenbach said. "The pilot opened the window and crawled out of the plane. The bombardier had put on his parachute and was too nervous to get it off by himself. I helped him take it off as he was blocking the exit."

As Crook's crew struggled to clear the wreck that had been their aircraft, the FW-190 that knocked them down made a firing run. "There were still five of us in the plane and shells were hitting everywhere," said

Breitenbach. "A shell hit an ammunition box and they started to explode, adding to our discomfort. It was a miracle that no one was injured in any way. We finally managed to crawl out, the men in the radio compartment having to wade in knee-deep, ice-covered water to reach the embankment."

All of Crook's crew made contact with the Dutch underground, and all but two of them were repatriated back to the Allies. Breitenbach was not among them. He was captured by German soldiers several months later, during June.

While Crook's crew was fighting for its life, the 303rd pressed eastward. The flak abated over the target, and the group made the best of it. Kirk Mitchell led the 358th, which was at the head of the 41st Combat Bombardment Wing. He was very satisfied with the bombing results. "We weren't bothered over the target and made a good bomb run. I think that we really smashed the place today."[4] George Angelo, the tail gunner aboard the 358th's *Connecticut Yankee* made a similar observation: "The bombs were really in there this time. I only saw three hit outside the target. It was a beautiful sight."[5]

Notwithstanding the excellent bombing results, the 303rd's crews still had to fight their way home. Not all of them were successful. George Underwood captained *Satan's Workshop*. The aircraft was badly damaged by flak, and Underwood faltered at the French coast before making a play to get across the English Channel. It was an unfortunate decision. Unable to reach England, he ditched the aircraft in heavy seas. The ship hit hard and broke apart. The entire crew perished in the crash or drowned. Only three bodies were recovered.

AFTER FLYING THREE big missions in succession, the 303rd, along with the rest of the Eighth Air Force, was grounded by weather on February 23. However, the group was at it again the next day when it hit Schweinfurt, and then again on February 25, the last day of ARGUMENT, when it was sent against Stuttgart.

The conclusion of ARGUMENT marked a turning point in the USAAF's air war against the Luftwaffe. Whereas the American air campaign grew gradually stronger through 1943 and into 1944, ARGUMENT—or "Big Week," as it came to be known—proved that the USAAF could go wherever it wanted, whenever it wanted. And from that point, it did.

The operation achieved a number of milestones, including, on February 20, a mission exceeding a thousand bombers; the massive effort hit twelve different targets. Throughout the week, operations were coordinated with the smaller Fifteenth Air Force—which was already hard-pressed to provide tactical support to ground operations in Italy—and with the RAF's Bomber Command. The emphasis was against industrial targets, particularly various aircraft assembly and component manufacturing complexes.

Of particular note was the fact that the USAAF not only flew more sorties and dropped more bombs than the RAF's Bomber Command, but it sustained a *lower loss rate* than its night-flying British counterpart.[6] And it was more accurate. The American daylight precision bombing doctrine was vindicated. Additionally compelling is the fact that the Eighth Air Force—built by Eaker but commanded by Doolittle—dropped nearly as much tonnage during Big Week as it had during its entire first year of operations combined. The USAAF had finally become the force originally envisioned by American planners.

Still, the effort was not a cakewalk by any stretch of the imagination. Rather it was a fiercely fought series of air battles during which the Allies sustained significant losses. The USAAF lost more than 250 bombers and their crews. Indeed, during the month of February, including Big Week, the Eighth Air Force alone lost 299 bombers—20 percent of its force. The 303rd's losses—12 aircraft—were consistent with the Eighth's loss rate.

On the other hand, aside from the damage sustained by German industry, the entire German Air Force lost one-third of its fighters and nearly 18 percent of its pilots during that same month. The loss rate among the units defending against the USAAF was much higher. The Luftwaffe, under assault from many fronts and failed by its leadership, was dealt a body blow by ARGUMENT. Although it would score occasional successes during the following year, its decline continued and it never again gained the upper hand.

German reports indicate that they understood how dire the situation was:

In number as well as in technical performance, the daytime fighter units assigned to German air defense activity are inferior to the American fighter aircraft forces. In spite of their demonstrated courage and their willingness to make every sacrifice for their country, in the long run our forces are fighting a hopeless battle.... The tactics presently employed by the German fighter units, i.e., going after the enemy bombers, should be revised and modified, since they are leading to heavy losses. Knowing that they need not fear an attack by the German fighter aircraft, American fighters are able to move into range and attack the German fighters from above. Because of our heavy personnel losses and the lack of sufficiently well-trained replacements, our daytime fighter forces are unable to maintain any degree of effectiveness in a lengthy combat.... Continuation of the present system is tantamount to the deliberate destruction of valuable personnel and materiel without hope of tangible results.[7]

Of course, as noted by the Germans, much of the credit for the success of the effort went to the American fighter escorts. Although there were often planned and unplanned gaps in protection, they made it difficult for the Luftwaffe's fighters to concentrate on the bombers. The P-47 was still the dominant fighter in the Eighth, and the increased range provided by extra internal fuel, external tanks and better tactics made a significant difference. Too, the long-range P-51 was increasing in numbers. The P-38 also had long legs and provided good protection, although it was trouble-plagued through much of its career in Northern

Europe. Ultimately though, the American fighters dominated the Luft-waffe from ARGUMENT until the end of the war.

FORREST VOSLER WAS RECOMMENDED for the Medal of Honor for his heroic actions during the mission to Bremen on December 20, 1943. As the recommendation wound its way through the USAAF's bureau-cratic machinations, Vosler, still crippled by his wounds and missing an eye, was released from the hospital.

However, George Buske barely clung to life. He was the critically injured tail gunner that Vosler saved from drowning after *Jersey Bounce Jr.* went into the North Sea. Shortly after he was evacuated to the Army hospital at Botesdale, Buske was put on the operating table again. His abdominal wound was hideously infected and much of the surrounding tissue was dead. It exuded a foul mix of digestive liquids and gas. The Army doctors cut away the rotten bits, cleaned the wound and additionally drained a large pocket of pus that had formed above the liver. The other two wounds had likewise turned empyemic and were cleared and cleaned. Still, there was little hope that the massive infections could be stemmed. It was likely that Buske would die.

"OUR FIGHTER SUPPORT WAS SPLENDID"

NO CITY IN THE WORLD boasted air defenses as powerful as Berlin's. Its approaches were guarded by an array of day and night fighter bases, and the city itself was ringed and embedded with closely coordinated layers and pockets of heavy antiaircraft guns. As the seat of the Third Reich, the heart of Hitler's power, it was considered the ultimate target—almost unassailable. Most aircrews from the early part of the 303rd's combat career never came close to reaching the city.

But although it had never been attacked by day, the RAF had been bombing Berlin since 1940. Those attacks, like most the RAF mounted, were area raids intended to de-house and demoralize the population. The British raids continued for the next couple of years, but Berlin was much too big and well defended to be rubbled by the relatively small efforts. However, by late 1943, Arthur "Bomber" Harris, the head of RAF Bomber Command, believed that his force was big enough to bring Berlin to its knees, and with it, Germany. He ordered a series of raids that ultimately numbered sixteen from November 1943 to March

1944. His ambitions were grand: "It will cost us between 400 and 500 aircraft. It will cost Germany the war."[1]

Actually, the tally Harris offered for his own aircraft losses was accurate. Bomber Command lost more than five hundred aircraft and suffered a loss rate of nearly 6 percent. Harris's other prediction was not as accurate. Berlin and Germany were very much in the war during early March 1944, as the USAAF readied to make the first-ever large daytime air attack against the German capital.

An air raid against Berlin would tick a lot of boxes for the USAAF. Firstly, it would be good for morale back home. It would demonstrate that the sacrifices made in sons and brothers and husbands—and material—were not just hurting Germany, but were striking the very heart of the Third Reich. And just as it would be good for American morale, it would help to undermine German confidence. That the German leadership and military were unable to stop the USAAF would be obvious.

Moreover, Berlin encompassed a number of important target sets, including transportation, manufacturing, government and power generation. And perhaps just as critical, especially as the time for the invasion of Europe approached, was the fact that the Luftwaffe would be forced to defend Germany's most important city. And, just as with ARGUMENT, if the German pilots came to fight, they could be killed. Dead men did not oppose invasions.

Everyone in the Eighth Air Force recognized that the first USAAF attack on Berlin would mark another turning point in the air war. In fact, Doolittle—the head of the Eighth Air Force—planned a stunt that was little more than stupid self-aggrandizement: "I wanted to be in on this first effort and have the honor of being the first air commander to lead a raid over all three Axis capitals. I planned to fly a P-51 with one wingman ahead of the bomber stream over the capital city."[2] As the head of the world's most powerful strategic air force, it was a notion that bordered on theatric spectacle.

Doolittle met with his boss, Carl Spaatz, the head of the USSTAF. "I had my argument all prepared mentally and launched into it with gusto. Tooey finally gave in and reluctantly said I could go. However, just a day or so before departure, Tooey changed his mind and said he couldn't afford to risk the capture of a senior officer who had knowledge of invasion plans." Doolittle guessed that his scheme might have actually been spiked by Eisenhower, who recognized that there was little upside to the stunt.

The first daytime mission to Berlin was scheduled to be flown by Doolittle's Eighth Air Force on March 3, 1944. That the USAAF was ready so soon after the losses sustained during ARGUMENT underscored the vast human and industrial underpinnings of the American war effort. However, notwithstanding the fact that the Eighth was materially prepared for a great, climactic air battle—and that it had the trained crews it needed— it exercised no control over the weather. And the weather forced the first American attack on Berlin into a series of stuttering false starts.

Vern Moncur was the pilot of the 359th Bomb Squadron's *Thunderbird*. "The target was the 'Big B.' The weather was so bad that we were forced to climb to 27,000 feet over the North Sea and were unable to get completely out of the clouds and poor visibility. This excessive altitude took a lot of extra gasoline since we had been briefed to go in at 20,000 feet. Therefore, because of the weather and shortage of gasoline, we were unable to get to the target."[3]

After bombers crossed the North Frisian Islands, the decision was made to return to England. The 303rd, together with the other groups that comprised the huge formation, started a great, arcing turn. Moncur recalled: "On our turn around in the haze, two Forts [B-17s from the 91st and 94th Bomb Groups] collided and exploded in midair. It was quite a spectacular sight. The bombs in these two planes went off like a Fourth of July fireworks display. None of the crew had a chance of getting out of either ship because it happened so quickly. Even had they gotten out, they would have been no better off because they were out over the water when the accident took place."

None of the Eighth's bombers made it to Berlin that day.

The results were scarcely better the following day, March 4, when the

Eighth sortied 502 bombers. Vern Moncur was at the controls of *Thunderbird* once more: "Again our target was Berlin, and again the weather forced us to go to 27,000 feet. Therefore, our briefed route was too long to allow for this added climb because of the possibility of running short of gasoline. Our combat commander decided to bomb a target of opportunity somewhere in Germany. We flew over the southern part of 'Happy Valley' and bombed Bonn, Germany. The flak was quite thick over the target, as it always was over the Ruhr Valley, and we were lucky to be flying as high as we were. We picked up a few flak holes, but all of them were small. There was no injury to any of the crew."[4]

Although twenty-nine bombers did find their way through the weather to dump their bombs on a Berlin suburb, the tremendous and decisive air battle that American planners had hoped to provoke failed to develop.

Doolittle waited two days before sending 660 bombers against Berlin on March 6. The Luftwaffe rose up in force, and the sort of air combat for which Doolittle and his staff had hoped was finally precipitated. Again, the 359th's Vern Moncur was airborne in his trusty *Thunderbird*: "Our fighter support was splendid, and even though the Krauts kept ripping through other wings, our combat wing was rather lucky in not getting too many direct fighter attacks that seriously threatened us. We had a few passes made at us, but no one in our group was hurt much."[5]

Although their escort kept the enemy fighters away, it could do nothing about the flak that exploded all around the 303rd's formation. It impressed Moncur: "Over the target it looked like the Fourth of July—flak bursting in red flashes and billowing out black smoke all around us. . . . It seemed almost thick enough to drop your wheels and taxi around on it. The Krauts were practically able to name the engine they were shooting at. We received hits in the No. 1 engine, the No. 2 engine and the No. 4 engine. . . . The horizontal stabilizer had a big hole shot through it, and the vertical stabilizer received a jagged hole in the top of it. We also picked up another hole in the right side of the fuselage, near the tail wheel. . . . A piece of flak came through the cockpit and cut the left sleeve of my leather flying jacket, but didn't touch me."

But for all their intensity, the air defenses around Berlin failed to knock down any of the 303rd's bombers. Of this, Moncur was proud: "Our group established a record on this mission. We put up twenty-seven ships, and every one of them went across the target, and every one of them came back."

In light of what happened elsewhere in the bomber stream that day, the 303rd's achievement—or luck—was remarkable. In fact, the losses the Eighth sustained on March 6, 1944, were the worst in the USAAF's history. When the last aircraft returned to base and the final count was made, it was determined that sixty-nine bombers had been shot down, mostly by enemy fighters. It was a loss rate that exceeded 10 percent. Other bomb groups were as unlucky as the 303rd had been fortunate; the 100th lost fifteen bombers, the 95th lost eight, and seven bombers of the 388th were shot down.

Doolittle got the fight he wanted, but the best result he could claim—and then only with some qualifications—was a draw. Bombing results through broken and scattered decks of clouds were poor. And although American fighter escorts claimed eighty-two enemy aircraft shot down, and the bomber gunners tallied an additional and certainly inflated figure of ninety-seven, these weren't the breaking point numbers that had been hoped for.

This is especially true since the claims, as usual, were overstated. Even if it is generously assumed that half of the claimed 179 German aircraft were actually shot down—approximately 90 aircraft—it was typical that it took three "shoot downs" before a German pilot was killed. Consequently, it is apparent that the Eighth Air Force paid 69 heavy bombers and their crews to kill approximately 30 German pilots. Notwithstanding the boost to stateside morale, the battle was a Luftwaffe victory.

BOTH THE ALLIES and the Axis exaggerated the numbers of aircraft they shot down. This was sometimes done on purpose, but mostly it was due to the fact that air combat was a swirling maelstrom in which machines were destroyed and men were killed in mere seconds. And then more machines were destroyed and more men were killed in the following seconds. During fights that sometimes lasted tens of minutes—or in some cases for an hour or more—it was difficult to track everything that happened. This difficulty was exacerbated by rushes of adrenaline and by the fact that the fighting sometimes covered every quarter of the sky. And of course each individual took away his own version of what actually occurred.

This can be seen to have caused particular problems when it is considered that the USAAF's bombers carried crews of up to ten men. And every man but the pilot and copilot had guns for which he was responsible. When an enemy fighter attacked a heavy bomber formation and was shot down, there might be a dozen or more men who reasonably believed it was they, personally, who destroyed it. Further, there were times when attacking fighters caught fire or shed parts and dived away, but managed to land safely. And the Me-109 belched clots of black smoke when the pilot advanced the throttle swiftly. This was sometimes mistaken by the gunners for mortal damage.

It was for these reasons—and more—that the heavy bomber crews grossly overestimated the numbers of aircraft they downed. Debriefing officers did their best to untangle conflicting and overlapping claims, but it was an impossible task. Everyone, even the gunners, knew and acknowledged that the numbers were inflated, but it was difficult to apply against the claims a metric that produced a realistic number. It was a problem that persisted through the war. Howard Hernan was a flight engineer and top turret gunner with the 359th Bomb Squadron, and he remembered the frustration felt by all:

I know that gunners made many claims and probably a lot of us got credit for planes that were not actually shot down. . . . In order to claim a fighter, you had to have two other witnesses. Heaven knows how many men were shooting at the same plane. Intelligence would ask for the exact location and it would sometimes take up to

45 minutes in interrogation if you were claiming an aircraft. By this time you were absolutely worn out, hungry, and trying to get warm, and it just wasn't worth the effort. . . . Eventually, intelligence told us we were claiming too many fighters. From then on I never claimed another fighter, even if I knew I'd got it.[6]

ANXIOUS TO KEEP THE PRESSURE on Germany, Doolittle sent the Eighth back to Berlin two days later, on March 8. The weather was clear, and for the first time since trying for the city on March 3, the target—the Erkner bearing works—was utterly smashed. The Americans put nearly six hundred bombers over the city and sortied more than a thousand fighters to escort them, including 174 of the newly arrived P-51s. Losses, at thirty-seven bombers, were heavy but not nearly as considerable as the previous mission.

Doolittle's Destroyer, piloted by Leo McGrath, was downed by flak, but otherwise the mission was unremarkable for the 303rd. This is borne out by the comments of Kirk Mitchell, who led the mission that day: "I know it's hard to believe, but we had absolutely no opposition at all. We saw 20 to 25 enemy fighters, but our P-38s and P-51s took care of them. The flak wasn't worth mentioning [except to the McGrath crew!]. When we got to the target, it was completely covered with smoke and fire, so we dropped our bombs right in the middle of it. I doubt if there is even an outhouse left there."[7]

Leon Witherwax, Mitchell's ball turret gunner, made a similar observation: "The only time I saw fighters was in dogfights. One FW-190 came in out of the sun on a P-38 and shot out his left engine. About that time two P-38s jumped the FW-190 and blew him to pieces. The other P-38 feathered his prop and flew home with us as far as the Dutch coast."[8]

The last of this particular series of raids to Berlin was flown the following day, March 9. Clouds obscured most of the assigned targets, and the Eighth's aircraft scattered their bombs all over the region. The 303rd

dropped its bombs through clouds and into the city generally. The Luftwaffe appeared disinterested, as only about twenty fighters were spotted. The Eighth lost eight bombers. The 303rd sustained no losses. It
was an anticlimactic finish that neatly bookended the anticlimactic start
of the missions on March 3. For the 303rd, the much anticipated series
of attacks against the Reich's most feared target was wholly unexcep-
tional. The group lost one aircraft in five missions. Ironically, to that
point, Berlin was one of the least lethal targets the 303rd had hit.

Ultimately, at some level, the Germans had a good grasp of their
situation. Wartime reports correctly noted that their fighters, when
employed in overwhelming numbers, were able to inflict real losses on
the American formations. "Whenever weather conditions permitted the
concentrated employment of all available forces in close combat formation in a single area, noteworthy success was achieved in bringing down
enemy aircraft and in keeping our own losses down to a reasonable
limit. The success of our defensive operations over Berlin on 6 and 8
March gave ample evidence of the fighting morale of our fighter crews
and of their ability to carry on effective combat despite the technical
inferiority of their aircraft, but such successes were not frequent enough
to represent any threat to the American offensive forces."[9]

EDDIE DEERFIELD HAD ASKED to be removed from flight status during
October 1943 pending the recovery of his injured pilot, Robert Cogswell. However, by the end of the year it was apparent that Cogswell
would not be returning to combat duty. Consequently, in early January
1944, Deerfield asked to be returned to combat operations. After two
months of administrative processing, the March 6 raid to Berlin marked
his return. "We didn't get so much as a scratch," Deerfield said. "I subsequently flew seventeen more missions with four different crews, until
my tally reached the magic number of thirty. The other crews were just
fine, but I never felt as comfortable as when I had flown with Cogswell."

"HURRY UP AND JUMP"

THE BRITISH STARTED BOMBING with ground-mapping radar—using the H2S system—during January 1943. The new technology gave them the capability for dramatically improved accuracy when they hit targets such as Berlin that were beyond the range of radio-beam bombing systems. And certainly it was more accurate than bombing blindly. The Americans needed the same sort of accuracy when clouds over their targets made visual bombing impossible. This was much of the time. The USAAF's leadership—especially Arnold—was much vexed by the notion that many hundreds of ready bombers and crews stood prepared to visit destruction on Nazi Germany but were grounded by an inability to put bombs on cloud-shrouded targets. Consequently, with British assistance, the Americans fielded their own radar bombing capability. Their first mission was against Emden on September 27, 1943, using the British H2S system.

The system the USAAF eventually developed was the AN/APS-15 H2X ground-mapping radar. Early versions were mounted below the nose, but later variants were installed in the belly of the aircraft in place of the ball turret. The H2X was a derivative of the British H2S but had a shorter wavelength, which produced sharper images and better accuracy. The radar transmitted pulses of energy that were reflected by features on the surface, to include rivers, cities and other significant anomalies. Using this information, specially trained crews could set up bombing runs that—theoretically—could achieve accuracies nearly as good as visual bombing. In practice the systems were not nearly so accurate. The USAAF later observed: "It cannot be said that this equipment was in any sense a precision bombing instrument."[1]

Nevertheless, radar bombing equipment did allow the USAAF to launch more—albeit less precise—raids. Aside from the value of the damage that these poor-weather missions caused, they also forced the Germans to defend at the cost of additional resources, which were increasingly difficult to replace. Indeed, the extra burden placed on the Luftwaffe to defend more frequently—and in bad weather—was very real. In fact, the green pilots that Germany was rushing into combat were poorly trained for bad weather operations and crashes were not uncommon. The impact was immediate and, together with actual combat, boosted the attrition rate of the Luftwaffe.

The aircraft that used the radar bombing systems were called Pathfinder Force, or PFF, aircraft; it was a term borrowed from the RAF. Another term commonly used was "Mickey," which was a code word. Radar operators were called Mickey operators, or simply Mickeys. Their combat careers were somewhat lonely or detached; rather than being assigned to a specific crew, they usually were scheduled individually to whatever crew was flying an H2X-equipped aircraft.

The 303rd's Standard Operating Procedures for its bombardiers described in plain words the duties of the PFF, or Mickey, operator.

PFF is Navigation and Bombing by means of Radar. The radar Navigator, or Mickey Operator, operates the radar set over the continent, or beyond Gee range, in order to obtain fixes, by which to aid the D.R. [Dead Reckoning] Navigator. PFF is most useful when weather conditions are 10/10 [complete undercast—ten-tenths cloud cover], and the D.R. Navigator can get no visual pin-points, but it can also be useful in visual bomb runs, since the Mickey Operator can set up the bombardier on the right course miles away from his target and before the Bombardier can get the target in his sight. The Mickey Operator can pick up any city of 25,000 [population] and over, and can thus avoid almost all heavy flak defended areas. His fixes should be accurate within two miles.

The pilots who flew the aircraft equipped with this specialized gear arrived at Molesworth long after most of the 303rd's original cadre of airmen had been shot down or sent back to the States. One flyer from this later generation was Don Stoulil, who grew up in Olivia, Minnesota. "I had always wanted to fly," he said. "Growing up, I hoped and dreamed and prayed that I would be a pilot. And I wanted to fly in the Navy—I loved that summer white uniform with those gold wings. At that time the Navy required its pilots to have at least a couple of years of college and I had none at all—and my parents couldn't afford to send me. So I joined the National Guard and was assigned to the 215th Coast Artillery, Antiaircraft. We got a buck for each day we drilled."

At that point—early 1941—the United States was racing to get on a war footing, and Stoulil's unit was activated. "They shipped us to Camp Haan, near Riverside, California," he said. "I realized at that point that the odds of me getting out of the Army and going into the Navy to become a pilot were pretty slim."

After training at Camp Haan, the 215th was sent to Kodiak, Alaska, during the late summer of 1941. By that point Stoulil was hard at work studying for his aviation cadet examinations. "I sent a letter to the superintendent at my high school and he sent me a box of books. And I got permission from my first sergeant to stay up past Taps in order to study; I spent a couple of hours each night reading under a blue light-bulb so that I wouldn't disturb the other guys."

Stoulil was sent from Kodiak to Fort Richardson, near Anchorage,

Alaska, for his aviation cadet examinations. It was then that the Japanese attacked Pearl Harbor. "I was standing in line at the mess hall on December 7, 1941, when someone said that we were at war."

It was several months later when Stoulil—who wanted nothing more than to be a pilot—learned the results of his examinations. "I was really nervous. The officer called me up in front of his desk and said, 'Stoulil, you passed the medical portion of the exams.'" Stoulil nearly panicked when the officer lowered his voice. "And then he said, 'And you also passed the academics. Congratulations.'"

"I was so happy I could have kissed him," Stoulil said. He left Kodiak for training as an aviation cadet during June 1942 and arrived at Molesworth at the end of 1943. His first mission was to Bremen on December 20. Several days later, on Christmas, he was sent to scour the North Sea to look for RAF crewmen downed the previous night. "We didn't find any of them," he said. From that point he continued to build his mission count as well as his reputation.

Once he completed fifteen missions, Stoulil was designated as a PFF pilot during March 1944; he was among the first USAAF pilots so qualified. The assignment was actually an acknowledgment of his competence. PFF aircraft were put at the heads of formations, where fools didn't belong. Still, he didn't like it. "I'd flown fifteen missions with the 303rd when I was selected to fly as a PFF pilot. So, my heart was always with the 303rd. But they reassigned us to the 305th at Chelveston, where they kept all the PFF aircraft for the 1st Bomb Division—it was easier to secure and maintain the radar sets in one location.

"But I didn't really feel like part of the 305th either," Stoulil said. "They maintained our aircraft and personnel records and such, but we flew long-range penetration missions with a variety of different groups—sometimes with the 303rd. The bottom line was that no one really took ownership of us after we were made a PFF crew. I felt like the man without a country."

It was also a wearying assignment. "When we got notice the night before a mission," said Stoulil, "I rounded up my crew and made sure the aircraft was ready. Then we flew to the base of whatever group we were assigned to lead. But they usually didn't have any billeting arrangements for us so we typically slept wherever we could find a place that was warm and dry. And then we got up early to get chow and go to the briefing. When the other crews saw us show up at a briefing, they often catcalled and booed us. It was done mostly in fun, but they understood that if we were there the mission was usually going to be a long and tough one. Anyway, we were pretty much worn out before we ever took off.

"Because there had been accidents taking off from Chelveston at night with fully fueled and loaded bombers, our aircraft were fueled, serviced and loaded with bombs by whichever unit hosted us," Stoulil said. "So we always had strangers working on our airplanes, and that was a little bit unnerving. And to add to the pressure, the group commander—or even the wing commander—usually sat next to me in the copilot's seat."

Aside from all those considerations was the fact that leading a formation of bombers required a good deal of skill. Getting the formation joined and to the right point, at the proper altitude and at the mandated time—on the correct heading—required the lead pilot to plan his actions well ahead. It was critical for him to consider how the other aircraft in the formation were affected by what he did. For instance, if he turned too tightly, the aircraft on the inside of the turn might have to slow down so much that they were in danger of stalling and falling out of control. On the other hand, the bombers on the outside of the turn might not be able to fly fast enough to stay in position. Or if they could, they would burn too much fuel in the process.

Power control was also critical. All the aircraft performed slightly differently depending on the condition of their engines, their drag and their trim—that is, how "bent" they were. Moreover, the bombers were not always of the same model or configuration. For instance, except for very late models, the B-17F was not equipped with chin turrets as was the later B-17G. And PFF aircraft had a radar installed rather than a ball turret. Too, aircraft weights varied widely as some crews carried extra ammunition or armor, or even additional crewmembers in the form of observers, photographers or radar operators.

Accordingly, the lead pilot could never use anything close to full power lest he leave the poorer performing aircraft in his formation behind. And when he adjusted his power, it was imperative that he do so only when necessary, and even then he had to be very smooth, slow and deliberate. Otherwise, the rest of the pilots were forced to jockey their throttles radically to stay in position. Doing so burned extra fuel and caused undue wear and tear on the engines, not to mention the fact that the pilots were quickly exhausted as they tried to keep position in a formation that compressed and expanded like an airborne accordion.

Indeed, keeping formation—so critical to maximizing the effects of the bombs and concentrating defensive firepower—was a special skill. It was impossible to simply fly an aircraft into position, set the power and leave it. Firstly, lead pilots were rarely able to fly perfectly straight flight paths at constant airspeeds. Instead large and small heading changes were nearly constant, as were deviations in airspeed. Consequently, to stay in position, wingmen were compelled to continuously manipulate their flight controls and power settings. And each adjustment required a counter-adjustment such that pilots flying as wingmen could never rest.

It should be additionally appreciated that the difficulties of staying in position were magnified for pilots at the edge of the formation. They made their adjustments on aircraft that were already making their own adjustments on the lead aircraft. Essentially, keeping formation demanded continuous, precise and grueling flying. Over many hours it was absolutely exhausting.

There was a final downside to flying PFF missions. German fighters commonly made head-on attacks against the American heavy bomber formations. The bombers at the front—among them, the PFF aircraft— were obviously in greater danger than those further back. Accordingly, crews who flew in the lead position were given extra mission credits so that their combat tours were abbreviated to a small degree. For instance a pilot who led three missions had his required mission count reduced by one.

As only a few aircraft carried PFF equipment in each group formation, it was imperative that the rest of the crews drop their bombs using the PFF aircraft as a reference. Accordingly, sky marker devices were created by filling one-hundred-pound bomb casings with a mildly acidic dye. The PFF aircraft usually carried one or two of these specialized markers along with their normal bomb loads. When released—together with the other bombs—they vented a brightly colored smoke that created long vertical streaks in the sky.

Dick Johnson had a bad experience with a sky marker when he was forced out of his position by another bomber: "This put us directly behind the lead plane so that when he dropped his bombs, his "Sky Marker" bomb enveloped our plane with a white acid fog which ruined all the Plexiglas in our plane. Flying home was difficult due to the milky looking windshield."[2]

THE FORMATIONS THE 303RD flew evolved during the group's combat career, but the common theme was that they were large, unwieldy and demanding to fly. As the war progressed, they grew even more so. On the other hand, training and procedures also improved, which, together with more experience, somewhat mitigated the difficulties.

The basic element was a three-aircraft flight with two wingmen—one on each side and slightly back of the leader—such that the formation resembled a flat triangle. A squadron was made up of four of these three-aircraft flights arranged, again, in a flattened triangle with one side having an extra flight of three. Each flight of three flew slightly stepped up or down from the squadron leader in order to clear fields of fire for the gunners and to ease the workload for the pilots. Separation from the various flights was approximately seventy-five feet, while the wingmen within flights flew as close as was reasonably safe and sustainable over long periods.

Generally, except for maximum efforts, only three of the group's four squadrons flew on a given mission. This rotation allowed the crews to get a certain amount of rest. Accordingly, the group generally flew a three-squadron formation: First, was the lead squadron; next was the low squadron, which flew offset to the left and slightly behind and below the lead squadron; finally, the high squadron flew offset to the right, slightly behind, and stepped up from the lead squadron.

The 303rd's Standard Operating Procedures, or SOP, directed its pilots: "To be effective, both offensively and defensively, this formation must be flown as close as safety will permit. When properly flown, the best possible bomb pattern can be obtained. One flight leader, or one wingman out of position, can disrupt the effectiveness of the entire pattern. The size of the pattern is also proportionate to the depth of the formation, so it will pay dividends on target hits to keep [the] formation as shallow as possible. In case an aircraft becomes disabled on the bomb run, the pilot should not disrupt his own formation or formations in trail."

The 303rd was one of three bomb groups that made up the 41st Combat Bombardment Wing. The wing formation of three groups was simply a larger version of the three-squadron group formation; a lead, high and low group comprised the wing formation. Finally, the 41st, as one of four wings of the 1st Bombardment Division, took its place within the stream of this larger organization. It should be noted that, in order to tighten the dispersion of the bombs and ensure maximum effects on the target, the various formations fell into a compact line as much as possible en route from the IP to the target.

Changes to formations—both planned and ad hoc—were constant. For instance, the 303rd grew as the war progressed, and was able to launch many more aircraft than was possible when it first started operations. Indeed, whereas the group struggled to get eighteen B-17s airborne during its early operations, missions of forty or more aircraft were not unusual during 1944. In fact, the group put fifty-eight aircraft up for the mission to Osnabrück on November 26, 1944. Accordingly the group sometimes went out as two, separate, multi-squadron formations typically designated Group A and Group B.

Formations also changed when aircraft went missing during botched assemblies, or when extra aircraft joined during those same botched assemblies. And under the fire of combat when aircraft were damaged and lagged—or were blasted out of the sky—the remaining pilots adjusted their positions to keep the overall formation as tight as possible. Ultimately, although formations were prescribed for virtually every situation, it wasn't always possible to achieve and maintain them. The pilots did the best they could.

BOMBER CREWS SOMETIMES took mortally stricken ships into neutral Sweden or Switzerland, where they were typically interned. It was markedly more preferable to be interned in Switzerland or Sweden than to be a POW in Germany and the men knew it. They also knew when their routes took them close to one of the neutral nations—it was something they noted during their briefings. That they considered recovering into Sweden or Switzerland if in extremis was only natural.

The route for the mission against the airfield at Oberpfaffenhofen on April 24, 1944, was one that took the bombers within about fifty miles of Switzerland. It was also one that saw the 303rd hit hard by enemy fighters. The area around Munich—Oberpfaffenhofen was about twenty miles west—was typically defended fiercely. This day was no different; nearly two hundred Luftwaffe aircraft rose to challenge the raid.

The bomber captained by Paul C. Stewart was badly damaged by antiaircraft fire over the target and he dropped the ship out of the 303rd's formation and turned south for Switzerland. The wounded B-17 was set upon by fighters almost immediately. A frontal attack killed Stewart as well as the copilot, the bombardier, the navigator, the flight engineer and the radio operator. The gunners in the rear of the aircraft were unable to make contact with anyone in the forward section. It was apparent that no one was flying the big bomber.

The ball turret gunner, Joseph Jasinski, climbed up into the fuselage but inadvertently deployed his parachute; yards of white nylon billowed about his legs. He dropped the tangled, fluttering mess and grabbed a spare parachute. The two waist gunners, James Cast and Raymond Cadlolo, hesitated as they watched him struggle to snap it onto his harness. He looked up and told them to "Hurry up and jump." They did. The tail gunner, Roy Sable, escaped from the rear hatch.[3]

Almost immediately the bomber fell off to the left and started into a sharp, downward spiral. Jasinski was likely pinned against the inside of the fuselage by the resultant centrifugal force. Still alive, he spun to earth with his dead crewmates and perished in the crash.

Two other bombers were badly damaged and made for Switzerland. But unlike Stewart's crew, they made it. The aircraft piloted by Thomas McClure was hit by fighters en route to the target. One engine was essentially destroyed, and McClure feathered its propeller. He ordered the bombs jettisoned and made a right turn to the south. Once again attacked by fighters, the right inboard engine was set afire and the chin turret stopped working. Cannon fire ripped the fuselage and seriously wounded one of the waist gunners and further crippled the big ship. Notwithstanding the ferocity of the German attacks, McClure wrestled the aircraft into Switzerland and landed in Geneva.

Like McClure's aircraft, Raymond Hofmann's bomber, *Shoo-Shoo Baby*, lost an engine to fighter attacks before reaching the target. More damage over Oberpfaffenhofen knocked out another. Hofmann's aircraft streamed fuel from its damaged tanks as the rest of the formation left it behind. With no good options, he turned the bomber toward Switzerland. Perhaps because they were occupied elsewhere, the defending German fighters failed to intercept *Shoo-Shoo Baby*, and Hofmann put it safely down in Zürich.

Don Stoulil—a veteran of fifteen sorties with the 303rd—was flying a PFF ship at the head of the 384th Bomb Group. "The German fighter pilots were really aggressive that day," he said. "Coming into the target we were hit and they blew a hole in the fuel tank in our left wing— it was really streaming out. At the same time our tail gunner, Calvin Turkington, was hit by cannon fire from one of the fighters; it hit the protective armor plate in front of his chest and splattered his arms with shrapnel. I had the crew drag him out of there and up to radio room, where they could give him first aid."

After the formation dropped its bombs, Stoulil faced a difficult decision. England was nearly six hundred miles away. Switzerland was only a tenth as far. "I didn't know if we could make it back," he said. "We were predicted to have a headwind of a hundred miles an hour on the return trip and we had lost a lot of fuel. And Turkington was wounded. So, I turned toward Switzerland. Immediately after I made that turn, the first thing that crossed my mind was that my parents were going to get a telegram saying that I was missing in action."

But aside from telegrams, Stoulil had other concerns. He was still understandably worried about the German fighters. "I asked our navigator, Harold Susskind, if there were any German fighter fields in between us and Switzerland. He said 'Oh yeah, there are.'" Stoulil weighed the odds again. "I turned back and caught up with the formation—I didn't want to give those fighters another chance at us. In the end, we made it back to England, but only barely.

"Calvin Turkington went into the hospital for a while but then later went back to flying combat missions with other crews long after we were finished. He was hit by cannon fire from an FW-190 on September 28, 1944, on a mission to Magdeburg. He crawled out of the tail position and died. He had been the only one of our crew who was married and had a kid."

Of the 754 bombers the USAAF sent into Germany on April 24, 1944, the day of the 303rd's mission to Oberpfaffenhofen, twelve went into Switzerland. During the next few months the number of USAAF bombers that recovered into Switzerland and Sweden rose at a rate that caused anxiety at the highest levels of leadership. During May, June and July 1944, there were eighteen, thirty-eight and forty-one diversions respectively. Rumors that many of the ships were barely damaged—or not damaged at all—greatly alarmed Arnold, the USAAF's chief. He wrote to Spaatz that reports indicated the attitudes of the bomber crewmen were lacking in many instances and characterized by "lack of respect (amounting to near hatred) for certain very senior leaders; disgust with the influence of political expedients on tactical and strategical [sic] employment; lack of desire to kill Germans; lack of understanding as to the political necessity for fighting the war; general personal lassitude with consequent lack of patriotic enthusiasm for their jobs."[4]

Of particular concern was the need to maintain the tempo of the strategic bombing effort without utterly breaking the crews. Arnold urged Spaatz to get green crews into action as soon as possible to relieve some of the pressure on hard-used veterans. There also followed various investigations and reports by Arnold's handpicked officers. It was concluded that although the numbers of aircraft landing in the neutral countries had increased, so had the number of aircraft that had been sent on operations. Moreover, it was determined that the accusations of cowardice had been greatly exaggerated and that the vast majority of landings in the neutral countries were justified. Ultimately, the issue was resolved to a great degree after D-Day as the Allies penetrated into France and advanced landing grounds became available on the continent. In the end, three crews from the 303rd diverted into Switzerland during the war while none recovered into Sweden, although a handful of damaged ships fell short while making the attempt.

AS A PFF PILOT, Don Stoulil often flew with squadron and group commanders. Indeed, he flew several times with Travis, the commander of the 41st Combat Bombardment Wing. "He sat in the copilot seat and took constant notes during the missions," Stoulil said. "He was all business. But he was a pretty good pilot too.

"I was flying as his pilot when he was hit," Stoulil said. "It was the mission to Berlin on April 29, 1944. We were on our way back and we ran into a little bit of flak near Magdeburg. There came a burst, and a little piece of shrapnel came through the windscreen and nicked him above the left eye. And he immediately slumped over. It wasn't a big wound, but it was bleeding."

Stoulil watched blood seep down Travis's left cheek and considered what happened to young officers who got their wing commander killed. "And then he started to regain consciousness," Stoulil said. "He finally sat up. I called the waist gunner [George Greene] up to the cockpit—he was pretty good with bandages—and had him fix the general up. He wound a big, white bandage around Travis's head so that it almost looked like he was wearing a turban. Anyway, he was fine and was so proud of that bandage that he showed up that night at the officers club with it still on! He got the Purple Heart for that cut above his eye."[5]

MEANWHILE, GEORGE BUSKE, the tail gunner aboard the *Jersey Bounce Jr.* who had been so horrifically wounded during the mission to Bremen on December 20, 1943, struggled to stay alive. He still fought infections and his abdominal cavity was afflicted with abscesses that refused to heal. Moreover, wounds on his legs that had initially seemed minor when compared to the massive trauma to his chest and abdomen became infected.

Buske's weight fell to eighty-eight pounds. His doctors, in an experiment to increase his weight and ward off malnutrition, administered reconstituted dried human plasma. Despite the intensive medical care, his condition deteriorated further. He fell into periodic comas and his breathing grew irregular. It was apparent that he was going to die.

"I WAS FINALLY FINISHED"

ALTHOUGH THE REQUIRED MISSION count—that is, opportunities to die—had been increased from twenty-five to thirty since he had stopped flying in combat, Eddie Deerfield returned to flight status on March 6, 1944, and flew sixteen more missions during the next two months. In that time a shot-out tail wheel on April 11 nearly ended in a catastrophic crash landing. And on April 24, during the Oberpfaffenhofen mission, the aircraft he was aboard was shot up so badly it nearly went into the North Sea. Deerfield had gone into the drink with the Cogswell crew several months earlier. "When the pilot told me to start sending SOS signals so that Air/Sea Rescue could fix our location, I thought to myself that there was no way I was going to be lucky enough to survive two ditchings; fortunately we made it back to England."

The mission scheduled against Saarbrücken on May 11, 1944, was to be Deerfield's thirtieth, and final, combat sortie. It was not the 303rd's finest hour. Of the forty aircraft the group scheduled for the effort, three were badly damaged when the brakes on one failed and it collided with two others.

The 303rd's remaining bombers made it to Saarbrücken, where enemy fighters were kept away by American escorts. But the escorts could do nothing about the flak, which was exceedingly accurate. That accuracy tested and broke Deerfield's string of luck; shrapnel blew a hole through the radio compartment wall and metal splinters from the skin of the B-17 lacerated the left side of his face.

The 303rd made two abortive runs against the marshaling yards at Saarbrücken, but haze obscured the target and the radar equipment aboard the radar-equipped ships was shot up. Only a portion of the aircraft released their bombs, and the results were poor. Rather than make a third run through devastating antiaircraft defenses that had already hit every one of the group's ships and sent one of them tumbling earthward in flames, the formation diverted to a target of opportunity—the marshaling yards at Völklingen—where the remaining aircraft dropped their bombs.

"It wasn't until we were back over the North Sea and descending that I realized I had been hit," Deerfield said. "My face was gashed just below my left eye, but at high altitude the wound froze almost immediately and there was no pain. It wasn't until we got into warmer air that the cuts opened up and started bleeding. I called the pilot on the interphone to tell him I'd been hit." An ambulance waited for Deerfield when his ship touched down. "I celebrated the completion of my thirtieth mission that night in the hospital," he said. "I was finally finished."

Milo Schultz remembered how the second run at Saarbrücken cost the lives of several of his 303rd comrades. "We turned at the I.P. and started our bomb run through very heavy flak. We ended by not dropping our bombs because [the] group bombardier [George Orvis] couldn't see the target for late afternoon haze and smoke blowing down from the Ruhr. [The] Group made a 180 degree turn and came back without changing altitude into that horrendous anti-aircraft fire. We were flying alongside Captain Johnny Long. . . . One of our waist gunners saw his plane get a direct hit and go down. Johnny was killed along with several of his crew. I always remembered him because he slept at the far end of our barracks and he had a nude picture of a beautiful gal at his bedside."[1]

The bomber crews hated to make more than one pass over a target as they did that day over Saarbrücken. Doing so was virtually equivalent to flying two missions. Arguably it was worse as the antiaircraft gunners had time to fine-tune their firing solutions during the time between the first run and the second or third or later runs. The formation leaders were often compelled to make more than one pass when weather temporarily obscured the target, or when the lead bombardier experienced equipment failures or self-induced targeting miscues. And, as described by Warren Kotz, a navigator with the 427th, bomb runs were occasionally aborted when other bomb groups mistakenly flew into the way. This was the case during the mission to Abbeville, France, on July 10, 1943: "No bombs dropped from our group. Groups 379, 381 and 384 cut underneath our group so lead bombardiers didn't drop bombs—SNAFU. We all saw target in our ship [and] could have bombed."[2]

AS EFFECTIVE AS THE GERMAN antiaircraft fire was, it would have been more so had the USAAF's fliers not developed tactics intended to foil it. Those tactics were built upon an understanding of how the flak guns worked and how they were employed. A training film solicited the men: "Let's have a look at this flak business."[3] It subsequently described in very basic terms how a typical German antiaircraft gun worked: "The heavy gun destroys aircraft by using a time-fuzed shell to put a large explosive burst in the near vicinity of the target [aircraft]."

The men learned that it took approximately one second for an antiaircraft round to climb a thousand feet. For instance, if a shell was fired directly at a formation at an altitude of twenty-seven thousand feet flying at two hundred miles per hour, the formation would have traveled nearly two miles before the shell reached the point at which it was originally aimed. Accordingly the German gunners were compelled to lead—or aim ahead of—their targets. This was explained by the training film:

> First the aircraft is picked up in an optical sight and held on the cross-hair[s]. The sight keeps tracking it continuously, obtaining its direction and angular height while a stereoscopic range finder determines the altitude. At night or in bad weather the aircraft may be tracked solely by radar. Whether tracked by optical sight or by radar the information is fed by electric cable to a director. This mechanical quiz kid digests the data and automatically computes the right lead. Setting the guns so that they will fire not at where the target is now, but at where it will be at the end of the shell's time of flight.

Exploiting this considerable time of flight was the key to survival for the American bomber crews. The Germans practiced a technique called continuously pointed fire wherein one or more batteries fired at a formation until it passed out of range. In heavily defended areas the formations often came into firing range of another set of guns, which received updated firing solutions. However, those updated firing solutions—accounting for altitude and course—took at least five seconds. The director subsequently pushed the new data to the batteries which set the individual guns. This required at least another five seconds. The shells, once fired, were on an irreversible course. And it took twenty-five seconds or so to reach the bombers, assuming they were flying at an altitude of twenty-five thousand feet.

The training film urged the bomber men to take advantage of the physical and temporal constraints to which the Germans were shackled. "Never fly one flight path for longer than the number of seconds you are up in thousands of feet. . . . Maneuvering every twenty-five seconds causes the flak to burst on a course you're no longer flying. The gunner must refigure a firing solution for the new course you just took up before he can fire again." Of course, so long as the bomber pilots made regularly timed—yet unpredictable—heading and altitude changes, it was impossible for the Germans to obtain a perfect firing solution. "Keep those gunners guessing," the film urged.

Certainly, the Germans understood this and adapted. One technique they used was to shadow the American formations with an aircraft whose crew radioed exact airspeeds and altitudes to antiaircraft direction centers. Charles Ziesche of the 427th Bomb Squadron was aboard *Miss Lace* during the August 24, 1944, mission to Merseberg. He recalled the Germans doing exactly this—with a twist. "Looking out to the rear of our formation, I saw a B-17 quite a distance behind, and I called to our tail gunner to check and see if he could make out the markings and whether she might be in trouble. As far as he could tell, she seemed to be flying at the same speed and altitude. However, as we approached the I.P., he called back to say she was peeling off. This confirmed our suspicions that the Germans had captured one of our B-17s, repaired it, and used it to fly behind our formation and call in our air speed and altitude to the anti-aircraft batteries on the ground, thus providing perfect accuracy."[4]

Whether or not the aircraft was a captured B-17 is uncertain. However, the Germans did indeed reconstitute and fly damaged B-17s that came down on the Continent. In fact, the first B-17 the Germans returned to flying condition was from the 303rd. *Wulfe Hound* was downed on the mission to Rouen on December 6, 1942. Shot up and harried by Me-109s and FW-190s, the pilot, Paul Flickinger, crash-landed it near Melun. The crew destroyed the ship's sensitive equipment and fled. Of the ten men making up the crew, four—including Flickinger—were captured and six evaded and returned to Molesworth. *Wulfe Hound* was repaired and flown by the Germans three months later during March 1943.

Another German adaptation made up with volume of fire what it lacked in finesse. Defending batteries were directed to simply saturate a portion of the sky—a "barrage box"—through which it was anticipated the bomber formations had to fly to reach the target. Maneuvering did no good as the antiaircraft fire wasn't aimed and there was a good chance that changes in altitude or heading would get a formation into more trouble than not. Caught in a barrage box, it was better to simply hold a steady course that got the formation through the flak as quickly as possible. Indeed, because the barrage boxes were often close to the target, the aircraft were in their bomb runs anyway and the crews had no other choice than to hold a steady course.

Robert Butcher's diary entry for the attack on Hamburg on June 18, 1944, describes what must certainly have been a barrage box. It was his sixth mission: "I never prayed so hard in all my life. It is just the Good Lord that brings us through. Low overcast over target. Bombed by PFF. The flak was a solid black wall just a little to our left. . . . I wonder now if I will make it."[5]

The primary German heavy antiaircraft gun was the 8.8-centimeter, or 88-millimeter, series of guns that were first prototyped in 1928. They were universally called "eighty-eights" by the Americans, or simply "flak guns." The word "flak" was an abbreviation of the German word for an air defense gun, *Fliegerabwehrkanone*. The weapons were improved through the 1930s and into the war years and were produced in prodigious numbers. Indeed, more than twenty thousand examples of three variants—mostly Flak 18s, Flak 36s and Flak 37s—were produced, of which more than ten thousand were in service as antiaircraft guns by late 1944. They were also used effectively as anti-tank weapons throughout the war.

The rounds weighed approximately twenty pounds and were fired at a rate of about eighteen per minute. Although the maximum firing altitude exceeded thirty-five thousand feet, effectiveness dropped off above twenty-five thousand feet. Ideally, each gun was serviced by a crew of ten men. In practice, as manpower grew short, the crew sizes shrank and were increasingly made up of old men, teenage boys and women. Indeed, one of those boys was Joseph Ratzinger, who eventually became Pope Benedict XVI.

As terrifying and effective as the German flak defenses were, it still required approximately forty-five hundred antiaircraft rounds, on average, to knock down a bomber; such defenses obviously consumed a staggering amount of resources. Had the Germans developed proximity fuzes—as did the British and Americans—their guns would have been much more effective. Instead they waited too long to field any significant improvements. It wasn't until April 1945 that an experimental round—a *doppelzünder*—was trialed with both a contact fuze and a traditional timed fuze. On April 9, 1945, flak defenses in Munich used the new round to knock down thirteen bombers at an average expenditure of only 370 rounds per aircraft.[6] New radar promised to enhance the effectiveness of the guns even more. Such improvements, had they been fielded only a year or so earlier, might have grounded the Allied strategic bombing offensive.

THE DAMAGE THE 303RD'S bombers sustained was not always caused by the Germans. Shell casings from other bombers' spent .50-caliber machine gun rounds sometimes lodged in engines or dented the aircraft. However, *The Floose* was hit by a more unusual object. Donald Birkenseer, the navigator, was surprised by a loud *pop* and the rush of air through a hole in the very tip of the ship's Plexiglas nose. He looked down at his feet and picked up a perfectly round piece of Plexiglas and a frozen peanut butter sandwich made from a hamburger bun. It had been tossed from one of the ships at the front of the formation.[7]

In fact, the guilty party could have been the 360th's James Geiger crew. He remembered the food that the crews were given: "They sent up peanut butter sandwiches but they froze solid so we couldn't eat them. We threw them out and hoped they'd hit a German on the head and shorten the war up a little."[8]

"YOU'LL BE SORRY"

RICHARD "DICK" JOHNSON was born on March 10, 1922, in Piqua, Ohio. "At this time Dad was working at a pool hall restaurant owned by Dick Shepard. He told Dad that if I was a boy and they named me after him, he would buy me my first pair of long pants. So my first name became Richard. Unfortunately for Dick Shepard, he never got to buy me those long pants, as his girlfriend did him in with a handgun when I was about four years old."

Johnson and his older brother went to an integrated grade school with a family of boys who later became famous as the Mills Brothers; they were the first black singing group to have a regular radio show. Don Gentile, who grew up to become one of the nation's greatest fighter aces, was a year older than Johnson and also attended the school. Johnson was surrounded by family at Piqua and—despite losing a younger brother to rheumatic fever—had many happy memories there. Sometimes the children picked up fallen apples from a nearby orchard. "Grandma Burt fussed about us gathering applies without being invited, but she made apple pies out of them anyhow. We were one big happy family in those days, but it didn't last."

The Johnsons hit the road as the Great Depression choked the nation. The family moved to Detroit for a short time and then headed to Houston, where they squatted in an abandoned house. There followed several more moves. The family sharecropped a derelict farm in the Piney Woods where much of what they ate—including armadillos—was scavenged. There followed another move to another abandoned homestead, in Arkansas. "One night Dad and the neighbor caught a groundhog that was so big that I thought it was a small bear. It was so tough that we couldn't eat it, and Dad later joked it was so tough that you couldn't even cut the gravy."

Following a stint on a strawberry farm, the Johnsons moved to Naylor, Missouri, where Johnson's paternal grandfather lived. Their lives stabilized somewhat, and Johnson attended Pig Ankle Grammar School while the family sharecropped cotton and sorghum. When the cotton crop matured, Johnson, his parents and his brother picked about six hundred pounds each day. "This made us about six dollars a day, which was better money than we had ever made as a family. But we still envied the black family that lived near us. They were so good at their job that they could pick four hundred pounds each. They told us that we too could pick that much if we didn't stop to straighten the kinks from our backs so often."[1]

The family eventually moved to Illinois, and Johnson's life became more normal. He graduated high school in 1940 and at the end of the year moved to Norfolk, Virginia, to find work. He eventually landed a job with the Prest-O-Lite company, which produced acetylene welding gas. He was there when the Japanese attacked Pearl Harbor. After more time at Prest-O-Lite he entered the aviation cadet program, earned his wings, was made a B-17 copilot and arrived at Molesworth during early May 1944.

As a B-17 copilot Johnson was a great deal of time and a greater deal of geography removed from his past as the cotton picking child of a struggling sharecropper. Although he was fully qualified on the B-17, he was still awed at the sight of the great flying war machine that was the 303rd: "There were so many B-17s that they couldn't be easily counted.

"After we got settled, and after hearing, 'You'll be sorry,' a few

times, we did the latest schooling. We learned that we had a forty percent chance of finishing our tour of duty without being shot down or
wounded, and if shot down there was a fifty percent chance of survival
from that, giving us an eighty percent chance of surviving the war."[2]
Indeed, those numbers were very much on the mark. The Eighth Air
Force put just more than a hundred thousand men into combat during
the period from 1942 to 1945. Of that number, approximately forty-
one thousand men were shot down. Of those who went down, nearly
twenty thousand were killed.[3] When it is considered that these numbers included fighter pilots—who enjoyed better survivability rates—it
is apparent that the information given to Johnson was quite accurate.

THE UNITED STATES recognized the increasingly sophisticated nature of
Germany's antiaircraft defenses even before becoming a combatant and
took steps to mitigate their effectiveness. The concept for one of these
efforts was a glide bomb, the GB-1, which was a winged, gyroscopically
stabilized bomb intended to be dropped from distances well outside the
ranges of defending antiaircraft guns. The GB-1's glide performance was
such that it flew one mile for each thousand feet it descended. For
instance, released from twenty thousand feet, it had a range of twenty
miles. It was considered that a weapon of this sort with a large enough
warhead—and accurately guided—might be capable of breaking up
strongly fortified submarine pens or other hardened targets.

Rather than a purpose-built, winged bomb, the GB-1 was a primitive,
twin-boom glider made of wood and steel and fitted to a standard two-
thousand-pound M34 bomb. It had a twelve-foot wingspan and was
designed to be suspended from the B-17—two per bomber—via shackles
fixed to each wing between the inboard engines and the fuselage. It was
a bulky arrangement that flew for the first time during November 1941.

Despite its crude appearance and rudimentary technology, the GB-1
and everything about it was highly classified, under the name of
"Grapefruit." The secrecy surrounding the weapon had nothing to do

with its effectiveness, as USAAF staffers were unimpressed with its poor accuracy long before it was sent overseas: When released from twenty thousand feet, the GB-1 could only be reasonably expected to hit targets the size of Dayton, Ohio.

Valuable work was in fact being done to develop an accurate radio guidance system during 1942, but Henry Arnold—ever impatient—ordered the GB-1 into production without it. Instead, the bomb was equipped with a crude autopilot that was readily available but could do nothing more than hold a heading as the bomb descended. The bomb could not be guided while in flight. Arnold's decision made little sense and guaranteed the GB-1's failure.

Ground crewmen were trained to assemble, check and load the GB-1s during late 1942 at Eglin Air Field in Florida before being sent overseas to one of the three bomb groups that made up the 41st Combat Bombardment Wing—the 303rd at Molesworth, the 379th at Kimbolton, and the 384th at Grafton-Underwood. The 303rd received nineteen of these specially trained men. That the program was poorly organized and executed is indicated by the fact that aircrews didn't train with the GB-1 until nearly a year later, during October 1943, at Brooksville, Florida. Following the specialized training the aircrews were sent to England.

GB-1 components started to arrive at Molesworth during mid-October 1943 despite the fact that the Eighth Air Force had earlier declared that it was not interested in the weapon. The specially trained ground crews—who had spent most of the year performing routine maintenance tasks on the 303rd's aircraft—went to work putting the secret weapons together. Robert Brassil was one of those men. "Our immediate job was an expedited effort to unload, assemble and prepare the glide bombs. Each assembled glide bomb had to be hoisted and delicately balanced prior to a final tightening of the two steel bands that attached the glider wing section to the 2,000 pound explosive. About 50 glide bombs were assembled, placed on steel cradles, and stored in an outdoor area of the bomb dump."[4]

A practice sortie was flown over the North Sea on November 11,

1943, during which a number of malfunctions were experienced. Not surprisingly a consensus was reached that additional training and more practice missions were needed. And then nothing happened.

One reason that the weapons weren't used immediately was that fine weather with almost unlimited visibility was required. The target had to be visible from well outside the ideal launch range of approximately twenty miles and the weather during late 1943 and into early 1944 was typically foul.

Moreover, at that time German fighters were a greater threat than antiaircraft guns, and the B-17s were especially slow, unwieldy and vulnerable when burdened with two of the cumbersome glide bombs. Without any sort of guidance system other than the autopilot that held a specific heading, they were aimed visually from long range. As directed by the bombardier, at about twenty-five miles from the target, the pilot nosed the aircraft into a shallow dive and descended at approximately fifteen hundred feet per minute, while accelerating to an indicated airspeed of between 190 and 200 miles per hour. After leveling off at roughly twenty thousand feet, he held the aircraft steady for twenty seconds in order to give the bombs' gyroscopes time to stabilize. At that point, at about eighteen miles from the target, both GB-1s were released. The rudimentary autopilot, if it worked, kept the bombs on course.

The GB-1s, because they were area weapons, were distinctly unsuited for the sort of precision bombing that the Eighth Air Force endeavored to practice. Because of that fact, and because the weapons were difficult to use—and additionally in light of the reality that they weren't available in large numbers—they were little more than the strategic bombing equivalent of a party trick. No one seriously believed that they were capable of making a meaningful contribution to the war effort.

An attempt was finally made to use the GB-1s on April 26, 1944. However, the weather deteriorated and the mission was recalled before the Continent was reached. The horse that followed that cart was a practice mission the next day. Dick Johnson arrived at Molesworth during that time and recalled the odd-looking weapons: "When our crew arrived at the 303rd Bomb Group in early May, a strange sight greeted us. The barracks for the 427th squadron to which we were assigned were on the airdrome and all along the armament roads were stacked row upon row of some strange flying machines."[5]

Little did Johnson know that he would be taking a pair of those "strange flying machines" into combat a short time later. Johnson, like most of the men making up the crews for the upcoming mission, was a relative neophyte in the context of the GB-1. Most of the men who had been so carefully trained on the secret weapon back in the States had already finished their tours or been shot down. Specially trained or not, a group of pilots was selected to take the GB-1 into combat on May 28, 1944. The target was the Eifeltor marshaling yard at Cologne. The 41st Combat Bombardment Wing's three groups were tasked with putting up twenty GB-1-loaded bombers each, along with another twenty aircraft to participate in conventional bombing operations that same day. The GB-1-armed aircraft made up only a small fraction of the 1,341 heavy bombers that the Eighth sent against targets in Germany on that date.

The 303rd's ground crews worked through the night of May 27 and into the morning of May 28 to get two of the crude weapons loaded onto each of the twenty bombers. Although one of the 303rd's aircraft aborted, the briefing and takeoff went well and the formations from the 303rd, the 379th and the 384th joined and started for the North Sea as they struggled to haul their GB-1s to altitude. Brigadier General Robert Travis, the commander of the 41st, led the mission from aboard the 303rd's *Tiny Angel*. Gordon Bale was the ball turret gunner aboard *Thunderbird* with the 303rd's 359th Bomb Squadron: "At the North Sea our fighter escort met us. It would have been difficult for any bandits to have challenged us this day. Fighter escort was below us and above us."[6]

In fact, the fifty-eight aircraft making up the unique formation were unmolested by the Luftwaffe's fighters as they made their way across France and into Germany. The weather over Cologne, as forecast, was spectacularly clear, and the formation took up a northeasterly heading preparatory to releasing the GB-1s. "About 20 miles from the city was a road running north and south," said Gordon Bale. "This was to be our dropping point. Spotting the road at a distance, we started a shallow dive. Airspeed built up quickly. The old lady began vibrating. Noise increased as George [Sirany] eased her up to the speed required for releasing the 'grapefruit.' My ball turret was whistling. Hank [Prussman], our bombardier, called bombs away. Away they went."

Dick Johnson was the copilot aboard *Betty Jane*, and his recollections were similar to Bale's: "We were to bomb by groups and our squadron, the 427th, went in first. Starting at 140 miles per hour [indicated airspeed] we started a shallow dive until we reached 208 mph. At this point, we leveled off for a few seconds and released the bombs nearly 18 miles from the target while flying at 195 mph. Unfortunately, our bombs, as well as those of the other two groups following, mostly spun in and exploded in fields 15 miles from the target."[7]

Bale remarked on the errant GB-1s: "They dropped about 300 to 400 feet straight down, straightened up and began gliding in a zig-zag course. Some of the bombs must have gotten their gyros dumped. Some went into tight, nose down spins. Some went into flat spins and some did acrobatics. It was quite a show. . . . We made a turn to the right and headed back to England." Black flak bursts appeared in the distance over Cologne, but the antiaircraft gunners were firing into empty skies. None of the GB-1 bombers came close to the city.

And for the most part, neither did most of the GB-1s. It is estimated that less than a third of the 109 weapons that were released—38 from the 303rd—actually made it to Cologne. "From the ball turret," Gordon Bale said, "I kept my eyes on the city of Cologne. We had been headed homeward for almost five minutes when I saw the first explosion. A giant burst of flame and smoke leaped skyward from one section of the city. A geyser of water leaped from the river running through the city. It must have been a half mile high to have been seen from such a distance at such clarity. We probably killed a few fish with that one. . . . I counted eighteen explosions before the city passed from view."

The effects of the raid on the Eifeltor marshaling yard were essentially nil. The mission, for all the effort and money that was spent on the GB-1—not to mention the secrecy and special training—was a failure. The Eighth's staff was unimpressed and the GB-1s were never used again.

When it is considered that the very real shortcomings of the GB-1 were understood beforehand, it is difficult to believe that there was a compelling operational reason for the May 28 mission against Cologne. Certainly it was encouraging that no aircraft were lost, but neither did the GB-1s inflict any meaningful hurt on the Germans. The GB-1 bombers would have done just as well had they never left their bases. It is likely that pressure from Arnold or his staff is what induced the Eighth to at least try the weapons on which so many resources had been spent.

It was speculated that the failure of most of the GB-1s to hold a steady course after being released was because the batteries that drove the gyroscopes were exhausted. Johnson recalled: "The stacks of bombs sat on the ground for so long that many of the batteries failed to hold charge, and so the [41st Combat Bombardment Wing] ordered a hundred new ones from the States. The Exide Battery Company said that they no longer made this type of battery, and that they would have to set up a complete assembly line, and therefore could produce no less than several thousand batteries. After all the hassle back and forth the batteries arrived at Molesworth after the mission was over. After it was decided to not fly any more glide bomb missions, the mechanics of the 427th Squadron used these batteries in an innovative lighting system for the barracks."

Aside from the batteries, the crates in which the GB-1 components were shipped to Molesworth were another windfall. They were constructed of furniture-grade black walnut. With the nation fully mobilized for a war in which expediency often took precedence over thrift, such waste was not uncommon. Happily though, the wood was salvaged, cut and finished into an exceptional bar at one of Molesworth's enlisted clubs. It was arguably the best thing to come out of the GB-1 project.

"I SURE DO GET HOMESICK AT TIMES"

THE NATURE OF AIR combat created scenarios and circumstances that could never have been foreseen. The reactions of the men to these situations generated unintended consequences. Such was the case on the May 19, 1944, mission to Berlin. Milo Schultz, the navigator aboard *Iza Vailable II*, recalled: "As we approached the target area of the city with the bomb bay doors open and prepared to drop on the lead bombardier's 'bombs away,' Ralph Sudderth, our bombardier, leaned back on his seat in front of me to kick the switch to drop bombs in train [one after another at preplanned intervals]. All of a sudden he fell off his seat and onto me. While he was on me the lead plane's bombs went away and the group started to turn away."[1]

With his crewmate flailing atop him and the 303rd turning away from the target, Schultz had precious little time to react. "I figured there was not time to let the bombs go in train so I reached over and kicked the salvo switch [releasing all the bombs at once]. Letting two-and-a-half tons of bombs drop all at once makes the plane jump very quickly. Don [Johnston] had to react fast to keep us from colliding with another plane in our squadron. I always wondered what damage I did or how many people I killed, maybe women and children, because those five, five-hundred pound bombs dropping in one spot was like a blockbuster. Only God knows."

ALLIED AIR COMMANDERS were growing increasingly frustrated that raids against the German aircraft industry were failing to achieve the desired effects. In fact, the Germans were in the process of dispersing their aircraft manufacturing centers to smaller plants that were less appropriate for aerial bombardment. Indeed, aircraft production increased through the spring and summer of 1944.

On the other hand those same Allied leaders began to appreciate that oil was a much more critical resource for the German war machine than they had previously supposed. Fuel was necessary to power trucks, tanks, ships and aircraft. Without it, the Third Reich would be crippled. Carl Spaatz, in particular, lobbied with some success during the early spring of 1944 for a hard-hitting campaign against oil targets. That campaign gained momentum slowly.

As part of that effort the Eighth sent more than a thousand aircraft against a set of synthetic oil plants on May 28, 1944. The raid was duly covered in the press just as most missions were. The *Lincoln Evening Journal*, of Lincoln, Nebraska reported: "The main force of Flying Fortresses and Liberators concentrated its fire bombs and explosives on synthetic oil plants at Merseburg, Zeitz and Latzkendorf (Lauchstedt) all within a 20-mile radius of Leipzig in central Germany. Ninety-three German planes were shot down, 32 by bombers and 61 by escorting fighters, against a loss of 34 bombers and 13 fighters."[2] The article did not dwell on the loss of the 34 bombers and the approximately 340 men who manned them, but went on to discuss other aspects of the raids.

That lives were lost in the raid is implicit in the article as well as others that covered similar missions throughout the war. Nevertheless, those lost lives are listed as numbers not names. Consequently it is worthwhile to examine the official and personal details of the loss of an individual within a crew, as it was men rather than numbers that died on the great bombing raids over Europe.

Acel Livingston was a B-17 crewman—a waist gunner—from Salt Lake City, Utah. During early 1944 he was the product of an American training machine that was in full stride, and he was one of many thousands of American flyers readying for overseas duty. The nation's plans to prepare virtually an entire generation for war had seemed overly ambitious even a couple of years earlier. But by mid-war those plans were being fully realized.

Livingston, part of the Alvin Determan crew, arrived at Kearney Army Airfield, Nebraska, on March 18, 1944. The crew's training was essentially complete by that date, and the men had already been given a new aircraft—a B-17G—to ferry to England. They stayed at Kearney only long enough to receive a clothing issue and a final flight physical before being ordered overseas. Livingston outlined what he believed was before him in a letter home:[3]

> We won't go to combat for awhile yet. First we will go to Scotland (probably) for some more training. After we get through with that we should be pretty well trained. Then all I have to do is to complete twenty-five missions and then I can come back to the states again. That shouldn't take so very long and from the reports they aren't losing very many planes on those raids any more.[4]

Acel Livingston and the rest of the Determan crew were assigned to the 303rd's 358th Bomb Squadron, and they flew their first combat mission on April 30, 1944. Livingston was at the right waist gunner position. The target was the Lyon/Bron Airdrome in France, and although the Luftwaffe made a showing, the only hurt the group sustained was a self-inflicted one. It occurred after the mission when one of the group's ball turret gunners injured himself as he unloaded his guns.

Bombs fall toward a target in Bremen. The wispy tendrils barely visible on the right are from smoke generators intended to obscure targets from bomber attacks.

The contrails of escorting fighters lace the sky above a formation of 303rd B-17s.

Military police provided security for the 303rd at Molesworth.

Unless otherwise indicated, all photos are courtesy of USAAF.

The tail section of *Helen Hiwater* after the mission of February 9, 1944, during which it had a midair collision soon after takeoff. Both aircraft returned safely.

Undoubtedly a staged photograph, it nevertheless emphasizes the skilled work required of the maintenance men.

The contrails created by the bomber formations were sometimes dense enough to provide cover for attacking German fighters.

Fabian Folmer, standing, was the crew chief for *Hell's Angels*. Not a single sortie would have been flown without hardworking men like Folmer and his comrades.

A tail gunner at his position. During actual operations the gunner would be wearing cold-weather clothing, an oxygen mask, goggles and head protection, as well as a flak suit.

A nice study of a B-17F in flight over Germany. *Meat Hound* was so badly shot up during the January 11, 1944, mission to Oschersleben that it never flew again.

The Ehle Reber crew gets a ride back from their aircraft sometime before being shot down on January 23, 1943.

Clark Gable, standing on the far right, flew his first mission of the war to Antwerp with the crew of the 303rd's *Eight Ball* on April 5, 1943.

Bombs fall toward the target from 303rd B-17Gs. Everything that was done by every man in every bomb group was done to deliver bombs onto the enemy. Note that the lowest bomb falling from the lead aircraft is a sky marker, just beginning to smoke.

ABOVE: A 303rd crew celebrates a milestone of some sort—perhaps their last mission.

LEFT: Jack Mathis was the first Eighth Air Force airman to receive the Medal of Honor. Mortally injured by a flak burst, he nevertheless stayed at his position and died as he released his ship's bombs on the submarine yard at Vegesack, on March 18, 1943.

A 303rd crewman demonstrates the close confines of the ball turret.

A radioman points his .50 caliber machine gun through the hatch at the top of his compartment. His worktable can be seen behind him to the left side of the photograph.

Robert Travis, the commander of the 41st Combat Bombardment Wing, just before leading the January 11, 1944, mission against Oschersleben. His sheepskin coat is personal. Also, note the necktie.

USAAF via Mark Forlow

Heavy antiaircraft fire marks the sky behind this 303rd B-17. A diving fighter can be seen in the upper left corner of the photograph.

A waist gunner at his position.

The three-dimensional nature of a bomb group's formation is apparent in this photograph.

A group of 303rd gunners receives a briefing. Eddie Deerfield is kneeling, fourth from right.

Crash personnel at Molesworth work to save a 303rd aircraft from fire.

Thumper was badly damaged on the January 23, 1943, mission to Brest. John Castle ordered the crew to bail out and made a wheels-up landing at Lulsgate Bottom. Billie Stander, the crew's right waist gunner, was killed when his parachute failed to open.

Carl "Tooey" Spaatz and James "Jimmy" Doolittle debrief with a 303rd crew near the end of the war. That the war took a toll on the USAAF's leadership is evident in Spaatz's face; he was only fifty-three when this photo was taken. Doolittle was only forty-eight.

Thunderbird, here pictured in April 1945 with her ground crew, survived the war as a veteran with 112 missions. Remarkably, no regular crew member was ever wounded on a combat mission while aboard the ship.

Irl Baldwin, the pilot of *Hell's Angels*, was the first bomber pilot in the Eighth Air Force to complete twenty-five missions.

Lieutenant Colonel Kermit Stevens, Colonel Charles Marion, and Colonel George Robinson celebrate the 303rd's first anniversary at Molesworth. Each of them commanded the group at some point, with Stevens being the most influential.

ABOVE: Princess Elizabeth of the Royal Family tours the 303rd on July 6, 1944. The *Rose of York* actually belonged to the 306th Bomb Group.

USAAF via Mark Forlow

LEFT: John Ford joined the service just before the United States entered the war. As an "old hand," he rose quickly in rank as a clerk and was indispensable to the smooth administration of the 303rd. *USAAF via John Ford*

Colonel Kermit Stevens and *Knock-Out Dropper* were two stalwarts of the 303rd.

Each aircraft was loaded with nearly 3,000 gallons of fuel before long-range missions.

Few men were in the 303rd longer than operations clerk Van "Rip" White. He joined the group at Gowen Field in Boise and was with it until after the war ended.

USAAF via Van White

Howard George Weinberg was the bombardier aboard the *Green Hill Belle*. He was killed on his first mission when his aircraft collided with another on April 6, 1945. The end of the war was only a month away. *Via Lois Brown*

As an enlisted man Mel Schulstad was selected for pilot training. He earned his wings to become a pilot and was one of the few who were with the 303rd from beginning to end. Here, he is a major.

Via John Schulstad

Another staged publicity shot of a ground crew working on B-17F *S for Sugar*. The ship was lost on the devastating mission to Oschersleben on January 11, 1944.

The combat crew and ground crew of *Hell's Angels*.

Old veteran *Thunderbird* is afire after its 102nd mission to Dresden on February 15, 1945. The ship survived and flew its last and 112th mission on March 22, 1945.

A contrail-creating formation of B-17s fly above a European cloudscape on the November 13, 1943, mission to Bremen. The contrails nearly hide at least two of the bombers.

The Grafton Smith crew was two men short after bombardier Bill Dohm and navigator Ed Gardner were forced to abandon their ship on the mission of January 10, 1945. Smith is center, standing. Al Dussliere, kneeling on the right, was particularly saddened when copilot Mel Alderman, standing on the right, was lost on his 35th and last mission on April 6, 1945.

The crew flew their second mission, a short hop to Sottevast in the Pas-de-Calais region of France, on May 8, 1944. The group's bombs fell wide of the target, which was a V-1 installation. Livingston wrote to his parents the following day, May 9, 1944:

> As yet I haven't heard from any of you yet but my mail isn't catching up with me very fast. I did receive a letter from Gloria [his new wife] last night and she wasn't feeling any too well. I sure do worry about her. . . . Well, I went to London on a pass and looked over the city. There were plenty of women there but I didn't bother with any of them because I already have one that I think too much of to go out with any others.

The Determan crew flew their next missions on May 11, May 12 and May 15, but Acel Livingston did not fly with them. Instead, a substitute, Edward Barteau, flew at the right waist gun—Livingston's normal position. Livingston did not mention these missed missions in his letters home, and it is possible that he was ill. He rejoined his crew on May 19 when the group hit Berlin. He wrote home three days later on May 22.

> I [sic] a letter from Gloria three days ago and she says that she would probably be down to visit with you soon. I sure do wish that I was where she could come to visit me every once in awhile. But I guess that I will just have to wait until this is all over and we can all be back home together. I sure do hope that it isn't to [sic] far off because I sure do get homesick at times. As long as they keep me busy I am alright but when they don't I get thinking about home and I sure do get lonesome.[5]

Livingston was indeed kept busy during the next several days. He flew the mission to Saarbrücken on May 23, the mission to Berlin on

May 24, the mission to Blainville, France, on May 25 and the mission to Mannheim on May 27.

On May 26, he sent another letter home.

Oh yes, she [his wife, Gloria] told me that she told you about the new addition we are going to have to our little family. I am proud and happy but I do worry about her health so much. I know that it is going to be hard on her but with the help of our heavenly father I know she will be alright. . . . Lately I have thought about being grounded but that would never do because I would never live it down and if my time comes to go, well it will happen wether [sic] I am in the air or on the ground.[6]

Livingston's mention of coming off combat duty leads to speculation that similar thoughts might have compelled him to miss the missions earlier in the month. Yet there is no evidence to support such conjecture. On May 28 the 303rd mounted two missions, one to Cologne and a second to Leipzig. The Determan crew was part of the mission to Leipzig, where the target was the Molbis thermal electric power station. It was the crew's fifth mission in six days, and it was marked by aggressive German fighter attacks. While the group made for an alternate target at Rotha because the primary target was obscured, a group of approximately twenty FW-190s hit the fifteen aircraft of the 303rd, heavily damaging three of them.

But it was antiaircraft fire that hit Determan's ship while the formation was turning toward the target. Francis Stender, a tail gunner in a nearby aircraft, described what happened in a statement for the Missing Air Crew Report: "The missing A/C [Determan's] received a direct hit close to #4 engine from A/A gunfire about 1435 hours in the vicinity of Leipzig, Germany. The right wing immediately caught fire. The A/C then slid under our A/C on out to the right past #2 position. The right wing came off, and the missing A/C then rolled over on its back and went down. As it did so, the tail came off about the entrance door.

Personally I saw no parachutes, but some of the others on the mission report seeing one."[7]

The Missing Air Crew Report, or MACR, for which Stender made his statement was an official USAAF document that described the circumstances associated with the loss of an aircraft, the personnel involved, eyewitness statements and serial numbers of important equipment such as the engines and machine guns—among other information. The AFPPA-11 was the Individual Casualty Questionnaire and was completed by a witness for each casualty. The closely related AFPPA-12 was the Casualty Questionnaire and was filled out by survivors. Robert Asman—the Determan crew's radio operator—completed these questionnaires postwar. When possible, as in the case of the Determan crew, German records supplemented the original report postwar.

In fact, the MACR shows that three men—possibly four—parachuted from the stricken ship. The pilot, Alvin Determan, was thrown from the aircraft with only one of his parachute snaps connected to his harness. Still, he made it safely to the ground and was captured at Pomssen by a German soldier who told him: "If you were English I would have shot you."[8] It is possible that the German was upset by the indiscriminate night bombing practiced by the RAF's Bomber Command.

Wayne Cope, who was flying as the right waist gunner—Livingston's normal position—was actually on the flight deck with Determan and copilot Ervin Pfahler after the aircraft was hit. Like Determan he parachuted to safety. Robert Asman was blown out of the aircraft at some point and was the third and last survivor. He recalled that a large section of the fuselage, from the radio room back, fell past him as he descended. Upon being made prisoner, he was told that three bodies were found in that particular piece of the bomber. Those bodies were of the engineer, Mervin Hendrickson; the tail gunner, Albert Carroccia; and Acel Livingston, the newly married father-to-be who had manned the left waist gun position.

In the front of the aircraft the navigator, Jackson Palmer, and the bombardier, James McCamy, also perished. It was McCamy's first mission with the Determan crew. The crew's normally assigned bombardier, Lamar Ledbetter, obviously missed the mission. He flew the following day and finished his combat tour on September 5, 1944. The copilot, Ervin Pfahler, was later reported by Cope to have been shot by civilians.

The body of the crew's ball turret gunner, Manuel Vasquez, was not found with the wreckage. The Germans tallied the crewmen they captured and the men they knew to be dead and realized that one of the flyers was still missing, as they noted in one of several reports included with the MACR: "According to state police and local police 1 (one) enemy flier was presumed to be still at large and was being looked for by army personnel and firemen."

But Vasquez was not alive. Rather, he and the ball turret had been blasted away from the bomber. Even had he survived the initial explosion he would have been doomed; there simply was not enough room in the ball turret for a gunner to wear a parachute or even to keep one close at hand. A later German report—included in the MACR—described the eventual recovery of his body: "On August 11, 1944, the corpse of the American flier Manuel Vasquez, Ser. Nr. 39693071 T 43-44 B, was found in the fields near Beucha, about 12 km east of Leipsig, in the process of decomposition." The report further detailed Vasquez's interment: "The dead flier was buried on August 12, 1944, 1100 o'clock on the 'Neuen Friedhof' (New Cemetery) of Beucha near Leipsig (western corner) in the presence of police chief John of Brandis and soldiers of Air Base Headquarters A 37/III."

There is no compelling evidence to support Cope's report of Pfahler's murder by German civilians. However, included in the MACR package is the German salvage report of the aircraft, which keeps the question open. It notes: "At the place of crash, west of Albrechtshain, 4 km southwest of Brandis, 5 dead crewmembers, whose identification was taken in hand at once, were found. Identification tags were found on four bodies [McCamy's was without]." This meant that one body, aside from Vasquez's, was not found with the wreckage. Yet six bodies were reported buried by the Germans on May 31, 1944. It is possible that Pfahler was captured and shot, and that his body was subsequently brought together with the bodies from the wreckage.

In fact, German records of the incident were quite extensive. Another document recorded the burial arrangements for the dead crewmembers: "The American aircraft (markings not to be found out, because they had been cut out by the salvage detachment) was downed May 28, 1944, 1430 English time (shown by the wrist-watch of a crewmember) above Beucha and crashed near Beucha west of Wolfshain. There the six dead [Vasquez's body had not yet been recovered] had been recovered by state police."

The report continued in detail: "The bodies were undressed in the morgue of the old cemetery of Beucha. Salvage detachment Oschatz furnished the coffins and took all military equipment and private property along. . . . Coffining and burial was accomplished by the detachment of the execution platoon 2, Brandis. The funeral took place in the presence of master of state police John from Brandis. The mayor of Beucha was not present." The report concluded with a description of the grave locations.

The Germans salvaged the bomber as outlined in a report dated June 1, 1944: "The aircraft, Boeing B-17G Fortress II, equipped with 4 radial engines Wright Cyclone 9, had crashed at two different places situated about 1200 m[eters] apart from one another. All secured implements, partly damaged very much, guns and ammunition are being shipped to the competent authorities. Wreckage of craft, saved to air base Brandis, is 90% destruction [sic]."

Among the other related documents that Livingston's kin later received was his Purple Heart Citation and, postwar, a letter notifying them of the location of his grave: "These [translated German] records also indicated that he was buried in the new cemetery of Beucha, grave number 5, on 31 May 1944, at 5:00 p.m. Beucha is located just north of Albrechtshain." Livingston's mother received a Gold Star Citation from the Salt Lake County chapter of the Service Star Legion "as visible evidence of its respect and lasting gratitude." It was the last citation in the world that a soldier's mother ever wanted to receive.

Finally, Livingston's mother received a letter of solace from Scottie Bergstrom, the nineteen-year-old wife of one of his friends from his time in training:

> We received your letter yesterday and have been feeling very badly about it ever since. It just doesn't seem possible anything could happen to Ace. He and my husband were together in Mississippi and were good buddies there, and slept next to each other. . . . Ace was a great guy Mrs. Livingston. He used to talk about his family a lot. Bergie [her husband] and I got a room in a hotel and Ace came up every night. He seemed to know everybody and was happy. . . . I know you all miss him terribly. Ace knows that, and he doesn't want you to grieve for him. Yes, he does know I'm sure, and I know that where he is, he's very happy. Let's be happy for him. He's better off than the rest of us. There's no night there.[9]

Ultimately, the families of 846 men of the 303rd Bomb Group received similar documents and expressions of sympathy and shared grief. These were the baby boys of 846 mothers and 846 fathers.

SEX WAS A UBIQUITOUS part of wartime life in England, especially London, the capital, and the locus of the Allied war effort in Europe. The urgency and danger of the war and the posting into the region of more than a million young, horny Americans—not to mention tremendous numbers of other Allied troops—created a sexually volatile dynamic. Dick Johnson recalled an experience: "While walking with a girl on Piccadilly Circus one evening, a newsboy hawking the London *Times* yelled, 'Hey, get your paper here!' Then in a sotto voice he said to me,

'Rubbers, I got 'em for sale.' When I didn't pay any attention to him he yelled, 'Give 'er a go, Yank, she's fourteen.'"[10]

"It was very embarrassing to me," Johnson said. "And nearly every newsboy or street urchin would yell the same thing. I think that they meant that the age of consent in England was fourteen at that time. I really didn't know."

And prostitution was very much a part of wartime England. This was especially so in London, where many Americans—sexually charged and with money to spend—were stationed, and where many more spent their time off. Van White remembered walking a girlfriend home from Rainbow Corner near Piccadilly Circus. "There was a little chapel on the way home. They kept a sign up front that said 'If you're tired of sin, please come in.' On this particular day there was a card tucked into the edge of the sign that said, 'And if you're not, call me at Mayfair 7345.'"

Dick Johnson recalled meeting a "nice looking young lady" at Piccadilly Circus during his first pass to London. The two of them went into a pub and chatted amicably. The conversation took an awkward turn when Johnson's companion guessed he was a virgin and declared that she could "relieve you of this burden" for the bargain price of three pounds.

"It finally dawned on me that this gal was a mercenary, a Piccadilly Commando," Johnson said. "I wouldn't have believed it when we first started talking." Caught off guard, a bit self-conscious and embarrassed— and mindful of the risks of venereal disease—Johnson declined her thoughtful offer. "So, I lied that I had to catch the next bus back to base. She seemed miffed that I had wasted her time."[11]

Ben Smith, one of the 360th's radio operators, discovered during a walk through St. James Park near Buckingham Palace that sex was oftentimes very public. "I was unprepared for what I saw, a plethora of ruttish couples gamboling and lying about the greensward quite impervious to the passersby. They simply spread newspapers over themselves to conceal their tender ministrations to each other."[12]

"I WAS TOLD SOMETHING BIG WAS GOING ON"

THE 303RD WAS IN ACTION—as was every Allied aviation unit in the European Theater—to support the defeat of Nazi Germany. However, notwithstanding the proselytizing of the most ardent airpower advocates, a second front in the West was imperative to victory. Eisenhower was determined that the Allied armies have every advantage possible when the time came to seize a foothold on the Continent, and he made that clear to the leaders of the Allied air forces. Accordingly, the focus of the Eighth Air Force was on tactical rather than strategic missions during the period immediately prior.

The Eighth, including the 303rd, was sent out to break anything and everything the Germans could use to resist the D-Day invasion. On June 2, 1944, the 303rd attacked gun emplacements at Dannes, France; a second raid on the same day hit railroad marshaling yards at Juvisy. During the next three days the group continued to hit gun emplacements all over northwest France even though B-17s—as strategic bombers—were not particularly well suited to hit targets of this sort.

Those tactically oriented missions aside, the effectiveness of the strategic bombing effort to which the Allied leadership had committed so many men and resources was validated. That leadership was overjoyed, even stunned, when the German Air Force offered no meaningful resistance whatsoever to the D-Day landings. Spaatz was particularly pleased and noted, "The concentrated attacks on the Luftwaffe, production and product, has paid the dividends that we have always envisioned, the dividend being beyond expectation."[1]

The 303rd's missions on the actual day of the invasion, June 6, 1944, were, like those of the Eighth's other heavy bomb groups, intended to break up lines of communication and to confuse and terrorize German ground troops. Accordingly, the thick clouds that blanketed the landing beaches and the areas beyond did not stop all the bombers from dropping their loads. Aim points were moved away from friendly positions as required, or the aircraft went to alternate targets. Don Stoulil, the PFF pilot, flew to Molesworth from Chelveston the night before D-Day. "I was told something big was going on and that we were flying with the 303rd. I gathered my crew and got over there okay, but couldn't find anywhere to sleep, so I spent the night in an easy chair in the pilot lounge."

Stoulil flew the lead aircraft on the 303rd's two effective D-Day missions. "General Travis flew with me on the second. It went well, but when I landed I bounced the plane a couple of times and he gave me a look. That bothered me a little bit because I had been up since the previous night and had already flown the lead aircraft on one mission that day—I was exhausted."

Still, Stoulil wasn't too exhausted to appreciate the history he not only witnessed through breaks in the clouds but also helped to create. "The stream of ships running across to France was incredible. There were so many and they were so well organized that it's impossible to explain the sight of it. During the first mission the battleships and cruisers and destroyers were still shooting beyond the beach and that was something to see."

By and large, the D-Day missions—of which the 303rd flew three— were anticlimactic. Thousands of Allied fighter sorties kept the Luftwaffe away, and there was little antiaircraft fire. Perhaps the biggest danger of the day for the 303rd's crews was the takeoff, as many of the aircraft were carrying not only full internal bomb loads but also a thousand-pound bomb under each wing. Indeed, after takeoff the 303rd's *Bonnie B* clawed through the air just a few feet above the ground and actually flew through a haystack before gaining altitude.[2]

UPI reporter Walter Cronkite was aboard the 303rd's *Shoo-Shoo Baby*, piloted by Robert Sheets. Like most of the 303rd's crewmen, Cronkite was dismayed that clouds obscured the formation's target: "Our bomb bay doors were open, our bombs were armed to go off on contact. But we couldn't see the target. And we couldn't see our own planes flying in close formation on either side. Any collision would probably set off a chain explosion, wiping out the squadron."[3] Cronkite was not a crewman, and he overdramatized the potential effects of a collision. Still, his hyperbole—considering the historic event, his avocation and his ignorance—is understandable. "Normally bombs would be jettisoned over enemy country, but our orders forbade that. No one knew in that first hour where our airborne [troops] had landed or even how far ashore the landing troops might have gotten." Ultimately, *Shoo-Shoo Baby* returned to Molesworth with its bombs, as did about a third of the 303rd's aircraft that day.

THE POST-INVASION PERIOD vexed Spaatz and Doolittle and their prosecution of the strategic bombing campaign. Firstly, the Eighth's priority, until released by Eisenhower, was to support Allied ground forces in France. This didn't mean that the entirety of the Eighth's operations were completely suborned to the ground commanders' needs, but the Eighth was obligated to provide bombing support on the battlefield if the requirement was considered great enough. Indeed, the requirement was constantly considered great enough, as the 303rd flew twenty-one more missions during the rest of June, of which only five were to Germany.

Additionally, the Germans began launching V-1 flying bombs against

England on June 12. The Allies had known of the V-1 and the more advanced V-2 ballistic missiles for some time. In fact, CROSSBOW operations had targeted the sites related to these two programs since late 1943. But when more than three hundred V-1s hit England on June 15, the general outcry was such that Churchill approached Eisenhower, and Eisenhower subsequently told Spaatz that CROSSBOW targets took precedence over all others. The problem was that V-1 targets, especially the launch sites, were widely dispersed, and heavy bombers were essentially incapable of hitting them. Consequently, masses of bombers bombed areas in which V-1 launch sites were believed to be hidden. The results were worse than dismal.

The problem with these other priorities was that they detracted from the Eighth's ability to pressure German industry. Bomber sorties that were wasted trying to hit unhittable V-1 sites were not available to strike oil or transportation targets. This was especially frustrating because summer was the "bombing season," during which longer daylight hours made very long-range bombing missions deep into Germany easier. Too, the weather was best during this time. It galled Spaatz to order Doolittle and the Eighth to chase after V-1 sites in the French countryside when those bombers might be better used against industrial targets in the heart of Germany.

Another use of the Eighth's heavy bombers during the summer of 1944 was their employment in support of Operation COBRA, the First Army's breakout from the bocage countryside of Normandy. The concept was for American troops to advance immediately after a massive air and artillery bombardment that included more than a thousand heavy bombers. It was a mission for which the B-24 and B-17 were not well suited. During two days characterized by sketchy weather, beginning on July 24, 1944, the big bombers mistakenly killed 136 American troops. A soldier on the ground remembered: "The first waves of bombers were on target but, the heavy cloud of smoke started drifting back over the infantry and, then the bombers started dropping their bombs on our own troops. Many of our infantry were killed, wounded, and stunned by this terrible error but, the attack went on as planned."[4] Of course, so too, were many of the German defenders.

WHILE THE REST of his 303rd friends quickly padded their mission counts with short missions that were mostly unopposed by German fighters during the period immediately after D-Day, Don Stoulil was idled. "That was another downside to being a PFF pilot. Everyone I knew was racking up easy missions really quickly. But most of those targets weren't appropriate for PFF operations—we were meant for long-range penetration missions against factories and such. So, after D-Day I sat around doing mostly nothing for a couple of weeks."

IT WAS A NEAR-MIRACLE. George Buske, the grievously injured tail gunner aboard the *Jersey Bounce Jr.* during the December 20, 1943, mission to Bremen, stopped dying during the spring of 1944. The abscesses on his legs and inside his abdomen began to heal and he gradually grew able to eat. He regained weight in part due to fresh eggnog made possible by a sympathetic Anglican vicar who provided the eggs. Additional operations closed Buske's wounds with skin grafts. Although his caregivers were awed at his recovery, they still worried that he might relapse as abdominal infections could be quick and deadly. Consequently, it was with real reservations that they evacuated him to the States during late June 1944.

TO MOST OF THE 303RD'S men, the Eighth Air Force's strategic air war against Germany seemed, understandably, to be a long grind of deadly sameness. But that wasn't so. Being so close to it, or perhaps being exposed to it for only months rather than years, they didn't see that it was a war made up of several phases, and of specific campaigns occasionally punctuated by exceptionally brutal battles such as Schweinfurt and Oschersleben. For instance, many of the 303rd's early missions were small, relatively short-range efforts that took off and landed during daylight. They were frequently sent against U-boat-related targets typically defended by aggressive fighter pilots as well as antiaircraft guns.

However, the U-boat war was being won at sea rather than ashore by late 1943. Consequently, the raids were biased toward more distant industrial targets. Moreover, per POINTBLANK, the Luftwaffe was increasingly targeted. It had to be neutralized prior to D-Day. This part of the air war reached a crescendo—with fighter escorts planned all the way to the targets—during ARGUMENT, although it continued through the invasion and beyond.

And then there was the crush of tactical missions that were flown in support of the ground war during the summer of 1944. These were short missions flown in quick succession, during which there often was little opposition whatsoever. These didn't resemble the missions of 1942 and 1943 at all. Although long-range strategic efforts were still flown, they were not so numerous, and crews consequently tallied large numbers of missions during a relatively short period.

The character of the air campaign changed again during the latter part of the summer of 1944 and into 1945 as the weight of the Eighth Air Force—and the Fifteenth Air Force in Italy—was thrown against oil, industrial and transportation targets located deep inside Germany and even beyond. The strategic forces were at full strength, and massive raids were mounted on an almost daily basis. Although German fighters were less numerous and regularly harried by the USAAF's fighter escorts, the Luftwaffe was still capable of deadly strikes; too, antiaircraft defenses were more concentrated and deadly. These were long, cold, bone-numbing missions that required the men to rise only hours after midnight. They often finished their debriefings and other duties just barely in time to get a few hours of sleep before rising and doing it all over again.

Indeed, it is reasonably argued that if the air war was made up of a series of phases and campaigns, it can also, from a historical perspective, be divided into two parts. The first was that period from the time of the first missions up until D-Day, and the second was from D-Day until the close of the war. Although this is not a crisp delineation, the series of tactical missions performed after June 6, 1944—in support of the invasion forces—represent the transitional period.

Certainly, the 303rd men who flew during this latter part were, by and large, not the men who flew during the group's initial combat operations. In fact, many of them were still in high school when the 303rd's original crews flew their first missions. They were, in effect, another generation who knew little or nothing of the men who preceded them.

Frank Boyle was one of them: "I was born in Montpelier, Vermont, in 1925," he said.[5] "My father worked in the lumber business and abandoned us when I was nine and my brother was five. All that my mother wanted was to be a good wife, a good mother and a good housekeeper. Instead, alone, she moved us to Nashua, New Hampshire, where she had grown up working in shoe mills and textile factories. There she raised us boys by cleaning other people's houses and doing their laundry seven days a week. She never received any child support—not a dime. I know it was hard for her when we asked why we couldn't have bikes and the other sorts of things that our neighborhood friends had.

"But my mother had eight sisters and a brother in Nashua," Boyle said. "And I had forty cousins. We were a typical French-Canadian family and tight as ticks. We yelled and argued and fought with each other all the time, but we always closed ranks around family. Woe to the outsider who tried to do harm to any one of us. Keeping the family together and safe was very important, and we always had help when we needed it.

"My priority wasn't schoolwork. And I know that I wasn't always the best son; there was no father to take a belt to me when I needed it. But I worked various jobs and helped however I could. I set pins at a bowling alley where a horse and dog booking business was run in the back room. And I worked in various department and shoe stores.

"Although I didn't study as hard as I could have, I did pretty well in school," Boyle said. "I had the lead in the senior play and I won the senior essay writing contest. I skipped fourth grade and was only sixteen when I graduated in the upper quarter from Nashua High School. But I was too young to join anything but the Boy Scouts, while all my friends had either been drafted into the service or enlisted. So, I took a job working the night shift at Nashua Textile Company. I folded Army blankets on an assembly line and was paid based on the number of blankets I folded."

All through 1942 and into 1943—a time during which the 303rd's first generation of crews were pioneering daytime precision bombing operations—Boyle considered how he might do his part in the war. "I didn't want to get eaten by sharks or get stabbed with a Jap or German bayonet. I got a call one morning from the mother of one of my closest high school friends. She asked if I wanted to go with their family to see her oldest son—Lieutenant Dick Messier—fly into Boire Field. He was flying fighters in the Navy.

"Well, I sure wasn't going to miss that. He came in with his cockpit open and a white scarf blowing in the wind. I'll never forget that picture and how he looked with his leather helmet and goggles. After we visited with him, he took off and waved to us. I knew that's what I wanted to do."

But Boyle was still too young. "I went to city hall to enlist in the Navy the very next day. They laughed at me when I gave them my high school records and birth certificate. The sailor I talked with said I had to wait until I was eighteen. He told me that I might want to go next door to see the Army. He said the Army cheated on that sort of thing."

The Army recruiter was happy to see Boyle and enlisted him immediately. "I was going to be a fighter pilot!" But his dream was shortlived. Early during processing and classification, on little more than pretense, Boyle was caught up in an unofficial draft for gunners. He was sent to aerial gunnery school and subsequently joined a B-17 crew. He arrived at Molesworth just after D-Day.

The war became very real very quickly to Boyle. "After supper we enlisted men went to our Nissen hut. They typically put two crews in one hut. As the new crew, we were assigned to the upper bunks, while the crew that had been there longer used the lower bunks. For a welcome we were each given a bottle of English beer—it was much stronger than what we were used to.

"There were boards ripped from the bottoms of bomb crates nailed to the ceiling above our bunks. The boards listed the mission numbers, dates and targets of the men who had slept in our bunks before us. None of the five boards above mine had more than fourteen missions. The guys who had been there awhile just shrugged and said that maybe I would be the first one to pass the fourteen-mission mark."

BEDS TO WHICH THEIR OWNERS would not return—and everything they signified—was a recurring and sobering theme in the 303rd. Indeed it was a reality shared by every Eighth Air Force flying unit. Eddie Deerfield recalled that "the empty bunks were as solemn as grave markers at a cemetery."

"I BECAME A SORT OF ORPHAN WITHIN THE BOMB GROUP"

THERE WERE INCIDENTS during which men were lost or killed for reasons that were never determined. An example occurred during the mission of June 10, 1944, which hit the airfield at Bouguenais, just southwest of Nantes. While the group formed after takeoff, the ship flown by Sam Oliver and his crew fell off to the left and into a dive.

Oliver recovered the ship, *Bam Bam*, and climbed back to rejoin the 303rd's formation. Nevertheless, the aircraft once more dropped into a dive and subsequently started to spin. A short time later an explosion blew the aircraft in half. Oliver, his copilot and four others were killed, while four crewmen parachuted to safety.

No cause was found for the mishap, although it was speculated that flight control problems were the culprit—that the controls might have been jammed somehow. Such a notion is plausible, but it seems unlikely that a pilot would choose to continue the mission after recovering from the first unplanned dive unless he believed that the problem was resolved. It is possible that the aircraft's automatic flight control equipment was somehow engaged and that it caused the aberrant maneuvers, but again, the pilot would likely have elected to return to base. And neither explanation accounted for the midair explosion.

The ship was a veteran of forty-four missions and had given good service to that point, although crewmen had earlier complained of strong gasoline fumes. It might be conjectured that fuel vapors doped the pilots stupid or unconscious. However the B-17 was not a pressurized aircraft and it was drafty. Consequently, it is questionable that the fumes could have become concentrated enough to cause such disorientation, or to ignite and blow the aircraft apart. Ultimately, regardless of the cause, six men were dead—and not due to enemy action. Nothing could bring them back.

That same mission provided an example that underscored another point. That is, when men were wounded badly enough to need extensive hospitalization, their association with the 303rd was abruptly terminated, usually for good. They went from their aircraft, to the ambulance, to a hospital and back to the States. Seldom were there opportunities for farewells. Men they had trained and lived and fought with were suddenly out of their lives forever.

Such was the case with Milo Schultz, the navigator aboard *Idaliza* on the June 10 mission to Bouguenais. He was fairly relaxed; the D-Day invasion was proving successful and losses had been light. Enemy fighters failed to show on the way to the target and there was little flak. But heavy antiaircraft fire rose to meet them as they approached Bouguenais. "Over the target, as [the] bombs went away, a blast below the nose kicked my left leg," Schultz said.[1] "I looked down and saw blood oozing out of my flying boot and running down the floor to the bulkhead. I called Don [Don Johnston—the pilot] on the interphone to tell him I'd been hit.

"There never was any pain, only numbness," said Schultz. "Don sent [Abraham] Barnum the engineer down to aid me. He gave me a shot of morphine and put a tourniquet on to stem the blood flow which was freezing on the floor at 26,000 feet and 20 below zero. I don't recall the toggler doing anything. Maybe he was in shock at seeing all the blood.

"We had to ease up on the tourniquet about every twenty minutes so that I'd have some blood in my veins," said Schultz. "With the morphine kicking in I was a pretty happy flier back to base. As we approached the field, Don fired off a red flare signaling wounded on board. This procedure gave the pilot priority for landing. I don't recall if they took me out the front hatch door or whatever. The last I remember I was in the operating room with the doctors taking my boots and shoes, and cutting my pants."

On the operating table, the doctors laid Schultz's leg open and scraped out all the bits of clothing, boots and shrapnel that threatened to infect the wound. Because his fibula was shattered, there was no clean way to close the jagged gash. A wheeled razor sliced and peeled a neat two-inch-wide strip of skin from another section of his leg. This unblemished skin was transplanted over Schultz's wound, medicated and bandaged.

"I awoke sometime during the night at the station hospital to see a beautiful blonde nurse next to my bed. I think I drifted back to sleep and awoke the next morning to finally realize I had a cast on my left leg up to my thigh." Schulz spent several weeks recovering while the war went on and his comrades at the 303rd continued to fly, fight and sometimes die. During the whirl of combat operations there was little opportunity to visit recovering comrades. "Don [Johnston] was the only member of our crew to visit me," Schulz said. Except for Johnston, the last time Schulz saw his crewmates was the day they pulled his bloody body from *Idaliza*. He was sent back to the States during October 1944 and was medically discharged almost a year later following the surrender of Japan.

There were other variations on the same theme. Because squadron rosters changed almost daily as veteran crews departed, new crews arrived, and crews were shot down, there was no way for every man to know every other man in his own squadron. Consequently, men pulled from their own crews and assigned as substitutes to other crews for a particular mission often found themselves flying with strangers. Indeed, it was not unusual for a substitute crewman to climb aboard his assigned bomber and prepare his position without meeting everyone on the crew.

William Fisher, a navigator with the 359th, offered an extreme example: "On my third mission, I was pulled from my original crew to fly in Lieutenant J.W. Bailey's plane as deputy lead. After briefing I entered the plane via the nose hatch. After our bomb run we had two engines shot out and we fell behind the formation. We were attacked by German fighters. The pilot ordered the crew to bail out, which I and the enlisted crew did. But as I heard later, the pilot and copilot remained in the plane for awhile and eventually bailed out into free France. The rest of us were captured and became POWs. To this day, I have never seen the pilot or copilot."[2]

Some of the men did stay in touch. Chris Balzano was a waist gunner and radio operator with the 358th Bomb Squadron. He finished his tour on May 12, 1944, and subsequently returned to the States. Upon arriving home, he wrote a letter on June 12, 1944, to a friend, Joe Worthley. Worthley was a pilot with whom Balzano had flown missions.

It was good to hear from you. I guess your [sic] darn near finished up, I hope, I hope. Say, how about me missing the big show [D-Day]? Wish I were there, wish I were there (heh, heh). I'm just a flag waver since I've been home. Boy what a place. Sunshine once again, steaks and stuff, no more blackouts. It's like a dream. You can't beat these good old United States and I'm not kidding.

Mail and personal news traveled slowly. Sadly, Balzano didn't know when he penned the note that his friend had already been dead for nearly three weeks. Joe Worthley and his crew perished during the mission to Berlin on May 24, probably before Balzano even stepped foot back in the States.

MANY BOMB GROUPS, including the 303rd, put a copilot in the tail gunner's position of the lead aircraft of each squadron, to include the group leader's aircraft. As an aerial observer he relayed details about the formation to the pilot, who could not see to the rear. The observer told him when the group was fully rendezvoused after takeoff, which crews were straggling or flying poor formation and which aircraft aborted or were shot down—among other information. Thusly informed, the lead pilot could make adjustments as required. Moreover, after the mission he could counsel crews who performed poorly.

Indeed, the 303rd's SOP required the aerial observers to act as snitches to a certain degree: "The lead squadron aerial observer will rate the lead aircraft of the high and low squadrons on the quality of their squadron leadership in relation to group formation on the basis of 'excellent,' 'good,' 'fair' or 'poor.'" The grading of individual pilots was required to be even more detailed: "The aerial observer in each squadron will rate all the pilots in that squadron on a numerical basis with the pilot flying the best formation as #1 and so on through #12. The pilots are to be rated on their overall formation flying throughout the mission with the greater emphasis placed on the correctness of formation flying during the bomb run."

Earl Douglass of the 358th Bomb Squadron flew more than his fair share of these missions. After arriving at Molesworth during the spring of 1944, his original crew was shot down while he was flying with an experienced crew to get familiar with actual combat operations. "So, I became a sort of orphan within the bomb group,"[3] he said.

"My squadron operations officer 'requested' that I volunteer to serve in the tail gunner position because the Top Brass wanted a qualified pilot to be the eyes behind the mission commander's head to make sure that all the planes in the group maintained proper formation. It was important for us to stay in a tight, carefully-designed flying formation to maximize our defensive firepower, and to keep all the bombs on target." Accordingly, Douglass flew most of his combat missions in the tail turret position.

However, Douglass's experience was the exception, as observer duty was generally a rotating assignment rather than a permanent one. Dick Johnson took his turn on the mission to the Pas-de-Calais on June 19, 1944:

> *When I got into the tail gun position with electrically heated suit and gloves, I was out of my element. I made out OK during formation and departure. But when I was about settled down, after advising the pilot that everything seemed good about the formation, I noticed that the [autopilot] that we called "George" was causing a good bit of movement at my new position. The swaying and yawing soon made me airsick. Not only that, I couldn't figure out how to fire the tail guns. I tried several times, finally giving up, as I figured that no enemy plane would attack from the rear, since all I could see behind me was hundreds of B-17s filling the sky for as far as I could see.*[4]

Johnson's airsickness grew worse and he took off his flak helmet, intending to vomit into it. He managed to hold his breakfast down, but his nausea continued. "It got to the point that I wouldn't have cared if I were shot down." As it happened, the short mission was entirely uneventful. There were no enemy fighters, nor was there any flak. The group dropped its bombs, missed its target and returned to Molesworth. Johnson couldn't have asked for an easier mission.

Some time later Johnson went off the base to relax at the Key Club near Molesworth. He enjoyed himself well into the early morning. As the crew's regularly assigned aircraft was undergoing heavy mainte-nance, he was certain he would not be flying if there was a mission scheduled. "I didn't get back to the barracks until about three AM and discovered with panic that the place was deserted. I quickly checked the manifest and saw that I was again assigned to fly tail gun position in the lead plane for an unexpected mission that morning."

Frantic—and sure he would find himself the object of court-martial proceedings—Johnson raced to the briefing room and breathlessly declared himself ready to go. He was stunned but relieved when he discovered there was no fuss at his absence; a replacement had been found. "I hadn't told them about my near fatal airsickness and I can imagine what would have happened to me if I had taken the flight. After having a 'few' drinks and no breakfast, I would have been in prime shape for a major barf."[5]

During the June 19, 1944, mission to the Pas-de-Calais area a milestone was achieved that was significantly more remarkable than Johnson's mission as an observer. The 303rd's John Tulloss had arrived at Molesworth on April 11 and flown his first mission as a pilot with the 359th Bomb Squadron on April 24. The June 19 mission—fifty-seven days after his first combat sortie—marked the completion of his combat tour. In that short time he was credited with thirty-one missions. It was an Eighth Air Force record.[6]

Tulloss's example underscores an interesting point. Although the maintenance men and other support personnel generally served in the 303rd for the duration of the war, such was not the case for the combat crews. Rather they flew out of Molesworth until they completed their required missions and then—for the most part—rotated back to the States. There were exceptions. For instance, Mel Schulstad flew his share of missions and more—forty-four—and was with the unit from the beginning of its combat operations until the end. Joe Vieira was another of those who flew many more missions than required. "I flew 58 missions which is more than two full tours. I came home in between and spent a few days with my old lady. When she heard I was going back, she didn't say twenty words to me."[7]

But for the most part the crews who flew the early missions and survived to go home would have recognized virtually no one flying from the base a year later. And many of the flyers who followed them to Molesworth during 1943 were gone before D-Day. Likewise, those who flew during the frenzied period before and after the invasion were rotated back to the States a few months later. And the crews who arrived during the last few months of the war considered as hoary ancients anyone who had been around even a year earlier.

Nevertheless, although the early crews were back in the States, dead, or being held as POWs, they were still, in a very real sense, part of the 303rd until the end of the war. The experience they gained at such a high cost in blood, exertion and spirit was incorporated into the group's operations, not only to increase its effectiveness but also to better the odds of survival for later crews. These lessons were shared across the Eighth, much as the 303rd embraced improved practices from other bomb groups.

For instance, formations were modified to better defend against enemy fighter attacks. Similarly, bombing procedures for the bombardiers and fire discipline for the gunners were improved. Less remarkable but still important were changes to the administrative aspects of mission operations, such as taxi, takeoff and assembly procedures.

In fact, a few of the 303rd's men dreaded the takeoff and assembly as much as they feared enemy flak and fighters. In order to lessen the risk, the group evolved stringent Standard Operating Procedures, or SOP, for takeoff and assembly in various sorts of weather. The normal procedures during daytime when the weather was clear were fairly straightforward: "Takeoff will be made at 30-second intervals for all aircraft in the group. The copilot will check [the] time and notify the pilot when the aircraft ahead has been moving 30 seconds. . . . The flight leader will climb at 150 I.A.S. [indicated airspeed] and at 400 FPM [feet per minute] straight ahead for 90 seconds from the time the aircraft started from takeoff position, then make a needle-width turn to the left, fly back to the field circling the East-West runway to the left at 2,000 feet altitude. Wingmen will turn inside flight leaders to accomplish 'join-up.' Right wingmen will fly under leader for 'join-up.'"

The procedures for takeoff and assembly during poor weather were more demanding and required the group to use the Harrington Buncher Beacon, twenty miles to the west. The beacon was a radio navigation aid that emitted a homing signal. "Takeoff will be as normal except that each A/C [aircraft] will continue for 90 seconds at 150 I.A.S. climbing 400 FPM straight ahead on runway heading, then make a needle-width turn to the Harrington Buncher Beacon, homing on the Buncher with an air speed of 150 I.A.S. and 400 FPM climb. In the event cloud tops are such that 303rd aircraft are still in the clouds on reaching Harrington Buncher, climb will be continued until aircraft are in the clear before turning to home on Buncher. At no time will any aircraft make a turn while in an overcast."

These procedures demanded strict adherence. For instance, the risk of a midair collision increased if just one of the thirty, or forty, or more crews flew ten or twenty miles per hour too fast or slow, or turned too early or late, or climbed at a different rate than prescribed. If more than one crew deviated from the procedures, the danger increased significantly. Another consideration that increased the chances of a mishap was the fact that two other bomb groups also used the Harrington Buncher Beacon, although each group was assigned its own particular altitude block.

Early morning takeoffs in the dark compounded the perils even further. "I hated taking off in the dark," said Don Stoulil. "The tail gunners in each aircraft used their Aldis lamps to flash the identity of their particular bomb groups in Morse code. For instance, our tail letter was 'C,' which was a flash, a shorter flash, a flash and then a short flash again. It helped everyone to figure out who was who. But still, when a mission was on, there were blinking lights everywhere, and it was often difficult to tell if they were coming or going, or turning or not. It could be very disorienting."

Squadron leaders fired flares to lessen the confusion. The B-17 had a socket, or port, overhead the pilots into which an M2 or AN-M8 pyrotechnic pistol could be inserted. The 303rd's SOP prescribed the procedures: "Announcement over V.H.F. as to when flares are being fired will be made by squadron leaders. Example: 'Hello all Cowboy Able [radio call sign for the 303rd's lead aircraft of the lead squadron] aircraft, this is Cowboy Able leader . . . standby for flares. Hello all Cowboy Able aircraft, flares away.'"

The 303rd also used war-weary assembly ships to help get its aircraft together. In some instances, as with the *Wabash Cannonball*, the aircraft were simply squadron hacks used to scout the weather before the main formation took off. They subsequently helped shepherd the group's aircraft together as they got airborne. However, the 303rd also specially modified one of its ships—the *Vicious Virgin*—as an assembly ship, as described by Dick Johnson:

> *The ground crews had installed 21 high intensity lights on the airplane which flashed the letter "C" in Morse code while it was acting as formation [assembly] ship. It was painted with red and white [and blue] stripes that were ten feet wide in a diagonal pattern. As a combat bomber it had been named* Vicious Virgin. *This was changed to* Scarlet Harlot *after the paint job, and I sometimes referred to her as* The Virgin Harlot. *Mostly though, we referred to the plane as* The Barber Pole.[8]

This practice became common within the Eighth Air Force as different bomb groups operated outlandishly painted aircraft on which their own aircraft would form after takeoff. Once the formation was established, the specially painted aircraft detached and recovered back to base.

The 303rd had one more tool in its box. Late in 1944, on a visit to an RAF base, the group's commanding officer, William Raper, discovered a P-47 that had diverted into the base with mechanical problems and been essentially forgotten. Raper made arrangements for maintenance men from the 303rd to make the aircraft flyable and subsequently took it home to Molesworth.

Raper ordered the P-47 painted with the 303rd's markings and had the aircraft's eight .50-caliber machine guns removed. He also had it waxed, named it *Peck O' Trouble* and subsequently used it to ride herd on the group's assemblies. He flitted here and there among the big bombers, directing, haranguing and cajoling until the group was satisfactorily assembled.

Despite all the special procedures, equipment and uniquely modified aircraft, post-takeoff assemblies did not always go perfectly. While the 303rd was getting together for the raid to Merseburg on July 28, 1944, Dick Johnson was forced to turn away from the formation to avoid a midair collision with another bomber that was obviously out of place. "By the time I returned to the assembly area, the 303rd Group was too far ahead for me to catch up, so I latched onto the 379th out of Kimbolton, which I knew was going to the same target. Many pilots aborted when they couldn't find their group and I didn't want this stigma attached to me."[9]

While joining with another group might seem an obvious choice, such a decision was not clear-cut. This was because bombers were not typically topped off with fuel before a mission, but rather carried only enough—with reserves—to make it to the target and back. As groups were often assigned to different targets, a crew that chose to join another group without knowing its destination might find itself out of gas before making it back to base. In fact, the 41st Combat Bombardment Wing's SOP gave very clear direction:

> The pilot will make every effort to join his assigned squadron. Failing to do this, he will attempt to join his own group. Failing in this, he will attempt to assemble on some other group of his combat wing. As a last resort he will assemble with some other group of _any_ [emphasis in original] combat wing, providing his fuel loading is sufficient for the mission assigned that combat wing. Abortives resulting from failure to rendezvous _will not be condoned_. Aircraft will not complete a mission individually unless so ordered.

The crews were able to distinguish aircraft from different groups by their tail markings. Each bomb group was assigned a unique letter, which was to be painted prominently on its vertical stabilizer—or tail. The 303rd was assigned the letter "C," and when it started operations during late 1942, each aircraft's vertical stabilizer was painted with a big yellow "C." However, as more groups arrived in England, the markings were modified during the summer of 1943 by painting the letters within a white, geometric shape. For instance, the shape assigned to groups of the 1st Bomb Division was a triangle, whereas the groups of the 2nd Bomb Division were assigned a circle, and the groups of the 3rd Bomb Division a square.

The 303rd thus became readily recognizable as the "Triangle C" group. At the same time the triangle was adopted, the markings were also added to the upper surface of the right wing and the lower surface of the left wing. The ultimate version of the marking, and the one by which the group is most remembered, was carried by the aircraft beginning during August 1944. A large, red triangle—twelve feet per side—was painted around the white triangle with its letter "C." This new scheme made the white triangle marking more visible on the bare metal finish that was typical of the aircraft assigned to the group beginning in February 1944.

The 303rd's squadrons could be distinguished from one another by code letters painted on the fuselage forward of the Stars-and-Bars national insignia. For instance the code letters for the 358th, 359th, 360th and 427th were VK, BN, PU and GN respectively. Individual aircraft call letters were painted on the fuselage aft of the national insignia.

As much as the 303rd worked to prevent midair collisions they remained a hazard throughout the war. Typical was the mishap on November 9, 1944, when two aircraft from the 427th Bomb Squadron came together. Both ships went down and only one crewman managed to bail out; the rest were killed. The group's commanding officer received a letter a few days later that included a one-pound note and a message: "Would you please place a small floral tribute on the graves of the boys, so far from home, who lost their lives near here?" It was signed, "A Wenlock Mother."[10]

* * *

ASIDE FROM THE BUNCHER BEACONS, there were also "Splasher" beacons that were used to navigate out of and back into England. They proved invaluable in helping crews recover during foul weather. That they were ubiquitous is indicated by a warning in the 303rd's SOP: "Care should be taken in tuning radio beacons and Bunchers because of the great number of stations in England." Too, the crews had to be wary of signals that were corrupted or co-opted by the Germans. More than one crew was tricked into flying out to sea, where they ran out of fuel.

Some aircraft, usually flown by lead crews, were equipped with GEE-H equipment. A British development, GEE-H used radio beams to derive a fairly precise navigational fix for bombing through the clouds. It was useful only to a range just beyond about three hundred miles from England and was susceptible to jamming. However, it was exceptionally useful as a navigational aid throughout the war.

"WE POURED THEM INTO THE BACK OF THE AIRPLANE"

"WE BOMBER PILOTS decided to throw a party for our fighter pilot friends [20th Fighter Group] who were at a base [Kingscliffe] about twenty miles away," said Mel Schulstad. "It was a hilarious evening of mostly drinking a lot of whiskey. As the party was winding down at about two in the morning [of July 24, 1944], the fighter guys were ready to go home, but the truck drivers who brought them over had left. So we were stuck with about twelve fighter pilots who wanted to go home."

Schulstad—who had partied through the evening—decided to fly them home in *Tugboat Annie*. There were few, if any, American aircraft still in service that had been in England longer. Originally named *Phyllis*, it was an old B-17E that entered service with the 97th Bomb Group during March 1942, months before the Eighth flew its first mission. It was subsequently passed from the 97th to the 92nd Bomb Group in August 1942 and was eventually transferred to the 303rd during May 1943. During its relatively long life it was repaired and modified a number of times and suffered major damage after a midair collision. The 303rd used it as a target tug for gunnery practice and as a formation assembly ship prior to missions.

"So I took my friends the fighter pilots out there," said Schulstad, "and we poured them into the back of the airplane. Then we flew them back to their base and told them to get out." Once his friends were clear of the hard-used bomber, Schulstad got airborne again in short order and turned south for Molesworth. His copilot was actually not a pilot but rather the group's administrative officer, Harry McDaniel, who had gone along simply for the ride. They arrived over Molesworth only a few minutes after taking off. "It was a beautiful moonlit night," Schulstad said. "It was calm and quiet and I flew the downwind leg and made a lovely turn onto base leg and put the landing gear down; I could hear it go 'round-round-round-round' and then *chunk* into place. And then I put the flaps down.

"I was sitting on final approach with everything just beautiful and my copilot sound asleep. And I thought I'd better check the gear and the flaps one more time." For whatever reason, Schulstad activated the switches rather than simply checking that they were in the proper position. The landing gear and flaps—which were already down and ready for landing—obeyed his errant command and pulled themselves back into the aircraft.

Schulstad didn't notice. An actual copilot—and one who was awake—would likely have caught the mistake, but Schulstad's ad hoc crewman was no help. "I flared out for this magnificent landing," he said, "and heard all four props hit the cement. We spread that ancient B-17 from one end of the runway to the other. At five o'clock in the morning. With no copilot." Schulstad knew he was in trouble.

No one was hurt, and the B-17 and the pieces it shed were scraped clear of the runway. "It was an incident that had to be reported," said Schulstad. "And it made its way up to the wing commander's [Travis] office, and he said something about a court-martial." Schulstad agonized for more than a week as he waited for the powers-that-be to determine what sort of action might be taken against him.

"About ten days elapsed," said Schulstad, "and I had chewed off all my fingernails worrying about what was going to happen." Schulstad's roommate, Mel McCoy, was the chief engineering officer for the 444th Sub Depot, which was responsible for performing major repairs to the 303rd's damaged aircraft. "He came in one day and told me that the airplane I crashed was built from other old airplanes. 'We never technically received that airplane,' he said. And I asked him if he meant that the airplane never actually existed. And he said, 'That's exactly right.'"

At Schulstad's urging McCoy talked to the proper people and made certain that the information made its way up the chain of command to Brigadier General Travis. "They brought it up to the wing commander, who was a very wise gentleman, and he said, 'Obviously, if the airplane never existed it could never have been in an accident and so then that's the end of that.'"

Although he did not mention it, it is quite likely that Schulstad was also given a pass because he was one of the group's original "old hands." Aside from having led and survived some of the 303rd's most dangerous missions, he was invaluable in planning operations and he lent expertise wherever and whenever he could. And unlike the vast majority of aircrews, he stayed at Molesworth until the end of the war.

In fact, he wrote home about his views on staying in England: "All in all, with my experiences, travels, meeting people, [and] opportunities, I wouldn't miss this, the greatest show on earth, for love or money. Matter of fact, I find it increasingly hard to understand these fellows who want to get home. Maybe it's because they have a wife and children, or maybe they are just too small-minded to appreciate their opportunities." Schulstad was correct in noting that there were opportunities aplenty to learn, gain experience and advance in rank. However, among those opportunities were many different ways to be killed.

SCHULSTAD'S STRONG AFFINITY for his fighter pilot comrades was near universal among the bomber men. A postwar study noted that the feeling of kinship was very strong indeed: "To combat crews few sights were lovelier than the prancing of friendly fighters around bomber formations during the quiet stretches of a mission, or more breathtaking than their sudden appearance—deus ex machina–fashion—at an instant of ultimate extremity. Bomber crewmen who had ever stared straight at an onrushing FW-190 for long seconds before catching a glimpse of a P-51 on its tail would not soon forget the emotions of that moment."[1]

DURING THE MONTHS following the D-Day invasion, the Luftwaffe was increasingly dominated by the American strategic bombing effort. At that point the USAAF's escort fighters handily outnumbered the defending Germans. Moreover, the American pilots were better trained, more aggressive and flew superior aircraft—excepting the new German Me-262 jet, which was only on the cusp of starting real operations. Still, the German flyers were not totally beaten or driven from the sky. Indeed, on a spasmodic basis, they still achieved startling successes. But for the most part those successes were realized only when the bombers were caught without their fighter escorts.

The 303rd was without fighter escorts at the wrong time on August 15, 1944. During the preceding three weeks—from July 24 to August 14—the group had flown eighteen missions without a single combat loss. It had never before enjoyed such a streak and would never again; it was an incredible achievement. However, the odds of air combat were not to be denied, and the mission to Wiesbaden on the following day was proof.

The group put up thirty-nine aircraft on August 15, 1944, and although they endured heavy and accurate flak in the target area, they were unmolested by fighters until about fifty miles west of Wiesbaden on the return leg. The mission report noted: "Up to this time friendly fighter support had been good, but the fighters had left the bombers and were not in sight."[2] At that point about thirty Luftwaffe fighters took advantage of the breakdown in the escort coverage and attacked the 303rd's low formation, which was made up of thirteen aircraft from the 358th and 427th squadrons.

The intensity of the attacks and the resultant slaughter were as gruesome as anything the 303rd sustained during its entire combat career. The incident underscored what had already been proven a year earlier at Schweinfurt: Unescorted heavy bombers could not defend themselves against determined enemy fighter attacks. That fact notwithstanding, the gunners still put up a curtain of gunfire. That curtain grew increasingly threadbare as bomber after bomber was hacked out of the sky.

Tiny Angel exploded under the onslaught and fell away in pieces. *Jigger Rooche* also went down, with six of its crew. The low group's lead aircraft, *Fearless Fosdick*, dropped out of the formation in flames. The navigator, Lawrence Wolf, was struck in the back by a 20-millimeter cannon shell and killed. The rest of the crew parachuted clear of the burning wreck and managed to evade back to England.

The right wing was blasted from *My Blonde Baby* and it fluttered to earth. An unnamed aircraft piloted by Alfred Smith was also shot down and three of its crewmen were killed. Another unnamed ship, this one captained by William Crawford, fell to the enemy fighters. All of its crewmen survived and were captured. A third unnamed ship, captained by John Cathey, was set afire by an Me-109; one crewman was killed, six were captured and two evaded. The Roman Charnick crew's B-17 literally blew up around them. Still, there were seven survivors, one of whom successfully escaped back to England.

FW-190s hacked away at *Hell in the Heavens*, and five of its crew dribbled out of the doomed bomber over a ten-minute period and were captured; the rest of the men were killed. *Bad Penny* was attacked and simply blew up. Pieces of flaming wreckage fell onto a farm and set several buildings afire. Incredibly, every crewman parachuted clear of the explosion. The navigator, Lester Reuss, came down in a tree. On the spot were two unarmed German soldiers, who came to help him down. A uniformed Nazi party official arrived soon after and shot

Reuss. Reuss was then beaten to death with a hammer and club by two German civilians. Fellow crewman Patsy Rocco was also murdered by his captors.[3]

Ultimately, nine of the low group's thirteen aircraft were shot down. The 358th lost seven while the 427th lost two. There were twenty-four men killed, while forty-eight were captured and ten escaped.

BEN SMITH RECOLLECTED the importance of alcohol to the lives of the men. "As a form of entertainment, nothing else was even close. We had a fine Red Cross Club with games and an excellent record collection. There were volleyball and other sports. But alcohol was the only thing that made our existence bearable, and we didn't miss any opportunities to put some away. I became a heavy drinker during the war and never quite managed to get the hang of social drinking again."[4]

Smith recalled that he and his comrades celebrated with gusto when the 303rd completed its two hundredth mission—a raid to Château-dun, France—on July 9, 1944: "So it began—non-stop drinking for days on end. The casualty lists mounted. The dispersal tents were booked solid. Bars were filled with wall-to-wall humanity, sodden and riotous." And, of course, women were an important element of the commemoration: "There was a bit of extemporaneous nudity, expecially [sic] among the females who knew that bacchanalian rites, such as we were observing, made this kind of costume imperative."[5]

However, alcohol wasn't at the heart of every diversion, and Smith noted that the men listened to the radio quite a bit. "The BBC was dry as dust; the Armed Forces Network was what we listened to." He remembered that German propaganda broadcasts were also an appreciated entertainment. "We listened to Axis Sally a lot. She would call some guy's name in the 92nd Bomb Group and tell him his wife was dating a lot. It probably was the truth. We thought these little gems were funny as hell; they delighted us to no end."[6]

Alcohol was officially administered on a voluntary basis to men who wanted it after flying missions. The alcohol was usually a shot or two of whiskey measured out by a medical officer. It was intended to relax the men and make them more predisposed to talk during debriefings. Sometimes it was overly effective: "This caused us to exaggerate greatly," Smith recorded, "but the I.O. [intelligence officer] dutifully wrote down everything we reported. At one of the debriefings later, we reported some striped flak. It was duly noted."[7]

Smith also recalled that some of the men sought diversion in substances other than alcohol. At the daily sick call, terpin hydrate—informally known as "G.I. gin"—was readily dispensed. "It was cough syrup with codeine in it. A guy could get bombed with a couple of swallows. There was always a long line and a lot of phony coughing going on." He also remembered a more grave issue: "The first aid kits in the airplanes were systematically looted for their morphine syringes. This was serious business, but it continued to be a problem."[8]

It is cliché to declare that the war changed men. To be sure, it is implicit that the furnace of air combat over Europe turned men into something they were not before. But sometimes it changed their lives in different, even humorous, ways. Booze often played a role. "My group commander came around to the bar on the night I was promoted to captain," said Mel Schulstad. "He'd already been to several other promotion parties that night so when he raised his glass to toast me he had trouble saying my name. Instead of Schulstad, he toasted 'Captain Tool Shed.' I've been 'Tool Shed' ever since."

BRIGADIER GENERAL ROBERT TRAVIS, the 41st Combat Bombardment Wing's commander, could be a mean-spirited, irascible blowhard. William Eisenhart finished his tour in 1944 and volunteered for a second. On September 21, 1944, he flew as copilot to Travis on the mission to the marshaling yards at Mainz, Germany, at the head of the entire 41st Combat Bombardment Wing. It was Travis's last mission. Coming off target, Travis made a mistake with the autopilot that put the aircraft into a steep turn and caused the group's formation to go awry. Eisenhart reacted quickly and turned the autopilot off, decreased the aircraft's bank angle and got the formation back together. Rather than congratulating Eisenhart for his timely action, Travis stewed in humiliation.

Later, clear of danger and at a lower altitude, Eisenhart's bladder grew more full than he could stand. The group's official policy—promulgated by memorandum—was that pilots were not to leave their position to urinate through the bomb bay as had been the previous practice. Rather, they were to crouch on their seats as necessary and relieve themselves through the side window.

Eisenhart did just this. Unfortunately, Travis's window was slightly open, as he was smoking a cigar. The pressure differential drew a goodly portion of Eisenhart's piss across Travis's face. The general nearly exploded with rage. "When we landed, he chewed me out like I've never been chewed out before," said Eisenhart. "He threatened me with a court-martial. And then I had to report to him the next day and he chewed me out again. He told me he was giving the Distinguished Flying Cross to other members of the crew for that mission, but he wasn't giving it to me."

Ultimately, Eisenhart was not subjected to a court-martial. But neither was he awarded the DFC for that particular mission.

THE EIGHTH SENT 1,049 BOMBERS against targets in central Germany on September 28, 1944. The 303rd was part of a force of 445 B-17s directed to hit targets at Magdeburg, and it put 28 bombers airborne by 0800; one aircraft aborted early. The remainder made their way toward the target unmolested—but without fighter escorts—until about seventy miles west of Magdeburg.

It was then that the 303rd's low squadron, the 360th, was set upon by FW-190s. The resultant butchery—reminiscent of the massacre the group had endured the previous month during the mission to Wiesbaden—was outlined by the group's intelligence officer: "There were twelve A/C in the squadron, of which only two returned to base. The remainder are missing. The formation was subjected to severe and intense fighter attacks about 1150 hours in the vicinity of the I.P. which was 52°11'N-10°35'E."[9]

The enemy made rear attacks from level and below in waves of up to six. By the time they completed their last passes, eleven 303rd Bomb Group B-17s had fallen to earth—afire and in pieces. The group's path was marked by clouds of dissipating smoke, falling debris, doomed bombers and the white blossoms of parachutes. William Miller, the pilot of *Miss Umbriago*, descended in his parachute along with a fluttering, flickering cloud of propaganda leaflets that had been part of his ship's payload.

Silver Fox, piloted by William Lay, was positioned to the rear of the 360th's formation and was ripped by fire from the first wave of FW-190s. Ray Miller, the engineer, was in the top turret and recalled that "the aft fuselage was 'popping' with fire caused by the explosion of 20mm shells." *Silver Fox* immediately caught fire. Crewmen aboard other bombers reported that the ship "was burning from the waist back when first seen to be in trouble. About twenty seconds later it burst into flames all over and went down."[10]

Confused calls came over the interphone. The bombardier was shot in the face and killed, and the radio operator reported that the ball turret gunner was killed by a direct hit. *Silver Fox* fell into a spin. Lay turned in his seat and signaled Miller to bail out. Miller delayed and helped copilot David Grenier out of his seat. "His arm and shoulder appeared to be completely blown off. I drug him to [the] escape hatch and pushed him overboard. His chute was attached."

Silver Fox exploded into pieces an instant later. Miller was knocked unconscious until very close to the ground. His parachute carried him safely down and he was captured. He was the only survivor; Grenier's body was never found.

Aside from *Silver Fox*, ten other 303rd B-17s suffered variations of the same fate. The unnamed aircraft commanded by Victor Howard was one of them. An FW-190 slowed, put its flaps down and stabilized behind Howard's aircraft. The pilot fired explosive cannon rounds into the B-17, setting its left wing afire and blasting pieces away. Aflame and disintegrating, the bomber dropped out of the 303rd's formation and spiraled earthward in a spin. Other crews reported seeing four men parachute from the fuselage hatch.

The radio operator aboard the aircraft was Sheppard Kerman; it was his first mission. A Jew, he was a big, handsome young man and the pride of his family—brave and strong but also kind and compassionate. When the enemy fighters were sighted, he moved from the radio compartment to the left waist gun.[11] At that point in the war, the crews included only one waist gunner; the radio operator was tasked with manning the other waist gun in the event of fighter attacks.

Kerman was injured when the bomber was attacked, but he remained mobile. When the signal was given to abandon the ship, he didn't immediately jump, but instead assisted the bombardier, Jack Timmins, who was wounded and struggling to get out of the doomed aircraft. Kerman made certain Timmins had his parachute on and shoved him from the bomber.

Once he saw Timmins safely out of the aircraft, Kerman leapt clear and pulled his parachute's ripcord. He drifted into the town of Wolfenbüttel, where his parachute snagged on the apartment building at 28 Krumme Street.[12] There, he hung down the side of the building with his arms raised in surrender. A crowd gathered and boys taunted him with cries of "Heil Hitler!" A group of soldiers and uniformed political officials rushed into the building and up to a window near where he was suspended.

"He was a big, beautiful man," said a woman who had been a girl at the time. She had watched through a window from her home across the street. "He looked very sad."[13] Kerman was pulled through the window and into the building, where his parachute was cut away. He raised his arms in surrender once more. An ardent Nazi and German army reserve captain, Wilhelm Kanschat, sent everyone out of the room save for two other men, Gerd Beck and Otto Weinreich. Once the room was clear, he ordered Beck to shoot Kerman. Beck took a pistol from Weinreich and, from behind, shot Kerman in the back of the neck and killed him.

Kerman's body left a trail of blood as it was dragged down the building's stairwell and into the street. Günter Rode was a seventeen-year-old eyewitness. When the body was dragged out of the building, he heard the police chief order, "If he's still alive, smash his head."[14] Townspeople stripped Kerman's body of its boots and jacket. From there, it was loaded into a cart, hauled to a local cemetery and interred.

Beck emerged from the building, his hands covered with blood. He later bragged, "Well, we took care of this one." Many years later Günter Rode rejected any notion that the actions of his countrymen were anything other than what they seemed: "It was murder."[15]

In fact, Claude McGraw, the crew's engineer, deduced as much soon after he was captured. "I was informed by the Germans that Sgt. Sheppard Kerman had died. I saw his personal effects at Brunswick, Germany, and inquired as to his whereabouts. Knowing that he was conscious and not too badly wounded when he bailed out, I suspected that he may have been murdered. I base this on my own treatment in that area by civilians." Likewise, Jack Timmins, the crew's bombardier, who had been helped out of the stricken ship by Kerman also had suspicions. He was told by the Germans that Kerman had "bled to death."

George Stewart, the waist gunner, was on the mark with his official statement made immediately after the war: "Based wholly on supposition it is possible that he died of his wounds but he had strength enough to assist another crew member out of the aircraft and then to bail out himself so he may of [sic] met with foul play. He should of [sic] come down in the same locality that I did which I believe to be a town called Wolfenbuttel, south of Brunswick."[16]

Sadly, Kerman was not the only 303rd airman murdered that day. The lives of Leo Waldron, Arthur Conn and Teddy Smith—all crewmen aboard William Miller's *Miss Umbriago*—were taken by civilians.

Similar slayings, at the urging of Hitler and other ardent Nazis, continued until the end of the war.

OF COURSE, KERMAN'S parents knew nothing of what happened to their son other than that he had gone MIA—missing in action. The next several months were a roller coaster of hope and despair and hope again that finally ended in anguish. The cause was a sequence of conflicting official correspondences and a well-meant but confusing and ultimately hurtful message from outside USAAF channels. The uncertainty was exacerbated not only by the nature of communications during that time—cryptic telegraphs and slow-moving mail—but also by the crushing volume of critical wartime information that had to be passed to simply keep the war going. The disposition of a single, missing crewman was not the highest priority.

The Kermans no doubt received the customary official notification of their son's MIA status within days of his loss. The 303rd's chaplain, Edmund Skoner, wrote a letter on the day after the mission in which he expressed genuine sympathy and a sense of shared loss. But he was careful to keep from giving any false hope: "I sincerely regret that I can give you no additional information about your son. I can assure you, however, that as soon as definite information is available, the War Department will immediately notify you. Although I can appreciate the fact that you are anxious for some word, any word, there is nothing I can say which would not be pure conjecture."[17]

The commanding officer of the 360th sent a letter to the Kermans on October 22, 1944. It was a sad part of his duties. He wrote: "Words cannot express the feelings of the squadron over the absence of your son, since he was a very popular member of this organization. We are proud to be able to say we were comrades-in-arms with him." Another paragraph confirmed that the 303rd had no official word of Kerman's disposition. "We would appreciate receiving from you any news you may receive from him. All of us sincerely hope that you will be reunited with him in the very near future."[18]

On October 30, 1944, probably before the Kermans received the letter described above, a telegram was delivered from the adjutant general: "Report now received from the German Government through the International Red Cross states your son Sergeant Sheppard Kerman who was previously reported Missing In Action was Killed in Action 28 September over Germany."[19] Certainly the Kermans were devastated at the news.

In response to a query by Kerman's mother about the circumstances surrounding her son's loss, the 360th's adjutant sent a letter dated December 8, 1944. It no doubt rekindled hopes that had been dashed by the previous telegram. Among other information it included a horribly imprudent paragraph: "I sincerely regret that I cannot transmit full details regarding the last mission your son participated in. I do not wish to raise false hopes but we have reason to believe your son will be reported safe. It is the hope of all personnel of this squadron that such news reaches you very shortly."[20] A statement such as the one above could have done nothing but raise hopes, false or otherwise. It was reckless.

But then other information was received that seemed to support the previous letter. A local Chicago paper carried a story about the Kermans on December 31: "But their grief was banished today by the news Sgt. Kerman is alive—a German prisoner. The good news came from the pilot of the ill-fated 'Mairzy Doats' in a shortwave broadcast message received by the pilot's mother in Saginaw, Mich., and relayed to Mr. and Mrs. Kerman." Another article noted: "But today they know he is alive, although they have not heard so officially. . . . The pilot said that the crew was all saved and were prisoners in Stalingluft [sic] No. 1 in Germany."[21]

In fact, everyone in the crew had survived, save Sheppard Kerman. This sad reality became more and more apparent as time went on and no word was received from him or from the authorities. Kerman's actual fate only became known to his family following the cessation of hostilities.[22]

THE HORRIBLE ENDS endured by the men who were shot down and killed on the same day as Kerman were alluded to by German records included in the MACR, which described the accounting of the various wrecks and men—living and dead—scattered across the landscape: "On 23 deads [of 23 dead] no identifications [*sic*] could be made on account of conflagration. Further inquiries are still going on. The burials were carried out by the communities of the different villages."[23]

THAT MOBS OF VIGILANTE CIVILIANS, the German police and the SS murdered flyers is undisputed, but it was not something that was widely known or understood among many German servicemen. Lothar Seifert was one of the thousands of young schoolboys drafted to man the heavy antiaircraft guns that defended against the Allied air attacks. During his time he never saw Allied airmen molested. "In my sector, we would watch the 'mushrooms' [parachutes] drift towards earth after the airplanes crashed, and would race each other out to meet the men. Sometimes we took the airmen to our barracks and entertained them until our soldiers arrived by playing some of the Louis Armstrong records we had." Seifert saw nothing that remotely approached the horrors that were visited on some Allied aircrews: "To be quite honest, the worst treatment I ever saw taken against a downed airman was not allowing him to use the latrine because the authorities were afraid to let him out of their sight."[24]

Eddie Deerfield and his comrades were naturally distressed by the possibility that they might safely bail out from a stricken bomber over Germany only to be killed by civilians on the ground. "I despised Hitler for starting a war that was costing so many lives, including those of his own people," Deerfield said. "I couldn't understand why the

Germans venerated him as their leader. Whatever sympathy I may have had evaporated when I learned that German civilians were following Hitler's orders to kill Allied airmen who had been shot down. If we had to bail out, we were better off when members of Luftwaffe or Wehrmacht units were first on the scene to make us prisoners of war."

THE RELATIONSHIP BETWEEN THE AMERICANS and their British hosts and allies was a warm and close one. The British welcomed their American cousins for obvious reasons and shared with them whatever they had. And certainly, for the Americans, there was a strategic imperative to be in England fighting the Germans. But there was also an emotional connection between the two nations. Notwithstanding the fact that the United States was a multicultural nation, the reality is that the foundation of that multiculturalism was English; American customs and laws were English at their roots. Although there is no denying that there were occasional frictions and disagreements at all levels of the relationship, the commitment between the two nations never wavered.

The 303rd's relationships with the British were typical. Susan Hamilton was one of the local girls, whose father operated a pub frequented by many of the men. Her memories of the 303rd were fond ones:

My father would wait every night for his regular G.I.s to come to our pub and drink a beer with him and bring him a cigar and sit and shoot the wartime breeze with him. Sad to say, he passed away before it was all over, but his friends all attended his funeral with us. They were such a great group of boys at Molesworth. Everyone took them into their homes like their own sons. We would watch them go on their missions every day and wait on their return that evening, and if they weren't on the liberty run that night to our pub, The Fox, one village pub would call the other to see if they were there. If not, we would wait news of them, often ending up with a card three months later from Stalag Luft #3, and some were never heard from again.[25]

Hamilton also drove a farm tractor at Molesworth. "I remember one cold day in January, I was on the tractor and a very thoughtful guy got out of a jeep, took off his big fur coat and gave it to me. He said, 'Susie, I know you are cold and I want you to have my coat.' I enjoyed it so much but it wasn't long and here came the provost marshal and took it away from me—I guess he thought I had stolen it. But a group of the boys got together and talked to him and got it back for me, and I wore it all through the war. I was so pleased to have it back!"

Nevertheless, the 303rd's men weren't above taking advantage of the English on occasion. Anthony Sacco of the 359th recalled that some of the men stole a hog from a local farmer, killed and butchered it, stuffed it with potatoes and carrots and dug a roasting pit. The men were enjoying their succulent but ill-gotten prize when they were approached by the military police, an English policeman and the wronged farmer. "The first thing he [the farmer] said was 'There's me bloody pig!'" recalled Sacco.[26] "To pacify the farmer we all dug deep in our pockets and collected around 120 pounds. When we gave this to the farmer a big smile came over his face and he said, 'Anytime you want to steal one of my pigs, go to it!'" The money the men gave him was several times more than he would have received at market.

Sacco recalled that the 303rd's men were not always so thoughtless—at Christmas they held parties for the local children. "The cooks made cake and cookies and we cleaned out the PX [post exchange] of candy, gum and children's delights to present to them on Father Christmas Day. Someone from the base dressed up as Father Christmas and the children were in awe. We didn't forget the dads of these children as they were given cigarettes, a short commodity in those times."

In fact, the group went to great lengths to make the experience a memorable one, as described by the unit diary: "A lone Flying Fortress circled for a landing at Molesworth, wildly shooting red and green flares, while 200 British children between the ages of five and 14 stood and gazed up with awe and anticipation on their faces. . . . were sweating out the arrival of Father Christmas, who was aboard the American bomber dispatched to ferry him from the North Pole." The children swarmed the bomber as it coasted to a stop and Father Christmas—Wightman Roach—stepped out and showered them with gifts and Christmas spirit.[27]

One English child, John Hilliard, remembered the large formations of American bombers:

My mother and I would stand in our back garden and count them going out in the morning, and then count a lesser number coming back. These B-17s were quite low, so we could easily see what sort of damage the returners had. Often an engine was stopped [and] sometimes smoke was still streaming out behind. Many times one could clearly see right through the main wings, and one I remember had one of its two tail planes missing. . . . I realise now that those aircraft must have been carrying many injured, dying and dead back to their bases. Very sad![28]

"I thought that the English were absolutely remarkable," recalled Frank Boyle. "They had already been at war—and living on rations—for several years by the time I showed up. Yet, they carried on in a very steadfast and admirable way; I never heard them complain. And they were very welcoming to us. For those reasons I always felt a little guilty when I complained about our situation on base. We had a roof over our heads and were well fed and well clothed. And we had hot water and electricity whenever we needed it. I came home to clean sheets every night. Not everyone in England had those things."

George Ashworth's first impression of the English was not favorable. He was the radio operator on the Armand Burch crew, which was the 303rd's first replacement crew. They flew to England via the southern route, which took them through Africa rather than across the North Atlantic. On the last leg of their journey they became lost over France but finally reached England, with their fuel totally exhausted. "We landed wheels up on a golf course in southern England," Ashworth said.

"I can still see the long-legged grounds keeper, come running out with coattails flying and holding onto his cap to complain about his golf course being dug up. The British antiaircraft crew nearby came running out to gather up the oranges that spewed from the nose of our new B-17. It didn't matter if we were hurt or the plane demolished—'Welcome to England.'"[29]

James Geiger recalled that he was treated well by the British but also remembered petty disagreements: "We were treated really good by people in . . . England when we went to a movie off the base when they played *God Save the Queen*. The British would jump up and ask us to stand and we would say the hell with the queen and they would say the hell with Roosevelt."[30]

Dick Johnson became friends with the Lowe family in the nearby town of Bedford. The Lowes had two daughters. "Beryle was in the Royal Air Force as a WAF, while Marjorie was still in high school. Beryle had a steady boyfriend while Marjorie was pretty well protected. A good thing, since she was a very pretty girl. I was attracted to her, but didn't have a chance to get to know her very well.

"Mr. Lowe sometimes took me fishing on the River Ouse, the beautiful little river that ran through the heart of Bedford. I caught a three-inch fish one day and was about to throw it back when Mr. Lowe reminded me that they never threw back a fish that size."[31] This was surprising even to Johnson, who as a young boy had subsisted on such fare as armadillos and groundhogs. "I found it difficult to imagine the rationing and hardships that the British had to endure for so many years. We had rationing in the United States at that time, but nothing approaching that of the British."

Ultimately, the lives of virtually all the 303rd's men were somehow changed by England and the English. Some more than others. In fact, more than three hundred men from Molesworth took English brides. Others planned to, but combat didn't care about those plans. Joseph Zsampar, a tail gunner with the 359th Bomb Squadron, fell in love with a beautiful English girl, Pauline "Bobby" Roberts, and the two were engaged. He presented her with a photo of himself on which he inscribed: "America lend-leased this soldier to England's fairer sex. Handle with care and return in good order."[32] Zsampar's ship was downed over the North Sea and his body was never recovered. The tragedy stayed with Bobby Roberts all her life.

One of Zsampar's fellow crewmen was Jack Snell, another gunner, who was also a close friend of Van White. Snell had worked for the *Sedalia Democrat* newspaper before the war and received issues while at Molesworth. "When Jack went missing in action," White said, "the issue of the *Sedalia Democrat* that described the mission arrived with Jack's mailing label at the bottom of the picture. It made my skin crawl."

BOMB GROUP OPERATIONS put hundreds of heavy machine guns in the hands of young men almost daily. There were bound to be accidents. George Hiebeler recalled an incident that occurred prior to the mission to Mannheim on October 19, 1944, when he was called to fly as a substitute navigator. It was his second mission. "While waiting in the crew chief's tent before start-up time, we heard a machine gun go off. The crew chief stepped outside the tent and then hollered, 'My plane's been shot and it's on fire.'"[33]

"We all piled out of the tent and indeed gas was pouring out of the wing between #1 and #2 engines and there was a pretty good fire going. The pilot said, 'I think we had better get out of here.' I figured he had a lot more experience than I did so I would stick with him." Hiebeler and another crewman in the tent sprinted after the pilot toward a nearby wooded area. "After a ways we stopped but the pilot said, 'I think we should get further away.'" Hiebeler and the other crewman didn't argue and the trio put more distance between themselves and the burning—and bomb-laden—B-17.

The fire crew extinguished the blaze, and Hiebeler and the other two men subsequently returned to the smoking hulk. Hiebeler learned that the errant rounds were fired by Harvey "Shorty" Kaber, the ball turret gunner from his own crew. "He had been called to fly at the last minute to replace a ball turret gunner who became sick. In checking the guns, the other gunner had hooked up the ammo belt with a round already in the chamber. Shorty . . . was not used to doing this and he somehow hit the trigger setting off a few rounds." Kaber was pulled from flying status and reduced in rank to private first class. He was later allowed to return to operations and completed thirty-five missions and regained his rank.

Accidents also happened while airborne. Indeed, during combat, with so many guns in action, it is certain that the bombers were sometimes hit by gunfire from other bombers. This was the case on May 11, 1944, as described by Clifford Fontaine:

> *Supposed to go to Saarbrucken, Germany, today but we tied onto another group and I don't know just where the hell we did go. It was somewhere in France though. Saw a couple of Me-109s today and some joker in another Fort shot a hole in the nose of our ship! I got a little scratch on my forehead but nothing to worry about. I damned near froze to death the rest of the trip because of the wind blowing through the nose.*[34]

Another gun accident actually took a life. Typically, when safely out over the sea, machine guns were test fired—just a few rounds each—to ensure they were ready for action. The men were always admonished to point their weapons in a safe direction. Nonetheless, this didn't always happen, as David Michael, a 360th Bomb Squadron ball turret gunner, cryptically noted in his diary entry for February 6, 1944, the day the group hit the Luftwaffe airfield at Lonvic, near Dijon: "Lt. Doering, Underwood's copilot, shot by test fire."[35]

Indeed, Creighton Doering was shot through the back of the head by a .50-caliber round—one of three that struck his aircraft. He was killed instantly. There was speculation that the misdirected rounds came from B-17s of the 379th Bomb Group, which was flying nearby, but nothing was ever proven. News of such incidents, as indicated by Michael's diary entry, spread rapidly through the unit and were obviously not good for morale. Too many of them were being killed at the hands of the enemy; killing one another was beyond senseless.

IT IS IMPLICIT that the 303rd's B-17s were of little value without bombs. In reality, they were nothing more than complex and expensive bomb delivery machines operated by intensively trained crews. The men who prepared the 303rd's bombs were organized on Molesworth as the 1681st Ordnance Company. These men were near the terminus of an enormous and complex ordnance manufacturing and transportation train that ended only when the bombs were released over the target.

It was these men who accepted and moved the bombs from the ports or railheads to the 303rd's bomb dump. There, the bombs were inventoried and stored until needed onboard the aircraft, as prescribed by the same field orders that directed the group to go on a mission. As the field orders nearly always arrived at night, the ordnance men were used to working in the dark—and often in miserable weather. Upon receipt of the orders, they moved into the bomb dump and earmarked the correct types and numbers of bombs. The bombs were subsequently hoisted onto trailers and transported to individual aircraft hardstands. From the hardstands, squadron ordnance personnel loaded the bombs into the aircraft and fit them with fuzes and safety pins. Although many fingers and a few bones were crushed and broken, there was never a major accident at Molesworth.

That is not to say that the work was never without drama. Maynard Pitcher described an incident that underscored the dangerous nature of the job. Pitcher and his comrades were tasked with loading the *FDR* with two 1,000-pound bombs. "It was a bitter cold winter night and the three of us were wearing heavy winter coats and gloves."[36] After getting the first bomb loaded and secured, the three men winched the second, fully assembled bomb up toward the bomb bay.

Pitcher recalled: "[Arnold] Gilsdorf's foot slipped from the step on the bomb bay door and fell that short distance to the ground, his coat catching the tail fin of the bomb and over-balancing it, causing it to fall tail fin first to the ground and standing upright on Gilsdorf's coat tail. The fall completely crushed the tail fin and broke off the tail fuse right next to the bomb. There was only a crunching thud." Stunned, but delighted to still be alive, Pitcher and the other loader, Smith [first name unknown], crawled out of the aircraft's waist hatch and freed Gilsdorf by cutting his coat away from the bomb, which had him pinned to the ground.

The bomb—which was stuck securely in the ground—extended up into *FDR*'s bomb bay. Consequently, the aircraft was trapped; it couldn't be moved without disturbing the now-armed bomb. Were it to explode, the aircraft and much of the 359th Bomb Squadron's billeting area would be destroyed.

An ingenious solution was contrived. The aircraft's propellers were removed and a large crane was moved to the site. Without the propellers to hang up on the ground, the maintenance men were able to hoist the aft fuselage high enough so that the bomb bay cleared the bomb and the aircraft could be rolled forward. "The bomb was then very carefully slung and transported to a safe area and disarmed," Pitcher said. "We were informed later that when the bomb crushed the tail fin and broke the tail fuse off, it also broke the long tail fuse firing pin and left a large burr on the firing pin which prevented it from detonating the bomb." Pitcher and the rest of the loading crew had only narrowly missed being blown to smithereens.

The science of matching the right combination of bombs and fuzes against specific targets—and determining how they were dropped—was one that evolved through the duration of the war. The numbers and types of bombs that were loaded on the aircraft varied with the type of target being attacked. Bigger bombs were used to destroy very large structures such as submarine pens. For instance, on its third mission the 303rd attacked the submarine pens at Lorient, France, with M34s, two-thousand-pound bombs. Each aircraft carried two. However, for attacks on airfields, many small bombs were carried so as to achieve greater effects on aircraft, hangars, runways and fuel supplies. As an example, the ships were loaded with twenty-four M30s, hundred-pound bombs, for the attack on the airfield at Gilze-Rijen on August 19, 1943. The default, general purpose load was ten or twelve M43s (later M64s), five-hundred-pound bombs. These were generally effective against most targets.

Most of the bombs the 303rd carried were conventional high-explosive types. There were many different weights and types, and updated versions became available during 1944. Incendiary bombs were used quite often against targets that were judged more vulnerable to fire rather than explosives. A weapon of another sort—a psychological weapon—was a canister that dispensed thousands of leaflets. The RAF codename for the leaflets was "nickels" and the name stuck with the American flyers. They were usually dropped in combination with high-explosive bombs but opened above the target so that the leaflets were scattered over a large area.

Occasionally, the ships carried a mixed load of bombs, which offered the advantage of combining different sorts of effects against particular target types. However, these mixed loads created aiming issues for the bombardiers, as each bomb type possessed different ballistic properties and fell to earth on a slightly different trajectory.

Fuzing the bombs properly was also critical in order to achieve the best effects. For instance, when targeting a factory, a fuze delay of a few milliseconds allowed a bomb to penetrate through the roof and into the factory itself before exploding. On the other hand, in order to keep the bomb's effects from being smothered by the ground, it was best that it be fuzed to explode immediately when attacking targets such as aircraft parked in the open.

Another consideration was the desired spacing, or interval, between the bombs as they fell across the target. The larger bombs were generally released at greater intervals so that they landed farther apart, while smaller bombs were dropped at reduced intervals. Bombs were usually only salvoed, or released all at once, when there was an emergency and the aircraft needed to be immediately rid of them. For that reason, there was a salvo release mechanism for the pilots as well as the bombardier.

AS THE USAAF—TOGETHER with the RAF—ramped up its air campaign during 1944, the effects on the German people grew more and more pronounced. The Franz Kaiser family lived in Munich, and their experience was fairly typical. Hildegard Kaiser, at fifteen, was the youngest daughter and lived with her parents and sisters. Her older brother had already perished in fighting on the Eastern Front. "We found out he had been killed when the soldiers came and banged on the door. When my mother opened it, they shouted, 'Heil Hitler, your son is dead!' And then they turned around and left, and we never learned anything at all about his death.[37]

"Everything was in short supply," Kaiser said. "Clothes and shoes were difficult to get, but I had older sisters so that I had enough hand-me-downs. Food was also in short supply—especially meat. We had ration stamps that we used very carefully, but the stores didn't always have what we needed, although there was always bread—black bread."

Kaiser's father was a school administrator but took extra work as a handyman and laborer on nearby farms. "He was very good at fixing things, and the farmers paid him with food—usually potatoes and turnips and such, and sometimes eggs and chicken. When the farmers slaughtered a cow or a pig, we sometimes had meat, which our father shared out very carefully at the dinner table. He was a very good provider. And even though we lived in an apartment, we also had a garden and we canned vegetables. An apple tree and a pear tree gave us some small amount of fruit. Mostly we ate potatoes that were purchased at the store. We kids also sometimes stole potatoes and turnips from nearby farms."

Still, food was never abundant. "One evening we had only a single potato," Kaiser said. "My mother cut it into pieces. I told her that she had miscounted because we were one piece short. She said that she wasn't hungry. But I knew she was. We were all hungry all the time."

Kaiser remembered the air raids in which the 303rd played a part on a number of occasions. "Even though we were on the edge of Munich—at Munich Allach—my mother made us go to the bomb shelter every time, even if we were in bed. The warning system was very good, and the sirens sounded at least thirty minutes prior to the bombs coming. We usually carried a blanket and a pillow to an enormous, purpose-built bomb shelter right next door. It had walls of concrete that were very, very thick, and I don't think anything could have hurt us when we were inside." Aside from the shelter, nearby defenses also included an antiaircraft battery deployed in a field adjacent to the Kaisers' apartment.

Kaiser was sent to work at a Junkers aircraft component fabrication plant when she was fourteen. "I went to school in the morning and to work in the afternoon. It was how things were done. They had me make coffee and tea and such and then started trusting me to do office work—typing and filing and that sort of thing. I gave half of my salary to my parents and they let me keep the other half.

"Everyone was very nice to me," Kaiser said, "but as the war continued, it became apparent that Germany was going to lose. The mood grew more and more somber. I was called into the office of the big boss one afternoon. I entered and said, 'Heil Hitler,' as we were required to do during that time. He just glared at me and said, 'And kiss my ass!' It was quite a risky thing to say as he could have been sent away to a concentration camp. But it was an example of how people felt toward the end of the war."

"YOU ARE GOING TO HAVE TO STAY IN THERE AND FIGHT THEM"

"IT IS MY CONVICTION that good group commanders insure [*sic*] good units and that poor group commanders cannot possibly have good units."[1] These words came from Ira Eaker who knew a thing or eleven about leadership. Consequently, if it is accepted that the 303rd was among the best of the best bomber groups, it must likewise be acknowledged that the men who led it were also exceptional.

In point of fact, it is difficult to identify a single 303rd commander as *the* key individual who set the tone and tempo for the group and put it on the right track. The command of the group changed sixteen different times, and the group's four different squadrons had more than twenty different commanders. Indeed, while still stateside, the 303rd went through several commanding officers before James Wallace took over during July 1942. It was Wallace who led the 303rd overseas and into combat, and it is certain that his leadership left some imprint on the organization. On the other hand, he was ordered to a staff billet during February 1943 after having flown only four missions. He did receive the Silver Star for his service, so it is unlikely that he was removed for cause or incompetence.

Command of the group was temporarily held by both Charles Marion and George Robinson into the summer of 1943. Marion, who was part of the 303rd's original cadre, flew only eleven missions by the time he was relieved in August 1943 by Kermit Stevens. Stevens, a stocky man with a dogged disposition, earned his commission and wings during the 1930s. Leading the group until September 1944, he was the group's first truly outstanding commander.

He was a dynamic leader known for his pre-mission pep talks and for his exhortations to the men to "bow your necks" to the task. "You are going to have to stay in there and fight them and get the job done or you are going to have to go back tomorrow and redo it."[2] In fact, his rallying call so impressed the men that one crew named their ship *Bow-Ur-Neck Stevens*. Stevens was the first of the group's commanders to complete a full tour. He flew twenty-nine missions, and because he led many of them, he was credited with more. It was Stevens more than any of the 303rd's commanders—because of his spirit, his example and the time he spent at the head—who left the greatest mark on the group. And the group was better for it.

Among the 303rd's squadron commanders, Lewis Lyle was the most notable. A native of Arkansas, he resigned his commission as an infantry lieutenant to become an aviation cadet during the spring of 1941. The pilot of *Ooold Soljer*, he was part of the group's original cadre of pilots and rose to command the 360th Squadron during January 1943—only two months after the 303rd began operations.

Lyle was cool, calm and capable, and no one in the 303rd had more combat credibility. He recalled his attitude about combat: "When I got in the airplane . . . I wasn't scared of the devil himself. I had so much adrenaline flowing and that's the way I went through the whole thing. . . . I know it sounds stupid and a lot of people won't believe it, but I never was afraid."[3] And he ran a tight and disciplined crew. "It was strictly business on my airplane and the only time they could shoot the breeze was when we hit the ground." It is likely that his crews didn't mind the discipline—they always made it back to Molesworth.

His reputation spread across the Eighth and was such that he was assigned to fly with the 351st Bomb Group's commander on that group's inaugural mission. Lyle completed twenty-five missions on July 17, 1943, and kept on flying. Not long after, he was the first Eighth Air Force pilot to reach thirty missions. He became so expert that he not only led the group on a regular basis, but often the 41st Combat Bombardment Wing and occasionally the entire 1st Bomb Division. Lyle was so intent on understanding every aspect of the Eighth's mission that he put himself through weeks of intensive bombardier training and flew as the group's lead bombardier on three missions, achieving excellent results. If the 303rd ever had a Most Valuable Player, it was Lewis Lyle.

Although he stated that flying combat didn't bother him, Lewis admitted that waiting to fly combat did. "Sitting around and waiting was agonizing to a certain extent and if I started to thinking about getting shot down or something, well, I just said that's a waste of time . . . why don't I think about how to keep from getting shot down? And that's what I did." Ultimately, Lyle was made the group's deputy commander and flew fifty-seven missions with the 303rd. In October 1944, he was made commander of the 379th Bomb Group at nearby Kimbolton. He flew on at least twelve more raids—other sources cite more—before being named commander of the 41st Combat Bombardment Wing during the last few days of the war. No bomb group commander in the Eighth Air Force flew more bombing missions.

The group's leadership was not always on the mark. This might be understandable to a degree when it is considered that air warfare of this type and scale had never been waged before. And especially when it is understood that fewer than two of each hundred men had been in uniform for more than five years. Regardless, leadership failures sometimes created ill will that was not easily forgotten. Ben Smith remembered that the combat crews were called together at some point during mid-1944 when the group had been especially hard hit. A colonel reminded them that their role in the war was "killing and being killed" and upbraided them as "cry babies."

The humiliating harangue infuriated Smith and many of his peers. "I can still see the hurt and anger on their faces as they listened unbelieving." It was especially hurtful because the men were volunteers. To a man, they could have refused to continue combat operations with no repercussions other than a reduction in rank to match the assignments to which they would have been posted. "The flight crews," Smith said, "never had any use for the colonel after this piece of gratuitous arrogance."[4]

Arrogance or not, no one ever accused the group's leadership of cowardice. "I had a lot of respect for our brass," said Dick Johnson. "They never avoided the missions that were expected to be especially dangerous. If it was going to be a tough one, they were right up front."[5]

There was mutual respect between the enlisted men and officers of the 303rd; military courtesies were expected to be rendered and returned. The group's leadership insisted on it and considered it key to maintaining discipline and morale. "I was talking with our squadron [427th] commanding officer, Edgar Snyder," said Dick Johnson, "and an enlisted man walked past without saluting. I thought about stopping him right then, but didn't want to interrupt Snyder. It wasn't but a few seconds later that he dressed me down for failing to discipline the enlisted man. Of course I was in full agreement with him, but I just stayed quiet and took the lesson."[6]

Where the aircrews were concerned, the responsibility for leadership belonged to one man—the pilot. It was his duty to make certain that each crewman at each position on his aircraft performed as required so that bombs were delivered on target on each and every mission. In most instances, the pilots were up to the task, but this was not always the case. A few pilots simply didn't *make* teams of the men they led. Many of them were simply too young and inexperienced to do so, while others were lazy, ignorant or selfish. It is arguable that in training these men as pilots, the USAAF didn't spend enough time to train them as leaders. Certainly, military protocol did not allow the officers to socialize or fraternize with their enlisted crewmen. However, such strictures were not intended to keep them from talking with their men, learning about them and coming to understand them. Indeed, this type of familiarity and empathy was a critical component of leadership. It built trust and loyalty as well as a sense of camaraderie. These were intangibles of great value during combat.

Frank Boyle, a ball turret gunner, rankled at his recollection of the officers in his crew: "In the three months we spent at the operational training unit in the States, the officers never shared a beer with us. We never went out to a bar or a restaurant to get to know each other. It was no better at Molesworth when we got to the 303rd. None of the officers on our crew knew where the enlisted men came from, what their families were like . . . or anything. We were second-class citizens, and we wondered if they even cared about us." Boyle recollected that one of his fellow gunners had a name for the dynamic: "He called it brass hat [officer] racism."

Still, it was rare when a pilot's leadership was so poor that it could not be compensated for by his crew's training, sense of duty and—perhaps especially—keenness to survive. Indeed, the forge of shared combat often brought the men together in a way that training could not. Crewmen who had previously barely tolerated one another did indeed sometimes become like brothers.

"Our crew worked pretty well as a team," said Tom Hardin. "But we had to let our original tail gunner go about the time we finished half our missions. He would get very upset and scream into the interphone for periods of time. Naturally this upset the rest of the crew. He was young and scared—like the rest of us—but just couldn't handle the pressure. When I finally finished my missions and left for the States, he was driving a fuel truck and was quite content."[7]

"I remember one instance," said Al Dussliere, "when one of our substitute crew members faked an injury to get removed from flight status. We were shot up pretty badly on a mission and had to crash-land. We all came through it just fine. In fact, I distinctly remember this particular guy doing the jitterbug pretty energetically not long after the crash. But a short time later he said that his back was hurt during the crash and he never flew again."[8]

There was at least one instance when a crewman fell out of favor, was sent away to fly with other crews and then rejoined his original crew. Warren Kotz, a navigator with the 427th's David Shelhamer crew noted that ball turret gunner Joe Keaton was removed from the crew for apparent incompetence: "Keaton off crew—made mistake on oxygen on an aborted mission. Passed out."[9] Nevertheless, Keaton continued to build his mission count with other crews before rejoining the Shelhamer crew to finish his combat tour.

Dick Johnson remembered the crew on which he was a copilot as a good team except for one member: "We had a waist gunner who was often insubordinate. He had a bad attitude and often mouthed off to the officers. We finally told him that it'd be a good idea for him to look for somewhere else to go. He actually finished his combat tour flying with several different crews."[10]

That these sorts of frictions were not more common is somewhat surprising as there was little in terms of age and experience to distinguish the officers from the enlisted men. In fact, many of the enlisted men were older than the officers under whom they served. It was sometimes difficult for them to take orders from officers who had no more combat experience than they did. Moreover, some of the enlisted men had been aviation cadets themselves and were washed out of training on little pretense when more aerial gunners were needed. Frank Boyle was caught in one of these unofficial aerial gunner drafts. "Early during our training we were all called into the auditorium and told that we had washed out. I was told that my depth perception was too poor." It is interesting to note that—with his deficient depth perception—Boyle was sent to aerial gunnery school.

This sort of heavy-handed treatment did cause resentment. Nevertheless, most of the men controlled their emotions, learned their assigned jobs, followed military protocol and performed admirably. And they did it both on the ground and in the air. An example of the sort of necessary teamwork that was routine and workaday, yet still saved lives, occurred during the 303rd's mission to Hamm, Germany, on September 19, 1944.

James Mickle, the pilot of the 359th's *Forget Me Not Olly*, described what happened: "We discovered we were short a flak suit for my copilot [Arthur Bergeron], so I asked the radio operator [Dennis Eagon] to bring up a spare."[11] Eagon found another flak suit in the rear of the aircraft and came back forward. As he reached the top turret, he found William Humphrey, the flight engineer, without an oxygen mask and unconscious. The copilot, Bergeron, noticed the problem and turned around to help. His own oxygen mask became disconnected as he did so and he slumped out of his seat, hypoxic.

"I called the navigator [Benjamin O'Dell] to help the copilot," Mickle said, "and told the radioman to help the engineer. The two men without oxygen looked purple in the face. I thought they were goners." Mickle, alone at the controls, tried to orchestrate the rescue while flying his ship in a formation that he remembered as very poor. "The navigator used his own mask alternately to revive the copilot, who then climbed back to his position in the cockpit."

With everything seemingly in control and everyone back on oxygen and breathing comfortably, Eagon headed back toward his radio compartment. But unbeknownst to him, his oxygen mask caught on something and was torn loose. "One of the waist gunners saw it happen," said Mickle, "and went forward to help put [Eagon's] mask back on him. Finally, all were okay."

The sort of teamwork exercised by Mickle's crew that day crossed the boundaries of rank and was essential to the success of the 303rd. William Heller, who finished his time with the group as the commanding officer of the 360th Bomb Squadron, understood this and described an encounter when one of his men referred to himself as "only" a sergeant. "I interrupted him," Heller said, "and told him to stand at attention and then said, Sergeant! No one in this squadron is an 'only.' You are a sergeant, and one of the best damn sergeants in the best damn squadron in the best damn group of the best damn air corps! And don't you forget it!" During the next few days as the story filtered among the men, Heller noted a subtle change in his unit. "I may have imagined it, but everyone seemed to walk more erect and more proudly."[12]

In fact, the performance of the 303rd and the anecdotal characterizations of its leaders closely mirror leadership attributes that were found to be critical by a postwar study on morale: "These included vigor, aggressiveness, fairness, firmness without arbitrary harshness, a lively interest in the welfare of all personnel, and, perhaps most important of all, the ability to inspire confidence by demonstrating both a grasp of the work at hand and a capacity for doing it."[13]

Finally, leadership aside, a nod must be given to the organizations, regulations and directives that kept the machine that was the USAAF functioning. If in doubt, new or confused leaders could always turn to "the book." Happily, these resources, in combination with bright, well-equipped men, ensured that failures were infrequent.

In contrast to the teamwork and close associations the men sometimes built when they served on the same crews, the relationships between men who shared living quarters were often less chummy. Officers lived with officers and enlisted men lived with enlisted men. Although they shared the same sorts of terrors when they flew missions, the enlisted men in Al Dussliere's Nissen hut shared little else. "It was really very impersonal for most of us," he said. "At any one time there were about twenty men in each hut, but the turnover rate was high and continuous. For example, one group of four or five guys might finish their required missions and get sent home. Then another crew might get shot down. Replacements oftentimes came in and disappeared just as quickly. Other guys would come or go in ones and twos as they got sick or recovered or just got moved in or out for one reason or another. Sure, guys made friends, but there was no way, or even desire, for everyone in the hut to become close with one another."

THE VAST MAJORITY of the men who served in the 303rd and the various support units were generally of fine character. Notwithstanding that fact, it was inevitable that among so many thousands of men—nearly nine thousand in total through the war—there were bound to be bad apples. A letter from Mel Schulstad to his parents showed that he was a victim of petty theft: "We had a very nice summer. English country-side is very beautiful in the summer in a pastoral kind of way. I suppose I will regret not taking more pictures but I've had my camera stolen and then too, film is hard to get."

An account from Keith Clapp, a bombardier with the 427th Bomb Squadron, gives another example. His aircraft was shot up by an Me-109 during the Stuttgart raid on February 25, 1944. The pilot struggled and only barely recovered the plane at an RAF fighter base at Brighton, where it was subsequently determined to need major repairs.

The crew left their bomber and returned to Molesworth the following day. On arriving at his quarters, Clapp discovered he had been robbed: "When we got back to Molesworth, from my foot locker was missing: my 45 cal. [pistol], my binoculars, fifty, one-dollar bills and two pair of ebony-handled Sheffield straight razors which I had purchased a week before in Sheffield. One pair I was going to give to the pilot when he finished his missions. These items were never recovered."[14]

The 303rd's command recognized that there were problems—especially when crews went down—and had the following notice published in the daily bulletin "for the information and guidance of all personnel concerned":

Private ***** (formerly staff sergeant) was tried and convicted by a special court-martial for the larceny of a Schick injector razor and blades, all of a value of about $3.00. The property belonged to a combat crew member who was reported to be missing in action. The accused himself has completed fifteen combat missions over enemy occupied territory. The court, however, considered the offense sufficiently reprehensible to sentence the accused to confinement at hard labor for six months and forfeiture of $40.00 of his pay per month for a like period.[15]

Ben Smith recalled related behavior: "There was always a mad rush back to the barracks to get the bicycles of some crew that was shot down. This was not intended as any disrespect to our friends who didn't come back." Nevertheless, it wasn't always easy to take away the newly-ownerless bikes as men were keen to keep those that were kept at their barracks. Smith recalled: "The crews in each barracks had a corral of bicycles. For some reason, it was important to us that our corral of bicycles remain intact."[16]

When crews were shot down, their personal effects at Molesworth were often collected by enlisted clerks. The belongings were sorted, and a special effort was made to make certain that nothing embarrassing or hurtful to the family was sent home. "I used to kid Milton Hamill," remembered Van White, the operations clerk. "Hamill was the radio operator aboard the *Jersey Bounce*. He was Jewish and a heck of a nice guy. And he always wore finely tailored uniforms—he was very particular about how he looked. He was a small guy like me, and I always told him that if he ever got shot down that I was going to take his gabardine flying suit; it was just beautiful. Well, when he finished his last mission he came and got me from my office and took me over to his barracks. Then he opened his foot locker. There was a sign inside that read: 'To Whom It May Concern: If anything happens to me, please make certain that my uniforms are given to Technical Sergeant Van White.' Well, that was such a generous gesture that I was really embarrassed. I felt about one inch tall."

Everyone dealt with the loss of friends and comrades in personal ways that varied from man to man. Dick Johnson recalled his own feelings at the loss of a friend, Charles Allen, during the raid to Berlin on June 21, 1944. He felt a small measure of guilt because his initial reaction was not concern for the welfare of his friend, but rather relief because he hadn't been lost on the mission himself. Still, he was taken aback at the astonishingly callous reaction of another friend when told that Allen had been shot down: "No shit? I wonder if his pants will fit me."[17] Johnson was stunned at the comment but tried to reconcile it in his own mind. "I figured that his attitude might have just been his defense strategy."

Johnson also recalled that some men dealt with their fears and anxieties by turning to the church. "After morning briefing, about half of the combat crews would go to the chapel for prayers or last rites. Some of our crew did this but I never did as I always relied on my own silent prayer: 'Thank you God, for taking such good care of me.'" It was a prayer he had offered since his teenage years in southern Illinois: "Never asking for anything in the future, but always thanking Him for keeping me alive and in good health."[18]

Still, religion and the almighty were no less confounding during the war years than any other time. Warren Kotz was a navigator with the 427th Bomb Squadron. Even though there were hearty exclamations of "Thank God" upon completing particularly perilous missions, he didn't believe that God had deserted those who did not return. "But we all said, 'Thank God we made it through that one,' no matter what we believed."[19]

ALTHOUGH THEIR GERMAN ENEMIES were expert at killing or hurting them, the airmen of the 303rd still found ingenious ways to hurt themselves. Dick Johnson offered an example: "One day I went over to the maintenance hangar to look around and the sergeant in charge had some .50 caliber bullets on the workbench."[20] Johnson watched, intrigued, as the man separated a bullet from its casing and poured out the gunpowder. "He then took a dull punch and set the casing on an anvil, placing the punch on the firing pin in the center of the base. With a light tap of a hammer on the punch, he fired the primer which made a subdued 'pop.'"

Johnson watched the man craft the disarmed shell into a base for a model airplane. He was quite taken with the idea and decided to do the same. With just a little practice he made a base for a replica of an RAF Hurricane as well as a couple of cigarette lighters. He enjoyed his new hobby, and it helped pass the time when he wasn't flying or otherwise obligated.

However, Johnson became a bit too comfortable handling the dangerous ammunition: "I had worked the projectile out of a casing and poured the powder out. The sergeant was not around and I couldn't find a dull punch to explode the primer so I picked up a prick punch." The prick punch had a very sharply tapered point and was used to precisely start holes in metal for subsequent drilling.

And it was the wrong tool for Johnson's purpose. "When I tapped the punch with a hammer the primer exploded, but the sharp point of the punch caused the brass surface of the primer to split and shoot back upward, thus imbedding all the brass fragments in my left thumb and middle finger." Blood poured from the wounds, and Johnson—somewhat sheepishly—walked himself to the dispensary. Had he sustained such a wound in combat, he would have been awarded the Purple Heart. In this instance, the only thing he earned was a raised eyebrow from the doctor who stitched his hand and fingers back together.

Not every injury in the 303rd or the Eighth was caused by German fighters or antiaircraft fire, or from hobbying with live ammunition. There were myriad ways to get hurt—sometimes badly—simply by being around the big ships. Slips and falls resulted in sprained or even broken limbs. And as well designed as the B-17 was, ergonomics came second to mission effectiveness and ease of production. Consequently, sharp corners and "head-bangers" were plentiful. Moreover, simply being around the aircraft could be dangerous; on at least one occasion, a man walked into a turning propeller.

Frank Boyle was injured when his ball turret failed on a mission during the latter half of 1944: "My turret just sputtered and stopped like a car running out of gas," he recalled. "I called over the interphone, and the engineer shouted at me to get out of there, which I did in a hurry. Then we got hit by a bunch of Me-109s, and I started carrying ammunition from the tail up to the waist gunners. I didn't have any headphones on, so I didn't hear when the pilot called out 'Geronimo.' That was his signal to us that he was going to take evasive action and that we should brace ourselves."

The heavy maneuvers caught Boyle completely unaware as he twisted while carrying a heavy ammunition box. "I was knocked off balance but kept my footing," he said. "I didn't feel any pain at the time and kept helping the rest of the crew. We made it back to base okay and I didn't think much more about it.

"But I couldn't move when I woke up the next morning," he continued. "I couldn't get out of bed. Finally, after doing a lot of stretching, I stood up and limped around well enough to actually fly a mission. But afterward, as we were coming back to base, I wasn't able to get out of the turret. The two waist gunners had to lift me out."

Barely able to move, Boyle struggled to the flight surgeon's office. "He said that he didn't have the equipment he needed to properly diagnose me. Then he asked me if I wanted to quit my combat tour. I told him no and left. I had torn ligaments and cartilage and such and walked with a heavy limp for the next seven years."

OF ALL THE B-17'S GUN positions, it is the ball turret—hung from the belly of the aircraft—that is the most fascinating. The Sperry ball turret, equipped with two .50-caliber machine guns, was intended to defend the aircraft against fighter attacks from below. An electrically actuated, hydraulically powered system rotated the ball through 360 degrees in azimuth and 90 degrees in elevation. In other words, the guns could point in any direction and from approximately level with the horizon to directly downward. The turret was cramped, only forty-four inches in width, and consequently was usually manned by smaller men. The gunner sat with his feet in stirrups and his knees close to either side of his head. However, he rotated with the ball, so that when the guns were pointed downward he was facedown. He sat on an armored seat that extended behind his back.

The turret was operated with two wooden handles located in front of and above the gunner's head. Moving the handles from side-to-side controlled the turret's rotation while the elevation of the guns was controlled by twisting the handles. The firing buttons were atop the handles.

The guns were aimed via a K-4 computing gun sight which projected two illuminated lines on a glass sight in front of the gunner's face. The gunner preset the wingspan of the target aircraft into the gun sight and then controlled the separation of the illuminated lines with a pedal under his left foot. A firing solution was achieved when the gunner framed an attacking fighter within the two lines.

In theory the ball turret was capable of protecting the bomber from attacks originating from any direction. However, firing forward was somewhat problematic. Firstly, the closing speeds were very fast and it was difficult to achieve a firing solution in time to use the guns. Moreover, obstructions from the fuselage cluttered the gunner's field of view, as did the propellers. Automatic stops prevented the gunner from accidentally shooting the propellers.

Frank Boyle recollected the dangerous peculiarities of the position: "As the ball turret gunner I was the only member of the crew who couldn't wear a parachute at my position. My chute and boots were wired to a steel triangle that was positioned immediately above the turret's exit hatch. If we had to bail out I had to position my guns so that they were pointed straight down, open the hatch, climb out, disconnect my heating wires, interphone, oxygen hoses and such, and then attach my parachute. From there I had to make my way to one of the waist positions and jump."

But the ball turret position could be even more dangerous. "If the turret's unprotected outer vertical cam gearing was hit and jammed," Boyle said, "it was impossible to roll the ball so that the exit hatch could open inside the fuselage. So, the gunner would be stuck."

Robert Butcher of the 359th recalled just such an incident in his diary: "Ship shot up. Out of gas. Jara (Felix) trapped in ball turret. Had to land that way. All of us were scared to death."[21]

If the ball turret was stuck and the aircraft had to be abandoned, the other crewmembers, usually the waist gunners, had to remove the bolts by which a long steel tube held the ball to the aircraft. Once that was done, the ball would fall free from the aircraft with the gunner in it. Then, while falling, the gunner had to open the exit hatch, rip the parachute from the steel triangle and fasten it to his harness. Then he had to grab his boots, unfasten all the wires and hoses, push away from the ball and pull his parachute's ripcord. And it was about fifty degrees below zero.

Moreover, the ball turret gunner's relative isolation from the rest of the crew was dangerous in its own right. "If I were hit by antiaircraft fire," Boyle said, "or if my oxygen was shot away or disabled, there was a good chance that I'd be dead before anyone from the crew could get me out of the ball—if they could at all." There is little wonder that the ball turret position was not one that was eagerly sought.

Boyle recalled the dilemma that he and his fellow ball turret gunners faced when the formations were hit by heavy antiaircraft fire. "I had two choices when we were getting hit by flak. I could put my guns straight down, which would allow me to climb through the hatch and into the fuselage if we had to bail out. But that left me facing downward with my genitals fully exposed, as there was no armor plate to protect them from that direction. Or, I could put the guns parallel with the bottom of the ship, which put protection between my family jewels and the bottom of the turret. But if the exposed vertical gearing on the turret got hit, there was no way for me to escape the turret. In the end I kept the guns pointed down so that I could more easily get out of the turret; I decided that my life was more important than my genitalia."

Boyle's relief at clearing enemy territory was typical of many of the 303rd's airmen: "Everyone smoked—I smoked Pall Malls. There is no way to describe the great happiness and relief I felt when I got out of the ball turret after we had descended down to below five thousand feet and were back over the English Channel. I'd sit on the floor in the radio room, light up a cigarette and smile. Hot damn—we got lucky one more time!"

"THE BACK OF THE ENGINEER'S HEAD
HAD BEEN BLOWN OFF"

THE MEN FEARED JUMPING from their aircraft for many reasons. Aside from the slim possibility that they might be fired on by enemy fighters, and discounting the greater possibility of being mob-lynched by German civilians, there was the actual—and dangerous—act of parachuting itself. Firstly, the parachutes were packed by young men who generally had been on the job for less than a couple of years. That they made mistakes was a given. Too, there was the fact that parachutes were relatively new; materials and practices were still evolving. Finally, in the heat of combat aboard mortally stricken ships, the men often forgot or were unable to follow correct procedures. All of these factors contributed to the 303rd's casualty rate to some small degree.

A case in point was the experience of the Cecil Miller crew aboard the 358th Bomb Squadron's *Paper Dollie* on the July 23, 1944, mission to Creil, France. The ship was low on fuel and made it back to the English coast with only one engine operating. Once over land, unable to hold altitude on one engine, Miller ordered the crew to bail out.

He and the other eight men jumped. The parachute of William Zweck, the tail gunner, was caught up in *Paper Dollie*'s elevators. Zweck was subsequently dragged behind the aircraft and finally killed when it struck the ground. Miller, the pilot, pulled his parachute lanyard, but the parachute failed to deploy. He was killed when he struck the ground. The navigator, Saul Cooper, broke his ankle upon landing.

Another example was provided by Grady Hodges of the 358th Bomb Squadron. He was a waist gunner aboard *Lady Alta* when it was hit on the Merseberg mission on November 21, 1944. Hodges was urged by his comrades in the back of the aircraft to jump first; he didn't want to.

> But if I was to go first I wanted to hook my parachute ripcord to the static line by the door. This way the chute would open without any action on my part. I was not successful in snapping the line onto my chute. Thinking I was nervous, I asked the radio operator [James Brady] to snap the line onto my chute. He did it so vigorously that the chute pack popped open, spilling the chute to the floor at my feet. The radio operator picked up the chute carefully and placed it at my chest, folding my arms across it. I went to the door and tumbled out headfirst to try to delay the chute from opening and to get away from the tail of the plane. The chute opened almost immediately after I had cleared the tail of the plane. It was nice to look up at the opened chute above me and good to be away from the roar of the airplane engines and the gasoline fumes that had filled the plane.[1]

THE B-17, THE FLYING FORTRESS, owed much of its reputation to the defensive armament it carried. Unmodified, the B-17E and B-17F each carried nine guns, while the ultimate model, the B-17G, was equipped with thirteen .50-caliber machine guns. Quite frankly, formations of the big bombers—bristling with so many guns—terrorized German fighter pilots. They coined a name for that fear: *Vier Motor Schreck*, or "Four-Motor Fear."

It took men to operate these guns, and consequently nearly half the B-17's crew was dedicated solely to doing so. The tail gunner and ball turret gunner each fired two .50-caliber machine guns. There were two waist gunners, each manning a single gun. The radio operator's gun protruded through a hatch at the top of the fuselage, where he had a limited field of fire. The top turret and its two guns were manned by the flight engineer, whose additional duties included the mechanical well-being of the aircraft while in flight. In the aircraft's nose section, the bombardier and navigator operated the forward guns.

Flexible aerial gunnery was a maddeningly complex skill—a gunner had to fire his weapons so that the bullets and the aircraft at which he was shooting arrived at the same point at the exact same instant. This required him to solve for the ballistics or flight path of the bullets, the speed of the bomber from which he was firing and the range, elevation, speed and flight path of the enemy aircraft. Some men mastered the science of gunnery through informed instinct, while others followed rote procedure. Still others—barely competent—simply trusted to luck. It was a very difficult craft to learn well.

For instance, men who were experienced hunters—as many of the gunners were—knew through experience to aim ahead of, or to "lead," a moving target. However, because an aerial gunner shot from a moving bomber, he often had to aim *behind* his target. The *Gunner's Information File* tried to put the concept into a familiar context with "The Newsboy's Lesson":

> *Every newsboy soon learns the basic trick of aiming from his moving bicycle. The first time he tosses a newspaper he discovers a simple fact: If he aims directly at a front porch, he misses, and the paper lands next door. The forward motion of his bicycle carries the newspaper forward too.... The same thing happens to a bullet fired from a moving plane.... It keeps the forward motion given it by the moving bomber.*[2]

Of course, aerial gunnery was much more complex than tossing a newspaper, and teaching it was something for which the Army Air Corps was ill-prepared when the nation began to prepare for war in earnest. As late as 1940 there were no schools dedicated solely to train-ing aerial gunners. Such training as existed was not well standardized and was performed incidentally by a variety of organizations. The results were unremarkable.

However, as Arnold hurried to put the USAAF on a war footing, action was taken to train the gunners necessary to man the enormous numbers of sophisticated bombers that were planned. The first flexible aerial gunner school was opened at Las Vegas, Nevada, where flying weather was outstanding but where officialdom noted that "moral conditions were less than ideal." Notwithstanding that judgment, the surrounding area was vast and sparsely populated, and there was little danger that gunnery operations would cause injury or damage.[3]

After getting off to a slow start during 1941, when just more than a hundred instructors were graduated, the school quickly got to busi-ness. More than twenty-seven thousand students were trained during 1942 and 1943 combined. These were augmented by students pro-duced by six additional schools, in Texas, Florida, and Arizona. Most of the 303rd's men trained in either Kingman, Arizona, or in Las Vegas, where schools were specifically organized to train gunners for the B-17. In the aggregate, the seven schools produced nearly a quarter million aerial gunners. It should be noted that this number included radio operators and flight engineers as well as bombardiers and navi-gators when there was spare training capacity.

Assignments to aerial gunnery were initially made on a volunteer basis, but the need for gunners was much greater than the numbers of volunteers. Consequently, involuntary assignments began during Janu-ary 1943, and standards were lowered. Originally, aerial gunners ranged from eighteen to thirty years of age, stood five-feet-ten-inches or less and did not exceed 170 pounds. Importantly, they were required to score at least 100 on the Army's General Classification Test, or GCT. In order to increase the pool of men available for assignment as aerial gunners, the height, weight and age limits were eased and the GCT requirement was markedly reduced to 85.

The general quality of the early graduates when they arrived at the operational training units—the organizations that trained them on the actual aircraft types that they would fly into combat—was not impressive. A wartime report described their shortcomings:

Upon interviewing these men, we have found that they have not been sufficiently trained to be aerial gunners in heavy bombardment equipment. They do not know how to harmonize turrets, load ammunition and install in turrets; they do not know the use of K-3 and K-4 sights; they do not know how to install guns on the turrets or time solenoids for firing; they do not know how to detail strip the .50 caliber machine guns, and they do not know how to take care of any malfunctions which may occur in the action of the .50 caliber gun.[4]

However, the curriculum and quality of instruction improved as experience was gained and training equipment became more available. But both were long in coming. Even as late as mid-1942, there was not a single turret-equipped aircraft in any of the flexible aerial gunnery schools. In fact, .50-caliber machine guns and ammunition—together with various training devices and gun sights—were scarce well into 1943. The shortage of aircraft to tow targets, and of aircraft from which to fire at those targets, was just as bad. The AT-6 pilot trainer was used early on. It could accommodate only a .30-caliber machine gun on a primitive mount in the rear cockpit. It was nothing like the sophisticated, twin .50-caliber turrets that the men would operate in combat shortly after finishing training.

The course was originally only five weeks and included just 150 hours of formal instruction. It was almost immediately recognized that the training was not thorough enough, and the course was extended to six weeks. The intensity of the training increased dramatically over time. By March of 1944 the course included 290 hours of instruction—almost double the original number.

Classroom subjects included the theory of aerial gunnery, instruction on turrets and sights, and aircraft recognition—among others. Aircraft recognition was an issue early in the war and remained an issue throughout. Because the P-47 appeared similar to the FW-190 at a distance, it was constantly shot at by B-17 gunners. Consequently, to aid in their recognition, the P-47s were painted with white stripes around their cowlings, wings, horizontal stabilizers and tails. The 303rd's James Andrus noted this in his diary entry for December 23, 1943: "The P-47s are now striped with white because of Fortress gunners' itchy trigger fingers."[5]

Outside the schoolhouse the men spent many hours learning how to clean and care for both .50-caliber and .30-caliber machine guns. They were required to know the guns well enough so that they could, while blindfolded, put together a completely disassembled weapon from a jumble of parts. Additionally, they spent time on the malfunction range, where weapons were set up to suffer specific failures. The men were required to recognize and remedy the malfunctions within a specific period of time.

And malfunctions were not infrequent. For example, guns frequently froze at high altitude and refused to fire. The 303rd's crews experienced this problem on a number of sorties, to include the mission to Osnabrück on February 4, 1943. The group sortied thirteen aircraft, five of which aborted early—two for inoperative guns. Frozen guns caused both *The 8-Ball Mk II* and *Hunga Dunga* to turn back before crossing over the Continent.

However, it wasn't apparent that the guns aboard *Memphis Tot* were frozen until the formation was over the Netherlands. The pilot, Lloyd Cole, elected to leave the group and return to England before penetrating any deeper. Doubtless, he hoped to reach the North Sea and safety without being molested.

But luck was not with Cole and his crew. Alone, the defenseless *Memphis Tot* was attacked by Me-109s and FW-190s. Cole was hit in the hip by a 20-millimeter cannon shell, and his copilot was shot dead. Cole put the ship down in the Zuider Zee, where two of his men drowned. The rest were picked up by a Dutch boat and transferred to the Germans. Cole died later of his injuries.

In truth, it was very difficult to get the guns to fire once they were frozen. The key was proper preventative maintenance as promulgated in a later edition of the 303rd's Standard Operating Procedures for its gunners: "On damp and rainy days, the receivers, barrel jackets, and barrel jacket bearing will be wiped free from moisture. This must be done to prevent <u>FREEZING</u> of the gun at altitude." The procedures also directed: "In oiling aircraft guns, be careful not to use too much oil. In low temperatures the oil will <u>congeal</u> and cause <u>MALFUNC-TIONS</u>. It is best to OIL by wiping with an oiled rag."

Safety was constantly stressed at the schools. The .50-caliber machine gun was a devastating weapon, and horseplay or inattention could be deadly. This was proven over and over again, even at Molesworth, where the 303rd was considered to be among the most professional of a very professional organization of combat groups. Raymond Espinoza recounted an incident: "I was driving a 'cletrac' on the perimeter road with Sgt. Erwin Heins when a jeep pulls alongside and the driver yells that they need us near the 360th parking area. A B-17 had been set afire from an incendiary that was accidentally fired from a ball turret across the field. Heins and I hooked up to the B-17 and pulled it away from the burning fuel on the revetment."[6]

Indeed, safety and an understanding of the weapons, turrets and sights were all very important. However, the point of it all was shooting down enemy aircraft. Consequently the real focus of the flexible aerial gunnery course was marksmanship. In some instances the gunnery students started shooting BB guns and small .22-caliber rifles, but most men began their training with shotguns. Although the value of trap and skeet shooting—firing at flying clay discs with shotguns—was questioned, it was still taught throughout the war. The men also fired on the moving base shotgun range. While atop a moving vehicle, often a jeep, they shot at clay targets launched from variously placed trap houses. They also spent time in turret trainers and camera-based simulators such as the curiously named Jam Handy, which permitted the "actual practice of gun firing in aerial combat with built-in means to indicate, accurately and easily on the films, where the point of aim was as well as where it should have been."

Nearing the end of the course, the men tested their skills while airborne. During 1942 and 1943 they typically fired a .30-caliber machine gun from the rear cockpit of an AT-6 at a target towed by another AT-6. Later they fired from other aircraft, such as the twin-engine B-34, which was a Lockheed Ventura variant. It had waist gun positions as well as a dorsal turret.

The results of all the effort and resources that were put into aerial gunnery training were confounding. Hitting an aerial target required skilled shooting, but the level of marksmanship attained by the gunnery school graduates failed to match expectations. And the USAAF, despite repeated calls from the combatant commands for better-trained gunners, never satisfactorily determined the best way to teach them.

Even as late as April 1944, a ranking officer at a specially called flexible gunnery training conference stated: "Please don't think that the Second Air Force [a stateside command responsible for aviation training] or anyone else today knows the solution."[7]

Much of the debate about how to improve results revolved about which of the two primary methods of flexible aerial gunnery ought to be taught—the "relative speed" method or the "position firing" method. The relative speed method was initially favored but was complex and awkward to execute in actual combat, as described by a contemporaneous critic:

The gunner was taught to use the following sequence of action in sightings: (1) recognize the enemy ship, (2) estimate the range with 600 yards as the critical distance for opening fire, (3) estimate the difference in speed between his ship and the enemy ship by holding the sight stationary for one second, (4) compute the lead according to a definite table which he had memorized, and (5) open fire. Under combat conditions there was usually no target in sight by the time the student had gone through this involved system of computing the lead.[8]

The position firing method received more emphasis later in the war. It was a technique used against fighters flying a classic pursuit-curve attack. A fighter making a continuous attack against a bomber necessarily had to fly a predictable curving flight path. Position firing took advantage of that predictability, and the USAAF's instruction prompted aspiring gunners to recall the principle of "The Newsboy's Lesson":

> *You have seen in the preceding pages that if you shoot in any direction other than dead ahead or dead astern, your bullets do not go where you aim. The bullets not only move away from your gun, but they are also carried forward—and they are carried forward regardless of whether you fire to the side, above, or below. Like the boy on the bicycle, you must allow for this forward motion. Make this allowance by using the* first *rule of Position Firing: Always aim between the attacking fighter and the tail of your own bomber.*[9]

Position firing was taught through the war, although the more advanced compensating gun sights that were fielded during the latter years offered better accuracy. Using these sights, the gunner had only to adjust the size of the reticle to match the wingspan of the fighter at which he was shooting. Then, once the fighter was in range, he simply put the aiming dot over it while he squeezed the trigger. An example of one of these gun sights was the K-13, which replaced the primitive steel ring-and-post sights on many waist guns.

One constant, regardless of how they were aimed and fired, was the fact that the weapons had to be cared for. Paul Sersland, a waist gunner with the 360th Bomb Squadron, recalled how the guns were handled before and after each mission: "Usually we—the gunners—stopped at the armory to pick up our guns before we went to the aircraft. Specific guns weren't assigned to specific aircraft; instead we just drew from a pool of guns. They were all interchangeable. Once we got to the aircraft, we installed the guns and readied the ammunition, which had already been delivered. After the mission we simply left the guns on the aircraft, and the armorers came by later to pick them up as well as the remaining ammunition. The armorers also cleaned the guns—we didn't have to."[10]

This policy later changed, and the gunners were required to clean their weapons on the same day they flew their missions. The change even applied to the navigators and bombardiers, who were officers and not normally expected to perform such work. Cleaning and oiling the bulky guns was a grubby and miserable task, especially when the weather was cold and wet. Still, the men made the best of it and often socialized or swapped stories about the mission just completed. Theodore McDevitt, a bombardier with the 360th Bomb Squadron, recalled a humorous encounter:

After a rough mission to Berlin, a lieutenant and I were in the armament tent cleaning our guns when he told me of an incident that had taken place while he was stationed at the Kingman, Arizona, gunnery school. As he was new to the squadron, he didn't know that I was raised in Kingman. He told me he had been in Kingman only three times—his arrival, his departure and a mandatory formation for a ceremony in front of the county courthouse. He recalled that a local widow was being honored on Memorial Day, 1943, because all her five sons had enlisted and were overseas in combat. The new lieutenant told me what he thought of any woman stupid enough to have five sons in the first place, much less to have them overseas in combat. I informed him that the foolish woman was my mother, Della McDevitt.[11]

Ultimately, it is impossible to accurately measure how effective the gunners were. In all of history there are no similar examples against which to compare them. To be sure, other nations had bombers with gunners, but their operations were trifling in comparison. Certainly bombers—sometimes many bombers—were shot out of their formations by enemy fighters. In those instances the gunners were obviously ineffective or, at a minimum, not effective enough. On the other hand it is undeniable that the gunners also shot down significant numbers of German fighters.

However, at the macro level, what is known is that the bombers could not—without escorts—conduct a sustainable daytime bombing campaign in the face of determined fighter opposition. The B-17 as a self-escorting bomber was a failure because the gunners could not keep back the German fighters. The second mission against Schweinfurt demonstrated this with absolute finality. No matter how the mission might have been trumpeted as a success by the USAAF's leaders, there was no way that such losses could have been sustained.

That this was so was not a black mark against the gunners. Regardless of whether the problem was with the equipment or the training or the concept itself, the gunners—as was demonstrated thousands of times during the war—performed bravely and capably. Tail gunner Joseph Sawicki of the 360th Bomb Squadron provided just such an example during the mission to Bremen on November 29, 1943. On that day his ship, *Dark Horse*, piloted by Carl Fyler, was hit by a flak burst that stopped both engines on the right wing, tore away the right horizontal stabilizer and shredded the rest of the tail section. It also ripped away Sawicki's left arm. Moreover, his chest and abdomen were lacerated by shrapnel, and blood gushed from his wounds.

He crawled out of his position to get help, only to find the two waist gunners, George Fisher and Martin Stachowiak, on the floor of the aircraft; they were badly wounded and bleeding. Aside from their other injuries, they both had broken arms. With no consideration for his own well-being, Sawicki crawled forward and put parachutes on both men. With the last of his strength—the last of his life—he dragged his two comrades to the rear hatch, kicked it open and pushed them overboard. Both survived as POWs.

Joseph Sawicki perished with *Dark Horse*.

The gunnery schools graduated nearly a quarter million students destined to serve in hundreds of different organizations, and classmates often crossed paths afterward. Those reunions were not always happy, as evidenced by the experience of William O'Brien, a flight engineer with the 359th Bomb Squadron:

On one mission, we were forced to land at an emergency strip for fuel. A B-17 from another group had just landed and I was told the engineer had been wounded and the crew needed help. I rushed over and climbed to the plane's top turret. There was no rush—the back of the engineer's head had been blown off. I disengaged the power train and rotated the turret by hand. When I then saw his face, I was look-ing into the lifeless eyes of a friend I had made at gunnery school.[12]

IT HAD BEEN nearly a year since George Buske, the tail gunner aboard the *Jersey Bounce Jr.*, had been so horribly wounded. He should have died. He didn't. Instead, following his release from the hospital and a three-week respite at home, his request to be returned to duty—rather than being medically discharged—was granted.

Buske's remarkable resilience and dedication to duty are even more incredible when it is considered that he knew firsthand the dangers of air combat before he ever climbed aboard the *Jersey Bounce Jr.* on December 20, 1943. Three months earlier, on August 19, 1943, he had been badly wounded by German fighters during the mission to Gilze-Rijen, Holland. A 20-millimeter cannon shell knocked out his left gun, set his tracer ammunition afire and sent shrapnel deep into his hip. Nevertheless, he stayed at his position, warded off more attacks and was credited with downing one of the aggressive fighters. It was an action for which he was awarded the Silver Star and which caused him to be hospitalized for two months.

Buske's crewmate, Forrest Vosler, was awarded the Medal of Honor on September 6, 1944, by President Roosevelt in a ceremony at the White House. He was only the second enlisted airman to be so hon-ored. Although news of the event was welcomed by the 303rd back at Molesworth, there were few men remaining there who actually knew Vosler.

"WE WERE ALL VERY FRIGHTENED"

PAUL SERSLAND WAS BORN on July 7, 1924, on his family's farm near Decorah, Iowa. Tragedy struck him young in life. "It was quite a shock when Mother died," he said. "I was four years old and my mother died of complications of childbirth. Consequently, the decision was made to send me away to live with my mother's parents. My two brothers and older sister were already in school, but I was too young to go with them, and my father couldn't watch me and run the farm too. I was so young and didn't really understand what was happening; I didn't lose just my mother—I lost my entire family and the only home I knew."

Sersland was returned home a few years later, and his childhood regained a level of normalcy. "Our farm was a hundred acres and my life on it was pretty typical. We practiced what was called 'diversified farming.' We raised corn and livestock—to include a lot of pigs. These were mostly Red Durocs and Poland Chinas. We also kept about ten head of milking shorthorns. We used horses a lot and had chickens for eating and eggs. And of course we raised a big garden.

"We came from a long line of Norwegians on both sides of the family—I had a strong Lutheran upbringing and I was always a good student," Sersland said. "I was athletic too. I played both offensive and defensive tackle on the high school football team at Decorah. My brothers and I learned to shoot on the farm. We had a .22-caliber rifle and we shot rabbits and squirrels, which we ate at the dinner table. I learned how to shoot pigeons as they flew out of the barn, and we also hunted pheasants in the fields; that was very useful when I went to aerial gunnery school later."

Sersland didn't give aviation much thought until he was a young teenager. "One of my uncles had a glider. Decorah sat in a sort of bowl, and evidently the area was good for gliding. My brother and I used to hold the wingtips of the glider and run alongside while my other uncle towed the glider airborne with his Graham-Paige automobile. That got me interested somewhat in flying."

Sersland enlisted in the USAAF immediately after graduating high school in May 1943. At that point, the 303rd had been flying combat for more than six months. "I decided to enlist rather than wait to be drafted, because I got to choose the branch of service. I actually would have started training earlier than I did, but the farmer I was working with pulled some strings without me knowing to ensure I was around long enough to get the harvest in that fall."

Although he took the exams and qualified for training as an aviation cadet, the USAAF needed aerial gunners at that point more than it needed pilots. Sersland was sent to Kingman, Arizona, for gunnery school, where he scored the highest marks achieved to that point. "They arranged for me to stay as an instructor, but I didn't want to do that. I told them that I hadn't enlisted to be an instructor—I wanted to fly in combat. They didn't care and were set on keeping me there. I went up the chain of command until I reached a major who was sympathetic and let me go."

Sersland was sent to Kearney Army Air Field, where he was assigned to the Thomas Hardin crew as a B-17 waist gunner. "We were from all over the country. We were three Lutherans, three Methodists, a Catholic and a Presbyterian. Our pilot, Tom Hardin, was an atheist." Following more training at Rapid City in South Dakota, Sersland and the Hardin crew returned to Kearney, where they picked up a new B-17G and additional flight gear. They also underwent a final physical examination—including dental work and inoculations—preparatory to proceeding overseas.

The crew was ordered to England as a replacement crew for the Eighth Air Force and took the oft-traveled route across the North Atlantic. The weather was just as horrid as it had been earlier in the war. "It was nighttime when we took off," Sersland said. "We got caught up in clouds and heavy icing, which we had never encountered before. Tom tried to climb us above the clouds but wasn't able to get high enough. And then he descended as close as possible to the water, where the air was warmer. There we waited for the ice to melt.

"We were all very frightened," said Sersland. "There was a good possibility that the ice would force us to burn all our fuel just to stay airborne. We knew that we'd die very quickly if we were forced to ditch in that icy water. And we'd be dead without ever having reached combat. I kept my Aldis lamp trained on the right horizontal stabilizer and watched through the dark for any sign that the ice was clearing. Tom Hardin called over the interphone every few seconds: 'Pilot to Waist—is it melting yet?'

"I could tell that Tom—the atheist—was getting very anxious," Sersland said. "Then, he called over the interphone: 'Shouldn't you religious types be doing some of that praying?' We assured him that we had already been offering prayers for some time. Finally, I saw a chunk of ice break away. And then another, and soon the airstream got under the ice and lifted it all clear."

Once across the North Atlantic, Hardin's aircraft was put into a replacement pool. He and the rest of his crew were likewise put into a replacement pool. After a few days they were assigned to the 303rd's 360th Bomb Squadron and arrived at Molesworth on October 4, 1944.

A postwar study described the importance of replacement aircrews such as Hardin's to the morale of a unit:

> *Prompt replacement of killed, missing, wounded and worn-out air-men was essential to the preservation or restoration of good combat morale. In the case of units whose attrition rates were moderate, a steady supply of new pilots or crews acted more as a preventative of trouble than anything else. But for squadrons and groups that had been numbed by disaster, an immediate influx of reinforcements had the life-giving quality of a blood transfusion. It counteracted tenden-cies toward disintegration, helped to bring the organization out of a condition of shock, and started the healing process.*[1]

Of course Sersland—along with the rest of Hardin's crew—was a replacement and, thus, part of that healing process. He recalled his impressions upon being shown his new living quarters: "I was a bit uneasy. There were a lot of empty bunks in the building. I asked the guy who was helping me get settled in if the other crews had finished their missions. He hesitated a bit and said that it depended on how my ques-tion was interpreted. In truth, yes, the missing crews had flown their last missions. In fact, the 303rd had lost eleven of the twenty-eight bombers it sent on the raid to Magdeburg a week earlier, on September 28. My new squadron, the 360th, lost seven of the eleven. The news was quite a shock to me, and I was uneasy for some time after that, until I had a few missions under my belt. But from that moment I had a keener under-standing of what was meant by the term 'replacement crew.'

"A few days later I was impressed again when Lieutenant Colonel Lewis Lyle, the group deputy commander, had a meeting with us new arrivals. He didn't pull any punches as he laid down the realities of the air war. He was clear about what was expected of us and didn't try to make it seem that people weren't dying. It was clear that the same could happen to us." Sersland's experience was typical and was one he shared not only with his peers but with virtually every young man who ever went to war. He had always understood at an intellectual level that he stood a real chance of being hurt or killed, but the reality became more visceral as he neared actual combat.

NOVEMBER 11, 1944—ARMISTICE DAY—was like any other day for the 303rd. There was no armistice in Europe, and the target was the Buer Synthetic Oil Plant at Gelsenkirchen, Germany. The weather was low, gray and wet, and the men speculated that the mission might be scrubbed.

Robert Sorenson, the waist gunner for Paul Stephan's crew, remembered the details passed to the airmen that morning. "In the briefing room we were told that this was to be a quickie; a short run to the Ruhr Valley. This was good news. If we did get off, we'd be back by noon. It was the eleventh mission for our crew; another reason for optimism. It seemed that if a crew got past ten missions they were riding a lucky star and had a good chance of finishing their tour."[2]

Almost immediately after Stephan lifted *Duffy's Tavern* from the ground, the ship was cloaked by the rain-sodden clouds. Flying entirely on instruments, Stephan reminded the crew to put on their oxygen masks as the ship climbed through fourteen thousand feet. Sorenson, already on oxygen, moved forward and pulled the safety pins from the bombs. "About ten minutes later, we must have been at about 17,000 feet, I noticed a bright red glow out the left waist window. Thinking we were breaking through the clouds and the glow was the sun, I stood up to look out. That was no sun! There was a ten-foot tail of flame coming from the number one engine!"

Sorenson called a warning over the interphone. "But I don't think the pilot ever heard me because almost at the same instant the plane flipped over, went into a spin, and exploded." Sorenson was making his way toward his parachute near the rear exit door when *Duffy's Tavern* blew itself apart. He never got there.

"As the plane flipped I was thrown against the floor with such force that I couldn't move a muscle. It probably was only a split second, but it seemed like a long time. Then came the terrible explosion which blew me out through the fuselage head first." Stuck between a pair of the aircraft's structural ribs, Sorenson struggled mightily to push himself clear of the falling wreckage that had been *Duffy's Tavern.*

"Once in the air, everything seemed to be floating and there was a terrific ball of fire. All at once, out of the debris, came a parachute pack. It fell right into my arms. I was conscious at the time and snapped the chest pack onto my harness."

Sorenson blacked out for a few seconds before regaining consciousness and finding that he was clear of the debris. "I counted fast and pulled the ring [to the parachute]. Nothing happened. I looked at my hand. I was holding the ring but there was no cord attached to it. I shook my hand and thought I threw the ring away then started clawing at the [parachute] pack. There was no sensation of falling but I knew I had to get that chute open."

Sorenson passed out again. "My complete life went through my mind; every good thing and every bad thing. I even saw my grandparents. It was almost like meeting them in a new world. They had been dead for 15 years but they seemed as real as they were when I was a kid on their farm."

Sorenson fell in and out of consciousness as the ground rose up at him. Each time he tore at the parachute pack. "Finally it opened partially but I was tangled in the cords. "As I struggled I noticed that part of the chute was burned and hung above me like a tattered rag. . . . The last thing I remembered was a large tree coming up at me fast."

For reasons never determined Stephan had flown *Duffy's Tavern* dramatically off course. It crashed near Much Wenlock in Shropshire, more than a hundred miles *west* of Molesworth. Pieces of the bomber were spread over several miles. Bombs exploded and larger pieces burned on and along the main route into town.

Edward Townsend was a local homesguardsman. He and another

homesguardsman, Harry Murdoch, raced toward the wreckage. "It was misty and we couldn't see too far, but in the second field from the road we thought we heard a faint 'help.'" Townsend and Murdoch headed in the direction of the pleading voice and found "an airman leaning over some wooden rails in the hedgerow."

The airman was Sorenson. "He looked in a very bad state and was only half conscious. He apparently had walked or crawled 60 or 70 yards from a large oak tree where we later found the burnt and torn remains of a parachute. He was still holding the metal grip of the parachute ripcord."

Sorenson remembered nothing of hitting the ground, and it is impossible to determine exactly what happened. It is likely that the heavily damaged parachute caught some air and slowed him somewhat before he fell into the branches of the hoary old oak. Those branches slowed him further, although not without injuring him gravely. After finding Sorenson, Townsend and Murdoch lifted him down to an old iron gate and used it as a litter to carry him to a waiting ambulance.

Sorenson woke up in Much Wenlock's hospital two days later. "They told me I had a concussion, was missing a few teeth, my spine was crushed, my neck broken in two places and I had a blood clot in my left eye. I was pleased to find that Sergeant [Dwight] Philips, our engineer, was in the next bed. They had found him eleven miles from where I landed. His back was broken in several places. He told me that we were the only survivors."

The rest of the group flew an uneventful mission to Gelsenkirchen that day and bombed through the clouds. No enemy fighters were encountered and the flak was light. *Duffy's Tavern* was the only ship lost.

EVERY CREWMAN OF THE 303RD struggled with fears of varying intensities. Ball turret gunner Frank Boyle spoke about his: "Starting with my 28th mission I got 'flak phobia.' I was frightened to roll the ball [turret] after the door was closed. I had an unreasonable fear that the turret was going to simply fall away from the aircraft with me in it. And of course, there was no room in the ball for a parachute. I went to the flight surgeon and told him that I was afraid and was putting the entire crew in danger. He told me not to worry—that I was normal."

Boyle was sent to a rest home to recover. "It was the Royal Hotel at Southport," he recalled. "It was on the coast of the Irish Sea and the British royals stayed there prior to the war. I had never been anywhere so nice. The toilet covers were padded purple velvet and the faucets were gold." The Royal Hotel was one of an eventual seventeen rest homes that were contracted by the USAAF beginning in 1942. They were typically good hotels, or converted estates or manor houses, intended to provide a brief period of respite—typically a week—to battle-weary men, or to those who had survived a particularly traumatic episode.

Although they were often jokingly referred to as "flak shacks" or "flak houses," they were overwhelmingly enjoyed by the men who recuperated there. One objective was to "demilitarize" the homes to the maximum extent possible; references to rank were discouraged and civilian clothes were worn. Crews were often separated; the enlisted personnel were typically sent to different homes than the officers, although care was taken to ensure that there was no distinction in the quality of the different arrangements. The homes were staffed by proper Red Cross hostesses whose chief duties were to make the men comfortable without becoming romantically involved or overly familiar.

Activities at the homes ran the gamut from archery, horseback riding and canoeing to less strenuous diversions such as playing cards, board games, watching movies and reading. Nearby towns or cities offered drinks, ladies, shows and other entertainments. Or, if the men preferred, they were allowed to do absolutely nothing.

Frank Boyle's preferences were toward quiet. "No card games, no dances, no girls and no excitement. Actually, it was just what the flight surgeon told me I needed—all quiet and no stress. I had never had such a mental problem, and it just didn't go away after a good night's sleep.

"The greatest thing about the Royal Hotel was my two rooms," Boyle said. "In the bathroom there was a brass reading tray on a flexible three-piece rod mounted to the wall. You could swing the adjustable tray with the *London Times* on it while you were sitting on the throne. And the tray had a flexible brass lamp screwed onto the arm right above the tray."

"There was no shower," said Boyle. "There was just a jumbo bathtub with gold faucets and a hose with a shower-type head. And there were terrific towels and wall-to-wall carpeting. There was also a bidet. Coming from Vermont and the New Hampshire mountains, I had no idea how to use it, and I was too embarrassed to ask. My bedroom had a very soft leather easy chair and an ottoman. There was a flexible brass floor lamp that gave superb light. Of course it was nothing like in our huts at Molesworth.

"I met other bomber crewmen in the bar and billiard room," Boyle remembered. "We talked and drank good British pints. We were all there for the same reason. 'They' called it 'flak happy.' It wasn't easy to talk with your peers about being scared in combat. It wasn't the manly thing to do when you were nineteen."

Boyle made a distinction: "Nobody was scared at being shot at by fighters—you could shoot back at those SOBs. But the flak from the IP [initial point] until you turned for the barn after bombs away was the worst. Especially for us ball turret gunners. We had the automatic seat cameras that followed the bombs down to the target through the GD [God damned] flak bursts.

"And we talked," Boyle said, "about the Brass Hat stupidity of daylight bombing without adequate fighter cover. I think that kind of talk is just what we all needed. We just needed to get it out—cry over so many lost buddies and yell about our Brass. Nobody got drunk . . . just mad.

"After eight days I went back to finish my tour," said Boyle. "The fears were gone—I was just mad. Everyone on my regular crew had finished their tour while I was gone, and I consequently lived the ball turret gunner's worst nightmare, which was to fly as a substitute with new crews who had little combat experience. They often didn't understand how important it was to check on the ball turret every few minutes. If the oxygen went out, a gunner wouldn't live more than about five minutes, and they needed to know how to manually crank up the ball and drag me out."

Boyle flew with five new crews during his last seven missions and successfully completed his tour on Christmas Eve, 1944. "When I considered that I had originally enlisted with the intention of becoming a P-40 pilot," said Boyle, "it had been a strange string of events. God works in mysterious ways."

BOYLE WAS FAR from the only man who grew to fear the ball turret. David Michael recorded a hauntingly cryptic passage in his diary: "I'm afraid of that ball turret. How I'd like to forget. Darkness scares me."[3]

"NOTHING SPECTACULAR EXCEPT THE EXPLOSION"

MORE THAN TWO YEARS after it began combat operations, the 303rd had evolved into one of the Eighth Air Force's preeminent bomb groups. It was among the most decorated, most experienced and most effective—both in terms of bomb tonnage delivered and the accuracy of those deliveries. Too, its crews were noted for their competence and bravery—Mathis and Vosler being two examples of the latter trait. Nevertheless, there were infrequent missions when lapses in judgment, poor weather, enemy action or just plain bad luck, alone or in combination, conspired to work ruin on the unit. Indeed, there were occasions when—after all the effort spent on a particular mission was held up against the results—it could be said that the USAAF would have been better off had the 303rd never left Molesworth.

One such mission was the one to the Leuna synthetic oil refinery at Merseburg on November 21, 1944. It was a target that the Eighth had visited many times before. Both the 1st and 3rd Bomb Divisions—a total of 763 B-17s—were thrown into the attack. The 303rd's contribution was 39 bombers, 2 of which aborted for mechanical issues.

The weather was poor over the target, with clouds, haze and thick contrails. Consequently, each of the three squadrons the 303rd launched that day, the 358th, 359th and 427th, made individual runs. Inbound from the initial point to the target, one of the 358th's bombers was hit by flak and the crew jettisoned its bombs. Seeing the jettisoned bombs, five other crews mistakenly believed they were over the target and likewise released their bombs. Similarly, when the 358th's lead aircraft was hit by flak and its crew dumped its bombs, most of the crews who still carried bombs released theirs.

The PFF equipment aboard the 359th's lead aircraft failed just before the squadron reached the initial point, and the lead was passed to the deputy leader. For reasons that are not recorded, the results were not just poor, but were staggeringly awful. In fact, the 359th's bombs hit *fifteen miles* north of the mean point of impact—the specific part of the target that was supposed to be hit. Along the way the ship piloted by Andy Virag was hit not only by flak but also by *The Duchess' Granddaughter*, piloted by James Green. Virag, along with many of his crewmen, was on his last mission. After falling away from the formation, his ship was set upon by Me-109s. No longer able to control the aircraft, he ordered the crew to bail out. All the men survived, although the engineer, James Jeter, whose leg was nearly blown away during the fighter attack, was shot twice by civilians upon reaching the ground.

The crew of the 359th's *Heller's Angel*, captained by Arthur Chance, was not so fortunate. Like the Virag crew, many of the men were on their last mission, but their number three engine was hit by flak, and Chance was unable to stay with the rest of the formation. He ordered the crew to abandon ship but rescinded that order once he controlled the fire in the stricken engine. However, two of the crew had already parachuted clear.

It is possible this it was Chance's ship that was attacked by Me-262 pilot Georg-Peter Eder, who recorded the following encounter: "We had been following this bomber formation, looking to see if there were any fighters around, as there usually were. I did not see any, and being low on fuel anyway, I saw this one B-17 smoking, and went in. I only had cannons, so it was a quick pass, nothing spectacular; except the explosion."[1] It might not have been spectacular to Eder, but it was terrifying to the Chance crew. Those still aboard bailed out. Sadly, at least three members of the crew were murdered upon reaching the ground.

The 427th was no more successful with its bombs than were the 358th and 359th. In fact, it was uncertain where the 427th's bombs hit. Photographs from the ships that were equipped with cameras showed no explosions whatsoever on the target.

The results achieved by the 303rd that day were anything but laudable. Worse, the group paid a heavy price for achieving nothing. Four aircraft and crews—more than 10 percent of the attacking force—were knocked down. Lloyd Hester was the togglier aboard the 427th's *Miss Lace*. He saw the Peter Cureton crew go down:

> When Lt Cureton's plane in the lead element was hit, a piece of his B-17 wrapped around our right wing, cutting the oil line to the number 4 engine. Our pilot, Lt [Auston] Caplinger, had to feather it on the bomb run. I released the bombs, but was unable to close the bay doors. The electric motor was shot away. S/Sgt [Francis] Duffek and I had to crank it closed by hand. After the Cureton plane was hit, I saw one of his crew in a free fall through space. I learned later that it was T/Sgt [James] Ellis, whose parachute opened late. He was the lone survivor on that crew.[2]

That the flak and fighters were vicious was borne out by the fact that twenty-six of the thirty-seven B-17s flying the mission sustained major damage. One of those aircraft was piloted by Charles Haynes of the 359th. "Our ship lost two engines over the target and received major flak damage," said the crew's bombardier, Charles Dando. "We were unable to keep up with the group and stayed hidden in the fog until we emerged north of Frankfurt in bright sunlight and unlimited visibility. We felt that at any moment the Luftwaffe would appear and pounce on us, but miraculously they did not appear; instead a lone P-51 eased in on us and flew with us for a short time until a sudden burst of flak from the Frankfurt area hit him and he plunged down—no chute was seen."[3]

Flying on only two engines—and still over the Continent—the odds were against the Haynes crew. "We were gradually losing altitude crossing the Dutch coast under 5,000 feet and hoping we could reach Molesworth," said Dando. "We were now 1½ hours late and dusk was falling. When we reached Molesworth a runaway prop on [the] #3 engine, due to a severed throttle cable, caused us to lose the engine. We came in on one engine and without hydraulics or brakes we used up the entire runway before finally coming to a stop on the perimeter." Aside from the aircraft being sieved with more than two hundred holes, its main spar was nearly cut in half.

ALTHOUGH THE USAAF was a mighty force by the fall of 1944, its aircrews were still dying in horrible ways. And many of those men were from the 303rd. Richard Healy was leading the 427th Bomb Squadron against an alternate target at Osnabrück on November 24 when his ship was hit by a flak burst. "The explosion blew off the bottom of the fuselage from the chin turret back to the bulkhead directly behind the pilots," said squadron mate Jim O'Leary. "Dutch Spooner, the GH navigator, Slim Steward, lead navigator, and Sandy Sandhagen, the lead bombardier, all fell out without their chutes. They tumbled out like tattered rag dolls. Sandhagen, to my horror, was blown forward through the Plexiglas nose and came back through the No. 3 fan [propeller], then rolled over the top of the wing."[4]

Remarkably, Healy and his copilot were uninjured and landed the stricken ship at an advanced fighter airstrip in Belgium.

* * *

THE 303RD'S MISSION to the railroad marshaling yard at Ehrang, Germany, on December 23, 1944, was largely uneventful except that weather closed Molesworth. Of the thirty-nine aircraft that were sent on the mission, thirty-eight recovered at Bassingbourn and one landed at the RAF base at Gravely. "We were cold and exhausted after we landed," said Paul Sersland. "We had spent about seven hours in the aircraft during the mission, and then we had to spend another three cold and miserable hours in trucks to get back to Molesworth. We didn't get to return until very late. They arranged to feed us, but all we really wanted was to get back to our bunks. When we did, the huts were freezing—the day's allotment of coke had been burned long before."

Sersland and his comrades crawled into their freezing bunks and quickly fell asleep. They didn't remain so for long. Only a couple hours later they were wakened to fly as part of the most massive bombing mission in history. The Ardennes Offensive—better known as the Battle of the Bulge—was at its height, and the Eighth ordered every available bomber to participate in the mission of December 24. Anxious to cripple the German attack from the rear, the Eighth sent its bombers after a series of communications centers and airfields.

"They woke us much earlier than usual," Sersland said, "because they had to take us back to Bassingbourn." After seeing to their ablutions, eating a quick breakfast and attending the mission briefing, the crews were loaded aboard trucks for the cold, dark ride back to their bombers. Although a skeleton crew of 303rd maintenance men had been sent ahead to help ready the aircraft, the crews were still apprehensive. "We had all the trust in the world in our own ground crews, but much less in anyone else, no matter what unit or base they were from," Sersland recalled. "Accordingly, we checked our aircraft very thoroughly after we arrived. We checked the fuel, the oxygen, the guns—everything that we could touch or see."

The weather was horrid and the visibility was essentially nil as recorded by one of the crews: "No visibility during taxiing and take-off. Could barely see wing tip lights due to heavy fog. Made instrument take-off."[5] Nevertheless, the mission was not scrubbed. "It was unnerving," said Sersland. "Normally, at takeoff, each individual aircraft was ticked off a roster by personnel in the control tower. But that morning, because the visibility was so poor, they had to put a GI in a jeep at the end of the runway." All told, the 303rd launched fifty aircraft from six different airfields. Although the majority of them flew out of Bassingbourn, many aircraft flew from bases into which they had diverted for various reasons during the previous week or so. In fact, some of those bombers were flown by crews from other bomb groups, and one was even flown by a mixed crew.

Although the visibility over England was horrible that morning, it was perfect along much of the route and over the target. The column of 2,046 heavy bombers—B-17s and B-24s—together with the 853 escorting fighters, was the most colossal assemblage of aircraft in history. Only two years earlier the Eighth could not muster a mission of even a hundred bombers. Sersland was awed at the sight: "There were bombers as far as I could see. It just didn't seem possible that there could be so many. We were toward the front of the column, and after we hit the target and headed back west, it seemed the formation was almost unbroken. There were still airplanes making landfall en route to their targets as we reached the North Sea."

The German defenses were virtually impotent that day, as only twelve bombers were downed. It was a loss rate of less than half of 1 percent. Although a few German fighters were spotted, the 303rd remained unmolested. Still, the gunners nervously fingered their triggers as a lone Me-109 skimmed over the top of the formation with a P-51 in hot pursuit. One 303rd aircraft, *Ole George*, flown by a crew from the 92nd Bomb Group, was lost over Germany. *The Floose*—a veteran of 102 missions—was cracked up and destroyed on landing while flown by another crew from the 92nd Bomb Group.

Notwithstanding the tiny loss rate, the Eighth lost one of its stalwarts.

General Frederick Castle, who had been part of Eaker's staff during the early days of 1942, was at the head of the entire formation that morning. His aircraft was attacked and downed by Me-109s and he was killed.

The results of the day's bombing were excellent. The Hell's Angels had been tasked to hit the airfield at Merzhausen, near Frankfurt, Germany. More than 75 percent of the airfield was cratered, and it was knocked out of operations for the near term. The effects of the overall effort on the ground fighting were impossible to quantify, but certainly they were real and significant. However, perhaps more important was the psychological impact of the enormous raid. If it wasn't clear to the German leadership beforehand that the Americans could establish air superiority whenever and wherever they wanted, it was massively clear afterward.

The weather was still poor at Molesworth when the bombers returned, and most of the 303rd's B-17s diverted to the 96th Bomb Group's base at Snetterton Heath. Bob Hand, the navigator on *Old Cock*, was quick to make himself comfortable at the strange base and celebrated Christmas Eve with enthusiasm:

> I fell in with the festivities at the base and lost track of time and was left with no barracks or bed and/or blanket, etc. By this time the well known pot bellied stoves had burned themselves out and it wasn't getting any warmer. I gently lifted a blanket from over 4 or 5 sleeping airmen and fashioned a sack on the floor with my head next to the stove and fell fast asleep. Sometime in the night a person wearing heavy shoes was making his way to the john in the dark and not seeing all that well accidentally kicked me full force in the head. By the time I got back from First Aid my blankets were gone and I spent the rest of Christmas Eve sleeping in a chair in the day room.[6]

THE MEN WERE ALWAYS COLD. It was less miserable during the summer, but the wet, bone-chilling cold of England was a constant source of griping. The various buildings and huts were typically heated by coke-fueled potbellied stoves, but they were too few and too small to provide much comfort. Even so, the men were issued only enough fuel to fire the stoves for a couple of hours each day. "We usually burned ours between about five and seven in the evening," said Paul Sersland. "But it was never enough.

"So we went to the maintenance shops and borrowed an oxygen cylinder, a valve and some tubing. We filled the cylinder with aviation gas and oil, hung it in the rafters and then ran the tubing down into the stovepipe. And oh, it worked—that stove got red hot!"

An inspecting officer was wholly unimpressed with the ad hoc furnace and the very real possibility that the hut might be caught up in a conflagration at any moment. He ordered it removed. Sersland and his comrades shelved their nascent engineering talent and pursued a more traditional means for getting what they wanted. "We made an 'unauthorized acquisition' to fill a big box with coke," he said. "We cut a hole through the fence that guarded the field where it was kept. But they eventually discovered our hole and we had to stop our acquisitions. So we went back to being cold."

"WE SHUT DOWN EVERYTHING THEN"

THE PREVIOUS TWO JANUARIES had been cruel to the 303rd. Very early in its combat career, the January 3, 1943, raid to St. Nazaire cost the group nearly a third of its fourteen bombers. It did lose a full third of its aircraft—seven of twenty-one—only three weeks later, on January 23. The following year the Germans shot down eleven of the group's B-17s on the January 11, 1944, mission to Oschersleben. But with the war entering its final months, January 1945 developed to be not nearly so gruesome. During that month the 303rd launched 208 more combat sorties than it had during the previous two Januaries combined. But it lost only seven aircraft.

Still, the dying was not any less grisly. James O'Leary underscored that point in his description of the January 13 mission against the Schlageter Bridge across the Rhine at Mannheim. He flew as the 427th Bomb Squadron's command pilot in the squadron's lead ship.

The 303rd attacked the target through heavy flak. O'Leary's navigator, Edwin Katz, was hit in the head. "Ed's body was wedged in an upright position. The green quilting was missing on my side and I could look between the rudder pedals for a full view of him. As his body would sway with the movement of the plane, I could see that the only part left of his face was a long strip of skin about two inches wide with an eyebrow and eyehole."[1] The bombardier, Lloyd Long, peered sorrowfully through the gap at O'Leary and informed him over the interphone that there was nothing to be done for Katz. O'Leary directed him to concentrate on the bomb run.

The flak burst also blew the ship's instrument panel to bits, severed a number of hydraulic lines—including those for the brakes—and knocked out the radio transmitter. "Meanwhile the spouts of hot blood spurting into minus 50 degree temperature created dense steam that rolled up the catwalk, into the pilot's compartment." Clair Reed, the lead pilot in the left seat, mistook the frozen blood-mist for smoke, declared that the aircraft was on fire, and started to unbuckle from his seat. "I yelled back," O'Leary said, "everything is okay, we are not on fire, keep flying."

The damage the antiaircraft fire caused to the 303rd's formation included mortal blows to three ships of the 427th Bomb Squadron. *The Red*, piloted by Jack Rose, was one of those. It was hit in the right wing, which caught fire. "Jack called me two or three times to say that he was on fire and going down," said O'Leary, who couldn't respond because his radio transmitter had been shot out. The entire crew, after evading for a week, was captured and survived the war as POWs.

"My right wingman, Oliver 'Tommy' Eisenhart, had taken a direct hit in his tail wheel well," said O'Leary, "and his empennage was in the act of separating from the fuselage as he went under the lead plane." The radio room camera on O'Leary's ship caught one of the iconic images of the air campaign. In it, the empennage of Eisenhart's ship can be seen tearing away from the rest of the aircraft. When it broke free, the aircraft flipped end-over-end until crashing. None of the crew survived.

Old 99, piloted by Martin "Marty" McGinnis, was hit in the nose and tail sections as well as the right wing. It caught fire. "McGinnis's copilot, Second Lieutenant F. C. Doscher, called me to say that Marty had lost both legs at the knee and had bled or was bleeding to death," said O'Leary. Doscher called again to let O'Leary know that he had given the order to abandon ship. "Lieutenant Doscher impressed me with his calm report. But I could not acknowledge his message." All the officers of *Old 99* were killed, while the enlisted men were captured and made POWs.

O'Leary and his crew survived the return flight to England, and he landed their damaged bomber at RAF Manston, which had a runway that stretched nearly two miles; with no wheel brakes, he needed it. As soon as the aircraft's tail wheel settled on the runway, O'Leary cut the power to the two inboard engines and used the two outboard engines and the rudder to steer. The airfield and the surrounding area were abuzz with other bombers in extremis. "I saw a B-17 on fire over the field with a long string of chutes trailing it," O'Leary said. "Two aircraft were landing to our right [and] a third B-17 was landing behind them at a slant.

"Down at the far end of the runway," he said, "a long line of aircraft were taxiing nose to tail. I opened my window, and leaning out as far as I could, waved frantically at the planes crossing in front of us realizing that we were going to run off the end of the runway. The leading ship's nose dipped as the pilot applied his brakes. God bless him. We shut down everything then, and went bouncing and sliding through tall grass and small trees. We came to rest in an RAF latrine ditch."

O'Leary and his crew sat silent and breathed in the stink of piss and shit and hydraulic fluid. And blood. An ambulance raced up to the bomber and an English medic checked Katz's corpse and reported to O'Leary what he already knew: "Sir we can't do anything for your man up front."

O'Leary spent a restless night at Manston along with a hundred or more other displaced crewmen. He groaned out loud in his sleep and woke up, self-conscious, only to see that no one in the room was disturbed. He was flown back to Molesworth early the next morning, and he stopped by his quarters before dropping his flight gear at the squadron's quartermaster hut.

> *Opening the door to what I thought was an empty room and easing my duffel bag to the floor, I glanced up in surprise to see my original navigator, Lieutenant Michael Kacere, sitting in the top bunk. He was staring at my duffel bag, and I then noticed that it was covered with dried blood, bone, hair and something that looked like gray chewed paper. I looked at Mike again and he was sitting there with tears running down his cheeks. After a long quiet minute, I picked up the bag and headed for the Quartermaster hut.*

ELECTRONIC WARFARE—WHICH CENTERED to a great extent around radar, radar enhancements and radar countermeasures—evolved rapidly during World War II. The RAF started using thin aluminum strips, codenamed "Window," on July 24, 1943, to scatter German radar signals during the highly destructive firebombing of Hamburg. The metallic strips reflected the signals and caused great meaningless blobs on the Germans' radar scopes. Because the RAF's aircraft operated at night and were impossible to spot unless illuminated by searchlights, the German antiaircraft defenses were greatly hampered.

Later, the Americans used similar metallic filaments or metal-coated paper strips called "chaff." This proved effective when operating above the clouds, when the Germans could not use visual targeting aids. The chaff was pushed by the radio operator through a chute in his compartment. Upon receiving a signal from the group's lead navigator—a radio call and two red flares—the 303rd's radio operators were directed to dispense bundles that consisted of two thousand strips each, at a rate of "4 units every ten seconds unless briefed otherwise."[2] Notwithstanding the initial effectiveness of these types of radar countermeasures, the Germans developed *counter*-countermeasures that somewhat negated their effectiveness.

Beginning in October 1943 the USAAF started using radar spot jammers codenamed "Carpet." Earphone-equipped spot jammer operators shared the radio compartment with the radio operator. The spot jammer operators detected and identified the frequencies of the German radars with a single receiver. Once that was done, they manually tuned one of three transmitters aboard the ship to jam a specific radar set. So a single jammer-equipped aircraft could neutralize three different radars at one time; the group's formations usually included from one to three spot jamming aircraft. Jamming was most effective when the formations were obscured from the ground by a layer of clouds. Otherwise, the German antiaircraft gunners could use visual sighting systems.

Another crew position that appeared late in the war, and about which very little information is available, was the Y-operator. The Y-operator shared the radio compartment with the radio operator on especially equipped ships and sat at a purpose-designed radio set. German-speaking, his job was counterintelligence. Likewise, the voice interpreter position emerged late in the war, and this crewman also operated special equipment in the radio room. He listened to German communications and took notes, sometimes passing that information—particularly as it related to fighter operations—to the pilot. Many of the men were cross-trained to serve as voice interpreters, Y-operators and spot jammers.

"WHAT THE HELL IS GOING ON UP THERE?"

ALBERT "AL" DUSSLIERE, or "Deuce" as he was later known, was born in Moline, Illinois, on July 21, 1924. "I was named after King Albert of Belgium. My father was Flemish and emigrated from Belgium to the United States in 1903 when he was nine, and my mother's heritage was also Flemish—she was from a family of fourteen."

Dussliere's childhood was almost a caricature of early twentieth-century America. "My father was a grocer and I grew up in the business. All of us boys—I had three brothers—worked in the store and we knew everyone in the neighborhood. It was a very important part of our lives. We had a classic Catholic upbringing; the parish was only a block from our house. Likewise our school was only one block away but in a different direction. John Deere was the major employer in the city. Actually, it was the heart of the community, and the company maintained a wonderful complex of athletic fields. As kids, we were free to use them and played a great deal of softball, which was very popular when I was growing up.

"We used to hang out at Bert Busconi's gym when I was eight or nine years old. Bert hosted boxing tournaments that toured the area. It was his idea to teach me and my brother trick wrestling moves and feature us in between boxing matches to help entertain the crowd. We were really kind of a novelty, and the spectators threw money into the ring at us quite often. One night we came home with twenty dollars; it was more than my father cleared at the grocery that day.

"We did other things to raise money too," Dussliere said. "We set up Flavor Aid stands outside the store and sold drinks to my father's customers—they were a captive audience. And I was a pretty good promoter too. We used to stage small carnivals, boxing matches, amateur stage productions and things of that sort on my grandfather's property. We had a lot of fun."

As idyllic as Dussliere's early life might have seemed, it was still marked by tragedy. "My mother died when I was twelve. Obviously, it was very hard on all of us, but my father did what needed to be done to raise me and my brothers. And he had lots of help. Not only did his family live in town, but all my mother's siblings were still there. We had cousins by the dozens and enjoyed all the advantages of a large, loving extended family.

"I was never one of those kids who were fascinated by airplanes," Dussliere recalled. "I wanted to go to college and be a lawyer. But in January 1943, with the war on, I went up to Chicago to see the Navy recruiter. We thought that flying with the Navy would be a good way to do our part. But at that time the Navy had all the pilot candidates it needed. The recruiter did put two of our group into flight training and enlisted three others. He told me that if I really wanted to fly I ought to try the Army. That's what I did. I passed the exams with no problem and started training as a cadet in June 1943." At that time, the 303rd was part of the initial effort to execute POINTBLANK. In fact, Ehle Reber, one of the 303rd's original pilots and one of its first casualties, had already been dead for five months.

Dussliere didn't complete cadet training. Rather he was sent to gunnery school and assigned to B-17s as a waist gunner. His training was much improved over that of his predecessors, as it had been informed by nearly three years of combat operations. He arrived in Molesworth during the late fall of 1944 and flew his first mission on December 18.

JANUARY 10, 1945, marked the 303rd's three hundredth combat mission. "I'm not sure that most people even knew it was the three hundredth mission," recalled Ed Gardner, the navigator on the Grafton Smith crew.[1] "If anything, our crew was a little unnerved because it was our thirteenth mission. And it was the hundredth mission for our airplane, *Buzz Blonde*. She was a great airplane. The nose art was a painting of a beautiful blonde—completely naked. Her arms were outstretched like she was flying and her breasts were taut and thrust upward. She had little propellers for nipples. But no one made a big deal during the briefing about it being the group's three hundredth mission. In fact, they emphasized the fact that it was expected to be a milk run."

Lack of fanfare aside, the three-hundred-mission milestone was one that no other bomb group had achieved, and it underscored the unit's reputation as one of the USAAF's premier combat units. It was highly regarded as an efficient and professional organization, and the argument could be made that no other bomb group had hit Germany so hard.

Notwithstanding the 303rd's reputation and experience, the mission developed to be a poorly executed mess. A number of factors—some over which the men had control and some over which they did not—came together to work against the group. First, it had snowed the previous night, which not only made the work of the maintenance men and bomb loaders difficult and miserable, but also required extra details of men to clear the taxiways and runways. The change in weather also brought a change in wind direction. This forced the group to take off from the north-oriented runway, which was counter to how operations were normally conducted. The deputy group commander, Edgar Snyder, described the effects of the change in a memorandum to the group a week later: "Under favorable weather conditions, taking off on the N-S runway is complicated and requires prompt compliance with and execution of instructions; under adverse weather conditions anything less than clockwork precision produces falling hair and a condition best described as FUBAR [Fouled Up Beyond All Recognition]."[2]

The runway change alone caused plenty of confusion, but the disorder was exacerbated when crews mistakenly taxied out of order and at the wrong times. Efforts to return some organization to the muddle were aggravated when a wheel on one of the bombers locked and trapped other aircraft behind it. The brakes failed on another bomber and it ran off the perimeter track. Ultimately, thirty-two aircraft got airborne more or less on time, but another seven aircraft were delayed an hour and never rendezvoused with the main body. Rather, they tacked themselves to another bomb group.

The 303rd's main formation, further reduced in size when two aircraft aborted, made it to the initial point on a northerly heading toward the target in reasonably good order. However, as Snyder noted in his memo, things unraveled quickly: "The main portion of our effort stayed together until the I.P. was reached. From the I.P. to the target we again ran the gauntlet of all the things that shouldn't happen to our worst enemy. Even the good Lord is confused as to just what went on."

The lead aircraft of the low squadron lost an engine and fell out of formation. The GEE-H set in the aircraft of the group leader, Major George Mackin, failed to work properly. This radio navigation device was used to bomb targets in poor weather. There appeared a providential break in the clouds near the target—the Bonn/Hangelar airfield—and the group set up for a visual bombing run, but a blanket of snow made it almost impossible to distinguish landmarks and the lead bombardier set up on the wrong target. Moreover, the bomb bay doors on the lead aircraft failed to open.

The high and low squadrons lost sight of the lead squadron as it maneuvered to attack the correct target. In a turn, for whatever reason, half the bombs from the deputy lead's aircraft fell away, and many of the togglers aboard the other bombers in the lead squadron mistakenly released their bombs at the same time. Mackin, at the head of the formation, erroneously believed his was the only aircraft with bombs remaining, and he consequently directed his bombardier to set up on whatever worthwhile target presented itself. This made more sense to him than taking the lead squadron back through the flak just so that he could drop his own bombs. As his bombs fell earthward, he was astonished to see the other half of the formation also drop its bombs on the ad hoc target.

The high and low squadrons executed their own attacks. "We came around for a second run on the target," remembered Gardner, "but had to abort it when a group of B-24s appeared below us. They were on time whereas we weren't. We finally released our bombs on the third try."

Blundering formations, blind dumping of bombs and other miscues aside, the 303rd's three hundredth mission was marked by tragedy as well. Al Dussliere, the waist gunner aboard *Buzz Blonde*, remembered what happened as the group finished its abbreviated run on the target: "Very shortly after the bombs were released, the squadron started a hard left turn, which put us into a blinding, low-angle sun. At full power and almost in the contrails of our element lead, we moved to our left and up to our left wing position on the high element lead.

"Our bombardier, Bill Dohm, leaned over to look out the nose so that he could see the bombs hit. But what he saw was not what he expected. There was the cockpit of another B-17 directly below him. He felt like he could reach down and shake hands with the flight engineer in the upper turret." Dohm immediately called over the interphone for the pilot, Grafton Smith, to pull up. At the same time he rushed to get out of the nose and shouted for Ed Gardner, the navigator, to follow him.

Ed Gardner remembered: "Bill Dohm disconnected his interphone, his oxygen and his electric flying suit and rushed by while shouting at me to get out of the nose. I also disconnected my equipment and started back, but right before I ducked down into the catwalk that ran under the flight deck I saw a giant black shadow rise up in front of our aircraft. It was the vertical stabilizer of another B-17.

"When we hit," Gardner remembered, "it sounded like a million tin cans being crushed all at once. The tail of the other bomber cut all the way through our nose and came right up to my feet. Then we separated for a few seconds before colliding again into the number two engine of the other aircraft."

Dussliere, the waist gunner, recalled the instant of impact: "In the back of the airplane we felt a tremendous jolt accompanied by a loud crashing sound. At the waist position, everything that wasn't fastened down was knocked around. I was slammed forward but managed to stay on my feet and get back to my gun on the right side. Looking out, I couldn't see the rest of the formation, and it seemed that we were pulling away to the left. Back at the tail position, Mel Howell seemed alert and was at his guns. Toward the front I saw George Parker in the radio compartment and he was okay too.

"The right wing was bent in two places and drooping like it was on a wounded bird," Dussliere continued. "And the number three engine was shaking like hell. In the back, we all thought we had been hit by flak."

Buzz Blonde's nose was torn away, but both Bill Dohm and Ed Gardner were still alive. Nevertheless, both of them were knocked unconscious. When Dohm regained his wits, he was on his back facing the rear of the aircraft with ammunition belts strung across his legs. Ed Gardner was down around his feet. A great, icy blast pinned the two of them where they were. Moreover, both had lost their helmets, gloves and oxygen masks.

The two men, trapped and without oxygen, were in danger of passing out and freezing to death. "I got up," Gardner said, "and stepped onto the catwalk that ran under the flight deck. I reached up and beat on the engineer's legs. Both Bill and I needed oxygen bottles." There was no response from the engineer, David Massingill. "I turned around and looked at Bill and he motioned at me to bail out from the escape hatch. It was then that I remembered my parachute. Thankfully, it was still in front of the bulkhead, but I was only able to get one of the snaps attached to my harness."

Suffering from shock, cold and anoxia, Dohm and Gardner struggled in the windblast. Gardner tried to get the engineer's attention again, and once more received no response. It was at that point that Gardner released the escape hatch on the lower left side of the nose below the pilots. They both hesitated to leave the bomber. Gardner and Dohm were operating on the very edge of consciousness and neither recalled how they finally cleared the aircraft.

Al Dussliere recalled what happened: "Ray Miller, the ball turret gunner, called out over the interphone and said, 'Someone just bailed out! And someone else bailed out! What the hell is going on up there?' Miller was told to get out of the ball and he did—in record time."

Smith and his copilot, Mel Alderman, wrestled with *Buzz Blonde*. Not only was the right wing broken and the nose smashed, but the right horizontal stabilizer was also mangled. Moreover, the ailerons were jammed and the two pilots were only able to turn the bomber— and just barely—with the rudder.

"Dave Massingill, the flight engineer, was flying with us as a replacement," Dussliere remembered. "He found some GI blankets and gave them to Smith and Alderman to wrap around their legs. They started descending the airplane and sent him back with us so he could get out of the wind."

"IT WAS A POPPING NOISE in my ears that brought me back to consciousness," recalled Ed Gardner. "It took a moment for me to realize that the cold, wet gray through which I was falling was the cloud layer that had been below us. I guessed that Bill Dohm had pushed me out through the escape hatch."

The cold was ferocious. "I touched my nose and ears," Gardner said, "and found that they were frozen nearly solid. I pushed harder on my right ear and was startled when the cartilage snapped. So I left my ears alone. Instead, I tried again to hook the second snap of the parachute to my harness, but my hands were frozen just like a chunk of meat in the grocery store. I just couldn't make them work. Then, I put my hands under my armpits to try to warm them. After a bit I tried the parachute snap again but still couldn't get it attached. At this point I shouted, 'God help me!'"

When Gardner finally tried to pull his parachute's ripcord, his hands were so wooden that he was lucky—after several attempts—to hook his little finger through the ring. When he pulled it, the canopy blossomed nicely, although—because it was attached at only one point—he was suspended lopsided beneath it. "I looked at the countryside," he said, "and it looked empty. I thought I might have a decent chance to evade. It was about then that I heard rifle fire and bullets ripping past me. I started swinging in my parachute to throw off their aim."

Gardner fell into a deep snowbank on the side of a hill. "When I finally dug myself out of the snow, I was surrounded by a group of farmers with rifles. A big, fat SS major in uniform was shouting at them to shoot me. He called me a *terror flieger*, and *luftgangster* and *Amerikanischer!* I was frightened that they were going to kill me right there. But they seemed unsure and not at all inclined to shoot me. It might have been because I was very youthful looking. I was twenty-one, although I could have easily passed for sixteen."

It was at that point that a pair of Luftwaffe soldiers arrived. "They drove up in what looked like a German version of a jeep [probably a *kübelwagen*] and just walked right up without saying a word. They helped me out of the snow and into the vehicle with my parachute. And then they drove me away."

Like Gardner, Dohm was disoriented when he regained consciousness. He was falling face up, and it took time for him to roll his body around and judge his height above the ground. When he estimated that he was below ten thousand feet, he reached to pull his ripcord. Again, like Gardner's, his hands were frozen, and it took time for him to release his parachute. Notwithstanding the fact that the parachute worked perfectly, he descended toward a farm and slammed into the roof of a barn before his parachute dragged him to the ground. He was captured immediately.

SMITH AND ALDERMAN still fought to maintain control of *Buzz Blonde*. "Without a navigator or any charts," remembered Dussliere, "they decided to head south toward France. The plan was to stay on top of the clouds as long as possible and then, if enemy fighters showed up, descend into the clouds. The tail gunner, Mel Howell, helped keep us on course by calling out the position of the sun."

The Luftwaffe never showed and the clouds soon dissipated, although the visibility was marginal. "As we passed through about six thousand feet, Smith gave everyone the option to bail out," Dussliere recalled. "He and Alderman planned to try to land the plane. The rest of us decided to stick with them."

It wasn't long before a C-47 was spotted lifting from an airfield. Without charts, Smith and Alderman didn't know exactly where they were but *Buzz Blonde* was obviously over friendly territory. They eased the power to the engines and let the big bomber drop toward the airfield. In the back of the aircraft the men readied for a crash landing.

"When Smith and Alderman turned downwind and lowered the landing gear," Dussliere said, "a voice came over the radio and told us to land alongside the runway. The airfield was a fighter base, and they didn't want us to crash and clobber the metal mat runway." Smith and Alderman raised *Buzz Blonde*'s landing gear and—steering by rudder alone—struggled to get the ship lined up for landing. It was no good. The two pilots added power to the three good engines and hauled the battered bird around for another approach.

Dussliere said prayers from the radio compartment, where he and the other four enlisted men assumed their crash positions. "There was a strong sense of relief," he said, "when we heard the power come off the engines and felt the plane settle on the ground. The pilots let it toboggan on the snow. As the plane slid down the side of the runway, snow poured down the open escape hatch and created a blizzard where we were sitting in the radio compartment. The airplane rotated slowly around to the left until we were pointed opposite the direction we were traveling. But it really was a very smooth landing. Unfortunately, we demolished a number of light aircraft as we slid.

"As soon as the plane stopped, we scrambled out through the escape hatch at the top of the radio compartment," Dussliere said. "We were fearful that there might be a fire. When we saw that the aircraft wasn't burning, we jumped back up on the wings to help Smith and Alderman through their respective windows. When the crash crew got there, we found out that we were at A-97 in Sandweiler, Luxembourg."

IZA VAILABLE III, piloted by Roy Statton and David Schroll, was the aircraft with which *Buzz Blonde* collided. *Buzz Blonde*'s number three engine hacked away the other aircraft's tail section. The tail gunner, Marion Mooney, fell away with it and was killed. Like Smith and Alderman at the controls of *Buzz Blonde*, Statton and Schroll got their mangled aircraft safely on the ground with an emergency landing in miserable weather, at B-53 in Merville, France.

One more loss marked the 303rd's three hundredth mission. The B-17 commanded by Cecil Gates was clobbered by flak as it approached the target. Three engines were knocked out, and maintaining control of the aircraft was almost beyond the physical capacity of the pilots. Gates stomped the left rudder to its limit while clutching the control yoke all the way back into his chest. With the help of his copilot, Benjamin O'Dell, he coaxed the steadily falling bomber through a turn to the west toward Allied lines.

Other than his backup compass, Gates had no flight instruments with which to safely penetrate the clouds below. An attempt to descend through them for a crash landing would surely have failed, and there was no good option but to abandon the stricken B-17. Gates sent O'Dell back to direct the enlisted men to jump. The Y-operator, Paul Hassler, was reluctant to do so. He spoke German and believed, with some justification, that he would be killed as a spy if he were captured. After O'Dell explained that Hassler had no choice—unless he wanted to stay aboard a pilotless aircraft—Hassler parachuted clear with the rest of the enlisted men. Gates, O'Dell and the crew's other two officers followed soon after. As it developed, Hassler evaded the German forces retreating through the Ardennes area and made it to the Allied lines, as did Gates, O'Dell and the other officers. Of the enlisted men, aside from Hassler, two were captured and killed, while three were made prisoners.

ALTHOUGH THE GROUP'S EXECUTION of its three hundredth mission was not something of which its leadership was proud, the fact that it reached the mark—and was the first heavy bomber group to do so—was. Nevertheless, it was little more than a number. The war was not over, and finishing it would demand more sacrifice. The group's commanding officer, Lieutenant Colonel William Raper, said as much in a congratulatory memorandum he delivered to his men on January 17, 1945, the week following the mission:

You have every reason to be very proud of our fine record and of our war effort to date. You have all worked very hard, putting in long hours under trying and adverse conditions. Your teamwork has been magnificent, and without it our accomplishments would never have been possible. However, this war is not over, and we must all continue to do everything in our power to keep this excellent record intact, and to improve it when and where we can. Our goal is a common one—total defeat of the enemy, so that we may again return to our families, our homes, and our normal way of living.

Accordingly, the men of the 303rd were compelled to continue the deadly grind.

Raper's memorandum mentioned teamwork. Certainly the 303rd was a team—a winning team—that proved itself every day. And the crews on each bomber made up smaller teams that worked toward the common goals of delivering bombs against the Germans and coming home in one piece. The public image of the USAAF bomber crews was of men who were "closer than kin." Within those crews, each man supposedly loved the others like brothers.

Such was the case many times. They crawled into their aircraft not for love of country, although virtually all of the men considered themselves patriots. Nor did they do it because their commanders issued orders that compelled them to go; they were volunteers and could have refused air combat at any time. And they didn't take to the skies to satisfy a sense of adventure and an urge to fight. Not after the first couple of missions, anyway.

What actually motivated them to fly mission after mission at terrible risk to life and limb was the difficult-to-describe bond of comradely love that manifests itself when men face danger together. Mel Schulstad articulated it with a pain that still throbbed decades after the war. He choked with tears and paused, then said, "You keep on going . . . because the other guys are going." He stopped again to blink back tears and then said, "And if they're going, you're going. It was a fantastic thing the way we came together as a group of people. We didn't know each other from Adam's off ox when we came together, but by the fourth or fifth mission we were blood brothers. You would do anything to keep your crew alive and well and happy. And you'd stay with them through hell and high water. And you did."[3]

But it was unrealistic to believe that eight, or nine or ten, men from different regions and backgrounds would come together in every instance and form strong fraternal bonds. The chemistry of personality simply worked against such a notion. There were too many screwups and sad sacks and bullies and other incompatible types. Some men just didn't like the way others looked or talked or walked or laughed.

Carroll Binder recalled how his crew became angry with their ball turret gunner when they learned that his guns—presumably due to his neglect—failed to fire during a particularly heated attack by enemy fighters. "We knew that, barring cold conditions not even approaching that day, guns would operate if properly cared for, and we were furious to find that Shorty had never succeeded in firing a single round from either gun, even more furious to see that, far from apologizing, he was now strutting like a peacock, telling the ground crew what it was like to be fighting the war. Under normal conditions, at least one of us would have taken a crack at Shorty's too-active jaw, but we were so tired that we let it go at a warning that a similar incident had better not take place again. Shorty said something about our always picking on him and sulked off to remove his guns."[4]

Paul Sersland recounted a mission to Sterkade during which a crewmember decided he was done being a volunteer. The aircraft, captained by Tom Hardin, had taken a beating. The left outboard engine was hit and set up a massive vibration through the entire aircraft. The fuel tanks on the right wing were also hit and streaming. The nose was badly damaged, and the bombardier and navigator had to be pulled clear. Just keeping the ship airborne required every bit of Hardin's considerable skill.

Meanwhile, a drama unfolded in the rear of the aircraft. Sersland, the waist gunner, looked back to see the tail gunner crawl out of his position and into the fuselage. "I asked him what he was doing—there was a good chance that we might be attacked by enemy aircraft. We were all needed at our guns because as a straggler we were easy pickings. He said he knew we weren't going to make it back to England and that he was bailing out.

"It wasn't unreasonable that he thought we might crash, but we were still flying at that point, and Tom Hardin hadn't yet given the order to bail out. He said he was going to jump anyway—the odds of making it back to England were poor. I stopped him. I asked him if he was sure his parachute was going to work. This caused him to pause as there certainly was no guarantee. Then I reminded him that even if his parachute did work, he could be shot by German fighters as he descended. This caught his attention even more.

"Then," Sersland continued, "I reminded him that intelligence reports indicated that it was not uncommon for German civilians to murder Allied flyers after they bailed out. It had happened many times. Finally, I told him to sit down by me. I let him know that I was pretty sure we were going to make it back, but if it got worse we would bail out together.

"He finally agreed to stay on the airplane," said Sersland. "But he said that if we did make it back he was never going to fly again. I told him that was fine. We were all volunteers and none of us had to fly if we didn't want to." As it developed, Hardin wrestled the ship back to England. The gunner was sent to a rest home but never flew again.

"DOWN IN FLAMES DOVE ANOTHER OF GOERING'S FANATICS"

THE AMERICAN BOMBER formations sent over Germany during early 1945 were massive. Raids of more than a thousand bombers became almost commonplace. In part because of the enormous numbers of men required to man the aircraft, the composition of the bomber crews was changed during this period. "Instead of two waist gunners," Al Dussliere said, "we started flying with just one. By that time, there simply weren't very many German fighters left. And even if there had been a lot of fighters, the waist positions could usually be covered by a single gunner because the attacks generally came from only one direction at a time.

"And, quite frankly," he said, "the waist gun positions weren't that effective. They were manually aimed and for the most part had only simple steel sights. Also, instead of having two guns as in the chin turret, the ball turret, the top turret and the tail position, each waist gun position had only a single gun. Finally, one less gunner meant that the aircraft had to lift that much less weight."

* * *

FOR ALL INTENTS AND PURPOSES, the Luftwaffe was finished. Some of the 303rd's success—and much of Germany's failure—was due to chronically abysmal leadership at the highest levels of the Luftwaffe. Its head, *Reichmarschall* Hermann Göring, was a decorated World War I fighter pilot and a charismatic, bright and sensitive personality. He was also a grotesquely selfish, corrupt and cruel narcissist and liar who failed to understand modern air combat and was too lazy, drug-addled and paranoid to put in place the people, policies and resources necessary for the Luftwaffe to succeed.

Another person who bore much responsibility was Ernst Udet, who was charged with development of new equipment and aircraft for the Luftwaffe. Like Göring, he was a successful World War I ace. Also like Göring, he was an ebullient personality who abused alcohol and drugs to the point that his work and judgment were impaired. The Luftwaffe's failures during the Battle of Britain and the invasion of the Soviet Union were major reasons for his suicide in late 1941. Another luminary was Hans Jeschonnek, the chief of the general staff of the Luftwaffe. He was a hardworking, dour martinet who—continuously stymied by Göring—was unable to right the wrongs that were being done to the Luftwaffe. In August 1943, like Udet, he committed suicide.

Erhard Milch, the air inspector general, and Albert Speer, the minister of armaments and war production, were capable administrators who were more successful than Udet and Jeschonnek in working around and behind the backs of Göring and Hitler. Indeed, Speer's dramatic and abrupt over-haul of German industry enabled the Reich to increase aircraft and arma-ments production during 1944 in the face of Allied attempts to bomb it into rubble. However, in the face of simultaneous attacks on fuel produc-tion, and in light of earlier German failures, there was little that Germany could do—barring a miracle—to save the Luftwaffe.

That miracle a year or so earlier might have been the Me-262 jet fighter. It was the one bright spot in the Luftwaffe's fighter force during the last few months of the war. Designed and built by Messerschmitt, it was a revolutionary, twin-engine design that was heavily armed and up to a hundred miles an hour faster than most Allied fighters. Speculating as to what might have happened had the Me-262 been introduced during 1943 rather than late 1944 is a never-ending exercise that excites experts on all sides. It is common to blame Hitler for the delay in its fielding due to his insistence on it being deployed as a fast bomber. The truth is, regardless of what Hitler did or didn't do, technical and material issues caused considerable delays, as did wrongheaded decisions up and down the Luftwaffe chain of command. Hermann Göring, Hitler's chief sycophant, could have done much to eliminate a lot of the friction had he been interested in leading rather than stealing great European art treasures.

In service, the aircraft was unreliable. Jet engine technology was still very immature, and the necessary metals were not available in Germany in the amounts required. Consequently, the engines were quite prone to failure and had to be changed after only about fifteen to twenty hours of flight time. Nor was the aircraft a good dogfighter. In a classic, hard-turning engagement it was easily outmaneuvered by the Allied front-line propeller-driven fighters. Its chief advantage was its speed, which approached 550 miles per hour. So long as its pilots flew high-speed slashing attacks, the jet was virtually untouchable. And armed with four 30-millimeter cannons or R4M rockets it was a superb bomber killer.

The jet's speed also made it less vulnerable to aerial gunners. Frank Boyle remembered that the fast new jets largely negated the effectiveness of his ball turret. "The Me-262s were so fast that we couldn't traverse the ball fast enough to pull the right amount of lead—we couldn't get our guns in front of them. And it really didn't matter anyway because the computing gun sight couldn't handle such high speeds. If they attacked us from the rear, we could pull enough lead but the firing time was so short that they were extremely difficult to hit."

Al Dussliere's diary entry for the 303rd's mission to Hamburg on March 20, 1945, captured not only the excitement of a young man in air combat, but also his wonderment at the new German Me-262 jet fighter. Also notable is his contemporaneous use of descriptors for his German enemies that were no doubt influenced by Allied propaganda.

> *First attack took everyone by complete surprise. The first jet attacked the high element with all guns blazing. The Jerry maniac came directly at #3 element. It seemed impossible that he could miss. . . . Wall of fire darted from top and ball turrets. The jet flew right through the squadron close enough for many (including myself) to see the black cross and swastika on the plane. I also saw the Nazi madman piloting the ship. The fighter attacks continued for a half hour. The greatest thrill of my life occured [sic] when I saw one jet knocked out of the sky. . . . When the jet got within 200 yards a thin trail of black smoke streamed out from its tail. Suddenly the vertical stabilizer flew off and a split second later in a mass of flames the tail crumbled. The plane fell off and went into a dive. Down in flames dove another of Goering's fanatics.*[1]

Guido Marchionda was a tail gunner with the nearby 360th and probably didn't know Dussliere, who was with the 427th Bomb Squadron. Yet Marchionda's description of the event dovetails perfectly with Dussliere's:

> *One of the fighters came so close by our ship that I saw the red marking it had on it's [sic] tail. I opened fire at him and as he was about 200 yds from us his tail broke off and caught on fire. The plane went in a spin and I didn't see the pilot get out. I believe I shot him down, but there were also other fellows shooting at him. One sure thing, he went down burning. . . . I was scared and I was praying while firing.*[2]

Unlike Marchionda and Dussliere, Charles Johnson didn't make it back to Molesworth to record his experience. A navigator with the 358th, he wasn't even supposed to fly that day. He was at the post exchange with his pilot and copilot—Francis Taub and John Cooper—when the call went out for all crews to report immediately to their squadrons. There followed a quick briefing before Johnson and the rest of the Taub crew were driven to a hardstand on which sat a spectacularly new and unblemished B-17G.

"The aircraft had flown less than five missions," Johnson said, "and appeared to be just off the assembly line, complete with carpet throughout and the latest technology including state-of-the-art heaters."[3] Johnson and the rest of the crew were quite impressed as many of the bombers they had flown were patched-up relics—some having completed well more than fifty missions. "As we prepared for takeoff, the crew chief said, 'Bring her back in the same condition as you got her.'"

Aside from heavy flak over Hamburg, the first part of the mission was unremarkable. The 303rd left the target, turned north and then winged west for England. Positioned on the outside of the formation—at the end of the "whip"—Taub and Cooper had a hard time keeping up as the group made the turn. "While in the process of the turn, which left our aircraft exposed on the outside of the formation, all hell broke loose," said Johnson.

The aircraft was rocked by a tremendous jolt. "As I looked to the right from my navigator position in the nose," Johnson said, "I glimpsed a German fighter going past our plane at a tremendous rate of speed. In an instant I realized that I had just seen my first German jet fighter." The tail gunner called over the interphone that the tail section was badly hit. Immediately after, Taub reported that he and Cooper were having difficulty controlling the ship and directed the men to prepare to bail out. Johnson, the navigator, advised that it might be a good idea to put as much distance as possible between their struggling aircraft and the city they had just bombed. "I suggested that we continue to fly in a northerly direction to reach a less hostile area, possibly Denmark or Sweden. Taub agreed."

Nevertheless, the German fighter pilots had other ideas, and the crew was attacked again a short time later. The Germans sieved both wings with cannon fire and destroyed two engines in quick succession. "This time there was no debating the decision to bail out. I buckled on my chute," said Johnson, "and moved to the escape hatch where I saw the engineer, Warren Chrisman, trying to jettison the hatch door." The door would open only partially and Chrisman became stuck as he tried to wedge his way out. Johnson helped push him clear and followed him out only after a mighty struggle that nearly exhausted him. The silver ship exploded an instant later.

Johnson pulled his parachute's ripcord, then realizing he was still too high, he immediately snatched the pilot chute before it could deploy the main chute. He fell, wind whistling past his body, until he judged he was low enough to release his parachute. "I then released the pilot chute and the main chute opened with a jerk. I misjudged the distance to the ground and was not ready for the impact. I landed on my right leg and arm, both of which sustained injury."

Upon Johnson's coming to earth, a gust of wind inflated his parachute and dragged him across the freshly plowed field into which he had landed. Stunned, injured and disoriented, Johnson struggled mightily as his face and body were dragged across the wet earth. His clothes scooped up soil as he was slammed from row to row. "Finally, the wind subsided momentarily and I somehow managed to unbuckle my harness. The wind again came up and the chute and harness became airborne and blew away."

Johnson hobble-trotted to a stand of young trees and hid there until nightfall. That night, cold and sore, he put his navigational skills to good use and used Polaris—the North Star—to make his way through more farmland until nearly dawn, when he hunkered down in a low spot and fell asleep. It was the noise of a fuss that woke him hours later. "When I awoke in the early afternoon," Johnson said, "I could hear voices and sensed commotion around me. I opened my eyes and saw eight to ten mostly elderly men with shotguns or pitchforks looking down at me. I knew instantly that, for me, 'the war was over.'"

The German farmers did not harm Johnson. Instead, they took his gun, knife, escape kit and money before bringing him to a nearby hamlet and turning him over to "some bureaucrat in a uniform. I was then directed to sit in the back of an old pickup truck with two armed guards pointing guns at me while the driver bounced across dirt farm roads." Johnson's trip ended at a town where he was put in jail.

Johnson left jail the following morning in the custody of two aged German army soldiers. "The younger of the two, about 55, had lived in New York as a ticket manager for the Hamburg-American Shipping Lines and spoke fluent English. The three of us walked to the Bad Degeburg railway baggage station and waited in a small room." There then arose a disturbance outside.

"The younger guard left," said Johnson, "and returned with a dozen Wehrmacht soldiers who were armed and promptly fixed bayonets to their rifles. Approximately thirty Hitler Youths were being led by a fat old man obviously trying to stir them up. The Wehrmacht soldiers went outside and formed a cordon around the building, menacing the boys with their bayonets until they backed off and dispersed."

Johnson's travails continued in the same vein when he climbed with his guards onto a train to the Neumünster southeast station. There they had to disembark and walk because the tracks to the northwest station had been destroyed in a bombing raid the previous day. "When civilians, mostly older women and young children, realized that I was a captured American airman, they started to converge on us," Johnson said. "The younger of my two guards shouted for us to make a run for it. I took off with him in spite of my bad leg. The older guard had fallen behind and was being pelted by sticks and stones."

The trio finally made it to the southwest station, where Johnson was temporarily put in the custody of four teenage soldiers. Their behavior was a marked contrast to what he had endured twice already that day. "They seemed delighted to see me and we discussed, in broken English, people and places in the United States. They were interested in Babe Ruth, Joe Louis and Benny Goodman, and in the cities of Chicago and New York."

After a short time, Johnson was back aboard a train with his two guards cum protectors. It was a short trip to a circular structure that was the station at Pinneberg, on the outskirts of Hamburg. It wasn't far from where Johnson's troubles had begun a couple of days earlier. "When we arrived, my two guards and the station commander cleared out everyone, including station personnel, locked the doors and went outside to speak to Wehrmacht soldiers milling around the building."

Johnson was torn with fearful anxiety. "I circled the inside of the station, stepping up on benches to peek out the windows." His two guards rallied the Wehrmacht soldiers to hold off a hostile mob that numbered in the hundreds and surged angrily against the station. Ultimately, the cordon of enemy soldiers held and the angry civilians were cleared."

It was time for Johnson's guards to leave. He had been with them only a day, but it had seemed much, much longer. "The one who had lived in New York asked if he could have the flight wings off of my shirt collar as a memento," Johnson said. "I readily and thankfully gave him the insignia. To me he was both a hero and a savior who could have abandoned me to the mob at any time."

From Pinneberg, Johnson was sent to an interrogation center, where he spent the following seven days alone in a small cell. "On the eighth day I was taken to interrogation. Although I feared the worse, it never transpired. On the contrary, the officer interrogator spent most of the time talking about the fact that he believed the war would be over in four weeks and what might then happen."

Johnson was subsequently joined with a couple dozen other American prisoners who were being readied for transport to a POW camp. They were addressed by a German officer before they left: "He said he could only assign six guards to defend us against civilians on the march to the train. He advised us not to create a confrontational situation, regardless of what happened. We did have to endure insults, taunts, spitting and threats, but refrained from any retorts and arrived safely at the train."

The men got under way, but the train pulled into a siding soon after. Johnson was able to see out of his car as another train was loaded with soldiers, presumably headed east to fight against the advancing Soviets. "Except for some officers, they were all boys of twelve to fifteen years of age. The flower of Germany's next generation being sent to slaughter for a cause long since lost. Of all the experiences during my service, this was and is my single, most poignant and saddest recollection."

JOHNSON WAS PROCESSED into the German POW system—as were 763 other men from the 303rd during the course of the war. The men were sent to *stalags*, a word derived from *stamlager*, which was a type of camp. A *stalag luft* was a POW camp specifically for captured airmen. The men called themselves *kriegies*, a bastardization of *Kriegsgefangener*, a German word for captured soldiers. Although there were exceptions, officers were generally sent to camps separate from the enlisted men. Some camps were for specific nationalities, or commonly, camps were segregated by nationality.

The Allies, with the exception of the Soviet Union—to the tragic misfortune of its men—were signatories to the Geneva Convention, as was Germany. Accordingly, the Germans treated their prisoners, except for the Soviets, in accordance with the rules set down by the convention. Men were not forced to work, and the wounded and ill received medical treatment; in many instances severely wounded men were repatriated back to the Allies.

The 303rd's men were held in at least seventeen different camps, but the conditions at each were generally similar. Although food varied in quality and quantity, it was enough for the men to survive, although never enough to keep them in the pink of health. Every man lost weight, with some shedding fifty or more pounds. Understandably, the power of hunger drove them to the brink of obsession, and food was always a favorite topic of conversation. Hal Gunn's wife sent him a photograph of herself in a bathing suit at the beach while holding a bottle of Coca-Cola. When Gunn showed it to his comrades they reacted as their instincts directed: "Ah, Coke!"

Red Cross parcels, weighing more than ten pounds and containing powdered milk, canned meat or fish, fruit, cigarettes, sugar, jam and other sundries and foodstuffs, augmented the German rations and contributed much to the well-being of the POWs. The men used cigarettes as an unofficial currency, and sometimes traded with their guards for additional food or for contraband.

Except for morning and evening roll calls, the men were generally left alone by their captors and entertained themselves as best they could, to include cards, board games, sports, walking and other diversions. Some of the POWs were experts in certain disciplines and gave classes or other sorts of instruction; many men learned a second language while in captivity. Philip Peed, a bombardier from the 358th Bomb Squadron, recalled his experience: "We had a fellow who wanted to start a class in accounting and I joined that, and it was a lifesaver. There was no pressure in the class and we got a good education in accounting in about 4 months."[4]

Keeping warm in the winter was a constant challenge as the barracks were drafty and heating fuel was scarce. Personal hygiene was likewise a challenge as water and fuel to heat it were usually in short supply. As a result, the men were typically infested with lice and other vermin, as was their clothing and bedding.

One of the greatest hardships the men endured was a paucity of news from home—letters were too few and sporadically delivered and men grew heartsick. Others did well enough and actually took the time and effort to write back to their comrades in the 303rd, as did Merle Cornish:

Dear Bob [Landry], Would you let Les know that I'm absolutely unhurt and that I'm sorry I had to stand her up? If the hose, sugar, or any of the cosmetics are around, let her have them. We are being well treated, with good quarters and enough nourishing food. Pay Les for the photos of mine and give her my love. The radio's yours, Bob.[5]

Although there were abuses, the Germans generally treated the POWs fairly, if severely. Gratuitous violence or harshness, although it happened, was not the norm. Philip Peed offered an example: "From the time of the invasion [D-Day] until about Christmas it was pretty tense. . . . They [German guards] were very anxious and anytime an air raid was called they made us stay in barracks with shutters closed. No one could look out. One of the enlisted men in the cook shack where they cooked the soup opened the door one day to air out the place and one of the guards saw him and shot and killed him. [It was] the only real tragedy in our compound."

Leadership was provided by the senior Allied man in the camp, and it was he who served as the liaison to the German leadership. Most of the guards—the POWs called them "goons"—were older men, or soldiers who had been wounded and were unfit for fighting. Their work was not overly challenging, as actual escape attempts were infrequent. In truth, for both the POWs and their guards, life in the stalags was, in the main, a cold, boring and dreary waiting game.

That waiting game came to a close as the end of the war neared. It was during this time that many of the POWs endured unnecessary and callous treatment when the Germans evacuated camps in front of the advancing Soviet armies. Many of these evacuations were begun at the height of winter during late 1944 and early 1945, and they continued to the end of the war. Movements were sometimes made in stinking, grossly overcrowded train cars, as described by Philip Peed: "We traveled about a day and a half before they finally stopped in a station and they let us out for a few minutes. We were animals, imagine 10 boxcars at once in a station, with 500 POWs and also civilians walking and waiting for their trains. The POWs from the train were the animals, they urinated and went to the bathroom right on the platform. The guards were not happy and finally got us back on the train."

But the majority of prisoners were made to march—sometimes hundreds of miles. Sick, cold and starving, the men frequently had no option but to bivouac in the open. Food was scarce, and the men were forced to scavenge from the countryside, bartering or stealing from farms and villages along their routes. George Emerson, a tail gunner with the 303rd's

427th Bomb Squadron, recalled a humorous encounter: "On one of the nights spent at a farm, Harry met the farmer. The farmer wanted to learn English, so what did Harry teach him to say? 'Buy American war bonds.' And after the farmer mastered this one, Harry motioned for our nearby buddies to form a circle around us. On command, the farmer used his new English phrase. Total laughter ensued."[6]

Although there were occasional amusing interludes, as described by Emerson, the marches were exceedingly miserable experiences that forced the POWs to struggle mightily to survive. Indeed, it is estimated that more than a thousand American servicemen perished on the road. Among many diseases, dysentery was rampant, and many of the men, unable to control their bowels, spent weeks in ragged, shitty clothes. Men who became too ill to move were either loaded on wagons— sometimes drawn by other POWs—or were left to die or shot. Sadly, the columns of prisoners were occasionally mistaken as German soldiers and strafed by Allied fighters: "The second day out," recounted George Emerson, "our column came under attack from our own P-47s. Three prisoners were killed and several more were injured. This happened near my particular position on the march."

There were opportunities to escape, but there was little point. The end of the war was obviously near, and the Germans had what food there was. Moreover, although they were enemies, the Germans were still organized and were charged by the Geneva Convention with protecting the POWs. They took those obligations more seriously as the Allied armies neared and it became clear that they would be held accountable. And men who fled the march risked being shot. If they made a good escape, they would be out of touch with events, in danger of being recaptured or shot, and without food or camaraderie.

The final destination for many of the marchers was Stalag VII-A at Moosburg, near Munich. It was a collection point of sorts for Allied POWs, and there were more than one hundred thousand men at the camp by the end of April 1945. George Emerson was there when the 14th Armored Division liberated the camp on April 29. "I can honestly say this is the happiest day I ever remember of [sic]. The artillery sounded close all night of April 28. The real fireworks for Moosburg, started about 9:00 A.M. this Sunday morning and lasted about three hours. A tank and two jeeps just came thru camp. Everyone is wild, P-51's, and little Elmer [an artillery spotting aircraft] have been buzzing this camp all day. What a beautiful sight."

Not all of the stalags were evacuated, and Charles Johnson's experience was typical of those POWs who weren't marched away from the front. He and the *kriegies* of *Stalag Luft* I discovered that their guards had completely abandoned the camp during the evening of April 30, 1945. That next morning he was one of many men who wandered through the surrounding area to see what they might:

> We proceeded to the road not knowing what to expect, but what we saw was incredible. There was a Russian horde of stupefied drunk, unkempt and unruly scavengers and pillagers. The rag-tag army, including many women, rode in expropriated old cars, which they could barely drive, or horse drawn carts piled high with loot taken from the Germans.[7]

Not wanting to get caught up in the rapacious riot, Johnson and his companions retreated to their POW camp. The next day, they sunned themselves at a nearby beach, and within a week, they were evacuated by the Americans.

Ultimately, of approximately ninety thousand American POWs held by the Germans, the vast majority survived the war to be repatriated back to the United States. Most of them passed through one of the "cigarette camps" near Le Havre, most notably Camp Lucky Strike. There they were deloused, cleaned, fed, clothed and otherwise nursed back to health before being sent home with pockets full of back pay. Their treatment, once back in friendly hands, was almost universally outstanding.

"I WAS BLOWN OUT"

NO OTHER DAY of the war saw more jets in air combat than did April 10, 1945. Walter Schuck was one of the Me-262 pilots airborne that day. He was a veteran of air combat in the Arctic. Fighting against the British and the Soviets, he was credited with nearly two hundred aerial victories—mostly against the Red Air Force—but he was called back to Germany during early 1945, where he transitioned to the Me-262. The Reich needed its best men to fly its best aircraft regardless of the fact that the war was already lost.

The Me-262 had been operational for many months by early April, but the Germans were still devising tactics that maximized its tremendous speed advantage. As the B-17s of the 1st Air Division—the 303rd among them—approached Oranienburg, just north of Berlin, Schuck, at the head of JG 7's 3 *Staffel*, led a flight of seven Me-262s in pursuit. He was careful to avoid the protective screens of American fighters. If his little formation was attacked and caught up in a dogfight, its chances of breaking away and getting to the bombers were slight.

It wasn't long before Schuck led his packet of jets to a point behind and above a long column of B-17s. "Once in position, and with the advantage of height, we launched our attack on the Flying Fortresses."[1] Schuck eschewed the traditional, curving, high-side attacks that were the German standard for much of the war. The Me-262 bled too much airspeed in a hard turn, and it took precious time to regain it. As speed was the jet's chief advantage, it made little sense to waste it. Too, the old method used too much fuel and took too much time. Moreover, the big, looping turns were predictable and made the Me-262s more vulnerable to ambushes by the overwhelming masses of American escort fighters. Consequently, Schuck formulated a different scheme of attack:

> As there were more than enough targets to hand, I decided that I would "surf-ride" along the length of the bomber stream; dive on the enemy from a height of 1,000 metres [approximately 3,300 feet] above, select a bomber flying out on one of the flanks, put a short burst of fire into an inboard engine, pull up and away while still at least 200 metres above the bomber in order to ensure safe recovery, climb back to 1,000 metres [above the bombers] and repeat the process.

Schuck's concept was akin to a running stitch, and because the attack followed the same flight path as the bombers, it did not require complex deflection shooting. Additionally, the B-17 was less well defended from above than it was from the side. Another advantage of the technique was that the Me-262s stood a good chance of escaping out of range before the defending gunners could spot them, bring their guns to bear, aim and fire. And although the jet pilots couldn't easily reverse course to finish off any cripples they created, their 30-millimeter cannons were exceedingly destructive and made cripples less likely. A single, well-placed round could bring down a bomber.

Schuck watched the B-17s release their bombs. "At this moment I didn't spare a thought for the pain and suffering that my cannon shells would soon be inflicting upon the enemy bomber crews. Vengeance, hate, retribution? No, those are the wrong words to describe the unbridled fury at the hundred-thousandfold deaths of innocent German women and children that filled my entire being as I opened fire on my target." Such were the ironic thoughts of a frontline airman who was likely unaware that the government he served had already murdered millions of innocent women and children.

The rounds from Schuck's cannons severed the tail section from the fuselage of his first target. The tail and what was left of the bomber tumbled earthward. He pulled on the fighter's control stick and chose another B-17 before nosing over into a second attack. His closing velocity was tremendous as he triggered the cannon once more. Schuck felt in his feet the *bump-bump-bump* of the big rounds as they arced away from the nose of his aircraft and into the bomber's right wing, between the two engines. He was forced to haul his fighter into a near-vertical climb to keep from colliding with the B-17. "As it tiredly lifted one wing prior to going down, I thought I caught a glimpse of a name written on the exposed nose section: '*Henn's Revenge.*'"

Henn's Revenge was a 303rd ship, of the 358th Bomb Squadron. The aircraft, a B-17G, flew its very first mission on October 26 and flew another thirty-five missions unnamed until January 23, when it was named by the Richard Gmernicki crew after their tail gunner, Thomas Henn. Henn had been badly wounded the previous day on the raid to Sterkrade. Shrapnel from a flak burst knocked his oxygen mask loose and punched into his skull. It was serendipity that swung the mask back and forth across his face and kept him alive until his crewmates came to his aid. Henn survived, but the flak wound left his left side paralyzed.

Since that time Gmernicki and his crew had finished their combat tours, and *Henn's Revenge* flew thirty-nine of the 303rd's next forty-five missions—it was a remarkable record that Schuck ended on April 10. The official statement from the Missing Air Crew Report, or MACR, matched Schuck's description of the ship's demise almost perfectly: "Missing A/C held course for very few seconds after being hit, then peeled slightly up and slid over and down to the right through the formation. Appeared at that time to be out of control."

Vito Brunale was the engineer aboard *Henn's Revenge* that day. The long seconds immediately following Schuck's attack were marked by chaos. The interphone lines of the pilot, Robert Murray, were shot away. He motioned to Brunale that the crew should bail out. Brunale turned to pass the signal to the radio operator, Theodore Bates: "When I last saw Ted, he was in the radio room and I motioned for him to bail out. He then closed the door of his radio room."[2] Brunale turned and ducked to look into the nose of the aircraft and saw the navigator, Harold Smith, bail out through the forward hatch. The togglier, Carl Hammerlund, was already gone.

And then the aircraft exploded. "When the plane blew up over Oranienburg," Brunale recorded, "all crew members with the exception of Hammerlund and Smith were aboard. I was blown out but had my chute on." Pieces of the aircraft fell past Brunale as he descended in his parachute. "I did see large shattered pieces of the plane floating down above my chute." Higher still, he saw the bomber stream continuing east.

Brunale was captured, interrogated and made a POW. None of the rest of the Robert Murray crew survived. Although Brunale spotted two chutes below him—presumably Smith and Hammerlund—they were listed as killed in action.

FOLLOWING HIS ATTACK on *Henn's Revenge*, Schuck spotted a B-17 staggering north, away from the bomber stream. The American aircraft was smoking, and the German pilot readied to finish it off. It was only after he closed the range that he saw that virtually the entire right side of the fuselage had been shot away. Inside he could see the crewmen at their different stations. The big ship was obviously doomed, and Schuck—despite the "unbridled fury" he had earlier felt—held back. "As the bomber's fate was already sealed, I flew a wide circle around it, not wanting to shoot at the defenceless crew members: the copilot was slumped forward in his seat harness . . ." Schuck counted nine men as they parachuted from the wrecked bomber.

But he didn't linger. He climbed up above the bomber stream again and made another high-speed run, knocking down two more B-17s in quick succession. And then, out of ammunition, he scanned the sky for his comrades. He collected a wing full of .50-caliber machine gun rounds for his trouble. An instant later he spotted a Mustang—piloted by Joseph Peterburs of the 20th Fighter Group—as it dived past. Reacting instinctively, Schuck winged down into a protective layer of clouds, but it wasn't long before his aircraft began to come apart. He bailed out, injured his ankles upon landing and never flew another combat mission. Ironically, Joe Peterburs, who had shot him down, was knocked down along with his wingman a short time later after strafing an airfield. Both men, like Schuck, survived.

"ALL OF US WERE DONE"

LATE IN THE WAR, although the slaughter continued unabated, thousands of American veterans were completing their combat obligations and returning home. The nation was still on a war footing but the fighting was far away and the end of the conflict—in Europe at least—was in sight. Most of the airmen who had served with the 303rd took training assignments where the demands on their bodies and minds were trifling compared to the terrors they had endured over Europe. Still, although it did not include action against a desperate enemy, life back home was as common and mean and everyday as it had ever been.

Following his combat tour, Dick Johnson took orders to MacDill Field in Tampa, Florida. There, the USAAF was still training B-17 crews, and Johnson was assigned as the assistant provisional group commander. The dichotomy between operations with the 303rd and stateside duty was marked. He was part of a booze run—officially characterized as a "goodwill" visit—to Cuba that included three B-17s crewed by officers, enlisted men and nurses. The liquor stocks at MacDill's various clubs were slim and there was liquor aplenty in Havana.

The delegation enjoyed three days of partying, exploring and sight-seeing before returning to MacDill. "After landing late that evening," said Johnson, "I was about to walk to the Bachelor Officers Quarters when Colonel [James] Carroll said that I could ride with him and his driver. I was flattered that the base commander would show an interest in me, a mere first lieutenant."[1]

Rather than taking Johnson to his quarters, Carroll took him to his own house, explaining that he was interested in the younger man's combat experiences. The two of them sat on the back porch, where Carroll dismissed his aide and poured drink after drink while showing a keen interest in Johnson. "Shortly I found his hand on my knee. Then he placed my hand on his leg. I removed my hand and he started trying to unbutton my trousers. As he was getting more aggressive, I sort of sobered up enough to say that I had to go to the bathroom and that the bushes would be fine." Johnson raced for the bushes and kept going until he reached his room.

"I was so angry about his attempted rape that I made no bones about the whole episode when I talked to fellow officers. Evidently the word had gotten around about my seditious talk, because Colonel Carroll suddenly retired right in the middle of a war. I had decided to face a general court martial if need be."

APRIL 1945 MARKED the last of thirty months of war for the 303rd. But regardless, operations during that month were still deadly. "I, along with the rest of Grafton N. Smith's crew, finished my thirty-fifth and final mission a couple of weeks earlier, on March 24," remembered Al Dussliere. "All of us were done except for our copilot, Melvin Alderman. He was from Casselton, North Dakota, and was a really wonderful person, but he was three missions behind the rest of us. That was because when we started flying actual combat missions on December 18, 1944, it was normal practice for an experienced pilot to fly with a new crew to make sure the men knew what they were doing; it helped transition them into combat. That meant that Melvin didn't get to go on the first few missions.

"The crew was given a three-day pass," Dussliere continued, "and we wanted Melvin to come along, but he insisted on staying on base so that he could finish his missions and go back to the States with the rest of us. The mission on April 6 was his last one—his thirty-fifth."

The Eighth Air Force put 659 bombers airborne that day. The target was the railroad marshaling complex at Leipzig. Pinched from both the west and east, the German Army was desperately repositioning units to make its final stand of the war. Neutralizing the railroad nodes—even for a few days—would help stymie that effort.

The 303rd launched thirty-nine bombers, of which two aborted. The rest of the formation joined the main effort and winged westward at high altitude. For the most part, the ingress was uneventful, as most of it was flown over Allied-held territory. At one point, a lone Me-262 made an ineffectual pass at the column of bombers and was chased by escorting P-51s toward the 303rd. A single gunner from one of the ships opened fire on the enemy jet, observed hits and was later given credit for a probable. Flak was described as meager and inaccurate. In terms of enemy action, the mission was wholly unremarkable.

Thick, puffy contrails—condensation trails—carpeted the path the bombers plowed as they continued toward Leipzig. The contrails were a normal part of high-altitude bombing missions, and aside from the fact that they made it easy for enemy fighter pilots and antiaircraft gunners to locate the bombers, they were—for the most part—little more than a nuisance. They were created when warm, moist engine exhaust mixed with the cold air typical at high altitudes. Depending on a number of factors, to include humidity, temperature and winds, the contrails could grow quite thick and persistent. And in some cases they grew dense enough to make it difficult for the pilots to see one another and maintain formation.

South of Leipzig, in the cloying cloak of the contrails, two of the 303rd's B-17s collided. Melvin Alderman, as the pilot rather than the copilot, was flying one of them—the *Green Hill Belle*. The other aircraft, piloted by Howard Lacker, was unnamed. Alderman's ship exploded in midair. Pieces of the bomber burned as they fell, and no parachutes were observed. Likewise, the other B-17 was critically damaged. Its tail section broke away, and the remainder of the aircraft fell into a flat spin. The engines, either disabled by the collision or shut down by the crew, spun their propellers slowly. As was the case with Alderman's ship, no parachutes streamed from Lacker's aircraft. The rest of the group continued toward Leipzig.

Both aircraft hit the ground in the vicinity of Loessnitz, approximately fifty miles south of Leipzig. The MACRs for both crews included a translated German police report:[2]

The factory building on the Loessnitz and Dittersdorf property was totally destroyed. Also the administrative and residential buildings were severely damaged and both cannot be used anymore. The restoration will take a long time. The factory buildings are beyond repair. The company employed 110 workers in an emergency program. The adjacent farmhouse of farmer Reimann was also heavily destroyed and cannot be restored. The farmhouse along Zwoenitzer Strasse and owned by farmer Guenther received also medium damage. The factory roof of Anton Jaehn in Dreihansen was heavily damaged, production continues though. Railroad and roads remain without damage.

The damage described was caused by the B-17 that Alderman piloted, *Green Hill Belle*. The police report mentioned that debris and bodies were scattered across a five-hundred-meter area. The bodies, except for that of the tailgunner, J. M. Moore, which was still trapped in the tail section, were taken to the local "cemetery hall."

Frau Johanna Tittmann was watching her daughter inside her home at Loessnitz when the air raid warnings sounded: "We did not take these air warnings serious[ly] anymore and we were all convinced that in such a lonely place we lived in, no harm would come. In such cases we would not even seek shelter anymore." Tittman was right in that Loessnitz was not a target. Still, two bomb-laden 303rd B-17s fell toward the town that morning. "I looked through the window in the direction of Oberer Bahnhof [the railroad station] and saw something fall from the sky."[3] What she saw were pieces of Alderman's bomber.

Tittmann bent protectively over her daughter. "Then we ran into the cellar. It happened all so fast and I cannot remember how I ended up there. I must have been still at the stairs when a loud bang, dust and rubble were flying all around us."

The doors and windows of Tittmann's house were blown out, as were various walls. She felt the heat from flames that threatened to consume the neighborhood. "Our wood pile, the building across and the farmhouse of farmer Reimann were on fire. Our roof was torn down, one kitchen wall gone. No windows and doors were left in the entire house. Thousands of tiny glass fragments were embedded into the furniture like crystals and months later still in the down beds when sheets were changed."

Lacker's aircraft crashed to the ground approximately five hundred meters to the northeast. The town's constabulary showed remarkable insight when it supposed—correctly—that the two B-17s had collided: "Since there was ANOTHER crash site 500 meters away, it is assumed that both bombers collided in midair. Additional bomb craters or delayed action fuses were not found."[4] Aside from the eight crewmen aboard Alderman's aircraft and the nine crewmen on Lacker's ship—all KIA—a Czech laborer and a French laborer were killed on the ground at Loessnitz. An additional eight civilians sustained injuries severe enough to require medical attention.

GUIDO MARCHIONDA WAS the tail gunner aboard *My Darling* on the mission to Leipzig. It was his last. The collision between the Alderman and Lacker ships unfolded directly in front of him: "The ship flying behind us collided with another aeroplane and they both blew up. I knew the boys for they slept in the same barrack[s] I did. I really felt bad for I knew them very well and associated with them. The planes were burning like paper and broke in a hundred pieces. I didn't see any chutes come out. I got a terrible feeling after that. I really sweated this mission out. Thank God I finished."[5]

THE 303RD'S REMAINING BOMBERS dropped a mix of general purpose and incendiary bombs—as well as leaflets—through the clouds at Leipzig. They returned to Molesworth just more than nine hours after taking off. Not a single aircraft sustained damage of any sort. It should have been the perfect last mission for Alderman.

"I was in a pub in Northampton with Ray Miller, our ball turret gunner, and George Parker, our radio operator, when we found out that Mel was killed," said Dussliere. "Early in the evening some other flyers from our squadron came into the pub. We immediately noted the somber looks on their faces; it was readily apparent that there was bad news. Naturally we wondered what and who. They approached us and one of them said, 'Alderman got it today.'"

Dussliere and his companions were staggered. They had given little consideration to the notion that Alderman might not live through his last mission. "Mel had always been very friendly and made it a point to spend time with us enlisted men. Moreover, he was a great copilot. He and our pilot, G. N. 'Smitty' Smith, brought us home from some very rough missions. And then he was gone. We left the pub and caught a ride home without saying much."

IT WAS DAYS before the family members of Second Lieutenant Howard George Weinberg—the bombardier aboard Lacker's *Green Hill Belle*—learned anything at all about the mission. They were at their home in Mount Vernon, New York, more than three thousand miles west of where Dussliere, Miller and Parker rode silently back to the base at Molesworth.

At that moment Weinberg's parents were likely going through their Friday afternoon routine. However, it was probable that they—like millions of parents across the globe—had sometime during the day said at least one prayer for their son's safe return. Lois Brown was Weinberg's younger sister. "I was 11 at the time of his death, the baby of the family. My next brother was 7 years older than I, my sister 10 years older, and Howie 12. Of all of them, it was Howie I adored. Howie was sweet, funny, gorgeous, sentimental, slender, 6'5-1/2" tall, athletic, popular, a charmer with the girls, the perfect son, the perfect brother. When he was home, our house was barely big enough to hold him. There was always noise, the radio turned up loud, music playing, his big friends dropping by. When I had to be dragged off to bed at night, the house would still be ringing with jollity, my lullaby.[6]

"We were blessed with parents who not only loved each other and were each other's best friends, but who loved us and were our best friends as well. They were happy, we were happy. It was truly a magical household. When I went to the movies, I thought those happy families up there on the screen were like my family, and not the other way around.

"Before we were prepared for it, war came to our house. Howie left Columbia University to join up. He wrote, 'Dad, I enlisted today. I want to finish the job you started in 1917.' Imagine. My sister accelerated at college, spending even her summers there, to finish in three years; my other brother was sent to a naval prep school (Dad arranged that, hoping he would go from there to Annapolis, which would draw out the time before he might have to serve overseas). I was alone. No more lullabies.

"For the next couple of years, we lived in a sort of limbo, waiting for the war to come to its climax. As young as I was, I knew as well as anybody what might happen to Howie. And then the telegram arrived bringing the terrible news. Our lives had changed forever. Our family never recovered from losing Howie. I can't imagine how my parents dealt with it; they never talked about Howie's death in my presence. My sister escaped her grief by getting married and moving as far away as she could from home. My remaining brother completely dissociated himself from the family; I don't even know where he lives today. Mother remarked to me once that he was as much a victim of the war as Howie. I imagine now she meant he was struggling with a penetrating guilt that Howie was the one taken, not he."

The tragedy that ripped the soul of the Weinberg family was repeated sixteen more times across the country because of the midair collision that day; the mishap killed a total of seventeen young fliers. And those deaths represented only an infinitesimal fraction of the twenty-six thousand men that were lost by the Eighth Air Force alone. "World War" was a label too innocuous and devoid of feeling to describe how the fighting hacked humanity apart.

"AND THEN HE FELL DOWN DEAD"

BY APRIL 1945 the strategic air campaign was essentially superfluous. There remained very few militarily relevant targets that merited the massive concentration of men, machines and material that made up a typical bombing mission. In fact, on April 5—the day prior to Alderman's death—USSTAF declared that all remaining targets were to be considered tactical in nature. Indeed, the war was going to be won regardless of whether or not the Allies ever put another aircraft into the sky.

That fact notwithstanding, many more missions were flown. The United States flew heavy bomber missions on all but six of the first twenty-five days of April; nearly fifty thousand tons of bombs were dropped on a Nazi state that was already all but defeated. The 303rd participated in nearly all of the final missions and the effort against the Friedrichstadt marshaling yard at Dresden, Germany, on April 17, 1945, was its third-to-last.

The 303rd launched forty-two bombers that day, with a mix of general purpose and incendiary bombs as well as leaflets. The weather was not good; there was an overcast layer at twenty-one thousand feet, and haze restricted visibility below that. More than two hundred P-51s patrolled the 303rd's route, and the Luftwaffe failed to make much of a showing. Still, three Me-262s were sighted, and one of them made a pass through the 303rd's low squadron from the rear without scoring any hits.

While the German Air Force failed to impress the 303rd that day, the antiaircraft gunners did not. Major combat damage was sustained by twelve aircraft—nearly a third of the bombers the group put airborne; eight other aircraft were also hit and sustained less damage. Although the war was nearly over, it was still only *nearly* over. In fact, two aircraft were shot down.

The antiaircraft fire was especially heavy over Brux, Czechoslovakia, about fifty miles south of Dresden. It was just north of there that *Sack Time*, piloted by Blaine E. Thomas, was hit. The ship, by Eighth Air Force standards, was a virtual Methuselah. It had flown 110 missions without a single abort.

Nevertheless, an 88-millimeter shell punched through the charmed ship's left wing. Fortunately, it failed to detonate. Still, the fuel tank was holed so badly that it failed to seal, and aviation gasoline streamed not only into the atmosphere, but into the fuselage as well. The crew opened the bomb bay doors to draw the highly inflammable fuel out of the aircraft.

Max Bartholomew was Thomas's copilot: "The target was obscured by clouds so the lead plane took us back to the IP, and again we had intense flak which hit our number two exhaust system, knocking out the turbo. We feathered the number two engine and tried to stay under the squadron. I checked the number one engine visually and thought I saw flames in the hole the 88-millimeter shell made so I had the engineer, Staff Sergeant Harry Haynes, in the top turret, look at it."[1]

At the same time, Bartholomew ordered the radio operator, Walter Smith, to get the ball turret gunner, Louis Contreras, out of his "fish bowl." Bartholomew and Thomas conferred and agreed that they would probably have to abandon the hard-worn bomber. Still, they stayed with the formation as it made another run against the target. "This time,"

Bartholomew recalled, "at the target there was a squadron of B-24s below us." Not wanting to drop bombs through the B-24 formation, the 303rd's formation leader, William Eisenhart, hauled the group back toward the initial point to set up for a third run at the target.

Sack Time was afire at that point. Both CO_2 bottles on the number two engine were discharged with no effect. Despite that, Thomas and the crew stuck with the rest of the formation until bombs were released on the third attempt at the target. "At this time," Bartholomew recalled, "the Tail Gunner, Sergeant Melvin Carlson, got on the intercom and said the flames were going by the tail. Blaine [Thomas] and I decided it was time to get out and gave the order to bail out and turned on the bell and hit the buttons to destroy the IFF."

Bartholomew's exit was not a smooth one. "Our autopilot evidently had received damage, as we had trouble getting the plane to fly level so we could bail out, which caused us to spend some extra time rolling in rudder trim. I checked the nose to see if everyone got out and then set down to go out the nose door and saw my shoes so I fastened them under my right leg harness. I evidently passed out from lack of oxygen and fell out. When I came to, I was looking at a couple of plowed fields and a fence line and pulled the rip cord on the parachute."

Bartholomew hit the ground hard and passed out. When he regained consciousness, he found himself surrounded by German troops. He had landed just a short distance from where they were encamped. He recovered his wits slowly, to discover that his parachute had disappeared, as had his shoes and his .45-caliber pistol. Worse, both his legs were broken. He spent the remaining three weeks of the war as a POW.

He was one of the lucky ones. Edward Eschinger was the crew's togglier and managed to safely escape the burning *Sack Time*. He came down at Halsbrücke, about ten miles southwest of Dresden. Horst Bayer, a young man living with his parents, recalled seeing three parachutes exit the stricken B-17: "One of the men came down over Halsbrücke and landed at Hohe Esse [a restaurant]. I ran to where the pilot was lying with his parachute. He was wearing a brown flight suit and nothing on his head. Hugo Schreiber and the peasant Rötzsch reached the site before me, the teacher Haufe, who lived in the Sand section of town, came after me. He tried to mistreat the pilot [Eschinger was actually a togglier] but Hugo Schreiber stopped him."[2]

But Hugo Schreiber could not stop everyone in town from abusing Eschinger. Bayer's account continued: "Gradually other residents assembled, one woman addressed the flyer in English, to which he replied that he spoke German. The air defense guards Otto and Hachenbuchner from Halsbrücke seem to have been among the last to come. The latter struck the defenseless man in the back of the neck, which immediately swelled up greatly." The two guards forced Eschinger to look for his .45-caliber pistol while they followed him. It was a fool's errand as he had thrown it away as he descended in his parachute. It was likely miles away.

Bayer described what happened next. "Otto stood behind him with his own pistol at the ready. At the moment when the flyer grabbed his swollen neck, he was fired on with one shot at close range by Otto. He looked at the sky, blood came from his mouth, and then he fell down dead. The two policemen of Halsbrücke, who now arrived, were unable to prevent the killing of the pilot. He was laid in a bower [wooded garden], the carpenter Kohl made him a casket and took him to the cemetery in Tuttendorf, where he was buried near the cemetery wall."

Eschinger was not the only crewman from *Sack Time* who was murdered by the Germans. The tail gunner, Melvin Carlson, was also killed. Louie Contreras, the ball turret gunner, was beaten and sustained a number of broken ribs and other contusions. He survived the war as a POW, as did the remainder of the crew.

Crewmen of the other 303rd bomber shot down that day, *Earthquake McGoon*, suffered a similarly tragic fate. The ship, piloted by Thomas Kahler, was hit by an 88-millimeter shell, and its right wing caught fire immediately; flames streamed over the top of the big bomber. The aircraft staggered momentarily in a puff of smoke before it exploded and fell away. Although no parachutes were observed, the entire crew managed to escape safely.

Six of the eight crewmen were captured and finished the war as POWs. However, two of the men, Thomas Kahler, the pilot, and Theodore Smith, the tail gunner, were not so fortunate. They were hanged from a tree—murdered—after being caught by *Schutzstaffel*, or SS, troops and a band of civilians.

"THEY ARE WORKING ME TO DEATH"

HILDA KAISER STILL LIVED in Munich with her parents as the war drew to a close. "Believe me; we were ready for the war to end. Nothing was moving in Germany. There was no food or fuel or anything. We were close to starving."[1] Kaiser's observations validated the sacrifices that the men of the 303rd—as part of the strategic air war—had made.

Munich was fortunate as it was surrendered rather than contested in a destructive and bloody battle. The city was doubly fortunate as it was given over to American forces rather than the Soviets; the Soviets murdered, raped and robbed wherever they went in Germany. Kaiser recalled the first Americans she encountered: "There were two soldiers and they walked down the street toward us. Something seemed wrong and I wasn't sure what the matter was. Then, it became clear that they had been drinking. They were so drunk that they could barely stand! But they were not brutal or vindictive. The Americans treated us very fairly."

* * *

ALTHOUGH THE AMERICANS dominated the daytime skies over Europe toward the end of the war, doing so was still dangerous and far from easy. The targets were distant and consequently the days were long—much longer than at the beginning of the group's combat career. A mission to Berlin or beyond could take twice as long as the short, pioneering "channel hops" the group made to Northern France during late 1942.

Arthur Shanafelt was a copilot with the 360th Bomb Squadron. His letters to his fiancée captured the sheer exhaustion of the men who were finishing the air war. Having only flown his first mission on February 24, he had completed twelve less than a month later. On March 23, he wrote: "Every day is rough but still it's that much more done and that much closer to getting home. I'll be so darn old and worn out when I get home you may not want me."[2]

Shanafelt flew twenty missions by April 1, and his fatigue is the main theme in his letter of that date. "Sorry I haven't written lately but if you've been reading the papers you know where I've been and how tired I am when I sit down at night. They are working me to death but as long as I get back, I love it and shall continue. Just getting back in one piece and breathing air is the main thing. Haven't the time to say more. I must hit the sack because it's rest I really need and must get. May get home soon if I keep going like I have. Hope I do get home quick as I'm tired of this life."

That thread of tiredness—with a touch of poor hygiene—continued on April 16. Shanafelt had flown three more missions since his letter of April 11:

Is it the 16th or 15th [it was Easter Sunday]? I didn't know it was Sunday until I got down this evening. Isn't that awful? All I do is fly, eat and sleep it seems, but I can rest when I finish. . . . I'm thankful as long as I always come back. I'm wearing a raunchy hat three fellows have worn through combat now so it is definitely lucky. I have to take a new crew up tomorrow and I'm sweating it out to be truthful. I'm sure we'll get along O.K. At least I certainly hope so. Water is scarce over here but you can manage a shower every three or four days if you are lucky. In spite of all I can do it will take me at least four months to get clean again. To top it all off I have contracted athlete's foot somewhere here and that isn't good. I'm really a nervous wreck.

On April 18 he wrote: "I've been so dead tired, scared or whatever you want to call it, at nights I would write you and not remember what I wrote." Shanafelt flew his last mission—his twenty-fourth—two days later, on April 20. He had flown them all within a fifty-six-day period. Worn out and dirty, but safe and whole, Shanafelt was finished with combat.

And one nine-hour mission later, on April 25, 1945, so was the 303rd. The target was the Skoda Armament Works at Pilsen, Czechoslovakia, against which the group sortied forty-two B-17s. An indication of the USAAF's dominance over Europe was the fact that radio broadcasts warned workers to stay clear of the Skoda complex. Consequently, the Germans knew when and where the American bombers were coming.

That fact notwithstanding, it didn't appear that they took advantage of the information. The Luftwaffe was nowhere to be seen, and antiaircraft fire was sporadic and inaccurate. However, that changed when the target was obscured by low clouds and the 303rd aborted its initial run. As the formation spun around for another attack, the flak increased greatly in intensity and accuracy. Indeed, twenty-four of the 303rd's bombers sustained major damage. One of them landed at a captured airfield at Würzburg, Germany, while another dropped into a base in Belgium. So many of the bombers landed back at Molesworth in various states of extremis—gear up, no flaps, no brakes, etc.—that the end of the runway resembled an aircraft junkyard.

The group lost one aircraft. Immediately after releasing its bombs, the B-17 piloted by Warren Mauger took at least two direct hits, one in the right inboard engine and the other in the lower fuselage. It didn't matter at that instant to the men aboard the ship that Germany was essentially defeated and that the mission was the 303rd's last. They were in a life-and-death struggle no different than if they had been caught at the height of the great air battles of 1943 or 1944.

Mauger was blown out of his seat by the impact, and the ball turret gunner, Francis Kelley, was killed instantly. This was supposed to be Kelley's last mission—number thirty-five. It was also to be his last because, although it was unknown at the time, it was the 303rd's last. Sadly, it was his last mission because it was the last day of his life.

Flames engulfed the number three engine, and the aircraft fell sharply to the right before dropping nose-down in a spin. Mauger regained his seat and righted the ship to some degree before a fire erupted around him and he ordered the crew to bail out. His hands and face burned, Mauger climbed down toward the forward escape hatch, which had already been jettisoned. The aircraft exploded as he knelt to leap clear. Knocked unconscious, he recovered his wits only just barely in time to pull his parachute's rip cord. Although he spotted only one other parachute, he and four other men managed to escape the pieces that had been their bomber, while three of their crewmates perished. Those three men represented the 303rd's last sacrifice in the fight against the Nazi state.

Mauger was the only one of the five survivors who managed to evade capture during the closing two weeks of the war. Wearing his burned uniform trousers and an old overcoat given to him by a Czech farmer immediately upon his coming to the ground, he steadily worked his way west. The combination worked well to disguise him, as evidenced by an encounter just a few hours later: "Ahead of me sat a German soldier with his girlfriend. I strolled by them practically unnoticed."[3]

His encounters at this late stage in the war were interesting, and he found the Czech people to be generally very friendly and accommodating, although German forces were practically ubiquitous. In fact, while digging a sleeping spot into an inviting haystack he found that an exhausted and dead-to-the-world German soldier had already claimed the space. One example of Czech kindness occurred a few days after he had been shot down:

> At about noon I came to a mountain stream, and just beyond the bridge, I could see a small town. After crossing the bridge, I rapped on the door of one of the houses. A young lad, about 12 years of age, answered the door and let me in the house. It appeared he was the only one home. He offered me some sour milk soup. He told me he was a member of the Hitler Youth and showed me his uniform. He said that it was all but mandatory to belong. Somehow I believed him and left feeling that he would not notify anyone of my being there.

Indeed, Mauger remained unmolested following his visit with the boy. Still he had several brushes with German troops during the next few days. While passing through one town, he was chased but managed to escape through several yards and onto a terrace. "I had no sooner stretched out on the ground when another German soldier came strolling up a small path toward my hiding place. It was too late to run. I had to do something fast. I put on the act of a man completely stoned. I got up, staggered around and fell down a couple times. He smiled while watching this and then turned and strolled up and over the hill."

Ultimately, Mauger was taken in for the last several days of his sojourn by a small Russian family that had been relocated to a village to perform farm labor. He was struck by their kindness and steadfast devotion to his safety through several more misadventures as the Americans advanced eastward and the Germans repositioned in the face of that advance. "The next morning, it must have been Sunday, for Andre had with him his wife and son. She had brought a nice lunch and a wash cloth, soap and a towel. We walked to a small brook where

I cleaned up. After this we settled back to a fine picnic lunch. Andre's wife and son never took their eyes off me. I must have presented a curious sight to them."

His hosts kept Mauger in a haystack during his stay. Buried in its dry warmth he experienced a perspective of the fighting that his comrades back in Molesworth could only imagine.

> *The artillery bursts were now getting so close that the ground shook. I could hear the distant sound of the cannon, the whine through the air and the explosion when the missile landed. I also heard something else now, machine gun fire. Sometime after midnight, the machine gun fire on both sides became intense. You could distinguish the American fire by its low pitch and slower rate than that of the Germans. The artillery on both sides were [sic] now firing. Toward morning I could hear many voices of German soldiers. I heard another sound, one I could not reconcile with the once mighty German army. Teams of horses were moving the biggest share of German equipment for this retreat. Evidently, the bombing of oil refineries had taken its toll.*

Mauger remained undiscovered as the German Army fled the advancing Americans. It was another day before his Russian host seized him from his hiding place and—with great excitement—led him toward the nearby village. There were three tanks and two jeeps. The tanks fired their machine guns into the distance. "I approached the last jeep and was about to identify myself when I took a second look at the helmets these soldiers were wearing. They had netting over them and their shape was hard to distinguish. Then, a G.I. spotted me and tossed me two packages of Camel cigarettes."

Mauger was safe. Aside from exchanging gestures and words of gratitude with his Russian friends, he left them with his wristwatch, which had earlier been much admired. "What a small price to pay for his great service!"

* * *

THE END OF THE WAR in Europe, VE Day, came on May 8, 1945. Ball turret gunner Frank Boyle remembered hearing the news: "At the time I was a phase check instructor on B-29 guns at Buckingham Army Air Field, in Fort Myers, Florida. We got the news just before dinner. Our first reaction was that it was a ruse to sucker punch us again with another Battle of the Bulge type of attack. Those of us who had fought them were convinced that the Germans would not surrender without a last-ditch massive air attack on our bases in England and France." But despite Boyle's suspicions, Germany was well and truly beaten. And he had played a role in administering that beating.

The 303rd hadn't flown a mission for nearly two weeks on the day that Germany surrendered. The killing and dying were over. There was a parade at Molesworth, a ceremony and celebrations. But it would take time, a lifetime for some, before the men reconciled themselves to the war and what it had meant and done to them. Because, regardless of what job or task they performed—combat or support—the war surely had imprinted them. They would never, could never, be the same.

EPILOGUE

ALMOST IMMEDIATELY FOLLOWING the cessation of hostilities, beginning at the end of May 1945, the 303rd was sent to Cases Air Base, Casablanca, French Morocco, where it operated under the direction of the Air Transport Command to return servicemen and equipment back to the States. As it developed, the unit was unneeded in this capacity and was inactivated on July 25. Most of its veterans had already left for home, and those that remained soon followed. The group was reactivated during 1947 but was soon put back into cadre status without ever being made operational. It was activated once more for a brief period from 1951 to 1954 before being shuttered again. Various organizations have been assigned the 303rd designation since that time, but any claims to the original group's lineage are nothing more than contrived.

RAF Molesworth is still extant and active seven decades after the end of the war. It is one of only two former Eighth Air Force bases that U.S. forces still operate. It is no longer an air base as the runways, ramp and most of the wartime structures have been plowed up or demolished.

However, the main hangar and two smaller hangars remain in service in various capacities. Although there have been many units based at Molesworth since World War II, the current tenant is the gracelessly named Joint Intelligence Operations Center Europe Analytic Center. It is operated by the Defense Intelligence Agency and staffed by servicemen from the United States and its European allies.

Regardless of what happened to the 303rd or to Molesworth, they both became part of the nearly nine thousand men who served with the bomb group from 1942 to 1945. Most of those men came of age during their wartime service, and those that survived went home to create new lives, new careers and new families. And as they turned their energies to things other than war, they transformed the United States into the greatest nation on earth. Their legacy and that of all the World War II generation is ubiquitous. The postwar stories that follow of various 303rd men are representative examples.

Frank Boyle entered the radio business several years after the war. He eventually went to work with Eastman Radio in Detroit in 1956 and retired as chairman in 1985. Today, at ninety, he still operates his own consulting business and brokers the acquisition and sale of radio stations. His service with the 303rd is never far from his mind. "I still have the same nightmare—a fear of opening the ball turret door at seven thousand feet and dropping my body into it—closing and locking the door. Then turning on all the operating machines, oxygen, heated suit, microphone cord, camera switch and automatic computing sight . . . and testing two .50-caliber guns over the Channel."

George Buske, whose chest and abdomen had nearly been torn away by enemy fighters on the mission to Bremen aboard the *Jersey Bounce Jr.* on December 20, 1943, returned home to Upstate New York after the war. Against all expectations he had a long career in the lumber business, and had children and grandchildren before passing away in 2003, sixty years after being so terribly wounded.

Medal of Honor winner Forrest Vosler was discharged from the USAAF in October 1944 before many 303rd veterans—who would complete full tours—had even arrived at Molesworth. He later went on to serve thirty years with the Veterans Administration. He went West in 1992, at age sixty-eight.

Eddie Deerfield went to school after the war and earned a BS in Journalism from Northwestern University. He was also commissioned as a second lieutenant in the Army reserve and was recalled to active duty during the Korean War. In Korea he commanded a psychological warfare detachment that transmitted radio broadcasts to the enemy. He later worked as a reporter and byline columnist for the *Chicago Daily Times* and was news editor at WGN-TV. Deerfield next served as a Foreign Service diplomat with the U.S. Information Agency for more than twenty years, retiring in 1988 as a counselor in the U.S. Senior Foreign Service. He had earlier retired from the Army reserve in 1983 as a lieutenant colonel. He currently resides in Palm Harbor, Florida.

Deerfield's pilot, Bob Cogswell, was killed while flying B-29s during the Korean War. He was part of a raid on the Namsi airfield on October 23, 1951. His aircraft was attacked by MiG-15s and caught fire immediately after dropping its bombs. It was last seen headed for the Yellow Sea, under control.

When the war ended, Richard "Dick" Johnson moved to the little fishing town of Deale, Maryland, east of Washington, D.C. He started a contracting business and remodeled homes while also working for the City of Annapolis. He bought a Piper PA-12 Super Cruiser in 1968 and still owns it. Johnson wrote the author recently: "I don't take it out very often anymore since the terror attacks of September 11, 2001. I am now required, because my airplane is only eighteen miles from Air Force One, to file a flight plan every time I want to fly." Johnson is ninety-two at the time of this writing.

John Ford, one of the 303rd's first "old hands," went to work for the Ford Company immediately after the war and was part of the magnificent American automobile heydays of the 1950s and 1960s. He worked in a number of different disciplines and rose to become the manager of industrial engineering at the massive Wixom assembly plant in Michigan—the factory that produced the Lincoln line. He retired from Ford after thirty-two years of employment. He also served as a reservist in the Army's quartermaster corps and retired as a major after six years of active service and thirty-four years of reserve service. He currently lives in Springfield, Missouri.

Mel Schulstad stayed on active duty and transitioned to the Air Force upon its formation as a separate service in 1947. He enjoyed a very successful career and retired as a colonel in 1965. Following his retirement, he was very active in promoting professionalism in counseling for alcoholics. A recovering alcoholic himself, Schulstad was the founding president of the National Association of Alcoholism and Drug Addiction Counselors, and was beloved and respected for his compassion and empathy. He had celebrated nearly fifty years of sobriety at the time of his death in 2012. Schulstad was a tremendous advocate of the 303rd, and although he was reluctant to highlight his own heroics, he engaged audiences for hours with the achievements of his comrades.

Van White—who had washed Jimmy Doolittle's aircraft so carefully in Kansas City before the war—was caught up in the great jobs upheaval as men returned from the war. He worked off and on with the Santa Fe Railroad in Winslow, Arizona, for several years before taking a job selling safes. After working out of his car for several years, he started the Albuquerque Safe Company; White had fallen in love with Albuquerque when the 303rd had been based at Alamogordo in 1942. Through tremendous hard work, he and his business prospered, and he retired in 1988. White still lives in Albuquerque and is a tremendous booster of the city and the surrounding area.

Charles Spencer's heroic actions during the January 26, 1943, mission to Bremen cost him his ears, nose and much of his face, as well as parts of his fingers, hands, toes and feet—victims to frostbite following a vicious air battle. He also lost an eye and much of his remaining eyesight. Spencer subsequently underwent thirty-six separate plastic surgeries in the States. With the support of his wife, he attended seminary. Soon after graduation, he began a ministry to the men of the Kansas State Soldiers Home at Fort Dodge. He stayed for thirty years. Despite his injuries and the loss of a son in a plane crash, he maintained his faith in God. He passed away in 1998, leaving his wife of fifty-six years, Jeanne.

Recon, the 427th Squadron's loyal terrier bitch, was killed by a jeep during the group's short stay at Casablanca.

THE 303RD HELL'S ANGELS: NOTABLE FACTS AND ACHIEVEMENTS

Combat crewmen from 1942 to 1945: 5,292

Total casualties (killed and wounded): 1,748

Total killed in action (KIA): 841

Total prisoners of war (POWs): 764

Total B-17 losses: 210

First Eighth Air Force bomb group to fly 200 missions, July 9, 1944, to Chatteaudon Airfield, France

First Eighth Air Force bomb group to fly 300 missions from England, to Bonn/Hangelar Airfield, Cologne Brillion and Euskirchen

Total combat missions flown: 364—most in Eighth Air Force

Total combat sorties flown (a combat sortie is one aircraft flying one combat mission): 10,721—second-highest in Eighth Air Force, of more than forty bomb groups

Total tons of bombs dropped: 26,346—second highest in Eighth Air Force of more than forty bomb groups

Total manning including support organizations from 1942 to 1945: 8,960

Total aircraft recovered in neutral countries: 3—all to Switzerland

First Eighth Air Force crewman to be awarded the Medal of Honor, Jack Mathis

One of four bomb groups in first Eighth Air Force mission against Germany, January 27, 1943—target Wilhelmshaven

First Eighth Air Force bomber to complete 25 missions, *Hell's Angels*

First Eighth Air Force bomber to complete 50 and 75 missions, *Knockout Dropper*

First Eighth Air Force pilot to complete 25 missions, Irl Baldwin

ACKNOWLEDGMENTS

As noted in the dedication and preface, Harry Gobrecht, a pilot with the 358th Bomb Squadron, committed himself—long years of himself—to the preservation of the unit's history. He catalogued the 303rd's achievements in his authoritative work *Might in Flight: Daily Diary of the Eighth Air Force's Hell's Angels 303rd Bombardment Group (H)*, from which his family graciously allowed me to borrow extensively. Edgar Miller was a fellow pilot who labored mightily to compile a list of known veterans of the 303rd and its support units. He began his task with a few hundred names on index cards. When he finished, he had produced eighteen hundred pages in six volumes. Many more 303rd veterans labored long, unheralded hours extracting information from, and organizing, official documents. Much of that work benefitted me in this effort.

Gobrecht, Miller and most of their comrades are gone. And the once-vibrant 303rd Bomb Group Association is no more. But Gary Moncur, the son of Vern Moncur, who piloted *Thunderbird* through so much peril, maintains the 303rd's legacy through the most extensive and professionally maintained Web site of its kind. It includes twenty-seven hundred pages and more than five million words. It can be readily accessed at http://www.303rdbg.com. Gary also knows as much about the 303rd as anyone living. His work belies a passion for the 303rd and the men who made it what it was—many of whom he grew to know very well during the past few decades. His help and encouragement during the writing of this book were of great value. Thank you, Gary.

The 303rd Bomb Group Association produced a regular newsletter from 1976 to 2006. Those newsletters grew in size and sophistication, and through the decades were a means by which the veterans told their personal stories in their own words. Those stories were an inestimable treasure to me. I thank the individual contributors as well as the hard-working and underappreciated editors: Al Martel, Jr., Harry Jenkins, Bud Klint, Hal Susskind and Eddie Deerfield.

Peter Park was, for many years, part of the Commander's Action Group with the Joint Analysis Center at modern-day Molesworth. He was also the base historian and an ardent supporter of the 303rd's heritage. As fellow historians, veterans and airpower buffs converged on Molesworth over the last many years, it was Peter who met and stewarded them about the base as special guests of the commanding officer. I had the pleasure of just such an experience and enjoyed the hospitality not only of Peter, but also of the commander of the JIOCEUR Analytic Center, Colonel Kristin Baker (U.S. Army), and the reserve management officer, Colonel Elizabeth Coble (U.S. Army).

Many 303rd members and families were gracious with assistance and material. I used much of it, but it was impossible to use it all. Nevertheless, that unused material was still valuable, as it furthered my understanding of the group's men and their actions as a whole. I am glad and thankful I had the opportunity to review it.

Ben Smith, Richard "Dick" Johnson and Brian O'Neill have written excellent books dealing with various aspects of the 303rd's history; they were useful to me. Smith's *Chick's Crew—A Tale of the Eighth Air Force*, is a remarkably candid account of his service that is a joy to read. Johnson's *Twenty Five Milk Runs (And a Few Others)* is remarkable not only for his wartime perspectives but also for the amazing story of his growing up. O'Neill's outstanding *Half a Wing, Three Engines and a Prayer: B-17s Over Germany* follows the actions of one crew but in the broad context of the 303rd's operations.

E. J. McCarthy has been my agent for more than a decade. He has always been unstinting in his support and superb in matching my work to the right publishers. He's done it again: Natalee Rosenstein, Robin Barletta and the rest of the staff at Berkley Publishing Group have done a tremendous job not only in presenting this work in the finest fashion possible, but in getting it in front of a broad audience. It is something that the men of the 303rd and the rest of their World War II comrades deserve.

Others who helped in varying ways include Dr. James Perry, who reviewed the manuscript and made genuinely useful critiques; Mark Forlow, who shared generously from his photograph collection; Ford Lauer, Gary Groth, and Bob Levandoski, who also shared photographs; and Ryan Bartholomew, who helped me with the Ehle Reber diary. There are others too numerous to mention to whom I apologize for not doing so.

Finally, my dogs shed a great deal, but they adore me. My daughters do daughterly things and adore me perhaps a bit less. My wife is beautiful, tender and engaging. And she lets me do what I will. When it pleases her. For all of this—minus the shedding—I love them with every bit of my heart.

BIBLIOGRAPHY

BOOKS

Air Ministry (A.C.A.S. [I]). *The Rise and Fall of the German Air Force (1933 to 1945)*. Richmond, England: The National Archives, 2008.

Bekker, Cajus. *The Luftwaffe War Diaries: The German Air Force in World War II*. New York: Da Capo Press, 1994.

Caldwell, Donald L. *JG 26: Top Guns of the Luftwaffe*. New York: Ballantine Books, 1991.

Craven, Wesley, and James Cate. *The Army Air Forces in World War II, VII: Services Around the World*. Chicago: University of Chicago Press, 1958.

Cronkite, Walter. *A Reporter's Life*. New York: Ballantine Books, 1996.

Davis, Richard G. *Bombing the European Axis Powers: A Historical Digest of the Combined Bomber Offensive, 1939–1945*. Maxwell AFB, AL: Air University Press, 2006.

_____. *Carl A. Spaatz and the Air War in Europe*. Washington, D.C.: Smithsonian Institute Press, 2006.

Doolittle, James H., and Carroll V. Glines. *I Could Never Be So Lucky Again*. New York: Bantam Books, 1992.

Freeman, Roger A. *The Mighty Eighth, Warpaint and Heraldry*. London: Arms & Armour Press, 1998.

Galland, Adolf. *The First and the Last: The Rise and Fall of the Luftwaffe: 1939–1945, by Germany's Commander of Fighter Forces.* New York: Ballantine Books, 1967.

Gobrecht, Harry D. *Might in Flight, Daily Diary of the Eighth Air Force's Hell's Angels, 303rd Bombardment Group (H).* Fort Collins, CO: Old Army Press, 1997.

Hammel, Eric. *Air War Europa: America's Air War Against Germany in Europe and North Africa, 1942–1945.* Pacifica, CA: Pacifica Press, 1994.

_____. *The Road to Big Week: The Struggle for Daylight Air Supremacy over Western Europe, July 1942–February 1944.* Pacifica, CA: Pacifica Military History, 2009.

Hansell, Haywood S., Jr. *The Air Plan that Defeated Hitler.* Atlanta, GA: Higgins McArthur/Longino & Porter, Inc., 1972.

Heaton, Colin, and Anne-Marie Lewis. *The Me 262 Stormbird: From the Pilots Who Flew, Fought, and Survived It.* Minneapolis, MN: Zenith Books, 2012.

Huston, John W., ed. *American Air Power Comes of Age: General H. "Hap" Arnold's World War II Diaries.* Maxwell AFB, AL: Air University Press, 2002.

Johnson, Richard Riley. *Twenty Five Milk Runs (And a Few Others).* Victoria, British Columbia: Trafford, 2004.

McCrary, John, and David Scherman. *First of the Many: Journal of Action with the Men of the Eighth Air Force.* New York: Simon and Schuster, 1944.

McNabb, Chris. *Order of Battle: German Luftwaffe in WW II.* London, England: Amber Books Ltd., 2009.

Mingos, Howard. *The Aircraft Yearbook for 1946.* New York: Lanciar Publishers Inc., 1946.

O'Neill, Brian. *Half a Wing, Three Engines and a Prayer—B-17s over Germany.* New York: McGraw-Hill, 1998.

Parton, James. *Air Force Spoken Here: General Ira Eaker & the Command of the Air.* Bethesda, MD: Adler & Adler Publishers Inc., 1986.

Ransom, Frank E. *Air-Sea Rescue 1941–1952.* U.S. Air Force Historical Study No. 95. Maxwell AFB, AL: USAF Historical Division, Air University, 1954.

Smith, Ben, Jr. *Chick's Crew: A Tale of the Eighth Air Force.* Waycross, GA: Yarbrough Brothers, 1978.

Spencer, Jay P. *Focke-Wulf Fw 190: Workhorse of the Luftwaffe.* Washington, D.C.: Smithsonian, 1989.

Spick, Mike. *Luftwaffe Fighter Aces, The Jagdflieger and Their Combat Tactics and Techniques.* New York: Ivy Books, 1996.

Stout, Jay. *The Men Who Killed the Luftwaffe: The U.S. Army Air Forces Against Germany in World War II*. Mechanicsburg, PA: Stackpole Books, 2010.

Wells, Mark K. *Aviators and Air Combat: A Study of the U.S. Eighth Air Force and R.A.F. Bomber Command*. London, England: University of London, 1992.

Westermann, Edward B. *Flak: German Anti-Aircraft Defenses, 1914–1945*. Lawrence, KS: University Press of Kansas, 2001.

GOVERNMENT STUDIES AND DOCUMENTS

Air Forces Manual No. 20, *Gunner's Information File: Flexible Gunnery*. Government Printing Office, May 1944.

Army Air Forces Historical Studies No. 31, *Flexible Gunnery Training in the AAF*. Assistant Chief of Air Staff, Intelligence, Historical Division, 1945.

Combat Crew Rotation: World War II and Korea. Maxwell AFB, AL: USAF Historical Division, Aerospace Studies Institute, Air University, 1968.

U.S. Air Force Historical Study No. 79, *Policies and Procedures Governing Elimination from AAF Schools, 1939–1945*. Maxwell AFB, AL: USAF Historical Division, Air University, 1952.

U.S. Air Force Historical Studies 158–160, *The Employment of the German Luftwaffe Against the Allies in the West, 1943–1945—The Struggle for Air Supremacy over the Reich, 1 January 1944–31 March 1944, Volume II*. Maxwell AFB, AL: USAF Historical Division, Air University, 1954.

INTERNET RESOURCE

Hell's Angels 303rd Bomb Group (H). http://www.303rdbg.com.

NOTES

NOTE: The reader should be aware that much of the material cited can be found on the 303rd's official website: http://www.303rdbg.com. This site—maintained by Gary Moncur—includes the official details of each mission flown by the 303rd, as well as related stories. It also includes relevant Mission Air Crew Reports (MACRs), personal journals, lists of missions flown by each combat crewman, information about each crew, lists of 303rd aircraft and their fate, thousands of photographs and other important and detailed information. Moreover, it is searchable. Nothing like it exists elsewhere and the interested reader is encouraged to visit and explore.

INTRODUCTION

1. John Donnelly, "A Treasure Found, A Brother Remembered—All He Wanted to Do Was to Fly," *Molesworth Pilot—Latest News from the 303rd Bomb Group* 3, no. 5 (May 15, 2011), electronic publication, http://www.303rdbg.com/news/2011-05-15 .html.

"AND THEN YOU SLEPT IN THE BARN"

1. Telephone interview, Van White, May 10, 2013. All subsequent quotes by or references to White are derived from this source.
2. Television interview, Mel Schulstad, KBTC, *Full Focus*, "The 303rd," premiere date, July 21, 2010. Unless otherwise noted, all subsequent quotes by or references to Schulstad are derived from this source.
3. Telephone interview, John Ford, July 5 and July 19, 2013. All subsequent quotes by or references to Ford are derived from these interviews.
4. Henry H. Arnold, *Global Mission* (New York: Harper and Brothers, 1949), 168–169.
5. Howard Mingos, *The Aircraft Yearbook for 1946* (New York: Lanciar Publishers, Inc., 1946), 477, 484.
6. Arnold, *Global Mission*, 178.
7. Ibid., 206.
8. Ibid., 356.
9. U.S. Air Force Historical Study No. 79, *Policies and Procedures Governing Elimination from AAF Schools, 1939–1945* (Maxwell AFB, AL; USAF Historical Division, Air University, 1952), 1.
10. Mingos, *The Aircraft Yearbook for 1946*, 482.
11. Arnold, *Global Mission*, 278.
12. Telephone interview, William Eisenhart, March 29, 2013. All subsequent quotes by or references to Eisenhart are derived from this source.

"NO PANTY WAIST UNION HOURS"

1. Headquarters, 303rd Bombardment Group (H), Office of the Group Operations Officer, Diary, February 16, 1942, Air Force Historical Research Agency Microfiche Reel #B0210, 4.
2. 303rd Bomb Group, "Memories of a G.I. January 1942–June 1945, S/Sgt Christ M. Christoff," http://www.303rdbg.com/journal-christoff.html.
3. Headquarters, 303rd Bombardment Group (H), Office of the Group Operations Officer, Diary, April 30, 1942, Air Force Historical Research Agency Microfiche Reel #B0210, 67.
4. Harry D. Gobrecht, *Might in Flight: Daily Diary of the Eighth Air Force's Hell's Angels, 303rd Bombardment Group (H)* (Fort Collins, CO: Old Army Press, 1997), 31.
5. Headquarters, 303rd Bombardment Group (H), Office of the Group Operations Officer, Diary, May 3, 1942, Air Force Historical Research Agency Microfiche Reel #B0210, 68.
6. Headquarters, 303rd Bombardment Group (H), Office of the Intelligence Officer, Diary, June 20, 1942, Air Force Historical Research Agency Microfiche Reel #B0210, 68.

7. Lester Hilliard, Letter to the Editor, *Hell's Angels Newsletter* 11, no. 3 (303rd Bomb Group (H) Association, May 1988): 318.

8. Headquarters, 303rd Bombardment Group (H), Office of the Intelligence Officer, Diary, June 20, 1942, Air Force Historical Research Agency Microfiche Reel #B0210, 119.

9. Ibid., August 21, 1942, 235.

10. Ibid., August 18, 1942, 235.

11. "Journal of Ehle Reber, Daily Diary of an Original 303rd Bomb Group Pilot," *Molesworth Pilot—Latest News from the 303rd Bomb Group* 4, no. 1 (December 18, 2011), electronic publication, http://www.303rdbg.com/news/2012-01-15.html. NOTE: The Ehle Reber diary is quoted by permission of Ryan Bartholomew, president of the Malin (Oregon) Historical Society. As dates from the diary are included with each quotation, individual citations are not provided.

12. Headquarters, 303rd Bombardment Group (H), Office of the Intelligence Officer, Diary, August 24, 1942, Air Force Historical Research Agency Microfiche Reel #B0210, 237.

13. Mike Spick, *Luftwaffe Fighter Aces: The Jagdflieger and Their Combat Tactics and Techniques* (New York: Ivy Books, 1996), 142.

14. U.S. Air Force Historical Study No. 118, *The Early Operations of the Eighth Air Force and the Origins of the Combined Bomber Offensive* (AAF Historical Office, Headquarters, Army Air Forces, 1946), 32.

"SHE IS A HELL OF A BIG SHIP"

1. Eugene J. O'Brien, *Memoirs from Molesworth, England*, n.d., http://www.303rdbg.com/journal-obrien-eugene.pdf.

2. Headquarters, 303rd Bombardment Group (H), Office of the Intelligence Officer, Diary, August 27, 1942, Air Force Historical Research Agency Microfiche Reel #B0210, 238.

3. Headquarters, 303rd Bombardment Group (H), Office of the Intelligence Officer, Diary, September 4, 1942, Air Force Historical Research Agency Microfiche Reel #B0210, 259.

4. Headquarters, 303rd Bombardment Group (H), Office of the Intelligence Officer, Diary, September 5, 1942, Air Force Historical Research Agency Microfiche Reel #B0210, 260.

5. Headquarters, 303rd Bombardment Group (H), Office of the Intelligence Officer, Diary, September 7, 1942, Air Force Historical Research Agency Microfiche Reel #B0210, 261.

6. Ibid, September 9, 1942.

7. Headquarters, 303rd Bombardment Group (H), Office of the Intelligence Officer, Diary, September 11, 1942, Air Force Historical Research Agency Microfiche Reel #B0210, 263.

8. Headquarters, 303rd Bombardment Group (H), Office of the Intelligence Officer, Diary, September 11, 1942, Air Force Historical Research Agency Microfiche Reel #B0210, 263.

9. Ibid, September 12, 1942.

10. Headquarters, 303rd Bombardment Group (H), Office of the Intelligence Officer, Diary, September 19, 1942, Air Force Historical Research Agency Microfiche Reel #B0210, 264.

11. William Neff, "I Almost Missed WW II," *Hell's Angels Newsletter* 20, no. 1 (303rd Bomb Group (H) Association, May 1998): 901.

12. Headquarters, 303rd Bombardment Group (H), Office of the Intelligence Officer, Diary, October 21, 1942, Air Force Historical Research Agency Microfiche Reel #B0210, 284.

"ONE MUST BE ABLE TO DEPEND UPON HIS CREW"

1. Headquarters, 303rd Bombardment Group (H), Office of the Intelligence Officer, Diary, October 28, 1942, Air Force Historical Research Agency Microfiche Reel #B0210, 289.

2. Headquarters, 303rd Bombardment Group (H), Bulletin No. 362, December 31, 1943, Air Force Historical Research Agency Microfiche Reel #B0210, 578.

3. Headquarters AAF Station ***[107], 303rd Bombardment Group (H), Special Court Martial Orders Number 39, December 26, 1943, Air Force Historical Research Agency Microfiche Reel #B0210, 590.

4. Eric Hammel, *The Road to Big Week: The Struggle for Daylight Air Supremacy over Western Europe, July 1942–February 1944* (Pacifica: Pacifica Military History, 2009), 172–173.

5. James Parton, *Air Force Spoken Here: General Ira Eaker & the Command of the Air* (Bethesda: Adler & Adler Publishers Inc., 1986), 214.

"I WAS TIRED OF GETTING HIT"

1. Gene Kuhn, "Snap! Crackle! Pop! Cereal's Slogan Helps Reunite Wartime Bomber Crash Parties," *Hell's Angels Newsletter* 3, no. 1 (303rd Bomb Group (H) Association, March 1979): 39.

"A CHARMED LIFE, MAYBE"

1. Parton, *Air Force Spoken Here*, 192.

2. Ibid., 217.

3. Ibid., 215.

4. Ibid., 220.

5. Ibid., 221.

6. George Ashworth, "Oranges and Boots," *Hell's Angels Newsletter* 19, no. 3 (303rd Bomb Group (H) Association, November 1997): 865.

7. Russell Ney, "A P-51 Tale," *Hell's Angels Newsletter* 19, no. 3 (303rd Bomb Group (H) Association): 863.

"THE KRAUT FIRED A BURST INTO THE SKIPPER'S CHUTE"

1. 306th Bomb Group, Intelligence Report, January 23, 1943, http://www.306bg .org/MISSION_REPORTS/24jan43.pdf.

2. Charles Roth, "Impact of Bomb Strike from Above Turns B-17 *Beats Me!* Upside Down," *Hell's Angels Newsletter* 28, no. 3 (303rd Bomb Group (H) Association, August 2005): 8.

3. Joel Wight, "1Lt Joseph E. 'Little Joe' Haas—A Loving Tribute by His Nephew Joel Wight," *Molesworth Pilot—Latest News from the 303rd Bomb Group 5*, no. 1 (January 27, 2013), electronic publication, http://www.303rdbg.com/news/ 2013-01-27.html.

4. Iris Drinkwater, "303rd Pilot Lands Stricken *Werewolf* on Grounds of British Mental Hospital," *Hell's Angels Newsletter* 21, no. 4 (303rd Bomb Group (H) Association, November 1999): 998. All Quotes by Oxrider and details about the landing at Langdon are derived from this source.

5. Sebastian L. Vogel, "The Evasion of Sebastian L. Vogel," 303rdbg.com, http:// www.303rdbg.com/vogel-evadee.html. All quotes by Vogel and details about his bailout and subsequent evasion to England are derived from this source.

6. Parton, *Air Force Spoken Here*, 212.

"I LIKE TO THINK SHE WAS PRETTY"

1. Headquarters, 303rd Bombardment Group (H), Diary, October 28, 1942, Micro-fiche Reel #B0210, 447.

"HOW ABOUT *HELL'S ANGELS*?"

1. Robert Yonkman, Letter to Editor, *Hell's Angels Newsletter* 10, no. 3 (March 1987): 265.

2. Eldon Audiss, Letter to Editor, *Hell's Angels Newsletter* 10, no. 3 (March 1987): 265.

3. 303rd Bomb Group, "*Hell's Angels* vs *Memphis Belle*," http://www.303rdbg .com/h-ha-mb.html. This site includes a detailed comparison between the missions of the two aircraft.

4. 303rd Bomb Group, "Famous Flying Fortress Gives 303rd Its Name: *Hell's Angels*," http://www.303rdbg.com/missionreports/097.pdf.

5. 303rd Bomb Group, "Original 303rd BG (H) Pilots and Their Fate," http://www .303rdbg.com/h-pilots.html.

6. Parton, *Air Force Spoken Here*, 298.

7. Ibid., 291.

"WE CHECKED OUR PARACHUTES"

1. Telephone interviews, Eddie Deerfield, December 28, 2012, February 13, 2013, and July 14, 2013. Unless otherwise noted, all subsequent quotes by or references to Deerfield are derived from these sources.

2. Robert Cogswell, "The Cogswell Letters—Rare Look into the Emotions of a B-17 Combat Pilot," *Hell's Angels Newsletter* 31, no. 1 (303rd Bomb Group (H) Association, February 2007): 10.

3. Ibid.

4. Editor, "Nine of the 303rd's Best Pinups," *Hell's Angels Newsletter* 28, no. 3 (303rd Bomb Group (H) Association, August 2005): 14.

5. U.S. Air Force Historical Study No. 95, *Air-Sea Rescue, 1941–1952* (Maxwell AFB, AL: USAF Historical Division, Air University, 1953), 28.

6. Ibid., 27.

7. Ibid., 44.

"COULD WE KEEP IT UP?"

1. Robin Neillands, "Luftwaffe Pilots Were Being Handed a Two-Course Feast," *Hell's Angels Newsletter* 30, no. 1 (303rd Bomb Group (H) Association, February 2006): 10.

2. Ibid., 12.

3. Gobrecht, *Might in Flight,* 233.

4. Ibid.

5. Arnold, *Global Mission*, 495.

6. Robert Cooney, "Schweinfurt Was the Worst of the Lot," *Hell's Angels Newsletter* 19, no. 4 (303rd Bomb Group (H) Association, February 1998): 881.

7. Letter from Louis T. Moffatt to Commanding General, 1st Bombardment Wing, August 10, 1943. http://www.303rdbg.com/MACR/00284.pdf.

8. Don Webster, "Do You Remember?" *Hell's Angels Newsletter* 11, no. 1 (303rd Bomb Group (H) Association, November 1987): 291.

"GOD WILL FIND OUT"

1. John McCrary and David Scherman, *First of the Many: Journal of Action with the Men of the Eighth Air Force* (New York: Simon and Schuster, 1944), 92–94.

2. James O'Leary, "Personal Diaries," *Hell's Angels Newsletter* 2, no. 4 (303rd Bomb Group (H) Association, November 1978): 35.

3. Willis Meyer, "Crew Chief Hugged By Grateful Pilot," *Hell's Angels Newsletter* 25, no. 4 (303rd Bomb Group (H) Association, November 2002): 15.

4. Curtis Olsen, "The Stirling Scare—Another Angle," *Hell's Angels Newsletter* 9, no. 1 (303rd Bomb Group (H) Association, February 1985): 207.

5. Lawrence Whippo, "Letter to the Editor," *Hell's Angels Newsletter* 9, no. 4 (303rd Bomb Group (H) Association, April 1986): 233.

6. Robert Cogswell, "The Cogswell Letters—Rare Look into the Emotions of a B-17 Combat Pilot," *Hell's Angels Newsletter* 31, no. 1 (303rd Bomb Group (H) Association, February 2007): 10.

7. Ibid.

"YOU COULD HAVE HEARD A PIN DROP"

1. Telephone interview, William Eisenhart, March 29, 2013. All subsequent references to, or quotes by, Eisenhart are derived from this source.

2. Telephone interview, William Heller, November 28, 2009. All subsequent references to, or quotes by, Heller are derived from this source.

3. End Note: VIII Bomber Command, Field Order 220. October 14, 1943.

4. Parton, *Air Force Spoken Here*, 315–316.

5. Arthur Tobkin and Matt Kremer, "'Black Thursday' Survivor," *Molesworth Pilot—Latest News from the 303rd Bomb Group* 2, no. 13 (September 5, 2010), electronic publication, http://www.303rdbg.com/news/2010-09-05.html. All subsequent references to, or quotes by, Kremer are derived from this source.

6. Gobrecht, *Might in Flight*, 272.

7. Parton, *Air Force Spoken Here*, 315–316.

8. John Huston, *American Airpower Comes of Age: General Henry H. "Hap" Arnold's World War II Diaries, Volume II* (Maxwell Air Force Base: Air University Press, 2002), 27.

9. Gobrecht, *Might in Flight*, 314.

10. Ibid.

11. Ibid., 342.

12. Ibid., 276.

13. Ibid., 275.

14. "German Area Smoke Screening," *Tactical and Technical Trends* 24 (Office of the Chief, Chemical Warfare service, War Department, Washington, D.C., May 6, 1943).

15. Gobrecht, *Might in Flight*, 294.

16. Philip Peed, unpublished memoir, n.d., n.p., via John Peed.

"I VOWED THAT I WOULD NEVER TURN BACK"

1. David O. Michael, personal journal, http://www.303rdbg.com/journal-michael.pdf.

2. John St. Julian, "Damn the Aborts—Full Speed Ahead," *Hell's Angels Newsletter* 21, no. 4 (303rd Bomb Group (H) Association, November 1999): 16.

3. Gobrecht, *Might in Flight*, 128.

4. Ibid., 213.

5. Bert Hallum and Jerry Hoffman, Sr., "Reflections on Being a Pilot in WWII," 303rdbg.com, http://www.303rdbg.com/reflections-hallum.html.

6. Editor, "Friends and Heroes," *Molesworth Pilot—Latest News from the 303rd Bomb Group* 2, no. 18 (December 28, 2010), electronic publication, http://www.303rdbg.com/news/2010-12-28.html.

7. Hal Susskind, "Portrait of Courage—Nothing but Grit and Courage Enabled This Man to Live," *Hell's Angels Newsletter* 11, no. 3 (303rd Bomb Group (H) Association, May 1998): 322.

"HE WAS LYING ON HIS BACK HOLDING HIS GUN"

1. James E. Geiger, unpublished memoir, n.d., n.p., via Jeanne Moon.

2. Gobrecht, *Might in Flight*, 299.

3. Brian O'Neill, *Half a Wing, Three Engines and a Prayer—B-17s over Germany* (New York: McGraw-Hill, 1998), 257–268. O'Neill's excellent account of the Vosler mission is detailed and thorough and was useful in informing the author's effort.

4. "Pappy Moody of Lewiston, War Prisoner," *Lewiston Evening Journal*, September 2, 1944, 1.

5. Stanley Moody, radio broadcast, BBC, February 21, 1944. Archived by Imperial War Museum, catalogue number 2183. All quotes from Moody are derived from this source.

6. Ivan Brown, Jr., MD, "Saving Sergeant Buske—An Account of Remarkable Valor and Amazing Survival from the Records of the 65th General Hospital, a Duke University Army Reserve Unit of World War II," *North Carolina Medical Journal* 60, no. 1 (January/February 1999): 22–25. All post-mission information about Buske's wounds and recovery are derived from this source.

7. Arnold, *Global Mission*, 441.

8. Parton, *Air Force Spoken Here*, 346.

9. Ibid., 320.

10. James Doolittle, *I Could Never Be So Lucky Again* (New York: Bantam Books, 1991), 344.

"THIS IS THE TIME WHEN I GET SCARED"

1. Travis's activities and quotes related to the Oschersleben mission are derived from his letter to the mother of William Fisher who was KIA on that day.

2. Harold Susskind, "If I Live to Be 200 Years Old. . . . ," *Hell's Angels Newsletter* 15, no. 1 (303rd Bomb Group (H) Association, March 1991): 442.

3. Jack Fawcett, "Remembering the Big O," *Hell's Angels Newsletter* 15, no. 2 (303rd Bomb Group (H) Association, July 1991): 451. All quotes by Fawcett are derived from this source.

4. U.S. Air Force Historical Studies 158–160, *The Employment of the German Luftwaffe Against the Allies in the West, 1943–1945—The Struggle for Air Supremacy over the Reich, 1 January 1944–March 31, 1944,* Volume II, (Maxwell AFB, AL: USAF Historical Division, Air University, 1954), 27.

5. Missing Air Crew Report (MACR) #1192, Headquarters, AAF Station 107, 303rd Bombardment Group (H).

6. Ibid.

7. Vern Moncur, personal journal, http://www.303rdbg.com/thunderbird/vlm-journal .html.

8. Fred Reichel, "Fly Your Missions and Keep Your Nose Clean!", *Hell's Angels Newsletter* 19, no. 4 (303rd Bomb Group (H) Association, February 1998): 883.

9. "One-Man Air Force Belittles His Feat; 'I Seen My Duty and I Done It,' Says Pilot Who Fought Off 30 Nazi Planes" by Frederick Graham, cable to the *New York Times,* January 19, 1944, 8.

10. Donald L. Caldwell, *JG 26: Top Guns of the Luftwaffe* (New York: Ballantine Books, 1991), 205.

11. Adolf Galland, *The First and the Last: The Rise and Fall of the Luftwaffe—1939–1945 by Germany's Commander of Fighter Forces* (New York: Ballantine Books, 1967), 203.

12. Richard G. Davis, *Carl A. Spaatz and the Air War in Europe* (Washington: Center for Air Force History, 1993), 304.

13. Cajus Bekker, *The Luftwaffe War Diaries: The German Air Force in World War II* (New York: Da Capo Press, 1994), 364.

14. Haywood S. Hansell, Jr., *The Air Plan that Defeated Hitler* (Atlanta: Higgins McArthur/Longino & Porter, Inc., 1972), 176.

15. Ruby Side Thompson, *World War II London Blitz Diary, Volume 4, 1944–1945: A Woman's Revelations Enduring War and Marriage,* n.d, n.p.

16. Clifford Fontaine, personal journal, via Dawn Higgins.

17. Harold Gunn, "Memories of Mission #35," 303rdbg.com, http://www.303rdbg .com/missionreports/035.pdf.

18. George Morrison, "The Story of Crew 20," *Hell's Angels Newsletter* 10, no. 1 (303rd Bomb Group (H) Association, September 1986): 242.

19. Lucius Arnold, "Empty Bunks a Devastating Experience," *Hell's Angels Newsletter* 22, no. 1 (303rd Bomb Group (H) Association, February 2000): 1023

20. Coleman Sanders, "London's Eiffel Tower," *Hell's Angels Newsletter* 19, no. 1 (303rd Bomb Group (H) Association, May 1997): 824.

"HE WAS MAD AS FIRE"

1. *Combat Crew Rotation: World War II and Korea* (Maxwell AFB, AL: USAF Historical Division, Aerospace Studies Institute, Air University, 1968), 13–14.
2. Telephone interview with Don Stoulil, July 8, 2013. All subsequent quotes by or references to Stoulil are derived from this source.
3. Clifford Fontaine, personal journal, via Dawn Higgins.
4. Wesley Craven and James Cate, *The Army Air Forces in World War II, VII: Services Around the World* (Chicago: University of Chicago Press, 1958), 420–421.
5. Richard Riley Johnson, *Twenty Five Milk Runs (And a Few Others)* (Victoria: Trafford, 2004), 185.
6. William Malone, personal journal (October 14, 1944).
7. Vern Moncur, personal journal (February 4, 1944). http://www.303rdbg.com/ thunderbird/vlm-journal.html.
8. Edgar Miller, "An Inch Is as Good as a Mile—A German 88mm Couldn't Get Me," 303rdbg.com, http://www.303rdbg.com/missionreports/163.pdf.
9. U.S. Air Force Historical Study No. 78, *Morale in the AAF in World War II* (Maxwell AFB, AL: USAF Historical Division, Air University, 1953), 48.
10. Clifford Fontaine, personal journal., via Dawn Higgins.
11. U.S. Air Force Historical Study No. 78, *Morale in the AAF in World War II* (Maxwell AFB, AL: USAF Historical Division, Air University, 1953), 56.
12. Johnson, *Twenty Five Milk Runs,* 173.
13. James E. Geiger, unpublished memoir, n.d., n.p., via Jeanne Moon.

"OUR FORCES ARE FIGHTING A HOPELESS BATTLE"

1. U.S. Air Force Historical Studies 158–160, *The Employment of the German Luftwaffe Against the Allies in the West, 1943–1945—The Struggle for Air Supremacy over the Reich, 1 January 1944–31 March 1944,* 111.
2. Orvis Silrum, "My Most Unusual 303rd Experience," *Hell's Angels Newsletter* 18, no. 3 (303rd Bomb Group (H) Association, August 1996): 762.
3. Gobrecht, *Might in Flight,* 352.
4. Ibid., 354.
5. Ibid.
6. Richard G. Davis, *Bombing the European Axis Powers: A Historical Digest of the Combined Bomber Offensive, 1939–1945* (Maxwell Air Force Base, AL: Air University Press, 2006), 288.
7. U.S. Air Force Historical Studies, 158–160, 84–85.

"OUR FIGHTER SUPPORT WAS SPLENDID"

1. Martin Middlebrook, *The Berlin Raids* (New York: Viking Books, 1998), 2.
2. Doolittle, *I Could Never Be So Lucky Again,* 368–369.

3. Vern Moncur, personal journal, http://www.303rdbg.com/thunderbird/vlm-journal .html.

4. Ibid.

5. Ibid.

6. Gobrecht, *Might in Flight*, 171.

7. Ibid., 368.

8. Ibid.

9. U.S. Air Force Historical Studies, 158–160, 169.

"HURRY UP AND JUMP."

1. Davis, *Carl A. Spaatz and the Air War in Europe*, 274.

2. Johnson, *Twenty Five Milk Runs*, 100.

3. Harry Gobrecht, "Last Mission," 303rdbg.com, http://www.303rdbg.com/358ste wart.html.

4. Davis, *Carl A. Spaatz and the Air War in Europe*, 449.

5. George Greene, "I Tied a Bandage on General Travis," *Hell's Angels Newsletter* 27, no. 1 (303rd Bomb Group (H) Association, February 2004): 15.

"I WAS FINALLY FINISHED"

1. Milo Robert Schultz, unpublished memoir, n.d., n.p., via Milo Schultz family.

2. Warren Kotz, personal journal, via Vicki Sharp.

3. *Flak*, official training film, T.F. 1-3389, First Motion Picture Unit, Army Air Forces, 1944.

4. Charles Ziesche, "Target: Merseberg! 'nuff said,'" *Hell's Angels Newsletter* 19, no. 2 (303rd Bomb Group (H) Association, August 1997): 841.

5. Robert Butcher, personal journal, via Brian Butcher.

6. Edward B. Westermann, *Flak: German Anti-Aircraft Defenses, 1914–1945* (Lawrence: University Press of Kansas, 2001), 282.

7. Alan Chesney, "My Most Unusual 303rd Experience," *Hell's Angels Newsletter* 18, no. 4 (303rd Bomb Group (H) Association, November 1996): 780.

8. James E. Geiger, unpublished memoir, n.d., n.p., via Jeanne Moon.

"YOU'LL BE SORRY"

1. Johnson, *Twenty Five Milk Runs*, 1–23.

2. Ibid., 93.

3. Mark Kendall Wells, *Aviators and Air Combat: A Study of the U.S. Eighth Air Force and RAF Bomber Command*, PhD thesis (London: Kings College, 1992), 305.

4. Robert Brassil, "Top Secret Glide Bomb Project One Frustration After Another," *Hell's Angels Newsletter* 26, no. 1 (303rd Bomb Group (H) Association, February 2003): 3.

5. Johnson, *Twenty Five Milk Runs*, 105.

6. Gordon Bale, "Grapefruits for Cologne," *Hell's Angels Newsletter* 19, no. 2 (303rd Bomb Group (H) Association, August 1997): 844.

7. Johnson, *Twenty Five Milk Runs*, 106.

"I SURE DO GET HOMESICK AT TIMES"

1. Milo Robert Schultz, unpublished memoir, n.d., n.p., via Milo Schultz family.

2. *Lincoln Evening Journal*, Lincoln, Nebraska, Monday, May 29, 1944, Page 2.

3. Letter, Acel Livingston to parents, March 18, 1944.

4. Ibid.

5. Ibid.

6. Ibid.

7. Missing Air Crew Report (MACR) #5340, Headquarters, AAF Station 107, 303rd Bombardment Group (H).

8. Gobrecht, *Might in Flight*, 431.

9. Letter, Scottie Bergstrom to Mrs. Earl Livingston, September 10, 1945.

10. Johnson, *Twenty Five Milk Runs*, 169.

11. Ibid., 167.

12. Ben Smith, Jr., *Chick's Crew: A Tale of the Eighth Air Force* (Waycross: Yarbrough Brothers, 1978), 66.

"I WAS TOLD SOMETHING BIG WAS GOING ON"

1. Letter, Spaatz to Barney Giles, June 27, 1944, Spaatz Papers, Diary.

2. Stanley Claster, personal journal, http://www.303rdbg.com/missionreports/172.pdf.

3. Walter Cronkite, *A Reporter's Life* (New York: Ballantine Books, 1996), 104.

4. John Lester, "Random Thoughts from World War II," 29th Field Artillery Regimental Home Page, http://members.tripod.com/msg_fisher/lester-2.html.

5. Telephone interview, Frank Boyle, February 23, 2013. All subsequent quotes by or references to Boyle are derived from this source.

"I BECAME A SORT OF ORPHAN WITHIN THE BOMB GROUP"

1. Milo Robert Schultz, unpublished memoir, n.d., n.p.

2. William Fisher, "My Most Unusual 303rd Experience," *Hell's Angels Newsletter* 18, no. 3 (303rd Bomb Group (H) Association, August 1996): 762.

3. John Vanzo, "Operation Mapquest," *Molesworth Pilot—Latest News from the 303rd Bomb Group* 3, no. 6 (June 12, 2006), electronic publication, http://www.303rdbg.com/news/2011-06-12.html.

4. Johnson, *Twenty Five Milk Runs*, 137.

5. Ibid., 139.

6. 303rdbg.com, *303rd BG (H) Combat Mission No. 185, June 19, 1944*, http://www.303rdbg.com/missionreports/185.pdf.

7. Joe Vieira, "303rd Relives Bloody Days in German Skies," *Hell's Angels Newsletter* 2, no. 1 (303rd Bomb Group (H) Association, November 1977): 9.

8. Johnson, *Twenty Five Milk Runs*, 150.

9. Ibid., 179.

10. Gobrecht, *Might in Flight*, 576.

"WE POURED THEM INTO THE BACK OF THE AIRPLANE"

1. U.S. Air Force Historical Study No. 78, 46.

2. Mission Report, 303rd Bombardment Group (H), August 15, 1944, Combat Mission No. 229.

3. Gobrecht, *Might in Flight*, 512.

4. Smith, *Chick's Crew*, 54.

5. Ibid., 107.

6. Ibid., 550.

7. Ibid., 45.

8. Ibid., 53.

9. Missing Air Crew Report (MACR) #9404, Headquarters, AAF Station 107, 303rd Bombardment Group (H).

10. Missing Air Crew Report (MACR) #9408, Headquarters, AAF Station 107, 303rd Bombardment Group (H).

11. Missing Air Crew Report (MACR) #9406, Headquarters, AAF Station 107, 303rd Bombardment Group (H).

12. "Krumme St. 28/Site of WWII Slaying of POW Sheppard Kerman," Panoramio, http://www.panoramio.com/photo/5580258.

13. T. McNamee, "Uncle's Heroic End: Nephew Finds Truth About World War II Tragedy," *Chicago Sun-Times*, January 7, 2008, p. 14.

14. K. Hueske, "Günter Rode *wird Tat nie vergessen*," *Wolfenbüttel Freitag*, December 9, 2011, n.p.

15. T. McNamee, "Uncle's Heroic End."

16. Missing Air Crew Report (MACR) #9406, Headquarters, AAF Station 107, 303rd Bombardment Group (H). Statements by McGraw, Timmins and Stewart are included in this MACR.

17. Letter, Edmund J. Skoner, Headquarters, 303rd Bombardment Group (H), to Simon D. Kerman, September 29, 1944. http://www.303rdbg.com/murder-kerman.html and http://www.303rdbg.com/shepkerman-chaplain.jpg.

18. Letter, Walter K. Shayler, Commanding Officer, 360th Bombardment Squadron, Headquarters, 303rd Bombardment Group (H), to Simon D. Kerman, October 22, 1944.

19. http://www.303rdbg.com/shepkerman-telegram.jpg.

20. Letter, Louis C. Jurgensen, Jr., 360th Bombardment Squadron, to Mrs. Simon D. Kerman, December 8, 1944. http://www.303rdbg.com/shepkerman-adjutant.jpg.

21. http://www.303rdbg.com/murder-kerman.html.

22. Sheppard Kerman's nephew, Matt Smith, was taken by a passion to discover more about his uncle and the circumstances surrounding his murder. He traveled to Wolfenbüttel, where he visited relevant sites and interviewed witnesses and others knowledgeable about the incident. He has shared the results of his efforts—to include many of the previously cited sources—on the 303rd's website: http://www.303rdbg.com/murder-kerman.html.

23. MACR #9406. http://www.303rdbg.com/MACR/09406.pdf.

24. John Pursley, "German Schoolboy Flak Gunner," *Military History*, August 2002, 50.

25. Susan Hamilton, "Letter to the Editor," *Hell's Angels Newsletter* 2, no. 1 (303rd Bomb Group (H) Association, November 1977): 12–13.

26. Anthony Saco, "Memories of Happy Times," *Hell's Angels Newsletter* 31, no. 1 (303rd Bomb Group (H) Association, February 2007): 16.

27. Gobrecht, *Might in Flight,* 303.

28. John Hilliard, guest remarks, 303rdbg.com, http://www.303rdbg.com/guest-rmks27.html.

29. George Ashworth, "Oranges and Boots," *Hell's Angels Newsletter* 19, no. 3 (303rd Bomb Group (H) Association, November 1997): 865.

30. James E. Geiger, unpublished memoir, n.d., n.p., via Jeanne Moon.

31. Johnson, *Twenty Five Milk Runs,* 168.

32. Jay A. Stout, *The Men Who Killed the Luftwaffe* (Mechanicsburg: Stackpole Books, 2010), 93.

33. George Hiebeler, "A Fire the First Thing in the Morning Could Ruin Your Day!" *Hell's Angels Newsletter* 19, no. 4 (303rd Bomb Group (H) Association, February 1998): 883.

34. Clifford Fontaine, personal journal, via Dawn Higgins.

35. David Michael, personal journal, http://www.303rdbg.com/journal-michael.pdf.

36. Maynard Pitcher, "We Dropped the 1,000 Lb Bomb!" *Hell's Angels Newsletter* 20, no. 1 (303rd Bomb Group (H) Association, May 1998): 901.

37. Personal interview, Hildegard Kaiser Franke, July 13, 2013.

"YOU ARE GOING TO HAVE TO STAY IN THERE AND FIGHT THEM"

1. Wells, *Aviators and Air Combat*, 260.

2. Kermit Stevens interview with Dr. Vivian Rogers-Price, National Museum of the Mighty Eighth Air Force, January 26, 2002.

3. John Cermin, "Lew Lyle, Pilot," *C.A.P.S. Intercom* 2, no. 1 (Combat Aircrew Preservation Society, January 2006): 8–19.

4. Smith, *Chick's Crew,* 113.

5. Johnson, *Twenty Five Milk Runs,* 182.

6. Ibid., 171.

7. Telephone interview, Tom Hardin, June 29, 2013. All subsequent quotes by or references to Hardin are derived from this source.
8. Telephone interview, Al Dussliere, February 23, 2013. All subsequent quotes by or references to Dussliere are derived from this source.
9. Warren Kotz, personal journal, via Vicki Sharp.
10. Telephone interview, Richard Riley Johnson, June 29, 2013.
11. James Mickle, "Oxygen Problems Plague Combat Crew," *Hell's Angels Newsletter* 20, no. 3 (303rd Bomb Group (H) Association, August 2000): 1064.
12. William Heller, 303rd discussion forum, July 23, 2002, http://www.303rdbg .com/303rd-talk/303rd-talk-archive-old/2002-July.txt.
13. U.S. Air Force Historical Study No. 78, 66.
14. Keith Clapp, "An Unusual Incident, or Was It?" *Hell's Angels Newsletter* 19, no. 3 (303rd Bomb Group (H) Association, November 1997): 864.
15. Daily Bulletin, Headquarters, AAF Station 107, August 9, 1944, Air Force Historical Research Agency Microfiche Reel #B02011, 98.
16. Smith, *Chick's Crew*, 51.
17. Johnson, *Twenty Five Milk Runs*, 178.
18. Ibid.
19. Warren Kotz, personal journal, via Vicki Sharp.
20. Johnson, *Twenty Five Milk Runs*, 174–175.
21. Robert Butcher personal journal. Entry made June 10, 1944. Via Brian Butcher.

"THE BACK OF THE ENGINEER'S HEAD HAD BEEN BLOWN OFF"

1. Grady Hodges, unpublished memoir, n.d., n.p., via James Hodges.
2. Air Forces Manual No. 20, *Gunner's Information File: Flexible Gunnery* (Government Printing Office, May 1944), S-8.
3. Army Air Forces Historical Studies No. 31, *Flexible Gunnery Training in the AAF* (Assistant Chief of Air Staff, Intelligence, Historical Division, 1945), 7.
4. Letter from Brigadier General E. L. Eubank to Commanding General, 2d AF, January 12, 1943.
5. James Andrus, personal journal, http://www.303rdbg.com/thunderbird/andrus -journal.html.
6. Raymond Espinoza, "Troubles on and Near the Runways," *Hell's Angels Newsletter* 21, no. 4 (303rd Bomb Group (H) Association, November 1999): 1003.
7. Army Air Forces Historical Studies No. 31, *Flexible Gunnery Training in the AAF*, 59.
8. Ibid., 54.
9. Air Forces Manual No. 20, *Gunner's Information File: Flexible Gunnery*, S-12.
10. Telephone interview, Paul Sersland, January 5, 2013. All subsequent quotes by or references to Sersland are derived from this source.

11. Theodore McDevitt, "Tribute to Mom," *Hell's Angels Newsletter* 21, no. 1 (303rd Bomb Group (H) Association, February 1999): 941.

12. William J. O'Brien. "Tragic Ending to an Old Friendship," *Hell's Angels Newsletter* 22, no. 2 (303rd Bomb Group (H) Association, May 2000): 1043–1044.

"WE WERE ALL VERY FRIGHTENED"

1. U.S. Air Force Historical Study No. 78, 43.

2. Robert Sorenson, "Was I a Survivor?" *Hell's Angels Newsletter* 8, no. 4 (303rd Bomb Group (H) Association, November 1984): 200–201.

3. David Michael, personal journal, http://www.303rdbg.com/journal-michael.pdf.

"NOTHING SPECTACULAR EXCEPT THE EXPLOSION"

1. Colin Heaton and Anne-Marie Lewis, *The Me 262 Stormbird: From the Pilots Who Flew, Fought, and Survived It* (Minneapolis: Zenith Books, 2012), 113.

2. Lloyd Hester, "303rd Crewmates 'Best Men in My Life,'" *Hell's Angels Newsletter* 20, no. 3 (303rd Bomb Group (H) Association, August 2000): 1063.

3. Charles Dando, *303rd BG (H) Combat Mission No. 275, November 21, 1944*, 303rdbg.com, http://www.303rdbg.com/missionreports/275.pdf.

4. James O'Leary, "Personal Diaries," *Hell's Angels Newsletter* 2, no. 4 (303rd Bomb Group (H) Association, November 1978): 34.

5. "Gobrecht Crew's Most Memorable Combat Mission Incidents," http://www.303 rdbg.com/358gobrecht.html.

6. Bob Hand, 303rd discussion forum, December 4, 2002, http://www.303rdbg .com/303rd-talk/303rd-talk-archive-old/2002-December.txt.

"WE SHUT DOWN EVERYTHING THEN"

1. James O'Leary, "As Rough as It Gets," *303rd BG (H) Combat Mission No. 301, January 13, 1945*, 303rdbg.com, http://www.303rdbg.com/missionreports/301.pdf.

2. Headquarters, 303rd Bombardment Group (H), Standard Operating Procedure 4D, October 29, 1944, Air Force Historical Research Agency Microfiche Reel #B0213, 803.

"WHAT THE HELL IS GOING ON UP THERE?"

1. Telephone interview, Ed Gardner, March 17, 2013. All subsequent quotes by or references to Gardner are derived from this source.

2. Memorandum, Heeadquarters 303rd Bombardment Group (H), January 17, 1945, Subject: Recapitulation of the Trials and Tribulations Encountered on Mission #300 Flown 10 January 1945.

3. Mel Schulstad speaking engagement to USAF Command Master Chief event, Denver, Colorado, circa 2008.

4. Carroll Binder, "That First Mission—From the Diary of Lt. Carroll 'Ted' Binder," *Hell's Angels Newsletter* 13, no. 4 (303rd Bomb Group (H) Association, December 1990): 429.

"DOWN IN FLAMES DOVE ANOTHER OF GOERING'S FANATICS"

1. Al Dussliere, personal journal.
2. Guido Marchionda, personal journal, http://www.303rdbg.com/journal-marchionda.pdf.
3. Charles Johnson, " 'Tremendous Jolts' Rock Taub's B-17 as German Me-262 Jets Attack," *Hell's Angels Newsletter* 25, no. 3 (303rd Bomb Group (H) Association, August 2002): 7.
4. Peed, Philip, unpublished memoir, n.d., n.p., via John Peed.
5. Air Force Historical Research Agency Microfiche Reel #B0211, pg. 1524, held in the collection of the 303rd's official records at the Air Force Historical Research Agency, Maxwell AFB, Alabama.
6. George Emerson, "My Short Life as a POW in Germany in World War II," 303rdbg.com, http://www.303rdbg.com/427barrat.html.
7. Charles Johnson, "Life in *Stalag Luft I* as the War Nears End," *Hell's Angels Newsletter* 25, no. 4 (303rd Bomb Group (H) Association, November 2002): 8.

"I WAS BLOWN OUT"

1. Walter Schuck, *Luftwaffe Eagle: From the Me109 to the Me262* (Manchester: Crécy Publishing Limited), 202–206.
2. Missing Air Crew Report (MACR) #13875, Headquarters, AAF Station 107, 303rd Bombardment Group (H).

"ALL OF US WERE DONE"

1. Johnson, *Twenty Five Milk Runs*, 216–217. See also, *Evening Independent* newspaper, "Mail-Away Edition," November 1, 1943, Volume XXXVI, No. 310, "Colonel Carroll Takes Command at MacDill Field."
2. Missing Air Crew Report (MACR) #13596 (Lacker crew) and #13719 (Alderman crew) Headquarters, AAF Station 107, 303rd Bombardment Group (H).
3. Frau Johanna Tittmann memories, 1995, Loessnitz, Germany, translated by A. Guenter Bier, via Al Dussliere.
4. Police report, Loessnitz, Germany, April 6, 1945, "Personal and Material Damage Due to Enemy Bomber Crash," translated via Guenter Bier, via Al Dussliere.
5. Guido Marchionda, personal journal, http://www.303rdbg.com/journal-marchionda.pdf.
6. E-mail correspondence between author and Lois Brown from May 2013 to February 2014.

"AND THEN HE FELL DOWN DEAD"

1. Max Bartholomew, "Did It Open or Was It a Streamer?" *Hell's Angels Newsletter* 19, no. 1 (303rd Bomb Group (H) Association, May 1997): 820.
2. Horst Bayer, eyewitness to death of S/Sgt Eschinger, 303rdbg.com, http://www .303rdbg.com/missionreports/362.pdf.

"THEY ARE WORKING ME TO DEATH"

1. Personal interview, Hildegard Kaiser Franke, July 13, 2013.
2. Arthur S. C. Shanafelt, "Excerpts from V-Mail Letters Home—28 February–14 May, 1945," 303rdbg.com, http://www.303rdbg.com/journal-shanafelt.html. All quotes from Shanafelt's letters are derived from this source.
3. Warren Mauger, "Three Die, Four Taken Prisoner, One Evades on 303rd's Final Raid," *Hell's Angels Newsletter* 21, no. 4 (303rd Bomb Group (H) Association, November 1999): 992.

INDEX